THE BROADVIEW BOOK OF

Canadian
Parliamentary
Anecdotes

THE BROADVIEW BOOK OF

Canadian
Parliamentary
Anecdotes

Edited by Marc Bosc

broadview press

Canadian Cataloguing in Publication Data

Main entry under title:

The Broadview Book of Canadian Parliamentary Anecdotes

ISBN 0–921149–28–X

1. Canada — Politics and government — Anecdotes.

2. Politicians — Canada — Anecdotes. I. Bosc, Marc.

II. Title: Canadian Parliamentary Anecdotes.

FC176. B76 1988   971   C88–094571–0

FC1026.B76 1988

broadview press   in the U.S.:broadview press

P.O. Box 1243   421 Center Street

Peterborough, Canada, K9J 7H5   Lewiston, N.Y. 14092

Printed and bound in Canada by

Gangné Ltd.

Preface

Anecdotes—narratives of detached incidents, or of single events, told as being interesting, amusing or striking in themselves—have long been a popular literary form. What makes them so appealing is not so much that they are a source of complete historical accuracy—although they do contain much that is true—but that they fulfill human curiosity. This is particularly true of political anecdotes.

Anecdotal narratives have always had an important place in political history and biography, but many of them languish half-forgotten in books, memoirs, reminiscences, letters and articles, unavailable or unknown to most readers. While I have included such pieces as T.P. Slattery's moving reconstruction of the death of D'Arcy McGee and a verbatim extract from Sir John A. Macdonald's great speech on the Pacific scandal of 1873, we also see Mackenzie King dim the lights for a seance, Nicholas Flood Davin dance across a bottle-laden table and Louis St. Laurent eat beans for lunch at a diner.

What I have tried to do in the following pages, therefore, is bring together those anecdotes most likely to satisfy our curiosity about federal politicians, from Confederation to the near-present. In part this book attempts an archaeology of the unguarded moment, while at the same time giving an alternative view of the "great moments" of Canadian parliamentary history.

Not surprisingly, the quantity and quality of material is much greater for Prime Ministers. In fact, one could fill volumes about many of these men, as was done by E.B. Biggar in his 1891 book the *Anecdotal Life of Sir John Macdonald*, a delightful collection from which I have drawn a few stories. There have been similar, although somewhat weaker, works concerning John Diefenbaker, another Prime Minister whose personality and manners spawned countless anecdotes. After Prime Ministers, Ministers of the Crown are most often the subject of these anecdotes, followed by backbench Members and a host of others, including Governors, Senators, and House officials.

This is a personal selection and it is by no means exhaustive. Some readers may search in vain for an old favourite I have not been able to add. Sheer volume and wealth of material explain some of the omissions—in other cases, I have had to accept, to my dismay, that no suitable narrative of an important political episode or a notable incident concerning a well-known figure exists. I have generally tried to accent the positive and to eschew sombre or depressing stories in favour of amusing, uplifting anecdotes. Naturally, some events, such as the assassination of Thomas D'Arcy McGee, simply cannot be excluded, however sad they may be.

Almost all the material is from published sources, and very few of my anecdotal subjects are now engaged in politics. To quote the authors of the Percy Anecdotes, "If it is unsafe to indulge a curiosity of this kind when the objects of it are living, we are under no such restraint with regard to the dead. We cannot offend them with our impertinent curiosity. Their movements are not compromised by our revelations." Although I have not followed this principle exactly, it has been a strong guide.

The book is organized chronologically, by name, using the usual appellation of the individual who is the subject of the anecdote. Occasionally, I have resorted to a general heading, such as "The House," when the anecdote concerns several individuals. Where the reader must know the context, a headnote has been included which briefly provides pertinent dates, full names and other strictly necessary information. References are given in short-title form below each anecdote and are also included in a complete form, in a separate section at the end of the book. In addition, an index of names makes it possible to find references to specific individuals who are either the subject of, or merely mentioned in, anecdotes.

This preface would not be complete without reference to the many individuals who had a hand in the project. To Roy MacLaren, and to Don LePan and the staff at Broadview Press, I owe an enormous debt of gratitude for getting the project going in the first place. The reference librarians at the Library of Parliament were unstinting in their assistance; likewise, the comments and suggestions made by my colleagues on the House of Commons staff as the work progressed were invaluable. Special thanks are due to Joanne Lacasse who tenaciously typed a mountainous first manuscript, and showed a remarkable forbearance as I made what must have seemed like endless modifications. Above all, my wife Peggy's comments on the many anecdotes she reviewed were indispensable, and I could not have completed the book without the extreme patience and support of her and our daughter Caroline.

Ottawa
October, 1988

In Committee

A glimpse of the proceedings in a Committee of the Whole House in the 1860s.

Some half a dozen or a dozen Members gather around the Clerk's table, and the clauses of the bill are passed one by one in rapid succession, while the rest of the Members, who have not escaped to the saloon, amuse themselves in various ways, somewhat after the manner of irrepressible school boys in the absence of the teacher. Some few, more staid and sober than the rest, settle down in their seats in the hope that they may be allowed to pen a letter or perchance read an article in their local paper. Unfortunate man! Vain hope! A huge paper ball, thrown from some skilful hand in the rear, scatters pen, ink and paper in rude confusion over the desk, while a seat cushion or a formidable blue book from another quarter comes thundering down upon the worthy Member's head, sending his ideas in a hurly burly race after his writing material, and arousing within him the spirit of retaliation. And thus the sport commences. Paper balls, blue books, bills, private and public, cushions, hats and caps of all styles, are brought into requisition, and are sent whirling through the room in every direction.

TWA, *New Brunswick Freeman,* 1868

Sir John A. Convivial

For 19 crucial years beginning at Confederation, Sir John Alexander Macdonald (1815–1891) served as Canada's Prime Minister.

Sir John Macdonald made no pretensions to oratory. He was, however, a clear, incisive speaker, and when upon his mettle he could hold his own with the best of them.

There were, however, times when he had his lapses, and in my early days I heard of one of these. Carried away by the conviviality which developed on a certain occasion, Sir John forgot all about his notes. He lost the thread of his argument with the result that had his speech been reported as he delivered it, he would have been made to appear ridiculous. There happened to be only one reporter at the gathering. He was a firm friend of the Old Man and realizing his dilemma he decided to see Sir John next morning before returning to the newspaper office, and ask him to dictate a summary of his address, as he had not been able to decipher his shorthand notes. Sir John divined what was behind the request and proceeded to give him a first class resume of his speech, for which the reporter was more than grateful. Thanking Sir John for his courtesy, the Old Chieftain remarked, "Now then, young man, before you leave, just a friendly word of advice. You have a career before you, and I think you will make good in the newspaper profession. But let me offer you this word of admonition — never attempt to report a public man when you are drunk!

Fred Cook, *Fifty Years Ago and Since*, n.d.

Sir John the Orator

Though always effective in debate, Sir John Macdonald lacked many of the qualifications of an orator. His voice, while pleasant, was not strong, nor remarkably distinct; and a slightly hesitating manner, which disappeared under the influence of excitement, rather impeded the flow of his ideas. He rarely prepared his speeches, preferring the impromptu semi-conversational style of the English House of Commons, to the more studied methods to which we are accustomed. Yet, while he could not be called a great speaker, there was no place in which he showed to more advantage, or was more at home, than in the House of Commons, where his lightest utterances always commanded universal attention. The report that the "old man was speaking" would always clear the lobbies and smoking-rooms of the House at any hour of the day or night. Much of this interest was no doubt due to his position, but more to his unique personality. His style, like everything belonging to him, was peculiarly his own. In the ordinary routine of debate he was clear and skilful in argument, possessing in a high degree the faculty of compression, of seizing the salient points of any argument in which he was interested. His speeches seldom exceeded an hour in length, and frequently occupied less time, forming a marked contrast to the set orations of Blake, who rarely spoke in Parliament without exhausting the whole subject he rose to discuss, and who, by reason of his desire to avail himself of everything that bore on his argument, frequently succeeded in producing weariness rather than conviction in minds less gifted than his own. Sir John, on the other hand, was somewhat impatient of detail.

He never wasted his time looking up authorities or wading through official papers. When he wished to speak on a subject calling for research, he briefly indicated the line he proposed to take to someone to whom he confined the task of getting up the facts. When these were marshalled in due order in the narrowest possible compass, he would devote a few moments to their assimilation, and then, often provided with nothing more than a few notes, generally on the back of an envelope (which he not infrequently contrived to mislay), he would deliver a short speech, presenting, despite the technical inaccuracies inseparable from extempore delivery, a luminous exposition of the whole subject. This was the nearest approach to preparation in which he indulged, save on rare instances, when the magnitude of the question demanded exhaustive treatment.

Joseph Pope, *Memoirs of Macdonald*, 1894

Sir John the Orator, II

In his style of delivery he was peculiar. He would run on for two or three sentences in a monotone in which but few words could be distinctly made out from the strangers' gallery; then he would throw out a single word with a tremendous jerk of the head, and such emphasis that it could be heard in any part of the Chamber. This explosion would sometimes be accompanied by a rapid glance round the whole House, taking in every part, from the Speaker on his left to those who sat behind on his right. He often spoke with his hands in his pockets, and seldom gesticulated with his arms, except to point a finger at some Member of the Opposition at whom he might be levelling a joke. In his early years he was more demonstrative on the floor, and his voice had a certain melody which he lost with advancing age.

E.B. Biggar, *Anecdotal Life of Macdonald*, 1891

Sir John and the Grit

In May 1870, Sir John suddenly became very ill—here is a report given to the House by Dr. Bown, a Member who, along with Dr. Grant, also a Member, treated Sir John during this time.

Yesterday upon entering the House I was requested to proceed to Sir John A. Macdonald, who had been taken suddenly ill at his office. I went there and I found Dr. Grant in attendance. I offered my services, but at the same time not wishing to press them returned to the House. After being in my seat about an hour I received a letter from Dr. Grant requesting my immediate attendance on Sir John A. Macdonald. I showed the note to Sir George-E. Cartier and then proceeded to see the Premier. I found him at his office lying upon a couch quite pulseless and in a state of collapse from the previous hard work which he had done and the wear and tear upon his system. The case became somewhat alarming because we could not use the ordinary stimulants we would have administered to other patients. Happily, however, the remedy used by Dr. Grant so far succeeded as to restore circulation. Sir John A. Macdonald suffered excruciating torture from what we supposed was the passing of a biliary calculus. From about 9 o'clock in the evening the spasms subsided, but during the whole night with the exception of a few moments' repose or sleep he passed a very restless night, and impressed my mind with great anxiety.

[Towards morning though, Sir John asked Grant what the stone was. Grant replied: "a small gritty material". At once Macdonald said: "Confound those grits, I knew they would be the death of me yet."]

John Bown, quoted in *Commons Debates*, 1870

Shrewd Sir John

Sir John was an adept at placating an opponent, and many Members of the Opposition who would have been "rabid" towards any other head of the Government were like lambs towards him. He had some curious ways of winning the personal good-will of Members of the Opposition, and suited his methods to the man. A certain country constituency returned a Reform Member who was not only below par in education and natural gifts, but had a fondness for drink. He was, in fact, what one would call a coarse man. Sir John had heard of him, and when he appeared in the precincts of the House went up, and in his most hail-fellow-well-met style introduced himself. After a few words, Sir John said to him: "Why, they told me you were a vulgar, coarse, unsociable fellow with nothing interesting about you; and good for nothing but to drink whiskey. But here I find you as good a fellow as ever I met — in fact you are just the kind of man I like. Let's go downstairs and have a chat." They went into the restaurant, where Sir John ordered a bottle of champagne, and told him some good stories — or, rather, stories that suited the ear of the listener. When they had become friends, Sir John said at parting: "Now, I expect you will vote against me. Of course, that is your duty. But don't think I will be offended at that. You vote just as you think right, because I'll expect it, but you and I will be friends all the same." The new Member considered himself enrolled in the great multitude of those who called themselves "personal friends" of the Premier, and it was observed by those who followed the career of the Member, that whenever a question of real danger to the Conservative interests came up he did not vote against them, but had some reason for absence.

E.B. Biggar, *Anecdotal Life of Macdonald*, 1891

Old Tomorrow

Sir John had the reputation of being a procrastinator, and to this idea is due his sobriquet of "Old To-morrow". Like many another popular idea, this estimate, so far as it ascribed his habit of deliberation to a constitutional defect, was fallacious. Rather was it the outcome of his quality of caution, which regulated his life, and ever prompted him to weigh all the circumstances of a case before taking action thereon. This was illustrated in many ways; for example, in his choice of colleagues, and in his administration of patronage. It is very easy for a Prime Minister to invite a man to enter his Cabinet, but it is very difficult to repair a hasty selection. It is equally easy to fill a vacant office, but the step once taken is practically irrevocable. It has often been remarked — by those who are not Prime Ministers — that, by promptly filling vacancies as they occurred, he would have saved himself much trouble and annoyance arising from the difficulty of deciding between the merits and claims of numerous aspirants thereto. Such a course might have saved him embarrassment, but, in his opinion, delay was often advantageous to the

State, and to the party interests he was commissioned to guard. He preferred, as a general rule, to "hasten slowly," to weigh well all the circumstances, to keep his hand free as long as possible, and to act only in the light of the fullest knowledge he could gather. Such a course, he has observed, often saved him from the disastrous consequences of hasty and ill-considered action. He was a firm believer in the efficacy of time as a solvent of many difficulties which beset his path, and his wisdom in this regard has time and again been exemplified.

In the matters of departmental administration there may have been some colour for the charge of procrastination, but his was due, not to indolence, but to the impossibility, even by working twelve to fourteen hours a day, of finding adequate time to devote to their administration.

Akin to this habit of caution was the patience to which he himself attributed no little of his success as a party leader. In this particular is seen his power of will, for by nature Sir John Macdonald was inclined to be impatient, and even at times irritable, yet, in spite of this, he acquired a habit of self-control which formed one of the most remarkable traits in his character. He often quoted Pitt's saying, that "the first, second and third requisites of a Prime Minister are patience," and no statesman every laid this truth more deeply to heart.

Joseph Pope, Memoirs of Macdonald, 1894

Sir John's Appetite

The callers at his house in the morning were, as a rule, confined to his colleagues, to whom he was always accessible, and to those who came by appointment, a large and constantly increasing number. Despite all the precautions that could be devised, his luncheon hour was often invaded to such an extent that he found himself obliged to resort to the French system of déjeuner at noon. This plan had its advantages, for while visitors might have no scruple in interfering with luncheon, the sound of the breakfast gong seldom failed to dislodge the greatest bore. In order to add to the obligation of these déjeuners, Lady Macdonald frequently invited a few friends to breakfast, and thus contrived to secure to her husband a pleasant relaxation of an hour in the midst of his busy day.

Sir John's appetite was small and easily satisfied. On rising he took a cup of tea in his bedroom. His déjeuner consisted of a minute portion of fish, game, or often a marrow bone, of which he was very fond; toast and butter without salt.

He generally managed to devote at least two hours a day to his departmental duties. His afternoons were spent in Council, which generally rose in time for him to dine at half-past seven. The half-hour before dinner was given up to his invalid daughter, whom he loved with all the warmth of his affectionate nature. His first words on entering the house frequently were, "Where is my little girl?" He would sit down beside her, and talk over the events of the day. Such conversations, brimful as they were of light badinage, in which they both excelled, were delightful to listen to. Sometimes he joined in a game with her, or read to her some story in which she was interested. His dinner was simple in character, a single dish and a glass of claret often sufficing for his moderate wants. His leisure evenings were generally spent in the library, looking over the newspapers, or playing a game of "patience" of which he was very fond, and in the mysteries of which he was always ready to instruct any of his little daughter's friends who displayed curiosity to know what he was doing.

What most impressed those who saw Sir John Macdonald at home, was the faculty he had of divesting himself of the cares of State. To watch him joining in a round game with a merry group of children, or sitting at the fireside chatting with Lady Macdonald and his daughter, reading amusing paragraphs out of the newspapers, or descanting upon the topics of the day, one found it hard to realize that he was the same man who, a few hours before, had been harassed by the grave and perplexing problems which awaited him on the morrow. He retired early, but as a rule, not to sleep, for to the very last he was much given to reading in bed. But sleep came when courted, and, after a good night's rest, he was always ready to approach the questions which he had banished from his mind the evening before.

Joseph Pope, *Memoirs of Macdonald*, 1894

Sir John's Correspondence

It is now many years since Sir John Macdonald found that the interruptions at the Government Offices were such as to render it impossible for him to do more than receive the constant stream of callers, who had, or who fancied they had, business to transact with him. He was therefore compelled to seclude himself many hours a day in the "workshop," as he called it, at Earnscliffe, a snug retreat into which only his secretary could venture unannounced. There he descended every morning about half-past nine to read and answer the pile of letters that awaited him. He attached great importance to the conduct of his correspondence, and made a point of answering all letters addressed to him as promptly as circumstances would permit. No correspondent was too humble or illiterate to receive a kind acknowledgement. Sir John wrote an easy flowing hand, and with the assistance of a secretary could despatch, in a quiet morning, an immense amount of correspondence. He preserved every letter written to him. To this rule there was no exception. He was not so careful to keep copies of the letters written by himself, though the omissions for the most part were confined to unimportant communications. He sometimes dashed off important letters on the spur of the moment, but after writing them he would frequently let them lie for twenty-four hours, especially if they conveyed reproof, or contained unwelcome intelligence of any sort. Sometimes the delay caused him to modify his original words and occasionally to recall them. He was always particular about a correspondent's initials or titles. "There are few things", he used to say, "a man resents more than to receive a letter in which his name is misspelled," and he would take a good deal of trouble to avoid such a fault.

Joseph Pope, *Memoirs of Macdonald*, 1894

Be My Friend

One of his best-beloved friends in Kingston in his early days of leadership was Dr. Grant, then Principal of Queen's University.

"Dr. Grant," he said on one occasion, meeting him on Princess Street, "I wish you were a friend of mine."

"But I am a friend of yours, Sir John," replied Dr. Grant. "I always support you when I think you are right."

"Ah!" said Sir John, "but that is not the kind of a friend I mean—I mean a friend who would support me when he thinks I am wrong!"

R. J. Manion, *Life Is An Adventure*, 1936

Shrewd Sir John, II

He was well read, and he had an immense experience of men and things, and he had also a curious philosophic streak in him, which showed out occasionally at a certain stage in the evening. Many of his remarks were not only shrewd but farseeing. I recall one occasion, when discussing our form of government and its peculiar difficulties, he observed, "Given a Government with a big surplus, and a big majority and a weary Opposition, and you would debauch a committee of archangels."

Sir Richard Cartwright, *Reminiscences*, 1912

Sir John Expressive

From my seat in the Press Gallery for four or five Parliamentary sessions I looked across at Sir John Macdonald. I was so placed that I could sometimes see shades of expression cross his face, the defiant jerk of the head when he was angry, the shrug of contempt for a mean gibe that was meant to wound, the quick, natural, human manifestation of pleasure over a generous word from an opponent or a tribute of affection and confidence from an associate. I think he liked best to have the word of praise come from the back benches as he was most attentive to those who spoke seldom and in sweat alike of brow and brain.

Sir John Willison, *Reminiscences, Political and Personal*, 1919

Father and Son

The 1891 general election, Macdonald's last, produced yet another Conservative majority. John A. was returned for Kingston, his son Hugh John for Winnipeg.

Parliament met on the 29th of April, 1891, and Sir John had the gratification of sitting down in the legislative hall with his son, Hugh John, who had been elected by a large majority for Winnipeg. The occasion, to his political friends at least, was a moving one. Just as the hands of the clock pointed to the half hour after twelve, a burst of applause from the Conservative benches greeted the veteran Premier as he entered arm in arm with his son. The old chief never looked better. He was dressed in a frock coat with light trousers, with the traditional red necktie and a "stovepipe" hat. His eye was clear, his step elastic, and every-thing betokened that he was in good condition for the hard work of the session. After the Premier had exchanged greetings with his followers, who pressed forward to grasp his hand, father and son together took the oath and together affixed their autographs to the parchment, the son signing on the line below Sir John.

E.B. Biggar, *Anecdotal Life of Macdonald*, 1891

Sir John Intoxicated

The Toronto Globe, in an article about an all night debate in April 1878, had some damaging things to say about Macdonald.

To say that Sir John A. Macdonald was on Friday night somewhat under the influence of liquor would be a grossly inadequate representation of the fact. He was simply drunk, in the plain, ordinary sense of that word. As the night wore on, he became still more so, and from six to eight on Saturday morning he was, to quote the conventional language usually employed on such occasions, "thoroughly laid out," and had to be hid away by his friends; if not in shame, at least in pity, and as an absolute providential proceeding.

The Toronto Globe, quoted in *Commons Debates*, 1878

On the Ropes

Late in 1873, Macdonald was in the final throes of the Pacific Scandal. In a supreme effort to save his political skin he delivered a compelling five hour speech. He closed with the following stirring appeal.

We have faithfully done our duty. We have fought the battle of Con-federation. We have fought the battle of Union. We have had Party strife setting Province against Province, and more than all, we have had in the greatest Province, the preponderating Province of the Dominion, every prejudice and sectional feeling that could be arrayed against us. I have been the victim of that conduct to a great extent; but I have fought the battle of Confederation, the battle of Union, the battle of the Do-minion of Canada. I throw myself upon this House; I throw myself upon this country; I throw myself upon posterity, and I believe that I know that, notwithstanding the many failings in my life, I shall have the voice of this country and this House rallying around me. And, sir, if I am mistaken in that, I can confidently appeal to a higher Court, to the Court of my own conscience, and to the Court of Posterity. I leave it with this House with every confidence. I am equal to either fortune. I can see cast the decision of this House either for or against me, but whether it be against me or for me I know, and it is no vain boast to say it, for even my enemies will admit that I am no boaster, that there does not exist in Canada a man who has given more of his time, more of his heart, more of his wealth, or more of his intellect and power, such as it may be, for the good of this Dominion of Canada.

Sir John A. Macdonald, quoted in *Scrapbook Debates*, 1873

Lady Agnes

Lady Agnes Macdonald (née Susan Agnes Bernard) married Sir John A. Macdonald in 1867.

There was no hauteur about her; she might be seen during the session going about the Library with a friendly word dropped now and then to an attendant or a stranger, or sitting on the bare steps of the Senate entrance reading a book. She would make most of her calls on foot. She was, by the way, a most vigorous walker, and when she drove it was in the same vigorous way.

In later years she became adept in politics. She was an almost constant attendant in Parliament, and a certain seat in the Speaker's gallery became hers by natural right. Here she would sit and listen to the debates, sometimes till three o'clock in the morning, and many a time she would persuade Sir John off to his private room, and, while he took a comfortable sleep, would watch the proceedings in the House. No one was quicker to note the appearance of a new member, and to take the measure of his parliamentary figure. She would take in every word uttered in a new Member's "maiden speech", and could gauge with an instinct almost equal to Sir John's the manner of man he was. She had learned the deaf and dumb alphabet, and occasionally she might be seen telegraphing to Sir John from the gallery by this means.

E.B. Biggar, *Anecdotal Life of Macdonald*, 1891

Cartier's Physiognomy

Sir George-Étienne Cartier (1814–1873) was Macdonald's long time friend and supporter, his Quebec lieutenant and most trusted minister. He possessed a number of striking personal characteristics.

Of medium stature, even small, about five feet six inches in height, he was of strong and robust build. Owing to his rather small stature, he at first sight did not impress the observer; it was only when he was animated that one realized that he was in the presence of no ordinary man. Without being fat, he was what may be described as rotund, and his limbs were so well proportioned as to give an appearance of uncommon vigour to the entire frame. His hands and feet were small but finely modelled. His well-proportioned figure was surmounted by a massive head — the most striking portion of his whole physical make-up. An expansive brow denoted intellectual power, the eyes were keen and piercing, the nose prominent, and the under part of the face strongly developed, denoting great strength of character and will power. The head, set straight on the neck, possessed an extreme mobility, and in speaking or when animated Cartier shook it in innumerable ways, each movement indicating something. This constant movement of his head was one of Cartier's most striking personal characteristics and sometimes caused surprise to strangers when they first met him. The head was covered with a generous growth of hair, brown in colour, which turned grey in his later years, and often as not it was in extreme confusion. His complexion when in good health was ruddy, and his whole appearance was replete with vigour and energy.

John Boyd, *Cartier, His Life and Times*, 1914

Cartier's Handwriting

In working Cartier wrote little himself, but dictated profusely. He had a peculiar method of dictating, making use of a kind of abbreviated or telegraphic style, and leaving to the secretary to fill in the details in writing out the document. When the completed document was subsequently read to him he would listen carefully to every part of it before signing it or ordering it to be signed. Invariably his signature was Geo. Et. Cartier, distinctly and legibly written. His handwriting generally was extremely poor, and frequently illegible. One day that distinguished French-Canadian statesman and littérateur, P.J.O. Chauveau, a warm personal friend of Cartier, from who he had received a communication, wrote to the Minister with that delicate wit which was one of Chauveau's distinctive gifts. "Your handwriting, which, however, is better than mine, makes it impossible for me to read what is in the envelope, which you addressed to me. I find, however, that these hieroglyphics have a kindly appearance and I thank you." Apropos of his poor writing, Cartier one day observed: "I have three kinds of writing, one which everybody can understand, one which I myself only can read, and one which only Sicotte and Sulte can decipher." [Sicotte and Sulte, who successively acted as Cartier's private secretary, were no doubt able, by long familiarity, to decipher their chief's poor handwriting.]

John Boyd, *Cartier, His Life and Times*, 1914

Cartier Entertains

During the earlier sessions after Confederation, Sir George displayed his hospitality by giving an entertainment to the Members on Saturday nights. None but gentlemen were ever invited, which quickly won for them the name of "stag parties," and as all political shades were freely intermingled, a more free and easy, jolly festivity could hardly be imagined. It was generally ten o'clock before most of the guests arrived, and the rooms were often so crowded that you could hardly get space to stand.

The chief event of the evening was supper at half-past eleven o'clock (when on time), but the evening was principally spent in conversation, French-Canadian boat songs, Scotch ballads, or other divertissements improvised for the occasion. Sir George himself set the example in jollity, and after welcoming those present liked nothing better than to grasp hands with two or three friends and jump around in a ring like so many *garçons* just out of school.

James Young, *Public Men and Public Life*, 1912

Plasticity and Expression

The legendary orator Thomas D'Arcy McGee (1825–1868) was elected the Member for Montreal West in 1867. He was assissinated in the early morning of April 7, 1868.

He had what is better than comeliness in the face of a man—plasticity and expression. The prevailing character was agreeable... it changed suddenly to correspond with the sentiment he was about to utter, and in addressing a public audience helped wonderfully the purpose of his speech. An unaccountable negro cast of features was a constant source of jesting allusions and induced his enemies, of whom he came to have a plentiful supply, to distort his name from D'Arcy McGee into Darky McGee; but if he was as uncomely as Curran, he was nearly as gifted.

Gavan Duffy, quoted in
Isabel Skelton, *Life of Thomas D'Arcy McGee*, 1925

McGee the Fighter

He had marvelous skill and ingenuity in defending his own party. Their course never looked so attractive nor their arguments so cogent and convincing as when enunciated in his glowing words and graceful, polished periods. He had a rich variety of weapons for attack. He excelled in banter, which very often became downright ridicule, but very seldom went so far as derision. Badinage and mockery, too, he studied with good effect. In a House and at a time when coarse chaffing and rude jeering often took the place of more refined weapons, even McGee's jesting was, comparatively speaking, on a scholarly plane. This was very irritating to his more clumsy opponents. It was very often not what he said, but the superior way in which it was said, that made the sting so unforgettable. Again, he was never at a loss for a pointed retort or a silencing rejoinder. In this he was without a peer.

McGee was a firm believer in the cumulative effect of constantly hitting on one nail—an adversary's well-known weakness, his amusing eccentricity, or vainglorious boasting. In days when there were few or no cartoons, his word-pictures took their place in making his warfare quickly and broadly effective and entertaining.

In McGee's Opposition days, Attorney-General Macdonald appeared decked out as "the Julian of the troupe." His post-prandial habits gave the needed foundation.

The Attorney-General East, George Étienne Cartier, appeared usually as an operatic singer in McGee's gallery. Cartier had a high-pitched, rasping voice in his speeches, but he prided himself upon his ability to sing French comic songs.

John Sandfield Macdonald was another whom McGee delighted to caricature. John Sandfield was a fiddler, and one of his most popular methods of keeping in touch with his constituents in those good old days was to enliven their various dinners, weddings and family festivities by playing Scotch selections on his beloved Cremona. Accordingly his role in D'Arcy's troupe became "Old Rosin the Bow."

Christopher Dunkin, secure to fame by his Confederation speech of two days and two nights, which filled one hundred and twenty columns of the official report, and analyzed with microscopic thoroughness every clause and phrase of the agreement, was born to enter McGee's gay procession. Sometimes he was the "petty politician" of Tom Moore's ditty, "There was a little man and he had a little soul," etc. This classic had some five or six stanzas of eight lines each and all of the same high order. The first time McGee hit on its applicability he treated the House to a complete rendering, and contemporary reports say, "roars of laughter and applause from all parts of the House prevented the honourable gentleman continuing his speech for several minutes."

At other times Dunkin reminded McGee, "as he rises and scintillates his little points," of the nursery rhyme, "Twinkle, twinkle, little star," but usually he was drawn, to counter-balance our neighbours' "old Abe the rail-splitter," as "Young Abe the hair-splitter."

Isabel Skelton, *Life of Thomas D'Arcy McGee*, 1925

McGee's Oratory

McGee's gestures were, as a rule, quiet, graceful and dignified. At times, however, when the eloquence or warmth of his subject demanded it, they were carried along with a fine spontaneity and vivid energy wholly in keeping with the animation and working of his face. As with all real orators, his speech was more than the words he uttered. It gained greatly from the play of countenance, the dramatic gestures, the whole movement and atmosphere of the moment which his fervour and the fervour of his audience both united to inspire.

Another great asset of the orator McGee was his gift of expression. Words never failed him. His vocabulary itself was noteworthy. It was wonderfully varied, precise, and scholarly. He had, moreover, an Irishman's peculiar delight in using it in all its breadth and variation. In another speaker his dictionary range of words would have seemed artificial, long sought after, and showy, but in his context it was natural, fitting, and pleasing.

Isabel Skelton, *Life of Thomas D'Arcy McGee*, 1925

The Assassination

D'Arcy McGee had finished writing when the House of Commons adjourned very late that night. In fact, it was another day. It was then ten minutes past two, Tuesday morning, April 7, 1868.

He walked down to the bar of the House, bought three cigars and lit one up with his chief, Sir John A. Macdonald. Then he chatted about Nova Scotia with Dr. J.F. Forbes, the Member for Queens of that Province, and waited while Robert MacFarlane, a younger Member from Perth, Ontario, had a whisky and water. In a few minutes they moved to the cloak-room in the west lobby. "Come, Bob, you young rascal, help me on with my coat," McGee said to MacFarlane. "Always ready to give you a lift," MacFarlane replied.

As they went out McGee asked Cartier to join them, but Cartier explained he was waiting to have a private word with Galt. So McGee and MacFarlane left together, relaxed and chatting easily. There were a number of Members leaving at that time, and some spectators were noticed near by. Going out the main door under the arches of the Tower among the Arnprior marble pillars, they passed the doorkeeper, Patrick Buckley, who had just seen Sir John A. off in his carriage to his home on Daly Street at Sandy Hill.

McGee was wearing an overcoat, gloves and a new white top hat. In his hand was his wheat-coloured bamboo cane with a silver handle and engraved band, presented to him five years ago by his friends in Montreal. Since the trouble with his leg, McGee had to walk slowly, so they took their time, McGee leaning on MacFarlane's arm, sauntering down the central path, across the broad terrace and out the front gateway to Wellington Street.

Veering to their left, they soon reached its intersection with Metcalfe Street close by. Keeping to the right side of Metcalfe, McGee on the inside, they walked one short block south to Sparks Street. Here, at the corner in front of Dwyer's Fruit Store, they had to part, MacFarlane to go east on Sparks, cross Sappers' Bridge and on to his lodgings in Lower Town, while McGee had merely to turn west and walk about a hundred and twenty-five yards to reach his room.

"Good night," said MacFarlane, and McGee replied "God bless you."

As he turned, MacFarlane noticed the doorkeeper's brother, John Buckley, and three others whom he did not recognize, following behind them at a faster pace. MacFarlane crossed Metcalfe, waved to Cartier and Galt, who were walking down the other side of Metcalfe, and followed Sparks Street past the Russell House. As he was crossing Sapper's Bridge he noticed the cabdriver, John Downs, returning from Sir John A. Macdonald's home with his empty carriage and iron-grey horse.

Meanwhile McGee had crossed to the south side of Sparks and was turning west, when John Buckley called out: "Good night, Mr. McGee."

"Good morning," McGee answered. "It is morning now." And those words were remembered as his last.

It was unusually bright that night and Sparks Street appeared deserted. The gas street lamps were not lit; but that was customary, as the city's contract with the gas company called for service only "during the dull period of the moon." Telegraph poles and a series of hitching posts for horses were spaced along the edge of the unpaved road, and the fourth pole up the street marked his destination. It was the Toronto House, better known as Mrs. Trotter's Boarding House.

Limping slightly, his cane clicking on the frozen sidewalk, McGee walked on alone, the red glow and the blue smoke from his cigar spreading, so it seemed, an air of peace.

Mrs. Trotters' House itself had three entrances, and McGee had the key to the middle one for the use of guests. So he passed the locked first door which led to the public bar, and then went by the large window. Then he stopped, took out his key and put it in the latch keyhole to let himself in.

At that instant the door was opened by someone from within. Simultaneously there was a sudden flash and the sharp blast of a shot right behind McGee. D'Arcy McGee stumbled to his right, shuddered, threw his head back high and fell flat on his back.

There was a commotion inside the Trotter House. Several people came running to the scene. But there was no sign of any assassin, no sign of any weapon. Nothing. No one but the victim.

He was on his back lying askew across the empty sidewalk. His legs were spread apart extending towards the door. They quivered slightly and then were still.

His body lay motionless, with his head towards the road. His right arm was stretched out, and the hand was gloveless. The left arm was extended at an awkward right angle and was hooked by his cane, pinned underneath his back. The glove was on the left hand, and the other glove was lying between it and the body. His new white hat was still on his head, but tipped forward. His face was distorted, and some froth had formed on his lips. A large pool of florid blood, oozing from his mouth and the back of his neck, had spread about four feet across the slightly warped planks of the sidewalk and was dripping into the gutter.

There was a latch key in the keyhole with two more keys tied to it by a red tape; and the lower panels of the door were spattered with blood. In the hall, inside the partially opened front door about a foot from the lower sill, were broken portions of three or four artificial incisor teeth, with a base of gutta-percha attached to fit an upper jaw.

Dr. McGillivray was called and he arrived within minutes. The body was quite warm but pulseless, and he pronounced D'Arcy McGee dead. Then he told Constable McVetty to summon the coroner.

Meanwhile someone had raced across Sapper's Bridge to Sandy Hill to tell Sir John A. MacDonald. He arrived about the same time as the coroner. The body was then lifted from the sidewalk with the Prime Minister supporting D'Arcy McGee's head, as they carried the body inside and placed it on a couch in a small front room on the ground floor of the Trotter House.

A careful examination followed.

Noticeable was a strong smell of gunpowder and some burnt hair on the back of the neck. The wound was evident, somewhat oval in shape, on the back of the neck on the right side of the spinal column. There was a corresponding hole right through the back collars of the overcoat, the undercoat and the shirt. It was evident that the bullet had entered from the back and passed horizontally through the upper part of the throat, along the roof and out by the mouth. The upper plate of artificial teeth had been ripped out, and the remnants found were identified as matching those missing.

It was a piteous spectacle. The lower part of the face was mutilated, and the greying beard was clotted with blood. His overcoat was still on with the top button fastened, and his cane and loose glove were close to his head. Near by was his blood-stained white hat. On his feet were woollen socks, and someone had removed his shoes and replaced them with carpet slippers. His bare right hand was lying across his breast.

Outside, a curious crowd was gathering and asking questions in low tones. A ladder had been place as a barricade to protect the area, and a policeman stood by. As Sir John A. MacDonald left Mrs. Trotter's a silvery dawn was breaking and a light snow was starting to fall around the pools of crimson blood. Lying there by the door-step was McGee's half-smoked cigar.

T.P. Slattery, *Assassination of D'Arcy McGee*, 1968

First Commoner

Timothy Warren Anglin (1822–1896) was Speaker of the House of Commons from 1874 to 1878. He succeeded James Cockburn, who occupied the Chair from Confederation to 1873.

The late Speaker was a little man, low voiced, retiring and apparently timid. His rulings were by no means infallible and there was no prestige about him to awe the House. Yet he got along very smoothly for seven years. Mr. Anglin, on the other hand, has a certain presence, plenty of self assurance, and a good sounding voice. Still he cuts a sorry figure.

In the first place, he talks too much. A ruling should be brief, clear as crystal and final as fate. One superfluous sentence spoils its effect. Mr. Anglin utters many superfluous sentences. He explains, expostulates, nay even argues from his seat.

Chaudière, *Canadian Illustrated News*, 1874

Honest Alex

Alexander Mackenzie, (1822–1892) was Prime Minister from 1873 to 1878. He remained a Member until his death.

I liked and admired him very much, and as fellow Members from York County we long shared an office in the Parliament Buildings together. He was the most impeccably honest man I ever knew, and, despite his solemn and almost melancholy countenance, a man with a sense of humour. During the 'Riel Rebellion' session of 1885 the House sat for an unusually long period, and Members on both sides felt that the sessional allowance — then only $1500 per annum — should be increased by special vote. The only Member who would not agree was Mackenzie, and he was emphatic in stating his opposition to any such proposal. One day when we were in our office together, reading our mail, he suddenly burst into quiet laughter, and tossing a letter to me said, "Mulock, r-read yon!" It was from a farmer, praising the stand he had taken, but suggesting that, as the House determined to vote the bonus, Mackenzie accept it and give the money to the writer who had a large family and sorely needed it.

Sir William Mulock, quoted in
Hector Charlesworth, *More Candid Chronicles,* 1928

Question Hour

Mackenzie had no gift of conciliation, no "sunny way," no faculty for compromising even in trifling matters. It was usually a blow for a blow, and the more his opponents winced the more was the sport enjoyed. He took a strange delight in making his opponents feel that he was their master. This characteristic often led him into trouble. Once during the question hour he replied to several Members of the Opposition so curtly and cynically as to arouse a general spirit of resentment on both sides of the House. My deskmate, Thomas Oliver, felt so strongly that Mackenzie acted unwisely that he took a sheet of foolscap, wrote on it in large letters, "A pint of molasses will catch more flies than a hogshead of vinegar," and, folding it up, sent it by a page to Mackenzie. We both watched him as he unfolded it and with a snap of his jaw tore it into fragments and threw it on the floor.

Sir George Ross, *Getting into Parliament and After*, 1913

Mackenzie the Orator

Alexander Mackenzie was not an orator in the generally accepted sense. He had, however, a reputation as one of the most accurate and knowledgeable debaters in the House.

He has not a fine or attractive voice by any means — his modulation is not in any way conformed to the rules — his action is nil, save a strange way he has of catching his spectacles by the two ends — it is rather an uncomfortable way he has of doing it, but doesn't like to — his pronunciation is at times extremely Scotch, but he speaks with more precision than any man I have ever listened to. His sentences as a rule are short, but at times he gets into an apparent confusion, and mixes his participles up so that one would imagine he was sure to break down. But no. He always comes out finished and elegant, every sentence complete and neat as if he were reading from a carefully revised manuscript. This is a faculty few speakers possess, and is only acquired, as is manifest in Mackenzie's case, from a thorough concentration of the mind on what it is about. The galleries may be crowded with the elite of the capital, and youth and beauty may be congregated so as to make most men feel flustered; but I question very much whether the leader of the Opposition ever looks toward the gallery at all; and if he does, its appearance has no visible effect on him. Another characteristic of his oratory is the wonderful memory he possesses as to Parliamentary facts and figures. It is all but impossible to trip him up. While many Members indulge in random statements, and throw off a date or so, without much regard to chronological accuracy, Mackenzie never does so. He is precise as a book, and his memory seems as retentive of impressions received in the House as is paper under the action of the printing press. This faculty is a great power in his hands, and it is at times sometimes amusing and sometimes painful to see some Members on the opposite side of the House wincing under the lash as he makes pass before them their old utterances, and recalls statements made long ago, which even they themselves had forgotten. Oftentimes an opponent will jump to his feet and deny some statement imputed to him, but it is no use. Book, day and date are always ready, and it often happens that Mackenzie proves himself to have been quoting almost verbatim.

Lounger, *Canadian Illustrated News*, 1873

Mackenzie and Macdonald

Mackenzie, during the later years of his Premiership, became the undoubted leader of the House of Commons during its debates. Sir John Macdonald and he frequently broke a lance with each other, and both gentleman enjoyed a good joke even when the laugh happened to be on the wrong side. Sir John seldom studied his speeches, and trusting for his words to the spur of the moment, he sometimes left a loophole for retort which Mr. Mackenzie, with his great store of facts and accurate memory, became remarkably expert in availing himself of.

A notable instance of this, and one well worthy of preservation, occurred one day in the Commons when the Conservative leader, wishing to close off an inconvenient discussion, pointed at Mr. Mackenzie during this remarks and in an offhand manner exclaimed: "Art thou he who troublest Israel?"

Sir John did not recall at the moment that he was quoting the words of Ahab, the wicked king, and not those of the prophet. But Mr. Mackenzie, who was well read in Biblical as in other literature, instantly saw the slip and as instantly retorted in the words of the prophet Elijah: "I have not troubled Israel, but thou and thy father's house, in that ye have forsaken the commandments of the Lord and followed Baalim!"

This happy retort convulsed both sides of the House, and with characteristic good nature Sir John himself joined in and seemed to enjoy the hilarity which followed.

James Young, *Public Men and Public Life*, 1912

Louis Riel

Louis Riel (1844–1885) was elected to Parliament in 1873 and 1874 and, although he once succeeded in taking the oath and signing the roll, he never actually took his seat in the House. The House declared him an outlaw in 1875.

The plans were made and the day selected. It was March, a cold day, with the snow still on the ground, cold enough to make the wearing of heavy coats and wraps a common enough sight on the streets of Ottawa. In the afternoon several figures crossed the Ottawa River from Hull and walked towards the buildings whose stone towers and metal spires dominated the city. Two of the men entered a side door and walked towards the office of the Clerk of the House, Alfred Patrick. One of these men, Romuald Fiset, the member for Rimouski and a former schoolmate of Riel's, asked Patrick if he would swear in a new member. It was a routine action, and Patrick paid little attention to what was going on. He did not even inquire the name of the new member, and noted only that he wore "a heavy whisker, not exactly black." He administered the oath of allegiance and listened indifferently as the reply came, "I do swear that I will be faithful and bear true allegiance to Her Majesty Queen Victoria." Patrick then produced the roll which the two men proceeded to sign. Then they turned to leave. "I did not pay particular attention," said Patrick later, "and did not look at the roll until they were leaving the room. To my astonishment I saw the name 'Louis Riel'. I looked up suddenly and saw them going out of the door. Riel was making a low bow to me." Fiset and Riel then left the building hurriedly, and Patrick, scarcely yet recovered from his astonishment, rushed along the hallway to inform the incredulous Minister of Justice of what had happened. Louis Riel, in spite of the efforts and plans of his enemies to secure his arrest, had actually entered the parliament buildings and had signed the register as the member for Provencher.

George F.G. Stanley, *Louis Riel*, 1963

The House on a Spring Afternoon, 1878

In the spring of 1878, Mr. Letellier de St. Just, Lieutenant Governor of the Province of Quebec, dismissed the Conservative provincial government there. While the new elections were underway, a debate began in the federal House on the Lieutenant Governor's highly unusual action. The Conservatives, under Macdonald, strongly disagreed with de St. Just's decision and they seized the opportunity to debate the issue at length. The debate began sedately enough, but by the afternoon of April 12 it was clear that members of all parties had been visiting the house saloon.

The scene which followed had no parallel before or since the Government was established at Ottawa. While points of order were being argued, members hammered at desks, blew on tin trumpets, imitated the crowing of cocks, sent up toy-balloons, threw sandcrackers or torpedoes, and occasionally hurled blue-books across the House. Often the babel of sounds was such that neither the Speaker of the House nor the Member who had the floor could be heard. Once in a while amid the din some Member with a good voice would start up the "Marseillaise," "God Save the Queen," "A la claire fontaine," "The Raftmans's chorus," or some plantation melody, and then the whole House would join in the song, with an effect that was quite moving. The feelings inspired by these songs would sway the House back into a quiet frame; but scarcely would the speaker who had the floor recover the thread of his discourse when such a pandemonium would be raised as made the listener think "Chaos had come again." When a speaker had at last made himself heard over the diminishing din of exhausted voices, and when he himself had exhausted his subject, he would keep the floor by quoting passages from law-books, books of poetry, philosophy and humor.

Mr. Cimon, one of these speakers, filled up his time by reading the whole of the British North America Act in French, making humorous comment upon each clause. In some of these passages "the grim features of Mr. Blake," writes a chronicler of the scene, "not merely relaxed into a smile, but broke into a laugh, that shook his big frame all over."

As the night wore on, the spectators became tired, and the galleries were gradually cleared. Now and again a Member strayed off, and would be found shortly afterwards stretched on a bench in the reading room, or curled up in an alcove of the library fast asleep. But there were always enough Members left in the House to keep up the fun. Even here, however, the exhausted figures of some Members would be found reclining on their desks, quite unconscious of the paper missiles that were being pelted at them. In the afternoon Lady Dufferin had sat in the gallery, listening with amused bewilderment to the babel of sounds. As she rose to leave, a Member struck up "God save the Queen," and all the House rose and joined in the anthem with a patriotic fervour that was remarkable. Mr. Mackenzie had just come in at that moment, and Mr. Blake and he, after looking at each other in hesitation for a few moments, threw off their dignity and joined in. Just as the signing ceased, Sir John, who had been resting in his private room, appeared on the scene, and was greeted with a rousing cheer by the Opposition.

At one stage Mr. De Veber rose to a point of order. The Speaker asked what it was, and De Veber said, "The Minister of Marine and Fisheries is sitting at the clerk's table in irreverent proximity to the mace."

"That's no point of order," said the Speaker, and in the midst of the laughter which followed some one struck up "Auld Lang Syne."

A party of Members organized an impromptu band, which was nicknamed "Gideon's Band," and began to play a species of music that was more discordant if possible that the voices and banging of desks which accompanied it. *The Citizen*, in its reports, compared the voices of the Members to the roaring of the beasts at Ephesus. The Speaker, after manfully battling against these insurmountable obstacles to order, at least gave up from a difficulty that was certainly "constitutional," — his voice having entirely given out. Mr. Cheval, a French Member, had procured some new instruments described as "squeaking machines," and these were added to the band. Some one wanted to put down Mr. Cheval and his music, upon which he pathetically appealed to the Speaker. "Mr. Speaker, I wish to know which is more worse, de man dat trows blue books 'cross de House, or de man dat goes in for a small leedle music." This entreaty was received with roars of laughter. The Speaker said both were unparliamentary, whereupon Mr. Smith of Peel, whose role was leader of the orchestra, led off the House in another song, while Mr. Cheval resumed operations on his squeaking machine. Mr. Mackenzie sometimes exhibited a face "as long as a family churn," and sometimes was beaming with goodwill, while Mr. Blake kept himself amused and awake "by performing some extraordinary finger-music on his desk." Mr. Smith of Peel got so hoarse from his orchestral performances that he simply croaked. At one point in the proceedings Mr. Campbell, horrified at this outrage upon decorum, came out near the clerk's table, and with the most violent gesticulations, swinging his arms and waving his hat, denounced the proceedings. Mr. Mackenzie demanded that the Sergeant-at-Arms should be called in to preserve order, but the Sergeant-at-Arms, ensconced in a private nook of his own, was enjoying the fun too much to do anything of the kind. Once when Mr. Plumb was speaking, Mr. Macdonnell of Inverness, with mock gravity, called the attention of the Speaker to the fact that the Member for Niagara was interrupting the music. "An ominous silence ensued," wrote the *Citizen* reporter, describing another stage of the proceedings, "when Haggart, the powerful but merciful Member for South Lanark, rises. He holds in his hands the memorial of Letellier de St. Just to Lord Dufferin. In front of him in a solid phalanx the ministerial battalion is roaring, howling, hooting, singing, whistling, stamping, shouting and caterwauling. That frisky kitten Dymond is suspiciously toying with a waste-basket; while the genteel Cheval, who looks as if he had strayed into the House by mistake, is expanding a toy bag-pipe, for the purpose of dropping it into the inverted crown of Dr. Brossé's [Dr. William Brouse] slouch hat. At last Dymond lets fly his waste-basket among a group of ministerial friends. The toy bag-pipe appeared in Dr. Brossé's hat again, and squealed to such a degree that he clutched it and threw it to another Member, who stopped signing in order to blow it up again. But not understanding how to manipulate it, the noisy object set up such a wail as fairly brought down the House." While this had been going on Lady Dufferin again came in, and when she left, the House once more gave "God Save the Queen," followed up with a cheer and such waving of handkerchiefs as would have led a stranger to believe that Queen Victoria herself was quitting the Chamber.

At last Mr. Cheval burst his toy bag-pipe and retired with a broken heart, amid the mock sympathy of his orchestra. A demand by Mr. Dymond for a speech from the Speaker was greeted with roars of laughter. At 4:15 a.m., that patient functionary left Mr. De Veber in his chair and went out to get something to eat. In a few moments pages began to bring coffee, which was greeted with cheers from both sides. About six o'clock (at which hour, had it been evening, the Speaker would have risen from the chair as a matter of course), Mr. Bowell rose and said he was willing to have six o'clock called, and go on after getting something to eat.

"There is no six o'clock to-day," added Mr. Holton. "Six o'clock was yesterday," added Mr. Mills. "Oh, it's six of one and half a dozen of the other," said Mr. Blake. "Then it's twelve," reasoned Mr. Bowell, amid laughter.

Debate continued in the same vein, as it had all night, before the House finally adjourned at six o'clock p.m., after sitting for twenty-seven hours.

E.B. Biggar, *Anecdotal Life of Macdonald*, 1891

Wild Prorogation

For most of the 1870s, relations between Donald Alexander Smith, M.P., later Lord Strathcona, (1820–1914) and the Conservative front bench were extremely poor. The conflict spilled onto the floor of the House at the close of the session of 1878.

The hour for prorogation arrived. All over the Chamber were evidences of early flitting, in open desks and torn and scattered papers, whilst the Members waited for Black Rod to appear. Donald A. Smith entered the House somewhat abruptly, and scarcely reached his seat before beginning to address the Speaker. He started to complain about an un-called-for reflection about his personal honour in a speech made the day before by Sir John A. Macdonald, a report of which had appeared in the newspaper which he proposed to read to the House. In one moment the House was in an uproar! Together with shouts for order, could be heard, "Treachery," "Liar," and other terms still more unparliamentary. The sound of the guns could be faintly heard, which announced that His Excellency had arrived at the Senate, and was awaiting his "Faithful Commons," but His Excellency's "Faithful Commons" was quite otherwise engaged. Sir John A. Macdonald, Dr. Tupper, Dr. Sproule, Mackenzie Bowell, John Rochester, and many others, were yelling themselves hoarse, and shaking their fists at Donald A. He waited quietly for a chance to continue, fearless as ever, not by any means wanting impressiveness and seemingly the least concerned of all there. The noise reached the lobbies and people came crowding in, some forced close to the Speaker's Chair, amongst them myself, by the crush behind. By a superhuman effort Dr. Tupper now got the floor and both sides took part in the chorus of shouts and yells.

Black Rod knocked. The Speaker tried to make himself heard. In vain! Both Liberals and Conservatives were determined to fight it out and to be recorded in Hansard. The Speaker resumed his seat. Outside, impatiently waited an indignant Black Rod. While in the House, communications between erstwhile friends, confidential and intimate, never intended for the public ear, were announced as from the house-tops. A shout in Dr. Tupper's stentorian tones, "You asked me to get you made a Privy Councillor," what piece of secret history was this? The Sergeant-at-Arms endeavoured to notify the Speaker that His Excellency's messenger waited. His efforts were in vain. Black Rod knocked, and knocked again. He might as well have knocked at the portals of the tomb. Finally the Speaker motioned to the door. Black Rod entered. He bowed, as usual. His lips moved, but no sound reached the frantic House. The Speaker stood up and evidently made an announcement. He was not heard — the "Faithful Commons" continued to shout at one another, with unabated fury! Finally, with what dignity he could muster, the Speaker stepped down from the dais, the Sergeant-at-Arms shouldered the mace, and preceded by Black Rod, they slowly made their way to the lobby leading to the Senate. The Cabinet followed, and then as excited a mob as ever disgraced a House of Commons.

In a determination to be in the middle of the stage I pushed my way through the crowd, close to Donald A. Smith. All around people were hustling and pushing, some of the Opposition with their arms uplifted as if to strike. Many besides myself had no right to be there, but messengers and door keepers had lost their heads. The crowd swayed to and fro, and the writer found himself beside Donald A. Smith, just as Tory Members reached out to strike his grey top hat. It was a shuffling and slightly dishevelled crowd that finally reached the Senate Chamber, but once inside those dignified precincts the excitement quickly subsided.

W.T.R. Preston, *My Generation of Politics and Politicians*, 1927

Smith and Sir John

There was much concern over the expected speech and attitude of Donald A. Smith over the Pacific Railway controversy. At Sir Charles Tupper's request Peter Mitchell, M.P., arranged an interview between Macdonald and Smith, who were not on the best of terms, with a view to a reconciliation. When Smith emerged from Macdonald's room the failure of the purpose was evident.

I saw by the expression and colour of his face that he was very much excited, and I feared it was all up with us. Mr. Smith came along to where I sat and said to me:

"Oh! Mitchell, he's an awful man, that. He has done nothing but swear at me since I went into the room."

Mr. Smith said: "I don't want to vote against your Government, and particularly on your account, Mr. Mitchell, because you have always treated me very fairly, but there is nothing else for me to do, and I will have to do it."

[Smith's arraignment of the Government that night marked the turning point, and the Government resigned next day.]

Peter Mitchell, quoted in M.O. Hammond, *Confederation and Its Leaders*, 1917

Cartwright and Macdonald

In the first Parliament, Sir Richard Cartwright (1835–1912), who prided himself on his credentials for the post of Minister of Finance, was passed over for the job by Prime Minister Macdonald. Shortly thereafter, Cartwright crossed the floor of the House and joined the Liberals, forever retaining a strong dislike for Macdonald.

In his time Sir Richard Cartwright was perhaps the most caustic and scholarly speaker in the Canadian Parliament. Too many of his speeches had the flavour of malice and the acid of bitterness. But every word carried its exact meaning. There was no verbiage or redundancy. The argument was direct, deliberate, compact and luminous. In his humour there was the frost of Autumn, but the radiance, too, of its piercing sunshine. Always stately and severe he relaxed nothing of his outward austerity when he was striking at a victim with biting irony or brilliant badinage. But the irony was always corrosive and the badinage often malicious and sometimes insolent. In social intercourse Cartwright could be gracious and intimate. As a host he was a simple gentleman, kindly without pretension. But in political warfare he knew only the law of the jungle. For Sir John Macdonald he had a consuming, incurable hatred.

When a sum was put in the estimates for a statue to Sir John on Parliament Hill he was determined to offer an amendment requiring that the facts of the "Pacific scandal" should be inscribed upon the monument. For days his Parliamentary associates pleaded and reasoned that he would injure only himself and the Liberal party if he should actually submit such a resolution. But it was long before he would yield and he yielded at last to the persuasion of friends who were brought to Ottawa

to reinforce the appeals and protests of the parliamentary party.
Sir John Willison, *Reminiscences, Political and Personal*, 1919

Doing Justice

About the year 1883 a life of Sir John Macdonald appeared written by
a certain John Edmund Collins. Sir John did not know the author, nor
had he any connection with the book. It was merely a well-ordered presentation of facts already known, and did not profess to be anything
more. Some of the government departments bought copies and the title
appeared in the public accounts, which came before parliament. This
gave Sir Richard one of those opportunities to attack Sir John of which
he never failed to take advantage. After saying some disagreeable
things, he concluded thus: "However, Mr. Speaker, I am bound to say
that I think it quite fit that a gentleman who in his day has done justice
to so many John Collinses, should at last have a John Collins to do justice to him." To the uninitiated it may be explained that "John Collins"
is the name of a rather potent beverage.
Sir Joseph Pope, *Day of Macdonald*, 1915

Sessional Hospitality

*Sir Richard did not bear the same animosity towards Sir John's son, Hugh
John Macdonald.*

In arranging for official hospitalities a great responsibility is thrown
upon the private secretary of the host, and once in a while he may make
a mistake. On one occasion Sir Richard Cartwright decided to give a
strictly party dinner at the Rideau Club for about twenty. His then
secretary, Mr. Frank O'Hara, who had been recently appointed, and was
not familiar with the Members of the House, was furnished with a list
of the gentlemen to whom he was to send invitations. Among them was
Mr. Macdonald, a Liberal Member from the Maritime Provinces.
There are always Macdonalds galore in Parliament. Sir Richard's
secretary, seeing the name "Macdonald" on the list, and knowing only
"Hugh John" of that name in Parliament, sent the invitation to him.
Hugh promptly accepted and on the eventful evening turned up at the
Rideau Club, the only Conservative in a Liberal gathering. Sir Richard

realized that a mistake had been made but promptly rose to the occasion. He made "Hugh John" more than welcome and gave him the seat of honour, to which precedence as a former cabinet minister entitled him. He proved to be the life of the party. He was full of good stories which kept the table in a roar, and Sir Richard was delighted with his guest. Next morning when he arrived at the office he remarked to his secretary, with an expansive smile, "Well, you picked out the right Macdonald for last night, Frank. It was the best evening I have had for a long time."

Fred Cook, *Giants and Jesters,* n.d.

Old Foes

Sir Richard Cartwright and Sir Charles Tupper faced each other for many years in the nineteenth century House.

The fiercest political protagonists usually entertained a sincere respect and even regard for each other. On one occasion during the early years of my leadership, Sir Charles Tupper was invited by the Speaker at my request to take a seat upon the floor of the House; he remained until six o'clock. No two men in public life had denounced each other more vehemently and bitterly than Sir Charles Tupper and Sir Richard Cartwright. I was a little surprised and greatly moved to observe Sir Richard, who was extremely lame, hobble from his seat around the Speaker's chair to greet and welcome Sir Charles before he left the precincts of the Chamber.

Robert Laird Borden: His Memoirs, Henry Borden, ed., 1938

Cartwright in Old Age

It was an interesting experience to visit the old gentleman, who in these later years was so badly afflicted with gout that he got around with difficulty with a cane in each hand, taking a step at a time. His brain, however, was working just as keenly as ever, and as he sat at his desk in his office he spoke with the same mathematical precision that he used in the House of Commons or the Senate. One of his favorite phrases in referring to any person whom he did not like or was opposed to was to speak of him as "Master" so-and-so, and he would deliver an address,

seated in his chair, upon any subject on which one happened to be looking for information, and characterize the opponent who might have
been connected with the matter in any way in this manner.

E.M.Macdonald, *Recollections, Political and Personal,* 1938

King of the Gatineau

*Alonzo Wright (1825–1894) represented the constituency of Ottawa
County in the early decades of Confederation. He was known as the "King
of the Gatineau" in part because of the lavish hospitality he dispensed at
"Ironsides", his Gatineau, Quebec estate.*

Like all good-natured Members residing near the capital, "Alonzo" was
much plagued by office-seekers of all classes. Among these was a certain Madame Laplante of Hull, whose aspirations did not rise above a
charwoman's place. She was unusually persistent. One day, as the
"King" was driving over the Sapper's Bridge, he saw a woman in front
of his horses waving her arms wildly as a signal to stop. He pulled up,
and saw that it was Madame Laplante. Being rather hazy as to her present fortunes, he ventured to express the hope that she liked the position which he had been so fortunate as to obtain for her. Madame
Laplante, with sobs, said that she was still without work. At this the
"King" feigned unbounded indignation. The rest must be told in his
own words.

> "Impossible," I made answer. "It cannot be." Upon receiv-
> ing renewed assurances that so it was, my resolution was taken
> in an instant. Turning my carriage I bade the weeping woman
> enter, and drove at once to the Public Departments. Brushing
> aside the minions who sought to arrest our progress, I strode
> unannounced into the Ministerial presence. "Sir," said I, "I
> have come to you as a suitor for the last time. You may remem-
> ber that you promised me that this worthy woman should be
> employed forthwith. I learned to-day that that promise, like
> many others you have made me, is still unfulfilled. There is a
> time when patience ceases to be a virtue. Sir, my resolution is
> taken. I am as good a party man as lives, but there is something
> that I value more than my party, and that is my self-respect. This

afternoon my resignation shall be in the hands of the Speaker, and I shall then be free to state publicly the sentiments I entertain towards all violators of their word, and by the aid of this victim of duplicity, to expose your perfidious treatment of one of your hitherto most faithful supporters." My arguments, my entreaties, my threats prevailed, and Madame Laplante that day entered the service of her country, which she continues to adorn!

Sir Joseph Pope, *Day of Macdonald*, 1915

King of the Gatineau, II

Mr. Wright, who was known near and far as the "King of the Gatineau" was a grandson of Philemon Wright, the first white settler in the Ottawa district. He was short of stature, and was the embodiment of good nature. His great delight was to entertain his brother Members of Parliament, irrespective of their political affiliations, members of the press gallery and other friends. At his Gatineau home "Ironsides", he dispensed bountiful hospitality. The Ottawa county member did not trouble the House with many speeches, but when it was known that Alonzo was "up," the Chamber filled rapidly. There was a musical rhythm in his voice and a grace and culture in his style which few men in Parliament could emulate. His wealth of language and classical quotations betokened the scholar. On one occasion he outdid himself.

For some years there had been friendly rivalry between Mr. James Trow, chief Liberal whip, and Mr. Wright, as to which should have the "last say" of the session. When all the business of Parliament had been transacted and the Commoners were waiting for the summons to the Senate Chamber to hear His Excellency's farewell message, it would be a struggle between these two veterans to catch the Speaker's eye. Generally Mr. Trow got the honour; as a matter of fact I think some sessions it was pre-arranged. For five or ten minutes the Member for South Perth would "josh" the ministerial benches unmercifully but always in a kindly spirit. However on the occasion I have in mind, the two members had reached an understanding that Mr. Wright was to have the floor, for a particular reason.

For some years Ottawa had been honoured by the presence during the parliamentary session of Miss Macpherson, the charming daughter of Sir David Macpherson, who was Speaker of the Senate from 1880 to 1883, and then minister of the interior until 1885. Miss Macpherson was one of the most attractive looking ladies I have ever seen. Tall, of regal bearing, and always immaculately gowned, she was the central figure at the different social gatherings of the capital.

The Hon. G.A. Kirkpatrick, M.P. for Frontenac, had been elected Speaker of the House at the beginning of the session, and it was not long before Members and newspapermen noticed the Mr. Speaker was paying great attention to Miss Macpherson. Later it was generally understood that they were engaged to be married, although there had been no official announcements.

Well, on the closing day of Parliament, Mr. Wright took the floor just before prorogation and proceeded to shower upon the Speaker the kindliest eulogies I have ever heard addressed to a public man. Remember that this was Mr. Kirkpatrick's first session in the Chair. The "King" was in fine form. In his opening remarks, he said:

Before the Usher of the Black Rod gives his three knocks, before that pleasant little raven from the Upper Chamber comes tapping at our door, I have been requested by a number of the Members of the House to say a few words concerning the manner in which you have discharged the important duties devolving upon you during this session. When we heard you read the solemn services with which we begin our proceedings, we thought a great mistake had been made when you devoted yourself to the law instead of the Gospel, to the evil instead of the good. But, Sir, we had to bow to the inevitable, and born as you were, under the shadow of the old fort of Frontenac; born, as your were, under the shadow of that great penal institution, where justice presents its malevolent rather than its benevolent aspects, we all felt assured that when you were selected by the Commons to perform the important duties of the office you hold, you would perform them with a singular grace and a wonderful charm—and I am free to confess that our expectations have not been disappointed. I am sure both sides of the House will agree with me that in all respects you have performed your duty in a manner to win commendation from all sorts and conditions of men; but while you have not been guilty of any sins of commission, I fear we must charge you with a sin of omission. We had reason to expect that the monotony of our Parliamentary life would have been relieved by a pleasant charm and an agreeable change. We thought that we would hear the rustling of divinity, the fluttering of angelic wings, and the odour of violets and orange flowers in our passages and corridors; but, Sir, a word to the wise is sufficient; and as an eminent writer says, it is never too late to mend, and we trust this matter will be mended before we meet again another Session. Sir, you have occupied a very distinguished position. You remind us of that picture by a great French artist which depicted the deluge. On a vast rock in the midst of a great expanse of waters, was seated a noble and distinguished figure, not unlike your own, who looked down on the struggling swimmers below. You have seen the ebb and flow of political life; the fierce assaults of my hon. friends of the Opposition on the serried ranks of their opponents, and you have heard the cry of many a strong swimmer in his agony, who went down in the terrible gulf—who, commencing his political life, found that in this arena, above all other, the principle of the survival of the fittest prevails; and I think, Sir, you have borne the criticisms of your friends as well as your enemies, which proves always the existence of the highest statecraft. In all respects, Sir, you deserve the highest commendation at the hands of your fellow-citizens, your colleagues and your countrymen; and we trust that when the period arrives, which comes to Speakers as well as to meaner organizations, when you will be exalted into the political arcana—we hope then when you will be transferred to another sphere, you will pass your time in studying, patiently, Parliamentary problems and curious constitutional questions so that you may enjoy the utmost happiness consistent with the state of things here below. And I am sure I express the opinion of every Member in saying we trust that when that time arrives, you will have so comported yourself that we will be able to join in saying: "Well done, good and faithful Speaker, enter thou into the new governorship, collectorship or the judgeship prepared for you from the beginning of this Parliament."

Mr. Kirkpatrick was more than embarrassed. His countenance was of the rosiest hue, and from our places in the gallery above him we could see how his nerves were being frayed by the compliments and personal references. Mr. Wright was a good prophet. The Speaker and Miss Macpherson were married that summer, and while he retained the position of presiding officer of the Commons until 1887, his good lady was the chief hostess of Parliament.

Fred Cook, Giants and Jesters, n.d.

George Brown

George Brown (1818–1880) one of the Fathers of Confederation and a founder of the Toronto Globe newspaper, was never elected a Member of the House of Commons. He was very active in Liberal party affairs and was rewarded with a Senate seat in 1874. He died of complications from a gunshot wound in 1880.

In November of 1878 George Brown turned sixty. With grey hair becoming white, and silvery whiskers framing his long, august-looking countenance, he had more the appearance of a grave and stately patriarch than the hearty, exuberant politician of earlier days. Indeed, this patriarchal image would come down to posterity, thanks largely to solemn engravings of the elder Brown, widely distributed by the *Globe*, that hung for years like Liberal icons in good Grit homes throughout the country. Yet the image was wrong, or at least superficial. The tall, white-headed figure in the black frock coat only looked austere and sombre in repose. And for him, that state was still very far from habitual.

For in these later years he continued to be vigorous, high-spirited, and full of quick enthusiasm. He tired more readily, no doubt; and he liked nothing better than to sit peacefully by the fireside with his wife. But there had always been this private tranquility in Brown, who could relax so contentedly and completely within his own domestic world. Certainly, he seemed as physically strong as ever. At Bow Park he kept up his favourite pastime of collecting and piling stones in the fields, chatting away meanwhile with guests who found much less enjoyment in the sport. At the *Globe* office he still liked to leap up the stairs four steps at a time—though Bob Gay, his old foreman, lamented that the Chief could no longer take six.

And it was in this era that he once settled a little friction with a badgering porter in the Montreal railway station by calmly picking up the man by the collar and the seat of his trousers and depositing him gently outside the station on the ground. The awestruck porter said afterwards that he had never felt so utterly helpless.

J.M.S. Careless, Brown of the Globe, 1963

Brown's End

March 25, 1880; four-thirty on a dull afternoon. Brown was working quietly at the *Globe* office in his room that opened off the landing of the staircase up from King Street, which went on to the editorial rooms above. There was a tap at the door. He looked up from his desk to see a sallow little man, not much more than five feet tall, thin-faced, with a straggling moustache and goatee, standing uncertainly in his doorway. George Bennett was his name, the intruder mumbled, employed in the *Globe* engine-room for the past five years, and now discharged by the shop foreman for intemperance. He would like a certificate from Mr. Brown that he had served five years. He had the paper with him—fumbling for it—and if Mr. Brown would sign—.

Brown was impatient. Gruffly he told Bennett to take his paper for signature to the head of the department where he had been employed. The foreman there had already refused to sign it, said Bennett, moving into the room and half closing the door behind him. Then take it to Mr. Henning, the *Globe* treasurer, who would have the record on the books—Brown grew uneasy. What did this man want? Bennett came forward to the desk. "Sign it—sign it," he demanded harshly. Brown rose. Angry refusal brought fierce insistence; the sound of rising voices could be heard in the editorial rooms. Now Brown's temper was soaring—when Bennett, white-faced and staring, suddenly snatched out his revolver and cocked it. The little wretch might be meaning to shoot me, flashed through Brown's mind. Impulsively he leaped forward, grabbing for Bennett's wrist. There was a moment of mad struggle. The gun fired as Brown managed to deflect it downward.

"Help, help—murder!" he shouted wildly. But his far greater strength quickly overcame his assailant. Forcing Bennett back out of the room and on the landing, he held him there against the wall as he wrenched the still loaded weapon away.

The shot, the cry, and the noise of struggle brought three editorial staff members, Thomson, Ewan, and Blue, pounding down the stairs from above. Aghast, they rushed to seize hold of Bennett, while Brown, grey and trembling leaned against the wall. "Are you hurt, Mr. Brown?" Blue asked anxiously. "I don't know," Brown answered in a daze. Blue pointed sharply at the other's leg. "There," he said urgently. On the outside of the left thigh there was a clean hole in the broadcloth trousers. Brown slowly ran his hand down, and behind his leg a little lower. It came up stained with blood.

They called the police and the doctor, while Brown went back into his room to lie down. Dr. Thorburn arrived and quickly dressed the injury. It seemed to be only a flesh wound, and quite superficial; the *Globe* director already appeared to be recovering, as he talked and joked about his "assassination" with excited members of the office staff. Undoubtedly it would make a good news story for a rather dull day. He even walked down out of the building to take his usual hired carriage from the West End Cab Company home to Lambton Lodge. He expected merely to have a short stay in bed while the wound healed.

J.M.S. Careless, Brown of the Globe, 1963

Blake and Macdonald

The brilliant lawyer Dominick Edward Blake (1833–1912) led the Liberal opposition between 1880 and 1887. Taciturn and lacking that political charm with which his rival Sir John A. Macdonald was so richly endowed, he often failed miserably in those little graces essential to successful leadership.

Sir John Macdonald was walking up to the Parliament Buildings one afternoon in the early days of the session, when Mr. Blake overtook him on the broad walk. Coat collar up, slouched hat away down on the head, Mr. Blake saw nobody; it was a habit with him. Just as he was passing Sir John, the latter hailed him with a hearty "Good-day Blake; feeling all right today?"

Mr. Blake looked up with a start and recognized the leader of the government. He fell into step with Sir John and remarked: "Ah, Macdonald, I envy that bright cheerful manner of yours — the way you accost people and make them feel contented with the world. How ever do you do it? I would given anything to have the same happy faculty."

"My dear Blake," Sir John replied, "it is as easy as rolling off a log, as the Ottawa river lumbermen say. You can acquire the same faculty without much difficulty. Let me illustrate. Supposing tomorrow I am walking up to the Buildings as we are today, and one of my supporters overtakes me as you did. He turns to me and says in a modest, retiring manner, 'Good day, Sir John. How are you today?' I reply, 'Splendid, Jones, splendid. And yourself?' He answers and then we continue our walk together. He then hazards the remark: 'Well, I think we are going to have a little snow.' At which I observe, 'Probably so, Jones, but 'sno matter.' Then we both laugh and Jones goes off to tell the boys the little joke we have had. There you are, Blake; these opportunities crop up all the time. Be on the lookout for them and they will soon come to you naturally." Mr. Blake gazed at Sir John with admiration and remarked, "Well, I will remember that one at any rate."

The story went that a few days later Mr. Blake had his opportunity. It was a dull day, with grey skies and all the portents of a downfall of "the beautiful." Striding along as usual up the walk to the Buildings, Mr. Blake overtook one of his own followers, a timid little backbencher, who ventured to give him greeting. "How are you today, Mr. Blake?" he enquired. "Oh, as usual, Smith." And then Mr. Smith remarks, "It looks as if we are going to have a little snow." At once Mr. Blake was reminded of the lesson which Sir John had given him. Now what was that joke? Ah, he remembered, and promptly replied to his follower, "Oh, yes, but it's quite immaterial". Pleased with himself, Mr. Blake continued to his quarters in the Parliament Buildings.

Fred Cook, Fifty Years Ago and Since, n.d.

A Soporific Speech

Sir Richard Cartwright's observations on Blake's speech on the Riel case in 1885 make plain Blake's lack of political instincts.

He delivered a speech of immense length which, it was said, and I believe correctly, it had cost him three months of hard labour to prepare, and which took him seven hours to deliver. From one standpoint this speech was a marvel of industry and ingenuity and a perfect store-house of minute information on a great many subjects for which no one in the House cared one straw, and it wound up in a maze of legal subtleties and disquisitions on points of medical jurisprudence, from all of which he deduced the conclusion that there was need of more evidence to clinch the question whether Riel was perfectly responsible or not. It was, in short, a speech which no man in the House except Mr. Blake could have made and which on such an occasion no man but Mr. Blake would ever have made. The effect produced on his audience may be best judged from one simple fact. I was sitting directly opposite to Sir John all through the harangue, and I had noticed at the outset that he was plainly nervous. As Mr. Blake proceeded I observed that Sir John grew more and more at ease, and at last I saw him turn round to one of his colleagues seemingly much amused. Mr. Blake had then been speaking about two hours, and the Chamber was very crowded and the atmosphere very close. Glancing round I saw that our friends were all, as in duty bound, in solid phalanx in their places, but also, alas that the majority of them were fast asleep. Knowing that if this circumstance came to Mr. Blake's notice he was quite capable of flinging down his manuscript and leaving the House, I succeeded in passing a note to one of our whips begging him to wake up the delinquents with all speed, but you may imagine how seven hours of such disquisition was likely to affect the ordinary hearer. As it was, after Mr. Girouard had replied in an effort of eight hours' duration, principally composed of traversing Mr. Blake's speech paragraph by paragraph, the whole life had gone out of the debate, and no power on earth could revive it. Had Mr. Blake on this occasion done himself justice and given us what everyone expected he would do, an impassioned invective of moderate duration, instead of this inordinately prolix dissertation, it was more than possible it might have turned the scale.

Sir Richard Cartwright, *Reminiscences*, 1912

Blake Morose

Blake did not cultivate to any extent the personal regard of his followers. He was often morose, and apparently depressed and discouraged, as if he thought the game was not worth the candle. He never appeared to rise above the serious side of life, or to be playful in manner or speech amid the companionship of his supporters. He enjoyed a good story, but never "swapped" with anybody. He could not make himself "one of the boys." He was always on his good behaviour.

As the Opposition was engaged principally in criticizing the Estimates and the legislation proposed by the Government, I suggested to Mr. Blake that it might be profitable, from a party point of view, if we brought before the House some questions of general public interest, to show that we had some power of initiative as well. After a review of several suitable topics it was agreed that I should give notice to reopen the question of Reciprocity with the United States in the form of a motion asking for correspondence between the Government of Canada and the United States bearing upon the subject. As the question was a comprehensive one, and might involve an expression of the policy of the Liberal party, it was agreed that I should submit an outline of my speech for Mr. Blake's approval, which I did. In the course of a couple of weeks my motion was reached, and I rose to deliver myself of a speech which I had carefully prepared, and which I felt confident would be a reasonably creditable presentation of my case. I spoke for about three-quarters of an hour, and was listened to with fair attention by both sides of the House. The Hon. Mr. White replied to my arguments, and with one or two other short speeches the debate closed. Though not particularly impressed with my effort to instruct the House, I ventured to say to Mr. Blake a few hours afterwards, "Well, I have done my best for Reciprocity. How did you like my speech?" "My dear boy," he said, "I did not hear a word of it. I slept the whole time you were speaking." Whether to take his repose as a mark of perfect confidence in my ability to do justice to the subject, or as showing a lack of interest in anything I might say, was my dilemma. It was, however, the last speech about which I asked his opinion, either before or after delivery.

Sir George Ross, *Getting Into Parliament and After*, 1913

Myopia

Was Blake's coldness due to poor eyesight?

Blake possessed a warm Irish heart, and what some thought was coldness arose solely from defective vision. I recall an incident which verifies this. One day when walking down Sparks Street, as we were leaving

41

Ottawa at the close of a session, he burst out with an exclamation of deep regret that he was unable to bow, shake hands or utter a passing word of leave-taking — as I was almost continuously doing — to the numerous Ottawa and other friends we chanced to meet. "The trouble is," he said, "my eyesight prevents me recognizing them until they are either passed, or it is too late for me to speak or greet them".

James Young, *Public Men and Public Life*, 1912

Blake Exacting

During Blake's period of office an old and faithful official of his department, who rather prided himself upon his discrimination in the use of words, wrote on a file of papers "Referred to the Minister for his instructions." When this came before Blake, he wrote underneath the memorandum: "My officers do not refer matters to me; they submit them.—E.B."

Sir Joseph Pope, *Day of Macdonald*, 1915

Blake the Orator

On the Opposition side of the House, the man who holds the first place as an orator is Edward Blake, and in almost every respect he is the very antipode of Sir John Macdonald. When any debate of importance is on, let the House be ever so noisy and languid, when the honourable Member rises, and his clear, ringing voice says "Mr. Speaker," the noise is immediately hushed and Members prick up their ears, knowing that something worth hearing is coming now. The first thing that strikes the listener about Blake is the methodical way in which he treats his subject. He starts off cool and deliberately. He lays down what he has got to do, and he sets about it in the most workmanlike manner. He takes up one argument of his opponent, deals with it and lays it down on the one side ruptured. He takes another and another, warming up to his work as the heap of damaged material increases; and when he has gone over them all, and begins to throw back to each his damaged goods, then it is that the man appears. He likes to wound, and as he sees those opposite wince at his blows, it seems to urge him to make them wince the more. And woe is to the man with whom he is dealing when he — the orator — begins to smile and jeer. I have seen men turn pale and press their knees with their hands as if restraining themselves from running away from that merciless shower of incisive invective. In some respects Blake's satirical powers are at once the ornament and the drawback of his oratory. To the on-looker, lounging with his chin on the rail of the gallery, what can be conceived as more delightful than to hear and see the spokesman of the Opposition skinning the Cabinet. He goes at it with such a will, and it seems so very sore to them that human nature cannot resist the fullest enjoyment at looking on. But it has frequently occurred to me that Blake gives way to his penchant in this respect too recklessly. I remember one night in particular when he marred the effort of a whole night by giving reins to his propensity for sarcasm. He had demolished all his opponents, scattered their arguments like chaff, and was so thoroughly master of the field that his opponents submitted almost deprecatingly. But the opportunity was too tempting. He could well have afforded to walk off with his laurels victorious. But no, he took up one of the conquered ones; and in a ten-minutes burst he scathed him most unmercifully; and I could well discern from my perch in the gallery that while his victim gained sympathy, he lost it in proportion. The great feature of Blake's oratory is his earnestness. Let the matter be ever so trivial, he deals with it as seriously as if it were a measure of the greatest importance; and one often wonders how, amid his arduous professional duties, he has gathered such a fund of information. He seems up in everything, even to the minutest details. While other Members keep plodding through their volumes enunciating precedents, Blake can rattle his off, seemingly as familiar with the whole thing as if it were the multiplication table. No wonder that at times he looks pale and nervous and exhausted, for while many Members of Parliament imagine they can gather political lore from the stem of a tobacco pipe, in the smoking-room, Blake grubs for his amongst the volumes of the library.

Edward Blake has little ostentation in his style, and his oratory derives little of its effect from action of any kind. He stands generally with his left hand in his pocket, and except when referring to a book, he rarely removes it. But when he bends forward, his eye glancing and his face suffused with passion, and his finger pointed at some unfortunate victim, there is more force in this simple action than in any amount of gesticulation. I have often thought what a grand scene it would be to see a field-day between Gladstone and Blake. Cool, earnest, honest, able but terribly merciless, they would make the best-matched pair of political gladiators I have seen. Gladstone, with his long experience and skill in fence, might win the fight, but he would have to acknowledge that he had vanquished a doughty foe.

Lounger, *Canadian Illustrated News*, 1873

Sarcastic Blake

Although Blake's mind was not of the constructive order, his critical and analytical faculties were highly developed. Always effective, often trenchant, sometimes cruel, his powers of sarcasm and invective were unrivalled. Once, when a former minister of Inland Revenue, not remarkable for his knowledge of the affairs of his department, had proposed a resolution to the effect that a barrel should no longer be considered a measure of capacity, Blake offered an amendment to the effect that "in the future the office of Cabinet minister be no longer considered a measure of capacity!" Again, in one of his orations against the building of the Canadian Pacific Railway, he prefaced a minute and exhaustive narration of events connected with the enterprise in these words: "Mr. Speaker, on the first of April—a fitting day—in the year 1871...." That was his estimate of the project as late as the early eighties.

Sir Joseph Pope, *Day of Macdonald*, 1915

Arthur Bunster

Arthur Bunster (1827–1891) was the Member for Vancouver from 1874 to 1882.

Bunster, a brewer of beer from Vancouver, was short-set, with enormous whiskers, always belligerent, and in language fierce and defiant he attacked the Government. He contracted a great dislike to Blake, and berated him fiercely for his reference to British Columbia as "a sea of mountains." On one occasion, when his feelings were more overwrought than usual, he drew from his pocket a buckskin glove, threw it on the floor in front of Blake and dared him to take it up.

Sir George Ross, *Getting Into Parliament and After*, 1912

Doctor Landerkin and the Mouse

George Landerkin (1839–1903) represented Grey South in the Commons for almost 30 years, between 1872 and 1900.

Many practical jokes were perpetrated by M.P.'s on the Press Gallery, and vice versa. I remember one day that a live mouse had been caught in the press room, and it was sent down from the Gallery to Dr. Landerkin in a small box, while the House was in session. The box was neatly parcelled but the doctor smelt a rat — I mean a mouse — when the package was delivered to him. I could see him, out of the corner of my eye, squinting up at the newspaper men, to ascertain who was responsible for the joke.

Naturally we were all busy at our work but still furtively watching him. The doctor undid the wrapper on the package, carefully raised the lid of the box and then replaced it.

The seat of Sir Louis Davies was immediately in front of Dr. Landerkin's. At the moment Sir Louis was absent from the Chamber. The doctor, with a broad grin at the gallery boys, leaned forward in his seat and placed the package upon the desk of his leader from Prince Edward Island. This was more than we bargained for.

Sir Louis Davies was the very embodiment of dignity, and we feared trouble. When he returned to the House Sir Louis, noticing the box, removed the cover, and out jumped the mouse. It was the most starling incident that the Island Member had experienced in the Chamber. For a moment or two he looked annoyed; then a smile flitted over his countenance, and he too gave a glance at the gallery. Of course none of the newspaper men could have seen the incident; they were all too busy with their duties, but just the same every man was taking a glance out of the corner of his eye. The little visitor was removed by the floor messenger, and nothing more was heard about the prank, except that at six o'clock Dr. Landerkin meandered into the press room and tried hard to ascertain who was responsible.

Fred Cook, *Fifty Years Ago and Since,* n.d.

Pope's Rejoinder

For years Sir John A. Macdonald's most trusted minister was John Henry Pope (1824–1889) of Compton, Quebec.

"John Henry," as he was familiarly called, had all the shrewdness and foresight of the statesman, and materially assisted in directing the policy of the party. He was not a polished or verbose speaker, but when he spoke, the few words he uttered always meant something. Once when fiercely attacked by Sir Richard Cartwright in the House, he made the shortest but most effective speech ever delivered in the Green Chamber. When Sir Richard had taken his seat amidst the loud applause of his followers, Mr. Pope slowly rose and quaintly said: "Mr. Speaker, there ain't nothin' to it."

The House cheered wildly, and Sir Richard warmly joined in the expressions of admiration. That ended the discussion.

George Ham, *Reminiscences of a Raconteur*, 1921

Pages

In the nineteenth century House, the page boys provided entertainment during the dinner recesses.

In the Canadian House of Commons there are a number of little pages who run errands for Members, and fetch them books and papers. These boys sit on the steps of the Speaker's chair, and when the House adjourns for dinner the pages hold a "Pages' Parliament." One boy, elected by the others as Speaker, puts on a gown and seats himself in the Speaker's chair; the "Prime Minister" and the Members of the Government sit on the Government benches, the Leader of the Opposition with his supporters take their places opposite and the boys hold regular debates. Many of the Members took great interest in the "Pages' Parliament," and coached the boys for their debates. I have seen Sir John Macdonald giving the fourteen-year-old "Premier" points for his speech that evening.

Lord Frederic Hamilton, *Days Before Yesterday*, 1920

Sir John Abbott

Sir John Joseph Caldwell Abbott (1821–1893), a Senator, was Prime Minister for just over seventeen months in 1891 and 1892. He was considered a poor and unenthusiastic successor to MacDonald, who died in office leaving no heir apparent.

Two days before Sir John Macdonald's death, he wrote a pathetic letter to an Ottawa friend in which he said:

"I hate politics, and what are considered their appropriate methods. I hate notoriety, public meetings, public speeches, caucuses, and everything that I know of that is apparently the necessary incident of politics—except doing public work to the best of my ability. Why should I go where the doing of honest work will only make me hated and my ministry unpopular, and where I can only gain reputation and credit by practicing arts which I detest, to acquire popularity?"

Fred Cook, *Fifty Years Ago and Since*, n.d.

Ingenuous Abbott

When I think of the ingenuous manner in which he treated the correspondents of the Conservative press I cannot withhold a smile. He was like a child so far as the news end of the Premier's duties was concerned, and frankly told us so the first afternoon we waited upon him after a meeting of the Cabinet.

"I know nothing," he said, "of the Prime Minister's relations to the correspondents of the party press. I think the best thing I can do is to tell you fully what takes place in Council and leave it to your judgement when and how you should use the information, if at all. I have every confidence in your discretion and feel that you will not get me into trouble."

A colleague was with me at the time and we had to explain to the Prime Minister that successive Governors-General, in the past, had been somewhat sensitive about Cabinet decisions leaking out before the Orders-in-Council were submitted to the representative of the Sovereign, and that Sir John Macdonald had repeatedly impressed upon us the necessity of withholding information, particularly about appointments, until we had made sure that the Governor-General's approval had been given. Mr. Abbott was pleased to get this information, and said he would arrange accordingly to advise us when Cabinet action, which was news, was a fait accompli.

Fred Cook, *Fifty Years Ago and Since*, n.d.

Decorum Breached

Sir John Sparrow David Thompson (1844–1894), Conservative Prime Minister from 1892 until his death, was Minister of Justice under Macdonald and Abbott. His outwardly stern demeanour belied an intelligent, if dry, wit.

What might be merely incidental in an ordinary gathering becomes entirely different under the ancient rules which regulate the decorum of the House. At times Members break loose from the repressions and behave like a lot of mischievous schoolboys. Nevertheless, they are strong for the traditional dignity. Sir John Thompson exemplified the spirit in every word he spoke and every move he made. He never ceased to be the judge on the bench. That must be borne in mind when I say he was very solemnly addressing the House one afternoon when Mr. Roulleau, the assistant Clerk, started to leave the Chamber. He took one step and then began to dance. First one knee would bend, and then the other. Several times he saved himself from rolling to the floor by grasping a nearby desk.

Sir John stood silent and scowled at this dancing and wobbling figure before him. The whole House gaped at the spectacle. Was the Clerk intoxicated? It looked like it, in which event the stern Minister of Justice would see to it that his head paid the penalty. If merciless, Sir John was nevertheless just, and poor Roulleau did not have to face the guillotine. The truth came out in time to save him. His feet were asleep!

J. Lambert Payne in Fred Cook, *Giants and Jesters*, n.d.

First-Class Clerk

The case of a chief clerk in the Civil Service, who had committed serious irregularities in connection with the public funds, once came up before the Cabinet. Thompson, always severe in such matters, considered that the gravity of the offence called for dismissal, but to this

Macdonald would not consent, holding that reduction in rank to a first-class clerkship, with corresponding loss of salary, would be sufficient punishment. It was seldom that Macdonald, in the ordinary course of administration, interposed his paramount authority as first minister, but, though the Council as a whole rather inclined towards Thompson's view, Macdonald insisted that the more merciful punishment should be imposed. Thompson was angry, but said nothing more at the time. Not long afterwards a third-class railway mail clerk, with a salary of $500 a year, got into similar trouble. "What shall be done with this man?" asked Macdonald at the Council Board. There was a moment's pause, which was broken by the bland suggestion from Thompson that, "following precedent, he be made a first-class clerk."

Sir Joseph Pope, *Day of Macdonald*, 1915

Thompson and the Inventor

A certain inventor of Toronto, who had devised an ingenious means for safeguarding level railway crossings, had long bombarded Sir John Macdonald with applications for Government patronage. When Sir John [Macdonald] became Minister of Railways in 1889, the inventor thought that his day had at last arrived. He went post-haste to Ottawa, obtained the requisite permission, and installed his models in a room belonging to the Railway department. One day Macdonald and Thompson happened to come along the corridor going to Macdonald's office. The inventor, who had been lying in wait, pressed them to step aside for a minute and inspect his models. Sir John, seeing no escape, said to his companion, "Come along, Thompson, and let us see what this fellow's got to show us." Thompson hated mechanical contrivances, but there was no way out of it, so he followed the chief. The delighted inventor... volubly descanted on the frequent loss of life at level crossings and proceeded to show his devices for lessening such dangers. The day was piping hot and he had taken off his coat. He rushed round the table and touched bells here and there, which caused gates to close and open, semaphores to drop, and all sorts of things to happen. As the ministers took their leave, Macdonald said to his companion, "Well, Thompson, what do you think of that chap?" "I think," replied Thompson with great energy, "that he deserves to be killed on a level crossing."

Sir Joseph Pope, *Day of Macdonald*, 1915

Thompson and the Cold

I went in for a bit & then drove to Government Buildings with Archie to see if Sir John Thompson, who was coming out to see His Ex, would drive out with me. I just caught him & conveyed him here in safety, for the ponies were pulling tremendously. Although the thermometer was at zero & the wind was bitter, Sir John according to custom had neck & ears uncovered, only a thin black overcoat & no gloves—he is extraordinary about not feeling the cold.

Canadian Journal of Lady Aberdeen, John Saywell, ed., 1960

Thompson and Cartwright

His calm exterior hid strong ambitions and intense party feelings which sometimes burned their way through in a revealing flash.

Sir Richard Cartwright was one of the men most successful in drawing Thompson's fire. Sir Richard himself spared no man; to quote a random instance, at a campaign meeting in Kingston, during a by-election in January, 1892, he had greeted the local Conservative candidate as a fitting choice—"as straightforward as Sir John Thompson, no more likely to eat his own words than Mr. Foster, as honest as Mr. Chapleau, as little likely to use his position to forward his own interests as Mr. Dewdney, as moral as Haggart, as modest as Tupper, Senior and Junior, and as loyal as J.J.C. Abbott." A few months later, in the House of Commons, he had denounced government boodling and patronage, judicial partiality, and public apathy. Whereupon Thompson thanked Cartwright for another of "those war, famine and pestilence speeches which have so often carried the country for the government," proposed a subsidy to keep him in parliament for the Conservative party's sake, replied to a taunt as to defending criminals by declaring that he had never shrunk from taking any man's case, no matter how desperate it might be, for the purpose of saying for him what he might lawfully say for himself, but had sometimes spurned the fee of a blatant scoundrel who denounced everybody else in the world and was himself the most truculent savage of them all, and ended by thanking God nature had broken the mould when she cast Sir Richard. This descent from "the language of Parliament to the invective of Billingsgate," as Mr. Laurier termed it in reply, was the last touch needed to establish Sir John's right to party leadership.

O.D. Skelton, *Life and Letters of Laurier*, 1921

Bowell's Temper

Sir Mackenzie Bowell (1823–1917), a Senator, was Prime Minister from 1894 to 1896. Before being elevated to the Senate in 1893, Bowell sat in the Commons for North Hastings and held various Cabinet posts, including that of Minister of Customs, in the governments of Macdonald, Abbott and Thompson.

Late one night when the customs estimates were being considered, Cameron, the champion heckler of the Liberal side, didn't seem to like some of Hon. Mackenzie Bowell's answers to his questions. So he lost his patience, and, I think quite unintentionally, flatly contradicted something Bowell had presented as a fact. The latter, perhaps unduly sensitive as to his veracity, cried out:

"Does the honourable gentleman call me a liar?"

Cameron may not have caught the question, and answered in words that implied the affirmative. Bowell sprang into action at once. Seizing a glass filled with ice water, he started to hurl it across the floor at his tormentor, but a benign and opportune providence saved him from this act of violence. Sitting right behind him, his head resting on his outstretched arms, Henry N. Paint, of Cape Breton, was peacefully asleep. As Bowell swung the tumbler backward, its cold contents got down Paint's neck. With a yell, the sleeper sprang to his feet and proceeded to give a fantastic imitation of a man swimming for his life. Arrested by the yell, Bowell turned around, and when he saw the little old chap, he stayed his hand. A tragedy was averted. Bowell was a journalist, and the free masonry of the craft saw to it that not a syllable of this incident got into print.

J. Lambert Payne in Fred Cook, *Giants and Jesters*, n.d.

Nest of Traitors

A temperamental and spiteful man, Sir Mackenzie Bowell had a difficult time keeping his administration together during the Manitoba schools crisis of 1896.

Seven Ministers intimated their intention to resign, on the ground that they found themselves unable to act in accord with the Premier, and they took the unusual course of communicating their intention direct to the Governor-General, requesting his permission to make their explanations in the House. To this I, of course, replied that I could only receive such resignations and give permission for explanations, through the Premier. Heated debates in the House of Commons followed, and on one occasion Sir Mackenzie Bowell, who, as a member of the Senate, and Prime Minister, had been occupying a seat near the Speaker's Chair, walked across to the front Opposition bench, on adjournment, and shook hands with its occupants, saying audibly, "It is such a comfort to shake hands with honest men, after being in company with traitors for months."

The Earl of Aberdeen, We Twa, 1925

A Good Hater

Sir Mackenzie Bowell was "a good hater," to use Dr. Samuel Johnson's well known expression.

An instance of this came under my observation after the defeat of Sir Charles Tupper's ministry in 1896. Sir Mackenzie had been to Montreal on private business and returning to Ottawa he travelled by the old Canada Atlantic Railway, now the Canadian National. It so happened that Mr. Foster was on that very train, and actually in the same parlour car, although seated some distance from the Old Man. As a matter of fact, they had travelled many miles of the journey before either was aware of the other's presence.

Having to go to the bookcase for a magazine, Mr. Foster noticed Sir Mackenzie reading a newspaper. Stopping directly in front of the ex-Premier, Mr. Foster said, "Bowell, we are both getting on in years; don't you think we should let byegones be byegones and shake hands," at the same time offering his hand. It was a touching amende honorable.

The Old Man, waving the proffered hand aside, retorted in an angry voice, "Go away; I don't want to have anything to do with you."

And so Mr. Foster left him, and they never spoke to each other again.

How do I know about this incident? Well, Sir Mackenzie told it to me with pride a day or two later. If he expected me to say that he had done the right thing, he must have been disappointed. I made no comment; as a matter of fact it saddened me to think that the old gentleman should carry his enmity for Mr. Foster to the grave.

Fred Cook, *Fifty Years Ago and Since*, n.d.

Voluminous Speaker

Always a good "second", Sir Charles Tupper (1821-1915), who was briefly Prime Minister in 1896, was the epitome of the stalwart Tory supporter in the early decades of Confederation.

Both on the floor of the House and on the political hustings, he was a voluminous speaker. Perhaps his briefest speeches would be an hour. Two hours would be more likely. I think it is claimed one of his budget speeches took five hours. He could be bold, tempestuous, audacious, imaginative. If his opponents regarded him with much dislike—and there would be the fullest reciprocity in that—no one questioned his loyalty or his steadfastness, while history readily concedes his constructive genius applied to the unity and upbuilding of his country. Even in repose, his opponents were given to the suspicion that he had a blizzard, secreted somewhere, about his person.

Charles Bishop, *Ottawa Evening Citizen*, 1945

Tupper and Howe

It was said, while engaged in a forensic duel with Joseph Howe on a warm night, that Sir Charles Tupper spoke with great volubility and at the same time consumed an enormous quantity of water. Howe's first remark on rising to reply was "that in all his experience he never before saw a windmill driven by water."

Sir George Ross, *Getting Into Parliament and After*, 1912

The Tupper Style

With a great many people he is, as an orator, placed foremost in the House. When real business is being transacted he makes no attempt at anything like fine speaking, and in fact is perhaps a shade too concise in his remarks, lacking altogether that discursiveness so characteristic of his colleagues. But sometimes all at once, without any warning given, and without any apparent cause, he will burst into most vigorous invective. His voice rings through the House like a bell; he throws out his right arm at full stretch, and with his fingers pointed at some opponent, and with his face showing the utmost earnestness if not passion, he asserts, denounces, contradicts, accuses, in a torrent perfectly irresistible. On these occasions the Members become attentive; the galleries are hushed; not a word is lost.

Lounger, *Canadian Illustrated News*, 1873

Pull

In 1899 Sir Charles Tupper travelled to Brockville to campaign for his old friend Peter White, the former Speaker of the House, who was running in a by-election.

Sir Charles Tupper went to Brockville to lend a hand to his old friend, Peter. The local Conservative committee, instead of offering their leader private hospitality, put him up at the Revere House, then the leading hotel in the town. Johnny Bann, the landlord, whom I knew well, was delighted at having Sir Charles as his guest over night and naturally gave him the best room in the hotel.

It so happened, however, that this particular room for years had been occupied every week-end by a prominent commercial gentleman of the road, and on the night of Sir Charles Tupper's visit he arrived in Brockville on his weekly business call. In the assertion of what he regarded as his prescriptive right to the room, and without bothering to register, the commercial man went straight upstairs and threw himself on the bed to sleep off the many "shots" he had imbibed that day. He was sound asleep when Sir Charles arrived about midnight from the political meeting at which he had spoken for Mr. White. The veteran statesman, not noticing that his bed was occupied, proceeded to divest himself of his clothing and make ready for a well earned rest.

He had donned the old fashioned nightshirt and then approaching the bed was staggered to find the intruder. Shaking the traveller vigorously, the old gentleman, in angry tones, asked him what he was doing there. The commercial man still in his alcoholic stupor, only responded with a grunt, and Sir Charles had to prod him two or three times before he could get an answer to his repeated question.

Presently the traveller, now awake, answered, "I was shleeping until you woke me. What the devil do you want?"

"I am Sir Charles Tupper, former prime minister," was the angry reply. "Get out of this room."

"Not much," the intruder retorted. "Thish is my room."

"Well, if you don't get out," said Sir Charles, "I shall pull you out."

"Pull? Nonshense," was the reply, "ex-prime ministers have no pull."

Fred Cook, Giants and Jesters, n.d.

Bossy Sir George

Sir George Eulas Foster (1847-1931) was a Minister of the Crown under seven different Conservative Prime Ministers, a record. When Laurier was in office, Foster was a strong second-in-command on the opposition front bench.

Foster was the first man whose voice I ever heard in Parliament. That was some years ago, when he was still the man who led all great debates on the Conservative side, snapped his fingers at the young orators whom he bossed like page boys, rather ignored the Opposition leader, and held the party at his back in a mass of thundering applause. He was talking about Liberal patronage-mongers, corrupt politics, and the low ebb of national life—all the commonplace ailments that mere diagnosis fails to cure.

No man ever took a hand in our politics who with a powerful brain and a copious tongue was quite so well able to twang the dismal lyre. Foster got the reputation of being a confirmed pessimist; largely because of his manner of speaking, which was entirely without plausible graces, studio poses, or genial struts. Foster needed an antagonist. He needed to convince, beat down opposition, scarify, repudiate, point the finger of mockery with a sort of cold creepy laughter. There was no Grit in the House who had not a casual wholesome dread of him. Sometimes even the Tories criticized him.

Angustus Bridle, *Sons of Canada*, 1916

Not an Easy Mark

He [Sir George Foster] was a dangerous man to cross, as many a member found to his sorrow. The 1911 election brought to the House a new Liberal member from the West, Dr. Michael Clark, member for Red Deer. He was an Englishman who had had considerable experience in politics in the Old Country before coming to Canada. He was one of the finest orators who ever sat in the House of Commons. He had a deep mellifluous voice, with a soft English accent, and was a master of well-rounded phrases. He was widely read in English politics and literature. Dr. Clark was a sincere Free Trader of the Manchester school and a Liberal of the Gladstone tradition. Foster was to him the high priest of protection and the symbol of the big interests "of the wicked East." One day shortly after he entered the House the eloquent "Red" Michael turned his guns on Foster, who, according to his custom, was sitting hunched up in his seat on the front bench, his hard bowler hat pulled down over his eyes—he was one of the last Ministers to wear persistently his hat in the House—and tugging his beard. When Dr. Clark finished Sir George straightened himself in his seat, rose on his long lanky legs and pointing his rapier-like finger at Dr. Clark he proceeded to demolish the new member. From that time Dr. Clark treated Sir George with respect.

Arthur Ford, *As the World Wags On*, 1950

Foster's Political Judgement

With regard to political strategy he was useful to us in a rather unusual sense. His emotional temperament made him a most unsafe guide. When any such question arose for discussion, several of my colleagues (notably Dr. Reid and Martin Burrell) listened carefully to Foster for the purpose of recording their votes in the opposite sense, as they firmly and invariably relied on the unsoundness of his judgement.

Sir Robert Borden's Letters to Limbo, Henry Borden, ed., 1971

You Can't Lose...

Foster was, assuredly, a creature of inconsistencies. Upon my entry into Parliament (1896), I looked up to him with profound admiration and respect as the exponent of careful finance. Sir Charles Hibbert Tupper told me that Foster had accumulated $100,000 by judicious investment in mining stocks. So, when Sir George invited me to subscribe for shares in a mining company of which he was president, I accepted the invitation with alacrity and acquired three thousand shares at eighty cents on the dollar. I was particularly impressed and attracted by his statement that the company was paying dividends at the rate of one percent per month. After receiving my contribution of $2,400 the company paid only one dividend ($30) which was accompanied by a notice that dividends were suspended for the future. Sad to relate they were never resumed. My contribution of $2,400 was used to pay that dividend. At the annual meeting, under cross-examination by the late Senator Clemow, Foster, thoughtfully stroking his beard, was obliged to admit that, from first to last, the company had never made more than its operating expenses. Dividends had been paid out of monies received from unfortunate subscribers of whom, alas, I was one. The sum of $2,370 which I thus contributed still remains a permanent investment. From that day to this I never heard a word on the subject from Foster or his company.

This incident does not alter my opinion as to Foster's fine idealism and perfect honesty. He seemed absolutely incapable of judging his own actions by the same standards which he applied to those of other men. But how he would have thundered against such a transaction if it involved one of his political opponents!

Sir Robert Borden's Letters to Limbo, Henry Borden, ed., 1971

Systematically Unsystematic

His biographer speaks of his success as an administrator. Among his colleagues in my government he was not so regarded. Undoubtedly he worked very hard; but he was systematically unsystematic. I was told that the appearance of his office was astonishing. Tables and desks were piled with files that should have been kept in their filing-cabinets; these files and other documents over-flowed the tables and desks and littered portions of the floor. He had a passion for keeping documents in his immediate possession. Despatches which I sent to him while he was Acting Prime Minister he carried away, although they should have remained as they were official and he had no right to retain them.

His lack of system was illustrated by his omission to take his code-book when he embarked upon the long journey to New Zealand, Australia and Japan, described in his biography. We sent cables in code which he was utterly unable to understand; eventually we were obliged to communicate en clair.

He had a passion also for extending the jurisdiction of his department in every possible direction, although its original scope was quite sufficient to absorb his whole energies. He was pervaded with an obsession to travel abroad, especially to spend many months as member of this or that commission, when his energies could more usefully have been employed in the duties appertaining to his department. I am quite convinced that he would have been willing to add to his department a very large proportion of matters appertaining to all the departments of the government, in which case he would still have been eager to journey abroad on occasion. While we were in opposition, he was made chairman of our parliamentary committee on organization. He gladly accepted the appointment with results that were absolutely negligible, indeed wholly invisible.

Sir Robert Borden's Letters to Limbo, Henry Borden, ed., 1971

Sir George Foster

When I first went to Ottawa one of the sights was Sir George riding on a bicycle to Parliament Hill, his rather ragged beard blowing in the wind. In later years it was trimmed into a more attractive Van Dyke. Probably no Parliamentarian was ever the centre of more bitter controversies. The possessor of a sarcastic and vitriolic tongue, he never spared it on his political opponents; on the other hand, he was pursued with almost vindictive cruelty. For years he was the stormy petrel of politics, although in later years he mellowed and looked with the eye of an old sage and philosopher from the serene Senate chamber upon the passing scene.

Despite his ability, his eloquence and his Parliamentary skill, Sir George missed being Leader and Prime Minister. He lacked the fine touches of an expert politician and he had too many enemies. He was no mixer with the boys, and he neither drank nor smoked. He had entered public life as a temperance advocate and orator. Once a year he relaxed to smoke his annual cigarette at the Press Gallery dinner. The Press Gallery programme was issued one year in the form of a parliamentary Guide; here is the sketch of Sir George which appeared in it:

GEORGE E. FOSTER

They say he could talk before he could walk,
And his words were never few,
And he made a name at the temperance game
Before his whiskers grew.
He could make men cheer, or dribble a tear,
He could wallop the Grits kerflop,
So Sir John took him in to tally the tin
And sit on the Treasury Top.
And he made good there and everywhere,
And at everything he did
But try as he would, and do what he could
He never quite got to the top.
For as Rufe said slow, one night below,
When the boys were having a smile,
"Say, George, ole man, you could run dis lan'
If you'd licker up once in a while."

Arthur Ford, *As the World Wags On*, 1950

Waiting in the Wings

Before becoming Leader of the Opposition in 1887 and later Prime Minister in 1896, Sir Wilfrid Laurier (1841-1919) maintained a decidedly low profile.

I made acquaintance with Laurier in the Dominion session of 1884. He was then in his forty-third year; but in the judgement of many his career was over. His interest in politics was, apparently, of the slightest. He was deskmate to Blake, who carried on a tremendous campaign that session against the government's C.P.R. proposals. Laurier's political activities consisted chiefly of being an acting secretary of sorts to the Liberal leader. He kept his references in order; handed him Hansards and blue-books in turn; summoned the pages to clear away the impedimenta and to keep the glass of water replenished — little services which it was clear he was glad to do for one who engaged his ardent affection and admiration. There were memories in the House of Laurier's eloquence; but memories only. During this session he was almost silent. The tall, courtly figure was a familiar sight in the chamber and in the library — particularly in the library, where he could be found every day ensconced in some congenial alcove; but the golden voice was silent. It was known that his friends were concerned about his health.

John W. Dafoe, *Laurier: A Study in Canadian Politics,* 1922

Laurier and Nature

Like Sir Robert, the Liberal leader was a lover of nature, although he was not a botanist like the Conservative leader with an acquaintance of the Latin botanical names. Apart from his books his chief delight was in the quiet contemplation of woods and fields and the birds and the animals, with whose habits and migrations he had been familiar as a boy.

Hon. Charles Murphy, who was probably closer to Sir Wilfrid than anyone else, wrote me a letter shortly after the death of the latter in which he referred to this side of his character. It is so interesting and throws such a light on this unknown side of him that I reproduce it:

One day while waiting to address a political meeting in my behalf he was sitting with a number of friends on the lawn of the late Senator Edward's residence at Rockland, when the song of an oriole in a nearby tree caught his ear. That started him talking about the birds that came to Arthabaskaville when he was a boy. He described their plumage, their different songs, the kind of nests they built, and the colour and number of eggs they laid. Then he explained that some species went away and never returned, and that in their places birds of other varieties came and these he also described. No more delightful reminiscences could be imagined. Had he been a professor of ornithology, he could not have given his group of listeners more information or pleasure than we derived from his chance talk about the feathered songsters that came to Arthabaskaville each spring.

How deeply Sir Wilfrid loved quiet communing with nature was illustrated by the way in which he enjoyed a fishing trip. His Quebec friends often took him to some angler's paradise among the hills of his native Province, and on his return to Ottawa one of us would be sure to ask him what kind of luck he had had. His invariable reply was: "I did all my fishing on the club verandah," and, even now, I can see the twinkle of the eye and the quizzical smile that used to accompany his answer.

Another of Sir Wilfrid's hobbies was his love of trees. He could not bear to see a tree mutilated or cut down if it possibly could be saved. Many a time he telephoned me, saying that linemen of the electric or the telephone company were destroying trees while stringing wires on some street through which he had just passed, and he would insist that my partner, who was then mayor of the city, would at once send some civic employees to stop the vandalism. If I was not prompt in reporting the result of his request, I was certain to get another telephone call from him.

Arthur Ford, *As The World Wags On*, 1950

Laurier and Finance

Sir Wilfrid aspired to shine in a field in which men like Sir George Foster and the Hon. W.S. Fielding were past masters. He spent a part of his vacation in the summer of 1899 preparing notes from blue books for such an effort; an unnecessary effort, be it said, for it had been arranged that Mr. Fielding should accompany him in the speaking tour projected for the autumn. The speech was made at Paisley, in the heart of Bruce County, Ont., the occasion being Sir Wilfrid's first visit to that region of Scottish Liberal stalwarts.

Sir Wilfrid thought it particularly fitting that he should address a Scottish audience in terms of dollars and cents, and genially announced his intention of making a financial address, though disclaiming that he was a man of figures. It was magnificent, but it was not war. It sounded well, but Mr. Fielding sitting at his side was driven almost to profanity in his efforts to make whispered corrections of the errors with which it bristled. The Scots listeners were frankly puzzled, but woke up to enthusiasm when Sir Wilfrid got back to his true oratorical métier.

After the meeting, which was held in the afternoon on the fair grounds, Sir Wilfrid announced that he was going to call on a friend or two, and entrusted his bag to Alexander Smith, the well-known Ottawa lawyer, at that time Liberal organizer, to carry to the hotel. This was Mr. Fielding's chance, "Get rid of that speech," he whispered to Smith. The organizer fell in with the suggestion and, as he crossed the picturesque bridge of Paisley, extracted the precious notes and scattered them on the bosom of the Saugeen River. Presumably they ultimately reached Lake Huron, and Sir Wilfrid never knew what became of the fruits of his summer's browsing among the blue books.

Hector Charlesworth, *Candid Chronicles*, 1925

Laurier Campaigning

When Sir Wilfrid was out campaigning, before he reached a new riding he had himself posted on the situation and the men he should know and call by their first name. John Tolmie, for many years member for one of the Bruces, used to tell a story of Sir Wilfrid visiting his constituency. He was told to make a fuss over a staunch old Scotch Liberal, "Sandy" MacDonald, and when he met him he greeted him like a long lost friend. Sandy was flattered, but much puzzled that Sir Wilfrid would know him. He came to Mr. Tolmie the next day.

"I have got it," he said to John. "Got what?" asked the member.

"I know now how Laurier remembered me. When I was a young man working on the building of the C.P.R. in Northern Ontario there was a Frenchman working with me called Laurier. It must have been Sir Wilfrid."

Arthur Ford, *As The World Wags On*, 1950

Matchmaker

Laurier frequently expressed misgivings about Mackenzie King's entering politics without financial reserves of his own. "In public life," he said in their first interview in 1905 on the subject of King's plans, "some independence was essential, if one had to worry over a livelihood it was difficult to do one's best." The "one or two thousand dollars" which to King looked fairly substantial he did not find very reassuring, and he suggested that King might enter journalism for a time to build up his resources. But King was apparently afraid of being side-tracked, and the suggestion was dropped.

In the summer of 1907 Sir Wilfrid tried another plan and endeavoured to interest the intending politician in an eligible widow twenty-four years of age. When he asked King why he did not get married, King replied that he had set his mind on a public career and had kept himself free from obligations which might make the course difficult. "On the contrary," said Sir Wilfrid, "the right person would be a great help to you in public life, and in securing a foothold.... Why do you not think of that young girl whom you met at our house on Sunday. She is a fine girl, I know of no girl of whom I think more, she is good, clever, kind, capable," and, raising his hand, "she will have a fortune." King expressed a moderate interest and Sir Wilfrid added: "Why do you not call at my house to-morrow afternoon and invite Lady Laurier and her to the theatre in the evening? There is the door opened for a beginning."

The "skirmishing expedition"—as King called it with some amusement—came off, but the divine spark was lacking.

R. MacGregor Dawson, *Mackenzie King: A Political Biography*, 1958

The Silver Tongue

In the seven years during which I reported Laurier in the House of Commons I never heard him speak in French. The reason was simple. He took the attitude that politics was the art of communication. If the majority in the country had spoken Hottentot, Laurier would have mastered Hottentot. His English was faultless, and in his grasp of every shade and nuance of both languages he was without a rival.

Grattan O'Leary, *Recollections of People, Press, and Politics*, 1977

Pumping Laurier

Laurier was notoriously stingy about giving formal interviews.

On one occasion Laurier was buttonholed in his office by an American reporter who, having been warned that the Premier of Canada never gave interviews, boasted that he would break the rule. After half an hour the American reporter came out to his confreres of the press gallery, sat down at a typewriter, lit three of four cigarettes, nervously aware that he was being watched for the forthcoming article, and after spoiling a number of sheets and tearing them all up he confessed, "Well, boys, I thought I was pumping Laurier, but it's a cinch he spent most of my time pumping me."

Domino (Augustus Bridle), Masques of Ottawa, 1921

Laurier's Wit

The element of humour was not predominant in many of Sir Wilfrid Laurier's speeches. He had, however, a keen wit and dearly loved a jest or a story. He was, in truth, fond of all clean humour, of gay badinage, of jovial company, of all kindly and sympathetic human companionship. Under such circumstances there was a lightness, a gaiety, a spontaneous and infectious wit in his conversation which his speeches seldom reveal. He could, however, counter readily upon an interrupter, he had an incisive and delicate satire, and if the occasion demanded he could be severely caustic. Parliament was greatly entertained when he clothed with judicial functions, elevated to the bench, and pronounced a grave and solemn judgement for each of the Conservative ministers who heard argument of counsel and judicially affirmed the necessity for the Manitoba Remedial Order. He once compared Sir Charles Tupper to the old blind king of Bohemia on the battlefield of Crecy, valiant but blind, striking to right and left and injuring no one but himself. Bantering the Conservative leader on his reminiscent exaltation of his own political services, he said that between Sir John Macdonald and himself they had sailed the ship of state pretty successfully; Sir John was at the helm and supplied the brains while Sir Charles supplied the wind; his blowing swelled the sails. And during the term of the Mackenzie government, Mr. Mousseau, a man of gigantic bulk, charged the ministers with fattening on the sweat of the people. Mr. Laurier, then tall, slim and delicate, pointed to his massive opponent and said: "If anyone here is fattening on the sweat of the people, which is it, he or I?"

Sir John Willison, Sir Wilfrid Laurier, 1926

Eminently Qualified

The distribution of patronage was the most important single function of the government. Sir Wilfrid frequently repeated the story of Lincoln, asked during a crisis in the Civil War whether it was a change in the army command or complications with foreign powers that wrinkled his forehead, and replying, "No, it is that confounded postmastership at Brownsville, Ohio." No other subject bulked so large in correspondence; no other purpose brought so many visitors to Ottawa. It meant endless bombardment of ministers, ceaseless efforts to secure a word from the friend of a friend of the premier, bitter disappointment for the ninety and nine who were turned away. While the members of the cabinet from each province usually determined the appointments which could be localized, all the more important ones came to Sir Wilfrid before decision, and to him the prayers of most of the seekers were turned. Some of his supporters tried to save themselves trouble for the moment by recommending to him each candidate in turn; in reply to a protest, one such practitioner naively replied: "True, I recommended both C and D. It was C I really wished considered. D is one of a class of people who hound my office, ask me for letters of recommendation, exalt their services or the services of their friends, whom they often bring along, and offer themselves to put the letter in the postbox. What am I to do?"

Some men worked through their friends, some applied direct. Particularly in applying for the higher posts, it was comme il faut to make it clear that it was only the insistence of the general public that had overcome the candidate's reluctance: "It has been represented to me that the Liberals of Ontario with whom the name Z is a household word would be much gratified if I were appointed to Government House," or "My friends insist that my tact and diplomatic talents would find suitable scope in the High Commissionership." For the Senate, the orthodox grounds were being "the only one left of the old guard who stood so loyally to their colours in the dark days of the eighties when there was no silver lining," or having "run six elections and paid all my expenses out of my own pocket." A Roman Catholic bishop would write to note that all the last five appointments, formerly held by his co-religionists, had gone to Protestants, or a layman would argue that because the last holder was a Catholic so should the next be, or that as the last holder was a Protestant, it was a Catholic's turn; a Methodist friend would write to point out that there were only two Methodist county judges out of eighty, and a Presbyterian to complain that the percentage of Presbyterian senators was falling. It was a Quebec follower who wrote Sir Wilfrid shortly after the election of 1896: "If anyone had told me when I was fighting the battles of Liberalism in my county, striving without fear of attack or hope of favour to advance the cause of the people, determined that no designing cleric and no corrupt politician would be allowed to shackle our noble country—if anyone had told me that six months after you took office, I would still be without a job, I would not have believed him." It was an eastern Ontario seeker who wrote: "To think that after naming my only son William Lyon Mackenzie, I am still denied any post by a government that calls itself Liberal." Acquaintance in youth; descent from the United Empire Loyalist great grandfathers; having seventeen living children, one named Wilfrid, and this in Ontario; being the daughter of a Conservative minister and the mother of ten potential Liberal voters; finding that "if poverty is not a crime, it is very inconvenient," were typical grounds set forth in the appeals which poured in upon the Prime Minister.

Oscar D. Skelton, *Life and Letters of Laurier*, 1921

"Pull Wit' Laurier"

Laurier had long been regarded as the Grand Seigneur in Quebec. I heard a delightful story about him up in the Gatineau country. The flag flew at half-mast on the post office at St. Cecile de Masham. Farmer Pierre Simard asked neighbor Sam Short about it.

"Queen Victoria is dead," Sam explained. "De h'old Queen's dead," ruminated Pierre. He took a few puffs of tobac Canadien... "Who's got her job?" he asked. "Edward VII," said Sam Short. "He's King now." "Dat fella Edouard," commented Pierre, "he musta had one helluva pull wit' Laurier!"

Charles Bowman, *Ottawa Editor*, 1966

Laurier Angry

Sir Wilfrid seldom lost his temper. I remember only a couple of occasions when he even showed anger. One was an encounter with Sir

George Foster in the session of 1909, and the second was when the Closure Bill was introduced during the course of the famous Naval Bill debate. The clash with Sir George occurred during a tempestuous debate on a report which Mr. Justice Cassels had made into the conduct of the affairs of the Department of Marine and Fisheries. There had been brought to light some rather unsavoury scandals. Sir George fiercely denounced the government and asked Sir Wilfrid, sitting in his usual seat on the front bench, what he proposed to do about charges of bribery of public servants. He pointedly inquired if he was going to proceed against those charged. "Why don't you do it?" he asked. "Is it because you share in it for party interest and party advantage?"

Sir Wilfrid, stung to the quick, retorted angrily: "I have never manipulated other people's money; I have never manipulated trust funds." He was referring to the charges against Sir George in connection with an inquiry into insurance affairs.

Foster was at once on his feet demanding a retraction. It was one of the stormiest scenes, if not the stormiest, I ever witnessed in the Canadian House. For a time it looked as if the chamber would become a bear garden, as Sir George, standing in the centre of the aisle by the Clerk's table, and backed up by the Opposition, insisted on a retraction and shook his fist at Sir Wilfrid. The Speaker was Hon. Charles Marcil, a delightful gentleman, but not a strong Speaker. He was unable to control the House and hesitated, perhaps naturally, to rule his leader out of order. In the Press Gallery that day by mere chance was Rev. J.A. Macdonald, editor of the *Toronto Globe*, who had been largely responsible for the charges against Sir George. His Celtic blood got the best of him and a couple of newspapermen had almost to hold him in his excitement over the scene.

It was Sir Robert [Borden] who succeeded in pouring oil upon the troubled waters and Sir Wilfrid, although objecting and objecting properly, to the character of Foster's remarks, agreed to withdraw everything he had said.

Arthur Ford, *As The World Wags On*, 1950

Have We Met?

Immediately after my first session in the House of Commons, during which session I was a whip, I was walking down Sparks Street in Ottawa, and met a farmer Member from one of the Western Provinces, one who possessed the good "horse-sense" of the soil, but who had also the retiring disposition so often displayed by his kind. We had lunch together, and asking him how he had enjoyed his session, I was somewhat shocked to learn that he had never met his own leader, Sir Robert Borden. This was no doubt due to some oversight on Sir Robert's part, although in those strenuous war days Sir Robert was bowed down under very heavy burdens, and was not quite the congenial companion that he has become in the fifteen years since he retired from the onerous duties of leadership.

"And you know, Doctor," my friend added, "as I came down in the elevator to-day, Sir Wilfrid was in it with me. He complimented me about those few remarks I made yesterday on the wheat situation. As he left me, he shook my hand and said: 'Well, good-bye, Mr.—— God be with you till we meet again.' And," my friend added to me solemnly, "I shall never forget those words."

R. J. Manion, Life Is An Adventure, 1936

Laurier Eloquent

No one in my experience has touched him as an orator: he was the greatest I was privileged to hear in sixty years of observing Parliament. Samuel Butler wrote of Bacon, "Men feared he would make an end." Such was the feeling when Laurier spoke. Enchanted, mesmerized, the silent House gathered unto itself the incomparable wizardry of his words. Mastery of language of course; depth of feeling and passion unrivalled; but more than anything the essence of the man shining through: Laurier's inner greatness inspired people to go with him. When Laurier spoke it was like a first night. Parliament is as quick to appreciate greatness as it is to turn away from the dull pretensions of mediocrity.

Anything but a dry intellectual, he had a thorough sense of literature and familiarity with history. The House of Commons was his theatre; a theatre in which he remained the leading player. He was a builder, not a destroyer; a unifier; not a sower of discord and division. The ambitions, the desires, even the recreation sought by others in other ways were for Laurier attainable only in the heady passion of parliamentary life.

I remember one of his last appearances, in St. Patrick's Hall in Ottawa, with Lady Laurier, half-blind, tapping the floor with her stick as he spoke. In London, Ontario I heard his last will and testament to the Young Liberals of Ontario.

"…remember that faith is better than doubt and love is better than hate…."

Such his creed. He was, as Goldwin Smith said to Gladstone, "in the best sense a man of the people; and the heart of the people seldom failed to respond…." Of Lincoln's passing, Walt Whitman wrote that it was as if a giant cedar crashed on a hillside, leaving a lonely place against the sky. So, with the going of Laurier, all of us knew a great light had gone from public life.

Grattan O'Leary, *Recollections of People, Press, and Politics*, 1977

Nicholas Flood Davin

Nicholas Flood Davin (1843–1901) was the energetic, outspoken and colourful Tory Member for Assiniboia West between 1887 and 1900. He took his own life in a Winnipeg hotel room in 1901.

Davin was adept at putting opponents down with witty, and often cutting, quips. He would respond to hecklers with phrases like "what animal is that I hear?" and "I thought at first that I heard the Klondike eagle, but it is the Yukon bray." On one occasion, he referred to a Member from a neighbouring constituency as "that man". When called to order by the Speaker, he responded with "Did I say that man? I apologize to the hon. Member for calling him 'that man'. It shows how one, in the heat of debate, is apt to forget himself. It would be impossible, with the deepest plummet that ever sounded the depths of the Atlantic to measure the depth of my respect for the hon. Member. I am sorry I called him a man. Nothing on this earth would lead me to repeat such a misnomer with regard to the hon. gentleman."

Bosc, quoting from *Commons Debates*, 1898

Blackfoot Dance

Davin's well-known drinking habits enliven an all-night sitting.

The Ministers have all beds in their rooms for the occasion and many other M.P.s ensconce themselves in blankets in various Committee Rooms. Others cheer themselves by other means. Mr. Taylor, the Conservative whip told me that last night they had what they call a Symposium and finally Mr. Davin, M.P. for Assiniboia was called on to give a Blackfoot Dance in the Smoking Room. They had a long table with refreshments put up and Mr. Davin wound up his dance by springing on this and jigging down the centre, kicking over bottles and tumblers and plates at every step.

Canadian Journal of Lady Aberdeen, John T. Saywell, ed., 1960

The Funnel

Davin, an ambitious man, was forever putting himself forward as the member who spoke for the whole of the North-West. In his own colourful way, he once characterized himself as "a funnel" through which the views of the North-West were brought to the House. This expression was an unfortunate one, and he was often taunted with it afterwards. On one occasion however, he struck back with characteristic effectiveness. "My hon. friend behind me speaks of a funnel, and the hon. Member for Bothwell (Mr. Mills), using a phrase that I used myself, compared me the other night to a funnel. I only wish I could taper the funnel a little so as to get some information into my hon. friends' heads, because the bottles are too small for the funnel."

Bosc, quoting from *Commons Debates*, 1889

Paterson's Thunder

William Paterson (1839-1914) was Minister of Customs in successive Laurier administrations. He represented the Brantford, Ontario area almost without interruption from 1872 to 1911.

Paterson is most remembered for his booming voice — loud, almost roaring, but not raucous. He used to assail Conservative budgets with great effect. "Did you hear Paterson on the budget last night?" Sir Wilfrid Laurier once inquired of a follower. The delinquent Member confessed that he had not. "Then," said his old chief, "you must have been out of the city."

Charles Bishop, Ottawa Evening Citizen, 1945

Sifton's Riches

Sir Clifford Sifton (1861–1929) was Minister of the Interior, and Superintendent of Indian Affairs under Laurier from 1896 until his resignation in 1905.

The opulence of Sifton's life was beginning to cause widespread comment. His splendid Ottawa home, called "Armadale," was lavishly furnished. According to one report, it had a music room, "devoted to a weekly dance"; a drawing room with satin furnishings, polar bear rugs, and beautiful paintings; a billiard room with still more valuable paintings; and a library, "full of books from floor to ceiling." Sifton also maintained a notable stable of horses, and in 1903 became president of the Ottawa Racing Association. In 1902 his old political enemy, Senator Kirchhoffer, was so busy regaling "the boys" back in Brandon with stories of Sifton's wealth that the minister's former law partner, A.E. Philp, wanted to launch a libel suit. Sifton naturally ignored the idea; but in Brandon, where many people well remembered the impecunious if hard-working young lawyer of nearly twenty years before, embroidered stories of his "magnificent institution," carriages, horses and footmen, his supposed interests in various companies and banks, invariably attracted a wide-eyed audience. But Sifton believed that his wealth was his personal affair, that it had been obtained perfectly legally, that it was no sin to be wealthy, and that there was nothing for which to apologize.

In the opinion of many, however—including some Liberals—a little discretion would have been appropriate. It hardly seemed decent for a minister of the Crown whose wealth obviously was increasing rapidly to be so ostentatious. The situation was perhaps best summed up in a story attributed to Sir Richard Cartwright, Laurier's minister of trade and commerce. As they watched Sifton step into his carriage one day, Cartwright supposedly said to a young Liberal acquaintance:

"Young man, do you note this display of affluence on the part of a minister so new and so young? Do you note those spirited horses, that silver-mounted harness, and the magnificent chariot behind? Shall I tell you what Sir John Macdonald would have said to one of his ministers if he'd appeared thus? Sir John would have said, 'My dear fellow, it is bad enough to do it, but for heaven's sake don't advertise it.'"

D.J. Hall, *Clifford Sifton: A Lonely Eminence*, 1985

Sifton's Trumpet

Whenever his immigration policy was attacked in the House, he was spared the discomfort because he was gradually growing deaf. And if at any time he chose to listen through his ear trumpet, he was well able to take care of himself in a debate.

Augustus Bridle, *Sons of Canada*, 1916

Blunt Sir Clifford

Sifton replies to a letter from a Member pressing on him an applicant for a post in the Klondike, well after the gold-rush had begun.

Let me express the hope that in other matters of business, professional or otherwise, you do not get so far behind as you are in this particular matter. All the inhabitants of Canada, except yourself, most of those in the United States and a great portion of the population of Europe are already on my list as applicants for positions in the Klondike, and much as I should like to meet your wishes I am obliged to say that your application is a little late. I hope and trust that the next unfortunate applicant for office who places his case in your hands will be able to get his application registered a little nearer the top.

Sir Clifford Sifton, quoted in John W. Dafoe, *Sifton in Relation to his Times*, 1931

Bijou Casgrain's Higher Calling

Joseph-Philippe Baby Casgrain (1856-1939) narrates his failed attempt to gain the Liberal nomination in Soulanges. He was summoned to the Senate in 1900.

"Many years ago, I became ambitious to represent my native county of Soulanges in the House of Commons. I went to my leader and I said, 'Wilfrid, how would you like to see me in the House of Commons as your supporter and member for Soulanges?'"

"'Bijou, I would be very pleased indeed,' he said, 'provided you can get the nomination.' So I resolved to try. I went to Soulanges, and hired a hall. That cost me $5. I put an advertisement of my meeting in the newspaper. That cost me $1.50. I told everybody I was a candidate for the Liberal nomination, and I spent $500 on 5-cent whiskies. If you are good at arithmetic you will know how many drinks that meant! Everybody slapped me on the back and I was very happy.

"The day of the convention came! I stayed in my office in Montreal to await results, and sent a friend out to Soulanges, who would bring the good news at the earliest moment. In the evening my friend returned, 'Well,' I said, 'how did the convention go?' 'Bijou,' he answered, 'the local doctor, your rival, got 750 votes.' 'Oui,' said I. 'But how many votes did I get?' 'Ah, Bijou, you did not get one vote.'

"I was shocked! I was amazed! I had spent $5 for a hall; $1.50 for an advertisement; $500 for 5-cent whiskeys, and yet the Liberals of Soulanges, the Liberals of the county where I was born, had not given me one vote. I was so sad I could have cried! I sat and thought, 'What shall I do to relieve my mind?' Then I said, 'I know what I shall do! I shall go to the St. James Club and get intoxicated!' I did, but I found that I could not get intoxicated, and I was not drinking 5-cent whiskey either. No, the very best! It was very strange because I had been intoxicated before and I have been intoxicated since. But on this night when I was so sad and needed to, the whiskey would not work. My sadness kept me sober!

"But not long after I received consolation. Sir Wilfrid said to me, 'Bijou, how would you like to be in the Senate?' I said, 'Wilfrid, my dear friend, you read my thoughts: I would very much like to be in the Senate.' And so it was arranged and I have been there ever since. I had not been there very long before a Liberal from Soulanges came to see me and asked me to help him with a political favour. I turned to him and said, 'You have not forgotten that I sought the nomination for Soulanges, my native county. I went there! I spent $5 on a hall; $1.50 for an advertisement; $500 for 5-cent whiskeys. I treated everyone of you with politesse but at the convention you did not give me one vote. Now I am in the Senate. I do not need to treat anyone with politesse: you can go to the devil.'

"He was angry and said, 'Such a man as you is unfit for public life.' But I laughed at him. 'All right, you can vote against me next time.'"

Senator "Bijou" Casgrain,
quoted in Hector Charlesworth, I'm Telling You, 1937

Captive Audience

For several years Senator Casgrain's chief pal in the Upper Chamber was the late Senator Lawrence A. Wilson, who could boast that he was a real Canadian, partly Indian, partly French and partly Scottish. Whenever he could obtain an audience with his friend "Bijou" present Larry Wilson delighted to tell this story. He was driving though rural Quebec one afternoon and heard that at a village 18 miles away "Bijou" was addressing a meeting. He swiftly made a detour and arrived full speed at the hall. It was locked, with a doorkeeper outside. He demanded admittance. He said, "I am Senator Wilson. I must get in to hear my friend Senator Casgrain. Unlock that door!" But the keeper said, "I cannot unlock that door. I must obey orders. The audience might get out."

Hector Charlesworth, I'm Telling You, 1937

Speaker Bain

Thomas Bain (1834-1915) was the Speaker of the House from 1899 to 1900. He was elected to serve out the term of Sir James Edgar, who died in office in 1899.

Mr. Bain was a dear old chap, but quite unfitted for the important post. It was always supposed that Sir Wilfrid Laurier had him elected to the chair as a compliment for his untiring devotion to his parliamentary duties and his faithfulness to the Liberal cause. He was very highly respected, but I am afraid some of the younger Members on the Conservative side, bent upon mischief, deliberately evolved plans to puzzle the old gentleman. One afternoon a member of the opposition rose to a point of order and asked Speaker Bain's ruling. Before this was given the "point" was debated by Members on both sides, and then the Speaker, naturally, decided in favor of the government.

This raised a storm of protest from the opposition; further points of order were submitted, until the Speaker, equally with the leaders on both sides, got hopelessly tangled up. The row had been going on for over an hour and it seemed impossible to get away from the impasse when Speaker Bain rose, hitched his robe well upon his shoulders, and spreading out his arms with the hands extended to the full, as if about to pronounce a benediction, remarked, "Will the brethren please come to order." For a moment the Members of the House on both sides were nonplussed. To be called "brethren", as if they were at a Methodist class meeting, was unheard of in Parliament. But quickly the request caught the entire House. The adjuration, so simply and kindly uttered, appealed to them and with one accord they burst into loud cheers and laughter. The points of order were dropped, and the House proceeded with its regular business.

Fred Cook, *Giants and Jesters,* n.d.

Sydney Fisher's Lectures

Sydney Arthur Fisher (1853-1929) served as Minster of Agriculture for all of Wilfrid Laurier's Prime Ministership.

He was a total abstainer, a prohibitionist, an inveterate talker and in general a most insufferable person. He would lecture the House for hours on the manners and customs of insect pests, the domestic intimacies of pure-bread swine, and the most effective if the most primitive method of fertilizing agricultural acres. His speeches were interminable and frequent and their only recommendation was that they appeared to occasion in him a distress almost as acute as that experienced by his hearers. It was a favourite practice of the Opposition to prod the Honourable Sidney as a means of wasting time and thereby deferring some other business for which the Conservatives were unprepared. Once when Mr. Fisher sat down, after one of his long and mutually painful orations, the Honourable John Haggart leaned across to his leader, Mr. Borden, and, in a quarter-deck whisper, roared, "Shall I ask the little beggar a question and get him going for another four hours?"

Paul Bilkey, *Persons, Papers and Things,* 1940

The Lost Pact

William Stevens Fielding (1848-1929) was Liberal Finance Minister for sixteen years under Laurier and four years under King. He negotiated the fateful reciprocity treaty of 1911.

One winter day, after prolonged negotiations at Washington, Mr. Fielding came back to Ottawa with the reciprocity pact in the bag; signed, sealed and delivered but requiring joint legislative sanction. We were all down to the depot to meet the Minister, not expecting much, if anything, but giving us anyway the chance of the first turndown. "Now, gentlemen," the Minister said in a tone discouraging our reportorial industry, "you really would not expect me...." Then, he walked away at the brisk pace at which he always moved.

Mr. Arthur Hannay of the Press Gallery and myself proceeded to the old Russell House to lunch. Mr. Fielding, that afternoon, was to deliver the great speech on reciprocity and give it "the works" but he had a habit of never rising to make such pronouncements until four in the afternoon and it would be an hour or more before he would bore through to the real milk of the coconut.

My friend was seized with the brilliant thought that, if we went down to Mr. Fielding's house, he might loosen up a bit enabling us to at least make an intelligent "stab" at the subject for our afternoon papers. The morning editions, otherwise, would have the first and last crack at it as they always do in budgets, to the intense envy of the evenings, their circulation enormously greater. It was reasoned that the minister might talk to two when he wouldn't talk to a crowd. I was extremely dubious but agreed to go along for exercise in the crisp air of a winter day.

As we were entering the Fielding residence ten blocks down Metcalfe street, there, lying right beside the sidewalk, was a portfolio, bulging with state documents, in all probability the reciprocity pact itself. The minister, or someone with him, had dropped it. We rang the bell. A maid answered. It was explained that we had just picked this up, that minute. "Thank you," she said. Could we see Mr. Fielding? She would inquire. The Minister, to whom the precious portfolio had been handed, meanwhile came out in the hall to thank us very much, at the time marvelling who had been so careless as to drop it — his secretary or himself. He was pleasant enough but efforts to draw him out, however slightly, were as abortive, when questioned by the two, as they had proven to be on behalf of the crowd.

So we went back to the Press Gallery to await the momentous hour with such satisfaction as comes from at least trying and also with the knowledge that we had retrieved a perhaps priceless parcel, delivering it promptly to the rightful owner. That was all. In life, virtue is its own reward, often the only one.

Charles Bishop, Ottawa Evening Citizen, 1945

Working for Fielding

Fielding was the combination of bigness and pettiness. Although he was a newspaperman by profession, he always acted as if he was suspicious of the Press, and seldom took them into his confidence. He was even suspicious of his officials and his colleagues. When he was dictating an important document he would close the transom and almost search under the desk to make certain that no reporter had concealed himself. When Budget changes were being considered Fielding hardly trusted himself, let alone his colleagues.

A hard worker himself, who often kept long hours, he was inconsiderate of his employees. A former secretary of Mr. Fielding told me an extraordinary and almost unbelievable story in regard to him. He said that one evening at closing time Mr. Fielding asked him if he could work that evening. The secretary said it was a little inconvenient as he had arranged to go to the theatre that evening. Mr. Fielding urged him to cancel his engagements as it was important, which he did, 'phoning his wife and arranging for someone else to go with her in his place. Mr. Fielding, before parting, asked him the name of the show, which was starring a well-known actor.

The secretary returned to the office after dinner, but there was no Mr. Fielding. He failed to turn up and the secretary delved into other work. To his amazement, after the show Mr. Fielding walked into the office. "Glad you reminded me of that show," said Mr. Fielding to the angered secretary, "I enjoyed it immensely."

Arthur Ford, As the World Wags On, 1950

Adultery

John Barr (1843-1909), a Conservative, was the Member for Dufferin from 1904 to 1909.

When Dr. Barr was on his feet members would flock in from the lobbies, and reporters to the gallery in quest of entertainment. One night one of Mr. Fielding's treaties was the subject of debate. With the assistance of Hon. Mr. Brodeur, a trade agreement had been effected with France, one clause of which was designed to encourage importation of French wines. Now Dufferin was nominally a teetotal constituency and Dr. Barr felt it his duty to oppose this clause. He noted the fact that no precautions against adulteration were provided in the Treaty. "Has the Minister of Finance looked into that?" he asked. "Are we to sit idly by and see the youth and maidens of this country debauched by these adulterous wines?"

Hector Charlesworth, I'm Telling You, 1937

Cinq-Mars

Ernest Cinq-Mars was a flamboyant Press Gallery reporter.

Cinq-Mars was the central figure in a spectacular incident of the Parliamentary session of 1906. It was the session following the insurance inquiry when Sir George Foster was under fire. Cinq-Mars wrote an article in La Presse bitterly attacking him in decidedly abusive and vitriolic language, of which he was a master. As a result Sir George presented a motion ordering Captain Cinq-Mars to attend at the Bar of the House. To summon a man before the Bar of the House is an ancient privilege of Parliament. In the days of the Stuarts when there was a prolonged struggle between Parliament and Crown, it was a right of which the commoners often made use. However, in modern times the right has fallen into disuse. When Sir George decided to summon Cinq-Mars to the Bar, there was much curiosity as to just what would happen and what, after all, the House could do with Cinq-Mars. There was no Tower where prisoners could be confined.

Sir George, in presenting the motion, said he did not complain of the personalities; it was the charge that he was daily "pouring out floods of gratuitous slander" upon the French-Canadians. That Sir George had some grounds for complaint is evident from the following excerpt from Cinq-Mars' article: "Our compatriots are represented as fools steeped in ignorance; our clergy as a collection of fanatics and hypocrites. And it is Mr. Foster, a politician of ill-fame, who sings this refrain in the House of Commons. He has but one principle, that of self-interest. He has only one desire, the desire to insult. He belongs to the school of lying, hypocrisy and cowardice. In his eyes the person to whom civic and political virtue are not vain words is an imbecile and a hot-head."

There was a considerable debate following the motion, Sir Wilfrid Laurier claiming that he had also suffered from religious and racial attacks. However, the motion was passed and Cinq-Mars was ordered to appear before the Bar of the House. On the day in question the House was crowded with expectant members; the Press Gallery was filled with anxious newspapermen and the galleries were crammed with spectators. As fitting the occasion Cinq-Mars appeared before the House with a frock coat and silk hat. Upon motion of Hon. Alan Aylesworth, the House decided not to limit the young journalist in his defence to the debates of the past session, or even to Parliamentary speeches. Mr. Cinq-Mars then read a statement claiming justification for his article, which he declared was not a report of proceedings, but an expression of editorial opinion. After some discussion the Prime Minister reviewed the case briefly and declared "that while I recognize in the fullest possible way the right of the press to criticize, while I recognize that the press should have the most ample liberty in criticizing, advocating, censuring and expressing its opinion in every possible way, at the same time, I think we must maintain the doctrine that the press, like everybody else, is amenable to the jurisdiction of this Parliament. There is, I think, much of truth in the article as a whole, but in the particular passage complained of the bounds of reasonable criticism have been passed and it constitutes a breach of the privileges of this House. The press must understand, while it is possible, and not only possible but fair and within their rights, to criticize the act of any public man, they must do it in the language that is fair, and not in the language of mere vituperation."

Mr. Cinq-Mars was discharged after the following resolution moved by Sir Wilfrid and passed unanimously, had been communicated to him by the Speaker: "That the passage in La Presse newspaper complained of pass the bounds of reasonable criticism and constitute a breach of privileges of this House, that Mr. Cinq-Mars, the writer of the article, incurred the censure of the House, that he be recalled to the Bar and that Mr. Speaker do communicate the resolution to him."

It cannot be said that Mr. Cinq-Mars went into mourning over the displeasure of the House. In fact, he was somewhat of a hero in Quebec for several years.

Arthur Ford, *As the World Wags On*, 1950

Swing Voter

Andrew Thorburn Thompson (1870-1939) was a Member of the House of Commons at the turn of the century. He was active in Liberal party affairs long after his defeat in 1904. On one occasion he was sent from Ottawa to the Okanagan Valley to handle a by-election campaign for the Liberals, and he made his headquarters in the charming town of Vernon.

Late one afternoon, a hurry up message came from another town some miles away asking Thompson to come and address a meeting at which the speaker advertised for the occasion could not appear. The Colonel sent for the only taxi-cab in town and set forth. He had proceeded but a short distance when the taxi-driver turned to him and said, "I hope the Grits win this fight; I've always voted Tory, but I'm going to vote the other way this time."

Thompson was guarded. As an old political hand it struck him that his companion might be laying the foundation for an extra charge. He asked, "What has happened to change your political views?"

"Well, it's this way," was the reply. "You see Vernon is an up-and-coming town and gettin' into city ways. Over on the far side of the town is a quiet little place with two or three good-lookin' girls that ain't too particular, you understand. Nice quiet girls they are too, but a stranger can get a drink there and have a pleasant evening. Well, a feller in my position has to earn a living, and the taxi-business in Vernon is dull some days. So I used to deliver parcels over there and maybe take out a bottle or two of whiskey or a case of beer whenever they sent me word. Things was going along all right, no harm done at all, until two fellers told my wife."

"What had that got to do with politics?" asked the Colonel. "Why just this, both of them snakes in the grass is Tories, so I'm goin' to vote Grit this time!" All Thompson could do was to commend his spirit of independence.

Hector Charlesworth, I'm Telling You, 1937

Too Old to Change

One night he [Thompson] was speaking at Penticton at the lower end of Lake Okanagan. In his audience he noticed a fine looking, bearded old gentleman, who seemed to be very interested. As is the practice of many speakers he concentrated on this listener, and was pleased to receive encouragement in the form of nods of assent whenever he made a really good point. Afterwards he fraternized with the audience, mainly composed of fruit-ranchers, and asked to be introduced to the old gentleman. He told him he had been pleased at the interest he evinced and that it had helped him in his speech. He added the hope that interest so aroused might be continued until election day. "Well, I don't know about that," said his new-found friend. "When I was a young man in England I was an ardent Liberal. But when Mr. Gladstone betrayed the Crown I became a Conservative, and I don't think I can change my politics again at my time of life."

Hector Charlesworth, I'm Telling You, 1937

Sir Robert Borden

Sir Robert Laird Borden (1854-1937) was Prime Minister from 1911 to 1920.

He goes with that Derby hat and thick overcoat, trudging a bit sideways up Parliament Hill on winter days to the office of the Premier in the East Block—the man who never laughs in public. Step by step he cogitates. Resolutely he holds his way. Courteously he bows to a Member or a Minister. On into his room, face chiselled like bronze for an Egyptian god, grey hair punctiliously parted amidships, faultlessly groomed, a thick grizzled moustache, and a steady eye—always seeming to have plenty of time, forever seeming to make up his mind, discreetly shuffling over papers, reflectively reading; such a serious, meditative man. His secretary is staccato; Borden—always slowly polite and for the most part gently reasonable. In an hour he may conscientiously get through a load of detail work and is ready for the first of a line of miscellaneous callers.

A green baize door opens and you face the Premier, at whose back a slow wood fire is burning, on his right a big Gothic bow window over-looking the campus.

He rises, greets the visitor in a thick basso voice of unaffected cordiality, and motions him to sit in a chair which is discreetly screwed to the floor on the end of his desk. And until the interview is over this man of slow mind and overwhelming sincerity says never a word that somehow does not seem to be part of a moral message.

He is the unstageable, unspectacular Borden; the man from Halifax, the lawyer who was born to be a judge, the citizen who was never cut out for politics, the gentleman who ordinarily never could have got through life without becoming a churchwarden.

Augustus Bridle; *Sons of Canada*, 1916

A Cultured Man

Before he studied law Sir Robert taught school for a time. If he had continued following the teaching profession he would doubtless, like many other Nova Scotian educationists, have ended up as a university president. He had every qualification, for such a position. Canada never had a more erudite, more scholarly, or more cultured Prime Minister. He could read both Latin and Greek in the original. It was relaxation for him to pick up Homer or Horace. He spoke both French and German. He was interested in botany although he had little time to pursue this hobby. His Ottawa home was on the banks of the Rideau River, and he had planted along the paths of the banks many Canadian wild flowers. He knew all the Latin botanical names.

Arthur Ford, *As The World Wags On*, 1950

Borden's Daily Routine

Borden describes his daily routine on first being elected to the House of Commons in 1896.

When his wife was not there Borden would busy himself with professional affairs. "The manner of my daily life is this," he explained during the first session.

"I rise at eight and at 8:45 tea and toast are brought to my room. Until about ten I read and then make any calls at the Departmental office or elsewhere which are necessary in connection with my work. Then to the House of Commons where I receive any letters and write for an hour or thereabouts. Then for a short walk or go to the Library of Parliament or to that of the Supreme Court. After lunch we go to the House at three which occupies the time until dinner. Then if the House is not in Session read in my room or in the Library or chat with friends at the Club."

The duties of a backbencher offered much work and scant reward. "It is a miserable irregular life that one has to lead," Borden complained, "and I am more than sick of it, I can assure you."

Nor were first impressions of Parliament very favourable. Borden remembered that he had entered public life "with a rather lofty ideal of the dignity of Parliament as the grand inquest of the nation." Doubts came quickly. The waste of time in Parliament, the onerous demands upon members, the iron-fisted control of the House by the Government to the point where debate seemed both mechanical and pointless, all added up to a feeling of frustration and uselessness.

Robert Craig Brown, *Robert Laird Borden: A Biography*, 1980

Borden's Mind

Borden lacked many of the qualities of popular leadership, though he always had the respect not only of his followers, but of everyone who came into contact with him. In debate in the House he always seemed to me more effective than Laurier, despite a hesitancy and slowness of speech which made him much less attractive. Yet Borden could always be depended upon to tear aside the non-essential, and to puncture any verbal balloons that his opponent sent so cleverly into the political atmosphere. Sir Robert was consistently sound and logical, and his training in constitutional law gave him a clarity of vision possessed by few. He never took a petty or narrow attitude on any subject. His mind was big—if one may use the term—and he could not descend to little things. Thus he was consistently one of the most effective debaters in my time. Personally he lacked the ability to secure a popular following in the country, and was somewhat neglectful of his following in the House, seeming, in those trying times of war, to be bowed down with his heavy responsibilities. Consequently, he did not inspire that type of idolatry given to Laurier, but he was nevertheless one of our great leaders.

R. J. Manion, *Life Is An Adventure*, 1936

The Other Side of Borden

He was a very human person behind the stern front and the stone face. The large fortune earned at the bar he conserved and expanded by rigid thrift. When he could spare the time he liked to go with his wife to the farmers' market in Ottawa and bargain for a fat capon or a mess of spring vegetables. Usually he rode to his office on a bicycle. He was an excellent raconteur among his intimates and enjoyed a rough joke over a drink. He loved the outdoors and the soil and understood them. Tobacco, which he chewed in private, was his only vice. Sometimes he showed flashes of humour unexpected and profane.

In his lawyer's punctilious language he once summed up a highly confidential meeting with his colleagues that was followed by immediate publication of important secrets in the press.

"I have endeavoured with no small expenditure of time and energy," he told one of his cronies, "to trace the origins of this extraordinary circumstance and have at last discovered the person responsible for a betrayal unprecedented in my experience." Then, referring by name to an eminent Canadian statesman, he added: "I am driven reluctantly, sir, to the considered conclusion that this gentleman is a dirty, low-down son of a bitch."

His humour occasionally extended to himself. Addressing the ball on the first tee of an Ottawa golf course, the Prime Minister was heard by a companion to mutter: "Now Borden, God damn you, keep your fool head down."

Bruce Hutchison, *Mr. Prime Minister*, 1964

Borden in 1917

After the Unionist election of 1917 Sir Robert never learned to know by name, or by sight, half of the supporters of the new government. There was a swarm of new members. Sir Robert, with the burden of the war on his shoulders, had little, or no time, for social amenities, or little opportunity to mingle with the private members even in the caucus room. He was in England, or Europe, nearly half the time. The House was sitting after the Parliamentary fire in the makeshift building, the Victoria Museum, and its environment did not make for close acquaintanceship. The story went the rounds of the Press Gallery that at one time Sir Robert mistook one of the new Unionist members from the West for a Parliamentary messenger and gave him a letter to deliver to one of his colleagues at his office. The amused member, not offended, rather than take the time to explain to the busy Prime Minister his mistake and as he was going in that direction anyway, delivered the message.

Arthur Ford, *As The World Wags On*, 1950

Borden Indecisive

His style of leadership contributed to an image of indecisiveness. He was deliberate and patient with his colleagues. A few of them chafed under that regimen. Foster, an impatient and impulsive man, wrote after one Cabinet meeting that Borden was "undecided as usual," adding the next day the simple condemnation, "Drift, Corroding Drift."

Robert Craig Brown, *Robert Laird Borden: A Biography*, 1980

Prayers

Thomas Simpson Sproule (1843-1917) sat in the House of Commons from 1878 to 1915, the last four years as Speaker of the House.

It is a well-established custom in the Commons that the prayers shall be read in English and French on alternate days. The two languages are on an equal footing in the Debates and Records of Parliament. Dr. Sproule, in common with many of the Ontario Members, was by no means enthusiastic as to the use of the French language; but he was very conscientious and upon his selection as Speaker he felt himself constrained to study this language, of which he was absolutely ignorant, in order that he might be able to read the prayers in French. Accordingly, he came to Ottawa before the opening of the session and engaged the services of a French teacher. For about three weeks the prayers were read in French by the Assistant Clerk but after that the Speaker considered that he was sufficiently fluent to undertake the duty himself. The equivalent or semi-equivalent of the French words was carefully marked on the card containing the French version of the prayers. At the first attempt Dr. Sproule did reasonably well. However, Sir Thomas White told me that on conclusion of the Speaker's effort, he (White) leaned over and made inquiry of his deskmate, Monk. Monk's countenance frequently was of a rather melancholy cast. He was sitting with his cheek on his arm and the following dialogue took place:

White: "That was very good, was it not, Monk? I thought the old man did fairly well, did he not?"

Monk: (in a very deep and rather sepulchral voice) "I have no doubt that Almighty God would understand it."

After a time the Speaker became confused between the French diphthongs "au," "eau," and "eu" and he read the Lord's Prayer with a pronunciation which greatly astonished the French-speaking Members, as his pronunciation of the French word for "heaven," sounded to them like the French word for "bucket."

Robert Laird Borden: His Memoirs, Henry Borden ed., 1938

Sir Sam Hughes

The mercurial Sir Sam Hughes (1853-1921) served as Minister of Militia during the early part of the first World War, before being sacked by Prime Minister Borden.

When I formed my Government in 1911, I was extremely doubtful as to including Hughes; while he was a man of marked ability and sound judgement in many respects, his temperament was so peculiar, and his actions and language so unusual on many important occasions that one was inclined to doubt his usefulness as a Minister. I discussed with Hughes when I appointed him Minister of Militia his extraordinary eccentricities. When I impressed strongly upon him the mischievous and perverse character of his speech and conduct, he broke down, admitted that he often acted impetuously, and assured me that if he were appointed I could rely on his judgement and good sense. This promise was undoubtedly sincere but his temperament was too strong for him. He was under constant illusions that enemies were working against him. I told him on one occasion that I thoroughly agreed that he was beset by two unceasing enemies. Expecting a revelation, he was intensely disappointed when I told him that they were his tongue and his pen. In my experience his moods might be divided into three categories; during about half of the time he was an able, reasonable, and useful colleague, working with excellent judgement and indefatigable energy; for a certain other portion of the time he was extremely excitable, impatient of control, and almost impossible to work with; and during the remainder his conduct and speech were so eccentric as to justify the conclusion that his mind was unbalanced.

Robert Laird Borden: His Memoirs, Henry Borden, ed., 1938

The Wrong Answer

Major George William Andrews (1869-1943) makes the acquaintance of Sir Sam Hughes.

Invalided out of the First Division in France, after being mentioned in despatches and awarded the D.S.O., Major George Andrews (later the Member of Parliament for Winnipeg Centre) reported at headquarters in Ottawa—on the way home to Winnipeg. Sir Sam entertained him to lunch.

After lunch, they went for a drive along the Rideau. Sir Sam broached the subject of Ross rifle proficiency. He suggested to Major Andrews that, having won prizes at Bisley with the Ross, he could well be the man—newly returned from the front—to testify to the superb qualities of that rifle.

The blunt, honest old soldier demurred. "For target shooting, under peace conditions, it worked fined," he said, "but in the mud of shell holes it was hopeless."

Sir Sam ordered the chauffeur to stop the car. He had no more time for Major Andrews. The chauffeur understood, and politely opened the door for Sir Sam's passenger. That sturdy veteran walked the several miles back to the Chateau Laurier.

Charles Bowman, Ottawa Editor, 1966

Meeting in Public

One of Sam Hughes' curious habits was to receive officers, or others who had business with him, at the time when his long office was full of newspaper men and a whole battery of female stenographers. It was often embarrassing to the visitor, as it was to us. All that could be done was to start a buzz of conversation by way of diversion.

One morning, W.F. Cockshutt, M.P., came in, wearing the full uniform of an honorary colonel, which rank Sir Sam had made for him. "I came to see you on private business," he said to the general, with no excess of deference, "I didn't think I was walking into the Press Gallery." "Oh, you didn't," replied the general, sarcasticly. "The truth, Cockshutt, is that they are a damn sight more welcome here than you are."

We started conversation and Colonel Cockshutt went on with his business, but the interview was strangely brief.

Charles Bishop, Ottawa Evening Citizen, 1945

Hughes' Conceit

In the hope of appeasing his huge conceit and making him easier to get along with, Borden arranged a knighthood for him and this did give Hughes much pleasure. Shortly after the honour was announced, a delegation from Elgin Country waited upon him to discuss a matter affecting his department. The spokesman began his presentation, very tactfully, by congratulating the minister. The conferring of a knighthood on Hughes, he said, had caused much satisfaction in the county of Elgin. Sir Sam interrupted him: "Just a minute, Dave. It has caused satisfaction not only in the county of Elgin but all across Canada. In fact, His Majesty said that there had never been an honour it had given him so much pleasure to bestow. Go ahead, Dave."

Roger Graham, Arthur Meighen: Door of Opportunity, 1960

Inviting Target

Hughes was under incessant heavy fire from the Opposition in Parliament and from the Liberal press. No other minister except Bob Rogers (also an inviting target) was hounded and harried so unmercifully. This abuse Hughes attributed to jealousy, malice or petty partisanship; he was positive, as positive as he was about everything, that no word or deed of his could justify it. Indeed, he seems to have thought his critics quite unpatriotic. After all, he was in charge of the war effort and to hamper him was to give aid and comfort to the enemy. Once, denouncing the *Globe* of Toronto for a virulent attack on himself, Hughes unconsciously cast a piercing light on his own colossal egotism. "'Cursed be ye Scribes and Pharisees, hypocrites!'" he proclaimed. "That's what our Lord said and I agree with Him."

Roger Graham, *Arthur Meighen: Door of Opportunity*, 1960

Camp Borden

Camp Borden was created in 1916 on a sandy plain north of Toronto as a training ground for Canadian soldiers and flyers in World War I.

The redoubtable Sam Hughes decided, as Minister of Militia, to inspect the camp, where there must have been some 30,000 or more troops, and, for reasons best known to himself, to hold a ceremonial review. The heat was tropical, most of the troops had been in the army for a very short time, and they were living in anything but comfort. The announcement of a review was, to put it mildly, most unwelcome. But the men in the ranks had their revenge. The field where the event was held was covered with dust and a great deal of ash left from the fires when the area was cleared of timber. A strong wind blew directly towards the saluting base and the troops realized that by dragging their feet the reviewing stand would be brought under attack. The result was that at the end of the march past, every one of the officers on the stand had a blackened countenance and, to complete the satisfaction of the troops, no one could be punished.

Vincent Massey, *What's Past is Prologue*, 1963

Keep Both Hands, etc....

I recall well the evening of July 26, 1904 when Lord Dundonald left the Capital on his way to England. All the way from Crichton Lodge, where he had resided, to the station, a distance of a mile and a half, he was greeted with cheering citizens waving flags. There were the wildest scenes of enthusiasm and excitement that Ottawa has ever witnessed. The horses had been removed from Dundonald's carriage and twoscore of enthusiastic militia men proudly drew him to the station with ropes. Arrived at the junction of Rideau and Sussex streets, one block from the railway terminus, Dundonald is supposed to have uttered the famous phrase. I made many inquiries from persons who had been in the locality mentioned, but could not find a single one who had heard the distinguished officer use the expression.

After the departure of the train to Montreal, Col. Sam Hughes hunted me up and inquired if I had heard Dundonald's final appeal to the Canadian people. I replied in the negative.

"Well," said Sam, "just as we were approaching the station Dundonald stood up in the carriage, and with his arms extended he called out, 'Men of Canada: keep both hands on the Union Jack.' Tip that off to the boys; it is good stuff."

I followed Colonel Sam's request and every Conservative newspaper from coast to coast next morning contained Dundonald's alleged final words. They made a great headline. I am certain that the credit for the expression is due to Sam Hughes. But here let me mention a curious thing. Reading the account of the Ottawa send-off in the Montreal Gazette next morning, which contained the famous abjuration with which he was credited, Lord Dundonald took it to himself and used it very effectively in his farewell addresses in that city and in Quebec.

Fred Cook, *Fifty Years Ago and Since*, n.d.

The Great Fire

A devastating fire destroyed the Centre Block of the Parliament Buildings on February 3, 1916. At the time there were rumours the blaze was the work of foreign arsonists.

I had been down to Nova Scotia on legal business and had only returned at noon on the 3rd. I had been in the House in the afternoon at question time, then went to dine with some friends in the Rideau Club and walked up to the buildings a little before nine o'clock. As I went to the House of Commons side I saw a strange, foreign-looking man standing on the left of the steps going up to the Commons chamber and I was struck with his appearance and said to myself, "That man is not a Canadian."

I hung my coat and hat in my cubicle in the corridor, which ran along the rear of the chamber, entered the House and was chatting with Mr. Graham when a page brought me a note from a Nova Scotian lady in Ottawa who said she had some friends who wanted to obtain seats in the ladies' gallery. I went out and took the ladies upstairs in the elevator, along the entrance to the ladies' gallery, in which there were very few people as it was a disagreeable evening outside. I was sitting pointing out different well-known Members in the House to them when a sudden puff of smoke came up to the gallery on the opening of the doors immediately underneath, and Mederic Martin, then Mayor of Montreal and Member of St-Mary's, came rushing into the House from the corner nearest the reading-room shouting, "The House is on fire! The House is on fire!"

I immediately suggested to the ladies that it would be prudent for them to go downstairs, took them safely to the elevator and suggested that it would be better for them at once to make their way home, as apparently very serious conditions existed.

Looking along the corridor where I had left my hat and coat I could see signs of flames at the other end, and volumes of smoke were coming through the corridor, so I decided that I would not venture to get my clothing and immediately took the elevator to the top floor where the Nova Scotia room was, went to my desk and took out some business papers, put them in my pocket and started to go down.

As I was returning to the elevator I met Bowman Law, the Member for Yarmouth, rushing from the elevator in the direction of the room.

I descended in the elevator, and there was a scene of wild excitement in the ante-chamber of the House, with Members frantically making their way from the Chamber. I went to the nearest telephone and telephoned to the Chateau Laurier, where I was staying, to send up a car for me, as I was without overcoat or hat. I went in the car to the hotel, procured both and started to walk back to the buildings. As I did so the fire had reached major proportions and it was seen that the buildings were doomed. I wended my way to the Rideau Club and from the verandah watched the progress of the fire, in company with numerous Members who had come there. Although three hundred yards distant from the buildings it was probably the best place available in the whole city to watch the scene.

The fire burned swiftly and steadily and one of the interesting and peculiar sights was the way in which the tower, which rose from the centre of the buildings facing the street, withstood the attack of the flames. All the under support seemed to have been burned away but the flames licked up the sides of the tower and reached the top. Slowly but surely, and then suddenly, the whole thing toppled in the burned out portion below.

E.M. Macdonald, *Recollections, Political and Personal*, 1938

The Great Fire, II

I was at a dinner given by the Minister of Militia, Sir Sam Hughes, at the Château Laurier. His dinners were not dry dinners. There were about eight or ten of us there, and one guest from the north of Ireland had a delightful baritone voice. He was in the middle of singing "Where the Mountains of Mourne Come Down to the Sea" when the door burst open and someone said, "Good God! What are you people doing here? Don't you know the Parliament Buildings are on fire?" We said, "We'll go up and put the fire out shortly. Now go away and don't bother us." But half an hour later someone else came, and then we thought we had better have a look. We streamed out to find a pall of black smoke obscuring Parliament Hill and the main tower of the Centre Block shooting great gouts of flame high in the night.

I dashed into the building to get my typewriter and made my way outside through corridors filled with smoke. By this time a great crowd had gathered. It was a bitterly cold night, and people caught in the building were coming down ladders or leaping into the snow beneath the windows.

What saved a lot of lives was that the House was practically deserted. The main speaker that evening was a man from New Brunswick called Loggie, and he was speaking on fish. So the House was absolutely barren, and Mr. Loggie was alone in his glory.

The Prime Minister, Sir Robert Borden, made his way hatless though the crowd from the Centre Block to his East Block office, where he watched from a window. Dr. Michael Clark, the Member for Red Deer, came reeling out into the snow, gasping and choking. Pierre Blondin, the Minister of State, and Dr. J.D. Reid, the Minister of Customs, brought out Martin Burrell, the Minister of Agriculture, who was badly burned about the face and hands. He had been working in his office next to the reading room where the fire started.

Dr. Edward L. Cash, the Member for Yorkton, and Mr. Thomas MacNutt, the Member for Saltcoasts Saskatchewan, saved themselves by climbing out a washroom window. Robert Rogers, Minister of Public Works, made his way out of the Chamber and down the main corridor in smoke so thick he couldn't see his hand in front of his face. Journalists were holding a ladder for John Stanfield, the Conservative party whip, to descend from a second-floor window. Madame Sévigny, wife of Albert Sévigny, the Speaker, was rescued through a window in her husband's office. Two of her companions, Madame Bray and Madame Morin, died. Madame Dussault, another of Madame Sévigny's guests, saved herself by jumping from a window. Five others were lost.

Fortunately, the aging Laurier was not in the House that night and was spared the holocaust. A number of famous paintings were destroyed, including the representation by Robert Harris of the Fathers of Confederation at Charlottetown.

When Sam Hughes saw the state of affairs, he summoned the 77th Battalion to aid the City of Ottawa firefighters and the government police. The Corps of Engineers, under Colonel Street, cordoned off the buildings to keep back the huge crowd. The fire had begun at nine o'clock. By eleven o'clock when the Governor General, the Duke of Connaught, arrived with his party from a performance at the Russell

Theatre, the fire was at its height, flinging a rippling curtain of flame hundreds of feet over the river.

Sparks rained on the snow-covered roof of the East Block; water from the hoses ran down in rivulets and froze in long, curling streamers. In the East Block were the Prime Minister's office and the offices of the Minister of Justice, the Minister of Finance, the Treasury Board, and the Governor General. Several members reported loud explosions when the fire began, and this no doubt helped to explain the cries of sabotage which immediately arose. The stories which came to the surface of mysterious foreigners, presumably Germans, around the building prior to the fire must be put down to wartime hysteria.

At three in the morning Sir Sam Hughes reported the fire finally under control. The Parliamentary Library alone had escaped undamaged. The government held a midnight Cabinet meeting in the Château Laurier suite of the Minister of Justice, C.J. Doherty. It was decided there would be no interruptions in parliamentary sittings. After casting about for other quarters the government settled on the Victoria Museum, a gaunt Gothic structure built on a swamp on Argyle Avenue in Ottawa.

Grattan O'Leary, *Recollections of People, Press, and Politics*, 1977

Ancient Senators

Following the fire, both the House and Senate met in the Victoria Museum.

Above the door of a room provided for the accommodation of the Senate some wag had affixed the following legend which he had found among the museum properties: "Prehistoric Fossils."

Robert Laird Borden: His Memoirs, Henry Borden, ed., 1938

Mortality

William Humphrey Bennett (1859-1925) sat as a Member of the House of Commons for Simcoe East for almost twenty-five years before being summoned to the Senate in 1917.

A favorite occupation of W. H. Bennett (Billy) was his senatorial mortality table. His ambitions to become a senator, in time, were unconcealed, but he wished the premature demise of no one to hasten his entry. He was prepared to wait, meanwhile keeping tab. I used to ask him now and then how the table stood. "Well," he would say, "I figure that old Senator So and So is due to check out before long." Strange to relate, his calculations worked out with an actuarial accuracy. In time Bennett went to the Senate in reward for long and industrious party service in the House. There, he had won laurels. In the Senate, he simply rested on them.

Charles Bishop, *Ottawa Evening Citizen*, 1945

Red Michael

Michael Clark (1861-1926) was the Member for Red Deer from 1908 to 1921.

When the estimates came up for the ports on the Atlantic most members from that region wanted to get into the debate. It went on all day and was getting pretty monotonous. Finally a Liberal member from Alberta named Michael Clark got up. Everybody called him "red" Michael, not because of his political views but because he had a great mop of red hair. He was quite a wag and he rose when the air was tense with the fulminations of the Maritimes against injustices they had suffered at the hands of the rest of Canada. Michael looked over the House and said, "Mr. Speaker, I have listened all day to these members from the Atlantic provinces. The last member said that the Maritimes produce more fish than any place in the world and that fish make brains. All I would like to say Mr. Speaker, is that the Lord Almighty, certainly put the fish where they were most needed. " It took three guards to get him safely out of the Chamber! He did not came back for a week.

T.C. Douglas, *Canadian Parliamentary Review*, Summer 1981

Red Michael, II

A great fault in the Commons is speaking too frequently. This applies to the new Member particularly, since the leader of a party or an able and old parliamentarian is expected to take part in many debates, but to the new Member too much or too frequent intervention in debate is almost fatal. Dr. Michael Clark, who in his early days was called "Red

Michael" because of his flaming red beard, was one of the most polished of the debaters whom I have heard in the House, and on one occasion shortly after my election we discussed this matter.

"I suppose, Dr. Clark," I said, "that a new Member should never speak in the House unless he is very familiar with his subject?"

"That is quite right, Manion," replied Red Michael, "and even then in most cases he should remain in his seat."

R. J. Manion, *Life Is An Adventure*, 1936

D.D. McKenzie

Daniel Duncan McKenzie (1859-1927) was chosen interim Liberal leader following the death of Sir Wilfrid Laurier in 1919. He was a losing candidate at the ensuing leadership convention which chose William Lyon Mackenzie King.

McKenzie, a lawyer, had been in the House a long time but, though active and voluble, he was by no means the strongest performer left on the Liberal side. He was given to making shrilly partisan accusations and the arts of insult and vituperation were more prominent in his arsenal than the gift of intelligent discussion. On the day the temporary leader was being selected a group of reporters crowded around the door of the Liberal caucus room to await the result. At last the door opened and the members began trooping out. "Who is it?" a reporter asked. "McKenzie," was the reply. "Yes, McKenzie," chimed in a French-Canadian member of Parliament, emerging at that moment. "He will always remind us of Laurier—he is so different."

Roger Graham, *Arthur Meighen: Door of Opportunity*, 1960

Henri Bourassa

Joseph-Henri-Napoléon Bourassa (1868-1952), founder of Montreal's Le Devoir newspaper, was an influential Quebec Nationalist and a Member of Parliament at the turn of the century and from 1925 to 1935.

Bourassa at the height of his influence in Quebec was also at the height of his vanity, a very lofty pinnacle. He was an excellent debater, dangerously logical and a master of the English tongue, but in Parliament at least he was never moving, a man without emotion and incapable of arousing emotion in others, except upon the hustings in Quebec. An egregious exhibitionist, it was his habit to enter the House of Commons, fold his arms upon the brass bar at the entrance, and gaze about him, and as he was no novelty in the Green Chamber, the irresistible inference was that he sought to engage the interests of the galleries. "Who is that man standing down there?" "Oh, that is Henri Bourassa, the famous nationalist leader."

Paul Bilkey, *Persons, Papers and Things,* 1940

Woodsworth and Bourassa

Woodsworth had many earnest conversations with Henri Bourassa, the Quebec nationalist who wanted to see Canada entirely on her own. Once when they had been discussing their views on various questions, M. Bourassa remarked with a twinkle in his eye: "Mr. Woodsworth, it is too bad you are not a Catholic, because if you were, you would be such a good Catholic!"

Grace MacInnis, *Woodsworth: A Man to Remember,* 1953

Meighen's Memory

Arthur Meighen (1874-1960) was Canada's ninth Prime Minister. A provocative, logical and powerful orator, with an enviable memory and strong powers of concentration, he was, ironically, notoriously absent minded. He was Prime Minister from 1920 to 1921 and for three months in 1926.

Meighen's ordinary custom when speaking in English was to have no notes, except perhaps certain statistics or quotations he intended to use. But in preparing for French-speaking occasions he took understandable precautions, drafting the speech in English and having it translated into French, then assimilating the French text in his mind so as to be as little dependent on his manuscript as possible. He recalled later having spoken in 1926 at the Montreal Forum for twenty-nine minutes in French without once looking at his manuscript but admitted that "this was more a feat of memory than... a true measure of my command of the language". Another time he had to perform the same kind of feat unexpectedly. He and Grattan O'Leary went together to a banquet meeting in Quebec which Meighen was to address. When he went to change his clothes for the dinner he discovered that his dress shirt had not been packed. O'Leary, more diminutive in stature, offered to lend him his and with some difficulty Meighen got into it. In the excitement of this crisis he forgot to put the text of his speech in the pocket of his dinner jacket and was seated at the head table before he discovered it was missing. He wrote a rather frantic note to O'Leary, who without a proper shirt was hovering discreetly on the outskirts of the crowd, and O'Leary obligingly went up to Meighen's room to get the speech. There were papers scattered all over the room but nowhere could O'Leary find what he was looking for so he went back down to the banquet hall and reported his failure. A less confident man would have extemporized some remarks in English, but not Meighen. When called upon he stood up and spoke in French for twenty minutes, delivering word for word the address he had prepared.

Roger Graham, *Arthur Meighen: And Fortune Fled*, 1963

The Green Coat

Meighen's lack of sartorial elegance greatly concerned his friends.

His clothes had a kind of home-spun, unstylish quality which reflected his casual indifference to them. He had few suits and he wore them until they were threadbare. Clothing, in his opinion, was worn for warmth and to cover one's nakedness; it had no other purpose. He neither noticed nor cared what others wore, nor was he at all aware of the dictates of fashion. Thus to some, especially to sophisticated easterners to whom Manitoba was only a name, he seemed a true son of the West, of that uncouth frontier where civilization had barely penetrated. Curiously enough, though Jack Garland, one of his best friends in Portage, was a tailor, Meighen for some reason habitually bought his suits from an English tailor who had settled in the town. That craftsman inexplicably chose to cut his trouser legs so that they ended prematurely above the ankles. But this troubled Meighen not in the least. There was, after all, nothing indecent about a male ankle and he wore the suits heedless, perhaps oblivious, of the fact that they were not exactly in style. Once the tailor outdid himself when he got an order for a new suit from his customer in Ottawa. Perhaps thinking that a glittering career would be furthered by a garment to match, he fashioned a suit of a spangled material that glistened brightly in the light. Meighen tried it on but his wife refused to allow him to wear it out of the house; so the ill-advised experiment resulted in a lamentable waste of cloth and money.

He did, however, wear out (in both senses of the phrase) an over-coat of weathered, rusty green, which was so long it reached almost to his ankles. That coat and the possibility of its disappearance became a subject of lively discussion among some of his friends. One day he and another Conservative member from Manitoba, William Sharpe, were steaming into Ottawa on the train. During Meighen's brief absence from their seat Sharpe decided to get rid of the coat. He did so by opening the window and throwing it out. Meighen, who probably left more personal articles behind him in railway cars and hotel rooms than any other Canadian politician in history, failed to notice the absence of the coat even when he got off the train, and was surprised to receive it in the mail a few days later along with a note. The writer had found the coat beside the tracks and, discovering Meighen's name on the label, had returned it. What had happened was now immediately apparent. With great enjoyment Meighen donned the coat, wore it into the smoking room shortly before the afternoon sitting of the House and triumphantly paraded it before Sharpe, whose astonished expression unmistakably betrayed his guilt.

Roger Graham, *Arthur Meighen: Door of Opportunity*, 1960

Meighen's Memory, II

Mr. Meighen visited Australia. On his return by boat the Vancouver Canadian Club decided that it would ask Mr. Meighen to speak to the club, presuming he would talk on his impressions of Australia. A Marconigram was sent to him extending to him an invitation and asking for the title of his address. He replied, accepting the invitation and adding that his subject would be, "The Greatest of all Englishmen."

Naturally the club was surprised and a little disappointed at his subject. They wondered who was "the greatest of all Englishmen." The club was even more surprised when he appeared before them and spoke on the subject of Shakespeare. Without a note he gave an oration which held them spellbound and made extensive quotations from his plays and poetry.

It turned out afterwards that he did not even have a copy of Shakespeare with him on the boat, nor was there one in the ship's library. His numerous quotations were stored in his amazing memory.

Later he gave the same speech in Ottawa to the Canadian Club and again swept the members off their feet. The newspapermen were unable to report correctly his speech, and afterwards they approached him in his office for a copy. He did not have a copy, but he offered to dictate it to them, and sitting at his desk gave the speech again exactly as it was delivered to the Canadian Club.

Arthur Ford, *As The World Wags On*, 1950

Meighen's Memory, III

Several years ago when Mr. Meighen was still in politics he was campaigning in Western Canada. Grattan O'Leary, associate-editor of the *Ottawa Journal*, accompanied him on the trip covering the tour. Mr. O'Leary had with him a book, a copy of the great orations of English statesmen. Mr. O'Leary was reading Peel's speech on free trade.

"I know that," said Mr. Meighen. "Try me out."

Mr. Meighen began to quote the speech. By the end of a page Mr. O'Leary called quits. Although it turned out that it was several years since Mr. Meighen had read this oration of Peel's, with a few minor errors he quoted it word for word.

Arthur Ford, *As The World Wags On*, 1950

Meighen Absent Minded

His forgetfulness about more or less trivial things, as distinct from things that really mattered to him, became a byword in Ottawa as it had in Portage. "I must ask you," he ruefully wrote Borden, "to accept my apology for so stupidly forgetting my invitation to your dinner to-day, but tender it is all I can do now. Long ago I adopted in self-defence a policy of advising my wife of my engagements and relying on her less treacherous memory but in this case I omitted that precaution. The circumstances in this case are so exceptionally unfortunate that I am utterly disgusted with myself. May I ask you to give my sincere apology to Mrs. Borden."

Roger Graham, *Arthur Meighen: Door of Opportunity*, 1960

Meighen's Forgetfulness

Partly because of speaking engagements and partly because business sometimes took him out of the city, Meighen continued to spend considerable time away from home, though of course much less than he had as a politician. But for years he had been accustomed to travelling usually with a secretary, who saved him the bother of arranging things with railway companies and hotels and coping with all the trivial nuisances that travel entailed. Now when he went away he was on his own and one never knew just what would happen, whether he might absent-mindedly get on the wrong train or what personal belongings he would forget to bring home. He was known to arrive at the railway station with just enough time to buy a ticket and catch his train, only to discover that he had forgotten to bring any money with him and would have to ask the railway company to cash a cheque. As often as not he came home minus one or two articles of clothing which he had left behind somewhere: a scarf in the train on the way home from Buffalo, which the Pullman Company and New York Central, despite his insistent urgings, were unable to find; his hat and topcoat in the Royal Alexandra Hotel, Winnipeg, which were obligingly forwarded to Toronto. Once after returning from Ottawa on the night train he arrived at his office to find a telegram: "Good morning. Expressed your hat. Return other Charles Bath, 77 Cartier St."

Roger Graham, *Arthur Meighen: No Surrender*, 1965

Meighen on the Links

Mr. Meighen came up to the first tee without a golf bag but he had one club in his hand—a putter. And I saw the strangest sight, a man hitting from a tee with a putter. He used only the putter all through the course. I thought to myself, "His score will be about two hundred." But the amazing thing was what he did with it. He always drove dead down the middle of the fairway, about 130 yards indeed, but even that was incredible. When he came within range of the pin he became more deliberate and cautious; the crowd behind yelling "Fore!" didn't disturb him. He would take a parliamentary stance and by some kind of calculus known only to himself he would assess all the factors and then he would strike. The pin was up there like a political opponent which had to be out-manoeuvred, not so much reached as attacked.

E.J. Pratt, quoted in Roger Graham,
Arthur Meighen: No Surrender, 1965

Meighen and Cars

He had always regarded the automobile, despite its usefulness on occasion, as more or less an instrument of the devil. There was little or no mechanical aptitude in his makeup and some who observed him in action behind the wheel thought he never really had learned to drive. Deep in conversation with a companion or in concentration on some matter, he would forget in his absent-mindedness to watch the traffic and the traffic signs—with considerable hazard to himself and those who crossed his path. His crony Hugh Clark was with him one day when he went through three red lights in the course of a three-mile drive, the last of them at the corner of Yonge and Bloor streets, where a policeman flagged him down and gave him a stern lecture. This greatly amused Clark, who never before had known Meighen to get the worst of an argument. Policemen on point duty at intersections annoyed Meighen, who thought they were more of a hindrance to the flow of traffic than a help, especially if the cars going his way had to stop when he got to the corner. "Arthur," Clark said to him once after an eloquent discourse on this subject by Meighen, "you Irish aspire to make, administer and enforce laws but you hate like hell to obey them." Another day Clark was with him when they got into a traffic jam at Avenue Road and St. Clair. Impatiently Meighen kept ordering the driver of the stationary car in front to "Go on! Go on!" At last Clark could stand it no longer. "He's going as fast as you are," he remarked quietly. Meighen's family finally prevailed on him to admit that driving a car was not his forte and he gave it up. Although he sometimes regretted this, he preferred in any case to walk wherever he could and was content to take the streetcar if need be. Taxicabs and their drivers he abominated as lawless, arrogant anti-pedestrians, but if an automobile had to be used Mrs.

Meighen could drive him in their Ford or, failing that, someone would see that he had a ride.

Roger Graham, *Arthur Meighen: No Surrender*, 1965

Brother Can you Spare a Dime?

If for some reason he [Arthur Meighen] could not be driven home he would ride the streetcar, rushing, heedless of the traffic lights, across the road to catch it, competing with all the others homeward bound to squeeze in through the door, then fumbling in his pockets for a ticket or some money. Once he could find neither, not even ten cents for a cash fare. He explained his predicament to the operator, assured him the fare would be forwarded in the morning and took his number. Convinced, the motorman extracted a dime from his changer and gave it to Meighen to put in the fare box. First thing the next day Meighen instructed his secretary to send ten cents to the Toronto Transportation Commission, along with an explanation. In due course she received an acknowledgment.

Thank you for your letter of December 4th reimbursing operator #1473 for a fare loaned to the Rt. Hon. Arthur Meighen. The 10 cents has been forwarded to the operator who has asked that we express his thanks. I understand he intends to keep it as a souvenir of the statesman he was privileged to accommodate.

Roger Graham, *Arthur Meighen: No Surrender*, 1965

All Dressed Up

Meighen was to catch the midnight ferry for Victoria. He left the dinner party about eleven o'clock, went to his hotel, had his luggage sent to the boat and then sat down to write one or two letters. Engrossed in that work he forgot all about the passage of time until, too late, he suddenly recalled that he had booked passage to Victoria. He rushed frantically to the dock, found the ship had already sailed, so returned to the hotel, re-engaged his room and went to bed. In the morning he put on of necessity the tuxedo he had worn the night before, walked across the street to a lunch counter and sat down unconcernedly to have his breakfast. Hearing that he had been seen eating breakfast in his dinner clothes, Clark got in touch with him and urged him to buy a ready-made suit before boarding the next ferry. There was no need of that, Meighen insisted. He had plenty of clothes in his luggage at Victoria and would be there in a few hours; he would just wear what he had on. And that is what he did.

Roger Graham, *Arthur Meighen: And Fortune Fled*, 1963

The Piano

At the height of the campaign a minor episode occurred which brought some consternation to the Meighen household and caused the head of the family rather acute embarrassment. It seemed to suggest that while Meighen, unlike Mackenzie King, had only one message to preach about the tariff—the message that it should be high enough to encourage the sale of Canadian products in Canada—he did not exactly practise what he preached. In October Mrs. Meighen bought a baby grand-piano—made by an American firm. This news was divulged to its readers by the Canadian Music Trades Journals and before long Meighen's private secretary, George Buskard, received a polite remonstrance from the general manager of the Canadian Manufacturers' Association, J.E. Walsh, who explained that Canadian piano makers were feeling somewhat aggrieved that none of their instruments was deemed worthy of gracing the Prime Minister's living-room. Meighen was away from Ottawa at the time so Buskard mentioned the matter to Mrs. Meighen "but, of course," as he wrote Walsh, "did not care to enquire as to the reason for her purchasing other than a Canadian made instrument." The reason was perfectly simple: she had bought it because she liked it and had never thought of asking about its place of origin.

When Meighen got home a few days later he found on his desk a rather stiff protest from the president of the Sherlock-Manning Piano and Organ Company against the purchase of the American piano. Although he had some other rather pressing matters on his mind, and cared as little about pianos as he did about motion pictures, stylish dress or dogs, he recognized both the enormity and the implications of his wife's crime and so took the trouble to dictate an apologetic reply. A friend in Toronto, whence he had just returned, had brought the subject to his attention:

his intimation was the first I ever had that the piano Mrs. Meighen bought was not made in Canada. No doubt I should have looked after this but with the pressure under which I live I really gave no attention to it at all and took it for granted that, as she was buying it here, it was a Canadian instrument. Certainly it would never have been bought if I had given the matter sufficient attention to ascertain the facts.

Am sorry indeed for this circumstance. I may add that until I examined it after the inquiry I had never been near enough to see even the name of the piano.

Fortunately the case of Mrs. Meighen's piano did not become a major issue in the campaign, and the piano itself continued to occupy its place of honour in the Meighen home.

Roger Graham, *Arthur Meighen: And Fortune Fled*, 1963

Meighen in Debate

Meighen aroused sentiments of fear, and of respect for his ability, and at the same time a certain dislike—I might almost say hatred—of his ruthlessness in debate. When I reached Parliament I found there was no doubt whatever of his ability, that in debating he was far superior to any of his colleagues, and that he was cold, ruthless, and efficient in any discussions.

Admiration for his great skill as a parliamentarian grew upon me, with the perhaps unwilling acknowledgement that in dialectic skill he was the superior of any one in the House. Towards Laurier he was invariably courteous and respectful and, even in his replies to other members of the Liberal party, strongly worded as they sometimes were, he never dismissed the arguments that they used with the disdain he later used towards Mackenzie King. There was no great reason, therefore, why I should have acquired anything like an intense dislike of the man, and whatever feelings of fear I may have had of him as a parliamentarian were overcome by admiration for his method of carrying his arguments.

He was never a friendly sort of man, and it cannot be said that he cultivated the admiration or friendship of his opponents. He lacked the urbanity of Sir Thomas White. He stood for straight, unadulterated Toryism, and never flinched in his stand. He never asked, nor gave any quarter. The members of the Liberal Party, and the majority of the members elected in 1917, were comparatively young. They were extremely wary of tangling with him. Of all our men I think the most successful in verbal duels with him was probably Lucien Cannon, who afterwards became very friendly with Meighen. Frankly, I enjoyed Meighen's performance in much the same way that I enjoyed the physical performance of opposing hockey players. I opposed these hockey players to the best of my ability, but was always willing to admit that they were superior players. In the same way with Meighen, there was nothing I enjoyed more than the manner in which he skilfully knocked out his opponents in debate and tore their arguments to shreds.

His manner, generally speaking, was cold and hard—no display of sentiments, little endeavour to persuade. He could make the fullest and most effective use of irony. He rose to perhaps the greatest heights of his peculiar and particular type of eloquence in his later days, in his treatment of Mackenzie King's somewhat long-winded and often, I am obliged to say, puerile arguments. Meighen's answers were almost invariably couched in terms of almost frigid contempt.

Meighen never seemed to attempt either to charm or to persuade; his efforts were aimed at confirming in his own people the belief that the course of conduct he was advocating was the only one that was sound, reasonable, and just. He was the Tory advocate, and his job was to justify Tory policy to themselves, not to convert opponents. His speeches gave the impression of improvisations; and, since he was a master of English, it is quite conceivable that they were: that having thought out carefully what he proposed to say and the conclusions he wished to draw, he had no difficulty in formulating his sentences. The style of argument approached the classical and academic: the listener could discern, first the major and the minor premises, and finally the almost irrefutable conclusions, which, however unpalatable, were usually clear, concise, and easy for anyone to understand.

Meighen, who was rather slim, stood up straight, with hands on hips, fingers outspread, and very occasionally pointed at his opponents. To those opposed to him Meighen looked and sounded as if he did not give a hoot whether or not we believed him, were interested in his arguments, or were prepared to agree with him. This was probably indicative of his thinking, and in all possibility may have been one of the reasons for his lack of success in appealing to popular audiences. Probably he was so strong a partisan and so strongly convinced of the value of the Tory party which he supported and afterwards led to the country that he paid too little attention to the feelings, sentiments, and views of his opponents and of the more independent voters in the country. This attitude could, of course, bring its own punishment.

Memoirs of Chubby Power: A Party Politician, Norman Ward, ed., 1966

Quick on the Draw

The only time I ever saw him really taken aback was one night when a very witty Jewish Liberal, Sam Jacobs, made a strong protectionist speech, and when he sat down Meighen rose and invited the honourable gentleman to cross the floor and come to his spiritual home: Jacobs got up and said, "Mr. Speaker, one of my ancestors did that sort of thing two thousand years ago, and the world hasn't stopped talking about it yet." Meighen raised his hand in salute.

Once, in a full flow of eloquence in the House, Meighen mentioned a policy he was particularly in favour of. "That's in the platform of the Liberal party," a voice cried from across the floor.

"Mr. Speaker," Meighen shot back, "I am sorry to hear it. Had I a wish dearer to my heart than all others, the worst fate I could fear for it would be that some day it would get into a Liberal platform."

I remember one night when he was speaking the back-benchers on the Liberal side started to boo. Meighen stopped and said, "Mr. Speaker, to an intelligent interruption I have no objection whatever, but I do object, sir, to those ejaculations which ceased to be the language of men ten thousand years ago." You could have heard a pin drop.

Grattan O'Leary, *Recollections of People, Press, and Politics,*, 1977

Upper Berth

In order that I could carry out my constituency obligations, I made a regular weekend train journey between Ottawa and Windsor that formed a very tiring part of my life. I used to get on board in Ottawa at four o'clock on a Thursday or Friday afternoon and arrive in Toronto about ten. Then I would change trains, waiting an hour before setting off for

Windsor, where we pulled in at seven the following morning. Sometimes, after a busy week in the House, I left Ottawa later in the evening and went overnight to Toronto. For thirteen years, when parliament was sitting, I made this weekly rail trip almost without fail; it took a long time for MPs to be given air passes — that was like extracting a tooth from a reluctant gum. Even with a berth it was frequently not a pleasant trip: the train was cold and steamy in the winter and stifling in hot weather. The cars usually would be full of members of parliament returning home to constituencies along Lake Ontario, in Toronto or in southwestern Ontario. From time to time, I saw Arthur Meighen, then Conservative leader in the Senate, travelling in a sleeper. Although he was well off, the frugal Meighen always took an upper berth, clambering up into it with one of the railway's brass spittoons. When I asked a porter about this ritual, he replied, "If you were his age, you might need one too!"

Paul Martin, *A Very Public Life*, I, 1983

Prime Minister Meighen

He did not change with the change in his circumstances. He continued to live in the large but unpretentious house on Cooper Street, and to walk to and fro each day between the house and office with his characteristic quick step and slight list to port. He went on buying his clothes ready-made from the racks of Ottawa stores, having by now discarded his Portage tailor, and with some reluctance purchased second-hand from Sir Charles Fitzpatrick a Windsor uniform to wear on state occasions when there was no honourable escape. His children continued to attend the public schools aware of their father's intense anxiety that neither in school nor elsewhere should they receive preferential treatment because of his position; aware, too, that however preoccupied with public affairs he might be, however little time he might have to talk to them, his mind still had room for thoughts about them and their welfare. It was true that in his absent-minded way he forgot to list Lillian as one of his children in the Parliamentary Guide until 1921, when she was eleven years old, and in the same tardy revision he at last corrected Ted's name from Theodore Rosewell, as it had appeared ever since 1909. But these small sins of omission were typical of a man who would scoff at those who fussed about keeping their sometimes long and self-laudatory biographies in the Guide up to date. Lillian was very much a reality and Ted's second name was Roosevelt, but whether these facts were made known in the Guide did not matter much to Meighen. What did matter was the right mental and moral development of the children and Meighen took that seriously.

Roger Graham, *Arthur Meighen: Door of Opportunity*, 1960

A Difficult Audience

The real climax of Meighen's 1921 electioneering in Quebec came in her capital city. There, in his first political address in the ancient capital, he spoke to a throng of eight thousand which packed the armouries on the Grande Allée.

He started out bravely with a few carefully rehearsed words in French which were well received, expressing his appreciation of the warmth of his welcome to the city and his regret that he could not give his speech in the language they all understood. He then began to speak in English, affirming his desire for reconciliation and amity between the peoples of Canada and denying that he had ever said anything in the least defamatory or derogatory about his French-speaking fellow citizens. He had repeatedly challenged his opponents, who were spreading vile slanders about him through the country, to find in the record of his career any evidence of his alleged bias against Quebec. They had completely failed to do so for the good and simple reason that no such evidence existed. The record was there for all to see; he did not regret what he had said and done in the past but was prepared to be judged by it and judged severely. Here he paused for a moment and gazed defiantly out at the audience, his arms folded. There was a burst of applause and as it died away a voice from the galleries called out, "Ton chien est mort quand même."

"I beg your pardon," answered Meighen, turning to the gallery, "but I don't understand French very well. If anyone has an objection to make, a question to put, I would ask that it be put in English and I shall undertake to answer it."

From that moment on the speech became, not the one Meighen had intended to deliver, but rather like a dialogue between him and individuals in different parts of the hall. Questions and comments, upwards of fifty of them, came thick and fast: about the tariff and railways and the merchant marine; about agriculture, taxes and unemployment; about the adoption of the closure rule in the Commons; and about the Levis munitions, mention of which provoked gales of laughter. For the most part the interruptions were good-natured—legitimate questions reasonably posed—and to each Meighen gave his reply in simple, concise words, looking directly towards the questioner. The answers did not win unanimous approval, of course, and were not couched in language intended to please or mollify. Some of them provoked sarcastic jeers, cries of "Non, non!" (which brought counter-cries of "Chut! Chut!") and someone bleated loudly like a lamb. On the other hand his remarks elicited frequent applause; one friendly soul called out in broken English, "You're alright," and Meighen could sense that all these interruptions and his handling of them were earning him a measure of sympathetic respect which in the beginning he would not have thought attainable. At least he had shown them that he for one was not going to be intimidated and take to his heels in ignominious retreat.

The dialogue went on for about an hour. Finally when the applause greeting one of his answers had subsided Meighen took a step forward, stood with arms akimbo, looked somberly out over the audience and said provocatively, "Well, gentlemen, any more questions?" For several seconds there was a profound silence in the vast room while the crowd digested this challenge. And then a thunderous roar of applause, a resounding ovation that went on and on in spontaneous tribute to the courage of the slight, gaunt, harrowed-looking, solitary figure standing there in defiance of them all.

Roger Graham, *Arthur Meighen: And Fortune Fled*, 1963

Chubby Power

Charles Gavan Power (1888-1968) was a Liberal Member of the House of Commons between 1917 and 1955, when he was elevated to the Senate, where he served until his death. A minister in the King Cabinet, he resigned in 1944 over the conscription issue.

Mr. Power has an informal, almost deferential way of speaking, tossing his head from side to side like a man with a tight collar or a horse harassed by gad-flies. Yet as he discourses in this offhand way, he gives you the facts, and he always provides you with a couple of first-class oratorical flights. He talks to the Commons as if he were addressing a group of boys, and had just begun: "You see, fellows, it's this way..."

In dress he is casual, and there is usually some hair hovering over his brow because he doesn't bother to control it. His suits look as if he bought them out of a catalogue.

There are a couple of stories that are typical of him. One has to do with a Chicago musicians' union trying to put the Royal Canadian Air Force Band off the air, and an unctuous Canadian broadcasting system helping out the Windy City unionists. I queried him about this. "What are you going to do?" I asked.

"Do?" he re-echoed. "No goddam dago in Chicago is going to tell me when my band can play and when it can't!"

"May I quote you?"

"You can quote all you like."

The other story is more delicate, and perhaps apocryphal. It was during the last war, and he got leave from the trenches of France, and went to Ireland, to visit relatives.

When he arrived there, he found some of his folks were Sein Feiners, and were fighting the British. So he jumped into the fight with the Irish Republicans, and fought with them against his Flanders comrades-in-arms, the British!

Then when his leave was up, he left Erin, donned again his Canadian uniform with the British coat of arms on it, and started fighting the Germans again.

Mr. Power has never denied this story.

Austin Cross, People's Mouths, 1943

Assemblées Contradictoires

Chubby Power describes his role in the 1910 by-election in Arthabaska, which the Laurier government lost. Many claimed the contest was a damaging litmus test for the Laurier administration.

Public meetings were held in almost every town or village in the constituency. Nearly all were assemblées contradictoires or forums. The assemblée contradictoire was then a unique feature of the Quebec electoral scene. Each party nominated its spokesmen who addressed the audience alternately. Our principal platform opponents were Bourassa, Blondin, Lavergne, Sévigny, and Lamarche for the nationalists, and F.D. Monk as the nominal head of the Conservative Party in Quebec. There was much heckling, but I do not remember a speaker being denied a full hearing. Years later tactics of noisy obstruction became a feature of the assemblée contradictoire. Disorder grew to such proportions that the meetings degenerated into riots, and it became necessary to abandon the practice. This I shall always regret. Radio and television may bring a party message in perhaps better form, to more people. But the Quebec assemblée contradictoire not only provided an ideal training for parliamentary debaters, it also supplied a lively medium for the exchange of political views and for the clash of political philosophies. I am inclined to think that, as a result, more people retained a livelier interest in politics.

There was a great deal of fun and excitement at headquarters each evening as the various speakers came in from their allotted missions. The horses were slow, the hour was late, the weather was often foul, and statesman who drove in from outlying districts often arrived cold and wet, sometimes covered with mud, but always thirsty for news and spirituous sustenance. The tales they told of exploits and of the manner in which they had vanquished their opponents were usually monumentally exaggerated, while they provided a great deal of entertainment to those of us who had remained at headquarters. We checked the results of the meetings as well as we could from the purely partisan sources from which we received them.

Needless to say, the orator who returned from what he considered to be a successful evening meeting was always sure that his arguments had convinced the particular locality where he had spoken, and if you were to believe the reports received of an evening you would retire early in the morning with the assurance that all was well and that the election was won. As a rule the next day brought different news from the local organizers returning with their recurring demand for more and more funds and their reiteration of the fact that our party was slipping in that particular district. "Oh yes, the meeting was a good one and so-and-so spoke very well, but we found that in such and such a village the opposition held a committee meeting last night with some of our most prominent friends who would appear to be abandoning our side." This story, repeated time and time again, left us at headquarters in some uncertainty as to what would be the final result.

On November 2, the eve of the election, I was given what I considered to be my first important job. Looking back, I am aware of its comparative unimportance, but at the time I regarded it as an indication of the trust and confidence that the organizer reposed in me. I was to interview party stalwarts in a number of parishes scattered from one end of Drummond County to the other. To help me in my task, I was handed a number of envelopes, each containing from $200 to $400, and was told to distribute these envelopes to specified individuals. Very little discretion was attached to this job, but since it was my first experience in the distribution of campaign funds, I look back upon it as the starting-point of what was to be repeated many times over in the future, often in circumstances involving too much discretion for my liking.

I started out at five o'clock on a rainy afternoon and drove all night in a buggy over muddy roads, stopping here and there for a cup of coffee or a drink of whisky-blanc, and for short chats with the constituents. I was received with open arms, especially by the recipients of the funds. I could see that the election was not going well, for there was no wave of enthusiasm in the hearts of those supposed to be our most faithful and loyal supporters. The job was finished about nine-thirty in the morning. I arrived back at headquarters about four o'clock in the afternoon to wait for the returns. When the first reports came in we were just about holding our own with only a slight margin in Drummond, and so we pinned our hope on the strongly Liberal town of Arthabaska. But when reports showed that we had a majority of only twenty-five votes there and were losing all through Arthabaska County, we knew that we were beaten. The over-all nationalist majority was 207.

Memoirs of Chubby Power: A Party Politician, Norman Ward, ed., 1966

Farm Delegation

It was estimated that three thousand Ontario farmers organized by the United Farmers and two thousand Quebec farmers under the leadership of the Quebec Minister of Agriculture, J.R. Caron, converged on the capital. When a small delegation from the group was finally permitted to interview the ministers in one of the halls of the Museum, where the House had been sitting since the parliamentary fire of 1916, I was an interested spectator. I was leaning against the wall, well to the rear, when two of the most typical theatrical farmers—tall, weather-beaten, bearded, and dressed in ill-fitting Sunday best—approached me. "Young fellow, do you know your way round here?" "Sure," said I, "what can I do for you?" "Show us around and let us see where the members meet." I took them on, although there was nothing much to see. Most of the museum exhibits had been stored away, and in due course we finished up in the gallery where the Commons was in session. While we were there, Sir Wilfrid Laurier rose to say a few words on some routine matter. My friends were delighted to recognize him. "A great reformer," said one. "I am sorry I voted against him. It was the first time and I can tell you it will be the last." I conducted them back to the hall where the delegation was still holding forth. They thanked me, and one of them handed me twenty-five cents for my trouble, which I pocketed with every expression of gratitude. I had wanted to say a word to Mr. Caron, but, for fear that my late charges might think it strange for their guide to be on familiar terms with a person of such importance as a Minister of Agriculture, I faded away.

Memoirs of Chubby Power: A Party Politician, Norman Ward, ed., 1966

O'Leary vs Lemieux

Grattan O'Leary (1889-1976) was summoned to the Senate in 1962 after a lengthy journalistic career and a long record of service with the Conservative party.

The election of 1925 was my baptism in backyard politics, politics at the riding level; such a baptism that it dulled for many years to come the bright edge of any political aspirations I might have had.

I had allowed my name to stand for the riding of Gaspé and, for want of a better Conservative candidate, they had nominated me.

Of course, I hadn't a chance from the beginning. My opponent, the Honourable Rodolphe Lemieux, a tower of strength in the Liberal Party, Speaker of the House of Commons, ran his campaign with a federal ship, the Lady Grey, up and down the coast. I was naive enough to denounce this blatant exercise of patronage until a very wise old Conservative, William Flynn (an uncle of Senator Jacques Flynn), pointed out to me that I was helping Lemieux to get re-elected.

"You're making him out a hell of a big man in Ottawa," said Mr. Flynn. I saw the logic and desisted. Well, of course, we had to have the classical encounter dear to Quebec hearts, the "assemblée contradictoire," at which each candidate was allowed an hour to speak. It was an endurance contest, the place packed to the rafters, wreathed in smoke from hand-rolled "Alouette" cigarettes, a situation in which the man with the loudest voice had all the advantage.

I didn't have the loudest voice, but I could make myself heard, and I was confident I could hold my own. Lemieux began with diabolical cleverness by paying high tribute to my career as a Press Gallery man in Ottawa, a young man of promise and brilliance, a credit to Gaspé.

Torn between being puffed up at these amazing and apparently sincere compliments and a suspicion that I was being had, I listened while he went on to express his distress at "coming down here and finding my young friend O'Leary the candidate of the Protestants and Jews." A rumble went round the room at this shot and I denied hotly that I was anyone's candidate except the voters'. The damage was done. I could feel the hostility creeping round me. I got through my remarks in stony silence from the crowd.

"That was a terrible thing to say," I accused Lemieux afterward. "I thought you were a gentleman."

"Don't take it to heart, young man." He laid a friendly hand on my shoulder. "It doesn't matter what we say here. There are no reporters. Chalk it up to experience." Whereupon he invited me to join a dinner party on the government ship. Of course, I refused. I went back to my hotel in a mood of disillusionment. There was more to politics than simply putting up your case and your party's case in the most persuasive way possible. I was beginning to feel like a fly in a web.

Lemieux's brother, an equally able politician, was Minister of Education in Quebec, and before the election there was a long delay in paying teachers' salaries. A week or so before voting day he came down and sat on the platform while Rodolphe Lemieux explained to the hall full of voters that the Minister from Quebec was here tonight and he had brought with him, at the particular request of his brother the federal candidate, the salary cheques for the teachers of Gaspé—which he proceeded to distribute to as many teachers as happened to be present; which was usually quite a few, since everyone who was able to walk went to the political meetings. By the time the election came on the voters began to get the idea Lemieux was a cross between God and Moses. They didn't dare vote against him. Some people think the art of running elections came in with the P.R. boys and the advertising agencies. The organizers of fifty years ago could show them tricks they never heard of.

My last meeting was held in a town called Chandler. The Liberals had packed the hall with, of all things, old ladies, and when I came out on the platform they beat the floor with their canes and cried out in a kind of sing-song chant in French, "Conscription! Conscription! Conscription!" It was unsettling to say the least. The idea was, of course, that Meighen was going to take all their sons and put them in the army to fight Britain's wars. I am sure they firmly believed this. That didn't make it easier for me.

The only place where I won a majority was a town of two thousand called Grande Rivière. Most of Lemieux's relatives lived there. They must have known him pretty well. I was not too discouraged by defeat. As a matter of fact, I felt rather relieved as I returned to Ottawa and the relative sanity of the Parliamentary Press Gallery.

Grattan O'Leary, *Recollections of People, Press, and Politics*, 1977

Laurier House

Despite having been the country's longest-serving Prime Minister, William Lyon Mackenzie King was one of the oddest, least-liked and least-understood leaders Canada has ever known.

When Lady Laurier died in 1921 and left her home to King—not to the Liberal Party, but to King personally—his domestic equipment was complete and the heirship legitimized. The ugly but commodious old pile on Sandy Hill was run down, all its furniture had been given to other heirs, and it lacked modern conveniences. King had no money to refurbish it. Happily, his admirers were only too proud to pay the bill.

There was no secret about these gifts. To any visitor King would explain that when he had envied a neighboring farm at Kingsmere his good friend Peter Larkin had delivered him the title to it a few days later and then, with other rich men who loved Liberalism more than money, had rebuilt Laurier House, installed the elevator, constructed a strong room where secret papers could be locked up, and turned the attic into the cluttered eyrie where the Government of Canada was henceforth centered.

By the time King had restored his mansion with this friendly assistance, it was, to most men's taste, a horror, a Bleak House straight out of Dickens.

The drawing room crammed with gilt and crimson plush, with gigantic vases and glass-covered tables to hold worthless ornaments, in all an assemblage of expensive junk sufficient to stock a high-class second-hand store. No piece was ever moved an inch. Everything, threadbare and with upholstery protruding, remained unchanged to King's last hour. A reception room on the other side of the massive hall contained items of sculpture, bas-relief, and painting which King had collected in Europe, most of it hideous.

The dining room, darkly paneled, with dim oil portraits of Laurier, Gladstone, the Rebel, and King's other predecessors staring down from the walls, was a candlelit cavern where a guest was likely to feel spirits at his elbow.

A chamber of contemplation was provided on the second floor, also packed with collected knickknacks, through which a visitor threaded his way with care.

In his bedroom King slept in Laurier's antiquated brass bed. Beside it on the floor, a warm basket housed the beloved Irish terrier, Pat, and his successors. On the mountainous bureau lay a brush, a comb, a bottle of eau de cologne, and a marshaled row of pencil stubs which King always liked to fondle nervously in his fingers. The bureau drawers were heaped to the top with shirts, socks, underwear, and the familiar high stiff collars, each item in its proper compartment. In the clothes closet suit on suit, from Windsor uniform to country tweeds, hung perfectly pressed and hardly worn. Twenty pairs of shoes, from dancing pumps to brogues, were arrayed in meticulous rows on their stand.

In the upper hallway, where no one could overlook them, hung a flattering oil portrait of King in the gown and hood of a university graduate and beside it, the most precious relic, a framed proclamation of the Queen's governor, offering a reward of £1,000 for the capture of the Rebel. On the third floor, its door cunningly concealed in the oak panels, was the "dark room." Here King was amassing the leaves of his daily diary and scrapbooks a yard square of newspaper clippings, invitations cards, Christmas cards, dance programs, and every sort of empty souvenir which anyone else would burn. Nothing was forgotten, nothing lost. When King died he left several large packing cases full of Christmas cards in the basement where his secretaries had persuaded him to move them, to make more space in the "dark room."

Finally, on the third floor, reached by the new elevator, King had made his study the perfect image of himself. It was lined on all sides with books, many of them in leather-bound sets—good, heavy books and classics all, none of the detective stories on which the great are said to relax. Most of this library had been read and reread. It contained on the margin of every second page a fine, illegible scribble in King's handwriting. Even the Bible, in fourteen stout volumes was penciled with his comments to remind himself and others after him what the Word meant.

Though spacious, the study was almost completely filled with tables, desks, chairs, a gigantic leather chesterfield, and various odd-ments like a cougar skin with a stuffed and snarling head to trip the unwary feet.

Every table top carried a cargo of silver-framed and autographed photographs of famous personages and other trophies of the chase. As King did not smoke, a box of pipes surprised the visitor. They were his father's. Nearby stood the piano which his mother had bought from her earnings as a music teacher. Her portrait in oils rested on a special stand to the right of the fireplace. It showed an aged woman of rare beauty who gazed wistfully into her own fire at Woodside. A shaded light, never turned out, gave this picture the look of a shrine. King could worship it at ease from the chesterfield, in which the great decisions of the nation's life were often made.

Here as nowhere else was he at peace. Everything had been done to make that peace perfect. The secretaries, stowed away in the barren rooms to the rear, could be summoned at any moment to take dictation. The Housekeeper would bring in tea on a silver tray and set the crumpets by the fire. Nothing to assure the master's comfort was neglected.

About all these little attentions he showed a woman's proprietorship. As if it were his own invention he would point proudly to the special table which had belonged to Matthew Arnold and now stood beside his desk, free of papers, so that it could carry a biscuit and a glass of milk when he desired them.

Bruce Hutchison, *Incredible Canadian*, 1952

King at Work

He is reputed to have worked harder than anyone in Ottawa. In fact, he never strained himself. He had learned to work with the least possible strain by regular habits, a long night's sleep, a nap during the day (he could stretch out anywhere and be instantly asleep), and by sweating his assistants.

His hours of work were no longer than those of his colleagues but they were unorthodox and peculiarly hard on his secretaries. Rising late, reading his Bible, spending an hour on his diary or dallying over a book, he hardly got well under way before noon and was seldom in high gear until evening. As he rarely left his office until seven o'clock, his staff was always late for dinner and the elevator man in the East Block must remain on duty to carry him down one story.

After dinner the real work of the day began. Almost every evening secretaries and stenographers were summoned to Laurier House and infrequently left before midnight. Being a bachelor, King had no notion of other men's domestic arrangements, cared nothing for their inconvenience, worked them unconscionably, and was amazed when a daring secretary asked a night off to see a hockey game. There was no rest even on Saturday afternoons when all government offices were closed. If the Prime Minister dined out he might summon an assistant from his bed in the middle of the night.

One secretary who waited on duty at Laurier House for King's return after a banquet foolishly sent a girl stenographer home. King was furious at this presumption. As a penalty he kept the unfortunate man working until three in the morning.

Another time King tried to find a letter for himself in the filing room and, baffled by the files, strewed them about the floor. Such fits of temper were unusual with him. While he constantly felt aggrieved by the failure of his assistants, he usually punished them without words by a manner of patient rebuke, a sort of silent treatment impossible for most men to bear.

No wonder his secretaries seldom lasted long. One new secretary after another was hired, broken by the strain, and released. Most of them left with resentment against King the man, and admiration for King the statesman. Some, like McGregor, were quietly promoted into bigger jobs.

King was capable at once of sudden kindness and unbelievable meanness.

A chauffeur who awaited him in his outer office one evening was instantly dismissed because he smoked a cigarette. After curtly ordering the man out of the East Block, King sent a secretary to rehire him.

Another chauffeur who had just returned from the town to Kingsmere with a guest showed by his manner that the was suffering from some secret anxiety, observing which, King asked him what was wrong. On learning that the man's little boy had suffered a terrible injury in an accident, King sent the father to him, paid all the hospital expenses out of his own pocket, and went without a car for the weekend.

On the death of two unknown children in a tenement fire he walked in the funeral procession, hardly noticed by the crowd.

Bruce Hutchison, *Incredible Canadian*, 1952

The Black Box

Just before King started out on his tour he called in Ralph Campney, one of his secretaries, and showed him a big, black wooden box. "That contains all my speeches and speech material," King explained. "Look after it, and make sure you get it on the train."

Campney took charge of the box, arranged for it to be placed on the train and then busied himself with a multitude of other chores. He thought no more about it until late that night when the train was roaring through the hinterlands of Northern Ontario. When he checked up he found that the box was not on the train. For a few frantic moments Campney thought of pulling the communications cord, getting off the train, and disappearing into the night. King was asleep and he dared not disturb him. He spent a sleepless night wondering what he would say to King next morning. When finally King awoke about ten o'clock Campney went in to see him.

"Mr. King," he began, "you know that black box...?" "My box of speeches?" nodded King.

"Well, sir, I'm afraid we haven't got it!"

Suddenly King's face broke into a big, broad smile. "You know, Campney," he said, "I knew something like this would happen some day and so (he reached under his berth and began dragging something out) I took the precaution of having a duplicate box prepared. Here it is!"

To Campney's amazement and relief King produced a second "black box" containing copies of his campaign speeches.

H. Reginald Hardy, *Mackenzie King of Canada*, 1949

Exacting Taskmaster

King was a difficult man to work for. In theory his office was in the East Block on Parliament Hill, but he had two offices in the House of Commons—a large office he rarely used and a small office behind the Chamber where he withdrew when his presence in the House did not seem necessary. When the House was not in session or on days when there was no Cabinet meeting he worked at Laurier House or even at Kingsmere and members of his staff were expected to accommodate themselves to his convenience. Any attempt to impose some organization was also frustrated because King was seldom punctual and kept no regular office hours. Nor did he have much respect for office procedures; he was always impelled by a sense of urgency, whatever his concern of the moment, and expected everybody to be at his beck and call. The confusion extended even to the stenographers and clerks who had to work evenings and weekends if King needed them; the fact that they were often not classified as civil servants and had no job security gave them little choice. Until 1938 there was some justification for King's frequent complaints that his office was understaffed and badly organized but he himself was partly to blame.

H. Blair Neatby, *MacKenzie King: Prism of Unity*, 1976

Daily Routine

In Ottawa his working day followed a regular routine. He was relieved of housekeeping responsibilities by a large staff which included at this time a cook, a maid, a butler, and a valet. He was a difficult employer because he insisted on his own convenience and the private life of his servants was not allowed to interfere. He usually got up around nine o'clock, read a passage from the Bible and from Daily Strength for Daily Needs, a collection of reassuring quotations on the rewards for religious faith and moral behaviour. After breakfast he read his mail. By eleven o'clock he was ready to attend a Council meeting or to receive delegations. He usually had lunch alone at Laurier House and might have a short nap before he began his afternoon dictation. If there was no official dinner or social function he might dictate or read official correspondence in the evening and then go for a short walk or drop in on the Pattesons. He rarely went to bed before midnight and usually read after retiring; his preference was for books with a spiritual emphasis or for biographies of English statesmen. He met many people by appointment and he was convivial when necessary but he carefully avoided casual meetings which would encroach on his time.

The summer residence at Kingsmere was necessary for King because there he could avoid these encroachments more easily. His chauffeur would drive him in to Ottawa for Cabinet meetings, interviews, and social functions but he usually returned to Kingsmere as soon as he was free. His secretaries were driven out to take dictation and his colleagues and important visitors had to make the same trip if they wanted a private talk. During the session and in the fall when the weather was cold, he visited Kingsmere on weekends and sometimes even made a brief visit on a sunny day during the week. It was always a sad occasion when he made his last visit of the year. He was sometimes criticized for isolating himself in the country and sacrificing the advantages which more frequent contacts with colleagues and visitors to Ottawa would provide, but this was for King a deliberate choice. He was never relaxed in company in spite of his apparent ease because he was always self-conscious. Kingsmere was a refuge from the pressure of public life.

> H. Blair Neatby, *MacKenzie King: Lonely Heights*, 1963

Working for King

It is well known that Mackenzie King was a demanding master. By the time I joined his staff, his personal routine involved a late start in the morning and unpredictable hours at night. Meal times, unless he were lunching or dining out, were irregular and fitted surgically to his own occasions. Cabinet colleagues as well as officials had to accommodate their timetables to his necessities and his whims. For us in his own office, and for Skelton and a few senior officers of External Affairs, virtually no personal or family occasion was immune from King's interruption. He would usually be charming when he telephoned at some abnormal hour, but there could be no question that he was expecting immediate attention to whatever was then at the top of his mind. It might be a matter of national or international moment; it might be trifling. In either case the call was inexorable.

> Arnold Heeney, *Things That Are Caesar's*, 1972

King at 49

King attends the Imperial Conference of 1923.

King arrived in London on September 29, forty-nine years of age. He carried himself well, though perhaps with too little assurance and too much self-consciousness. His face was full and unlined, his eyes unusually level and direct, and both eyes and mouth appeared ready to break with little provocation into a broad friendly smile. His frequent horseback riding had not prevented his putting on weight, but the chief sign of age was an increasing baldness, which was ill concealed even at this early stage by long locks brushed over towards the right side. His clothes were conservative in cut and material, and showed a tendency to fussiness with white piqué along the top edge of his waistcoat and the corner of a handkerchief peeping from his breast pocket. A part of his week in London was devoted to the selection of a number of suits, a new silk hat, and several pairs of shoes, and, thus fortified, King was prepared to face whatever might lie ahead.

R. MacGregor Dawson, *Mackenzie King: A Political Biography*, 1958

King Whimsical

King could be whimsical when he felt so inclined. The sober intensity of the dedicated public servant was occasionally belied by a lighter touch in his private correspondence. He received an awkwardly printed letter addressed "Dear Government" from a little girl in South Africa who was worried about the "Red Skins" being locked up on reserves and not being allowed to shoot "Grizzly Bears".

Ottawa, March 28th, 1925

Dear Elizabeth:

I cannot begin to tell you how very pleased the members of the Government of Canada were when they received your letter. Some of the letters they receive are so very hard to read—not beautifully written as yours was—and sometimes people ask for the most extraordinary things! You would hardly believe me, I am sure, were I to tell you all the things the people in Canada ask for! The only difficulty about your letter was that each Minister thought he should answer it. However, I was very firm and told them I was the one to do it. I then spoke, at once, to the Minister of the Interior, who looks after Indians, and he tells me, Elizabeth, that there is nothing you need worry about. It's like this. Supposing the Indians had all gone a-hunting, some one might come and settle on their lands or steal their tents—all kinds of dreadful things—while they were away. So the Government just puts up big signs "This land is reserved for our Indians," —and no one dares to touch anything. But the Indians are never shut up, Elizabeth, and if any Grizzly Bears come, they can always shoot them if they feel like doing so. You say you are coming to Canada when you are fifteen. That is splendid. The Minister of the Interior says that if he is still Minister of the Interior (you never can be quite sure), he will see that we have a good supply of Indians on hand.

The Minister of Defence says that if he is still Minister of Defence, he will give them plenty of ammunition with which to shoot the bears. And I feel sure that some one else—probably the Minister of Agriculture—will arrange for the grizzly bears—so that's all right, Elizabeth.

But there is something I want you to tell me—about South Africa. This Government has never been there but perhaps some day they might feel like going. Now is it true, Elizabeth, that when you have your tea in the garden, lions sometimes come and sit down beside you?

And when you go for a walk, do you have to be careful, for fear a rhinoceros or a hippopotamus might want to walk with you?

It would be apt to make the Government very nervous. There is so much you must tell me when you come. Of course, I know you always ride on elephants.

But I shall have to say good-bye now. It was very nice of you to write (we all thought the letter paper beautiful!) Will you let me thank you again for the Government and with all good wishes, say at present Good-bye Elizabeth.

Yours sincerely,

W.L. Mackenzie King

> H. Blair Neatby, *MacKenzie King: Lonely Heights*, 1963

King's Belief in His Own Virtue

King's belief in his selfless devotion to his party and his country is an example of his fundamental naivety. He was not a hypocrite because he deceived himself. This self-deception was not the result of complacence; few men have made more prolonged efforts to understand themselves. His diary was in part his conscience. In it he constantly criticized himself for wasting time with social frivolities, deplored his weakness in taking a glass of whisky, or regretted that a speech had been too hastily prepared. These criticisms were always coupled with resolutions to exert more will-power in the future and to devote himself more unsparingly to his work. But he saw in himself only minor shortcomings. He never doubted his innate goodness. Even in his diary he never questioned his motives. Why had he consented to a dubious political compromise or disappointed a colleague? Instead of facing such questions,

Mackenzie King produced detailed and sometimes tortured justifications of his behaviour—always he was working for the good of the party or the country or of humanity. He must have had occasional misgivings, for he sometimes protested too much, but he always seemed to have convinced himself. His introspection was an exegesis of his faith in his own goodness rather than a harrowing soul-searching. "Above all else I want to be a good man," he had written in his diary after the election of 1925. "The rest can go as it may I shall be happy. May God strengthen and guide me and enable me to fulfil his purposes in my life."

H. Blair Neatby, *MacKenzie King: Lonely Heights*, 1963

King at 52

Mackenzie King's face was full but still firm and unlined. The most visible sign of age was the bald spot on his head, now so large that he was left with a fringe of hair around his head, greying at the temples, and a forelock which concealed his baldness from the front. This forelock was fine and wispy and was always ruffled or falling down over his forehead. Already it was the delight of cartoonists. King was also inclined to put on weight and was close to two hundred pounds on his return from England, although fifteen pounds were soon removed by exercise and restraint at mealtime. He regretted his unimpressive appearance. "I do not like my appearance anywhere—a little fat round man, no expression of a lofty character, a few glimpses here & there of the happier self" was his reaction to some newsreels made at this time.

H. Blair Neatby, *MacKenzie King: Lonely Heights*, 1963

Loaves and Fishes

King depended on his friend Mrs. Joan Patteson for a great deal of his entertaining.

As Canadian president of the Zionist organization, A.J. Freiman invited Sir Ronald and Lady Storrs out especially to meet the Prime Minister. Sir Ronald had served as military governor of Palestine during the British occupation after World War I.

With memories of the Chanak crisis, and the subsequent revolution in Turkey along modern lines, Sir Ronald's experience keenly interested

Mr. King. He invited the Storrs to lunch with him in Ottawa next day, but they were leaving for Toronto that night. As a last resort, he invited them to come over, after tea at the Freimans', to dine with him at King-smere. They were pleased to accept.

Now Canada's bachelor prime minister began to wonder what there would be in the Cottage larder for dinner. He had no cook: only one man-servant to prepare and serve a simple meal. He took hasty leave of the tea party, to make domestic arrangements for dinner. Sir Ronald and Lady Storrs would drive over later, in the Freiman car.

At the Cottage, Mr. King found that the fare available for dinner consisted of cold boiled potatoes, suitable for frying cottage-style, corn on the cob and apple pie. They had no meat, but a bit of cold roast... and no butcher's shop nearer than Ottawa.

Came a sudden inspiration. A field away, the Patteson neighbors were comfortable living country dwellers: almost formal in the serving of sumptuous meals. Neighbor King hastened across the field.

The Patteson kitchen door stood open, giving off a gratifying smell of roast beef. Mrs. Patteson >had just put the roast on a serving platter. Much to her surprise, Neighbor Rex—as she called him—suddenly entered, picked up the platter and, with no time to explain, invited Mr. and Mrs. Patteson to come over to have dinner with him—and Sir Ronald and Lady Storrs.

They followed in procession across the field, with Yorkshire pudding, gravy, vegetables and whatever else they could load on trays.

When the distinguished guests arrived from Freiman's, a savory repast awaited them. They congratulated Mr. King on being able to serve such a fine meal in the woodland remoteness.

Charles Bowman, *Ottawa Editor*, 1966

King on a Hot Day in 1928

The first time I saw Mackenzie King in person was when I was about ten years old and at a summer resort on Murray Bay where, on a hot August day, without a breeze to stir the humid air, my Quebec sisters and I had been invited to a tea party given in honour of the distinguished Ottawa visitor. The men were wearing tropical suits, and the ladies their lightest gowns. We were all gathered in a lovely garden, sweating profusely under the boiling sun. At 5:30 p.m., the guest of honour appeared and shook hands all around. He was dressed in a heavy Irish tweed jacket, gold knicker pants, and had on knee-length woollen stockings and a pair of heavy brogue shoes. A high celluloid collar encircled his puffy neck, and no one failed to notice the widest possible tie knotted in a lump fashion and held together by a discreet diamond pin. The chubby pale features wore a fairly friendly smile, and the same greeting was handed to each guest. We were all told that he had been walking vigorously for one hour, and yet after all this exercise there was not even a bead of perspiration on his forehead. After sipping his tea and munching on a few crumpets, the leading statesman of Canada asked to meet the children. We were duly called, and then after a gentle pat on our respective cheeks or heads, the Prime Minister pulled out a few melted chocolate bars from a tweedy pocket, broke each in half, and distributed the pieces evenly to the members of the group. This munificence was accompanied by a paternal suggestion to be good to our parents. We agreed but we were not impressed, and only a few gains were scored among those present for the Liberal cause.

Pierre Sévigny, *This Game of Politics*, 1965

King and Meighen

In the real world King's methods by now were well known to Parliament and public—the gentle and cumbersome reply, the long and heavy-laden speech, the rambling sentence, the politeness to his enemies. Parliament and public also had found, to their surprise, that the man of peace could fight.

Year in and year out he maintained his running feud with Meighen across the floor of the House. The Opposition leader, hardly hiding his contempt under the amenities of debate, continually flung questions at the Prime Minister, interrupted his speeches, leaped up to argue every detail. Usually King, well briefed by his secretaries, had a reply to the most obscure question, a statistic or quotation to match Meighen's. When Meighen caught him out in some factual error, his method was to assert blandly that "the facts are as I have stated them," or "I hold, Mr. Speaker, to my statement," or "the record will bear me out," and then to hurry on to something else.

King suffered under Meighen's pinpricks as he never suffered from any other opponent. As soon as Meighen stood up to speak, one could note from the gallery the Prime Minister's sudden congelation. His pencil stub began to tap on the desk. A line of scarlet rose slowly up the back of his neck until it had flooded his bald scalp. As Meighen, erect, gestureless, and glacial, poured on his vituperation, King oozed pure hatred. The friends of student days had learned to loathe one another.

Bruce Hutchison, *Incredible Canadian*, 1952

King vs Hanson

When his back was to the wall he could fight like a tiger and like a tiger he was dangerous when cornered.

One recalled the occasion, during the war, when the late R.B. Hanson, the House Leader for the Progressive Conservatives, had been attacking King all one evening. Patiently and without outward sign of embarrassment or concern King had sat there in his seat calmly listening to Mr. Hanson's seemingly endless diatribe. At last, however, King began to tap his desk nervously with his pencil, the blood rose to his face, at first faintly then suffusing it completely. Suddenly his eyes grew cold and hard and a moment later he was on his feet shaking a threatening finger at Mr. Hanson.

"I warn you..." the Prime Minister shouted angrily. "I warn you!"

The warning was sufficient. Mr. Hanson's attack quickly ebbed and died. To save face he continued on for a few minutes but he chose his words more carefully. It was easier to change tack and run before the impending storm than attempt to face into it.

H. Reginald Hardy, *Mackenzie King of Canada*, 1949

Ideal Companion

For Mackenzie King, his Irish terrier was the ideal companion. Dogs express affection without making many emotional demands in return. Pat slept in a basket in King's bedroom, had breakfast at the same time as his master, greeted him at the door when he returned from Parliament Hill, and always listened alertly when King talked to him. After one guest had left Laurier House, King recorded the "real sense of rest & freedom in being again alone with Pat at breakfast and no need to be thinking of engagements of others etc." Mackenzie King could be charming and gay and also thoughtful and sympathetic but his life centred on his own career. He quickly resented even the pleasantest distractions if they interfered with his work.

H. Blair Neatby, MacKenzie King: Lonely Heights, 1963

King and Pat

Despite the difference in our ages, Mr. King thought of Pierre and myself as friends and we were often invited to Laurier House. One evening, after dinner, when we were drinking our coffee in the library, where there was a portrait of his mother, always with fresh flowers beside it, Mr. King walked over to the piano, announcing to the guest of honour, a titled Englishman, "My dog is going to sing." Somewhat startled, I wondered what was about to happen. The other guests, who included Mr. and Mrs. Lapointe, Mr. and Mrs. Gustave Lanctot and Mr. and Mrs. Maxime Raymond, were also bewildered. Our host then sat the dog on the pianostool with its paws on the keyboard and, standing behind it, began to sing while the dog howled in unison. On our way home, Pierre said to Mr. Lapointe, "That was frightful! You who are so close to Mr. King, couldn't you have a word with him? What will our foreign guests think?" To this, Mr. Lapointe replied wryly, "I think we'd better speak to the dog." Despite the strangeness of the scene we had just witnessed, I confess that I was glad the Prime Minister had at least this faithful companion beside him.

Thérèse Casgrain, A Woman in a Man's World, 1972

Pat

On one occasion during the war he invited a small group to the Kingsmere farmhouse to celebrate a victory, and one of them was his neighbour, Duncan Campbell Scott, the unofficial poet laureate of the time, who said he would write a poem to mark the occasion.

When the party assembled, King announced that his beloved dog Pat had learned a new trick, and he called the animal into the parlour to demonstrate.

"Pat!" he commanded. "Lie down and roll over."

The dog sat motionless.

"Pat!" he commanded. "Do your new trick. Lie down and roll over!"

No response.

The command was repeated again to no avail. King sighed, patted Pat on the head, and said: "Pat will do the trick later. Very well, Scott, let's have the poem!"

Charles Lynch, *You Can't Print That*, 1983

(Auto) Biography

King had already spent most of his weekends during the session arranging for the publication of his own biography. A decade before John Lewis had produced a campaign biography and King had initially suggested to Norman Rogers that Rogers might add a few chapters to bring it up to date. Rogers must sometimes have regretted undertaking the task because King insisted on supervising every detail. Not surprisingly, King had found the first draft "inadequate and disappointing"; somehow King's dedication to humanity and his great achievements were not adequately presented. He found it necessary to redraft many sections in order to bring out the full story of his family heritage and his "life's work in politic & reform." King was a little more satisfied with the revised version; it gave the proper emphasis to his moral courage, his sincerity, his vision, and his ideal of public service. The biography appeared in the summer of 1935 with Norman Rogers listed as the author; King's contribution to the volume was not mentioned.

H. Blair Neatby, *MacKenzie King: Prism of Unity*, 1976

King and Bennett

King usually managed to conceal his feelings — he believed that politicians should behave with dignity and propriety — but he could not always resist the temptation to remind Bennett that he had been defeated. During the 1938 session, with the Conservative leadership convention scheduled for July, King found the temptation almost irresistible. When Bennett's retirement was announced in March King paid a tribute to his devotion to public affairs and expressed sympathy for his poor health because, as he commented in his diary, "it was the right thing to do." When Bennett's sister, Mildred Herridge, died in May, King provided the government railway car to bring the body to Ottawa and went to the station to see Bennett off. Again it was the right thing to do but the gesture also gave King the satisfaction of feeling that it must have been galling for Bennett to have to endure such kindness from a man who had so decisively defeated him.

By the end of the session, however, some cracks appeared in his veneer of propriety. Bennett was partly to blame. He was a proud man who knew he had worked unremittingly for five years, and who believed that he had sacrificed his health to save his country, only to find that his efforts were unappreciated and unrewarded. It was all the more galling to have lost to King, with his unctuous manner and his unprincipled lust for power. The death of his sister had also been a deep personal tragedy for Bennett because Mildred had been his confidante and his hostess at social functions until her marriage to W.D. Herridge, and her death intensified his loneliness. It was not surprising, therefore, that he became more than usually partisan late in the session. On one occasion in June when Liberal backbenchers were heckling him Bennett reacted by criticizing Mackenzie King for his absence from the House. A few days later he accused Norman Rogers of personal patronage in his administration of relief and when a Liberal retaliated by producing correspondence which linked federal expenditures on roads with the Conservative election campaign in 1935, Bennett lashed out at King, the man who pretended to be so honourable but who encouraged his followers to be so despicable.

Mackenzie King was outraged. In the House he launched into a bitter diatribe against a man who in two elections had tried to win political power by demagoguery. "In all Canadian history there has never been an exposure of corruption and corrupt political methods so disgraceful." When Bennett interrupted with "Beauharnois! Beauharnois," King reminded him that for all his talk of Beauharnois in the last election Bennett had come back "with his party emasculated, well-nigh annihilated" and that his record would "follow him to the end of his days." It was a petty and untypical outburst but King had no regrets. Bennett would go out of politics "discredited as he deserves to go."

H. Blair Neatby, *MacKenzie King: Prism of Unity*, 1976

The Missing Page

In March 1939, King made a statement in the House concerning what Canada's attitude would be if Britain were attacked.

In the usual cumbersome, infuriatingly detailed, and exhausting way and in the atmosphere of tension and short temper in which all of King's major speeches were produced, the final text of an intended statement in Parliament was being hammered out in his East block office as the House of Commons was about to assemble. The last typing and checking was still in progress as the carillon struck three o'clock and the Speaker's procession began to move towards the chamber. The Prime Minister got to his feet, was helped into his overcoat, and the papers were thrust into his hand as he descended to his car and was whisked over to the Centre Block. Hurriedly he took his place in a chamber which was crowded and expectant. He was recognized immediately and began to speak. Well into his text he seemed suddenly to have lost his place. He stopped and fumbled amongst the papers in his hand and on the desk before him; then, with a perfunctory bob in the direction of the Speaker, he bustled out of the astonished chamber. Out to the Speaker's entrance and back to the East Block he hurried to locate a page he had discovered to be missing from his typescript. In the scurry of final preparation it had somehow been detached. King recognized at once that its omission would distort the careful balance of his statement and give an opening to those who suspected him of disloyalty towards Britain and the Commonwealth. After some minutes of embarrassed pause, the Prime Minister returned to his place and started again.

Arnold Heeney, *Things That Are Caesar's*, 1972

Telegraphic Verbosity

During the later part of the second World War, Lester Pearson was stationed at the High Commission in London.

On one occasion Pearson reported long telegrams from King about the appointment of the Earl of Athlone as successor to Lord Tweedsmuir and simultaneously a phone call from Tommy Lascelles at Buckingham

Palace, asking whether something could be done about King's tele-graphic verbosity. "He complained that they had received the other day an 11 page telegram from him [the Prime Minister] in secret cypher, which meant that it had to be decoded at night, that the use of the cypher in such a long telegram was prejudiced, and that it took hours of work on the part of their staff. He said there was nothing in the telegram that couldn't have been sent in one page of ordinary code. We have had the same trouble here, namely Ottawa's using of the cypher in unimportant messages. It is a very ticklish thing to bring to the attention of the Prime Minister, however, who may be naturally inclined to think that anything he sends from Ottawa is of enough significance that it should go in secret cypher. I tried to draft a tactful telegram gently suggesting that for long messages of this kind the ordinary code was adequate."

London was hit by an intensifying series of German air raids. One night Pearson, as duty officer, got a call from the code clerk at his flat in Roehampton.

"Well, Mr. Pearson, I've got one of the 'most immediates' in," he reported, "and this is going to make you smile. I hope you don't have to come down four miles through the air raid to deal with it."

"If it's a war secret, I'd better come down," Pearson said, "but if it isn't, perhaps you could read it to me, even if it's against the rules."

"Oh, I can read it to you," said the clerk.

It was from Mr. Mackenzie King. He had heard that in the previous night's raid Westminster Hall, part of the House of Commons, had been damaged by Nazi bombs. One of Mr. King's hobbies was to collect old ruins for his Kingsmere estate, and he wanted someone from Canada House to see if he could get a few stones from the historic building in which the British Parliament had developed.

Dutifully, Pearson visited the works office next day and arranged to have two stones from the rubble retrieved, crated, and shipped to Ottawa, although officials at the office received the request with something less than enthusiasm. "I can't blame them," Pearson remarked. "They're not worrying about the exportation of ruins, they're worrying about the creation of ruins." It was characteristic of King that he could intrude trivial, personal requests at time of national crisis.

John Robinson Beal, *Pearson Phenomenon*, 1964

The Ruins

Relieved of the burdens of office in the early 1930s, King found a hobby to fill his time.

It began one day in May when King, returning from a visit to Kingsmere, saw an old Ottawa house being demolished. He decided on impulse that the bay window would make a marvelous ruin for his estate. Once it had been dismantled, transported, and re-erected at Kingsmere, King was so taken by its beauty that he decided it should be integrated into a building—"something in the nature of a chapel or a library"—a building worthy of the site, an edifice that would somehow combine the beauty of the Parthenon and of Westminster Abbey! The cost, at a time when the Farm House renovations were underway, was of some concern, but the political risk weighed even more heavily. The abbey, he decided, would have to wait. "Meanwhile," he convinced himself, "no one is likely to be critical of a ruin as an extravagance — and the public mind can be prepared for its completion later on."

The ruins were never completed. There were some subsequent additions — including a fragment of the British House of Commons after it was damaged by a war-time bomb — and doorways and arches from other buildings were salvaged and erected around Moorside, but King's enthusiasm for construction at Kingsmere was a passing phase. Once back in office he had neither the time nor the need to indulge in such fancies. He soon forgot his bizarre plans and developed a great pride in his unfinished ruins.

But why did Mackenzie King think that a bay window on a Kingsmere hill-top would be a thing of beauty in the first place? King was not a man of cultivated tastes, and he preferred the old-fashioned and the familiar. He was shocked by modern styles in clothes and in art. Modern bathing suits, for example, seemed quite indecent; surely "a woman of refined feelings would find it impossible to exhibit her naked self to all sorts of men." He reacted in much the same way to the "frightful" paintings of the Group of Seven; his preference was the Venice of Canaletto or the romantic landscapes of Homer Watson. The scenery to which King responded was not the imposing Rockies or the untouched wilderness but the quiet country side, with stone fences and hedgerows with paths where a man could walk and quote Wordsworth and feel he was communing with nature. He was a Victorian romantic, unsophisticated but sure of what he liked. Gothic ruins might be out of place in the Gatineau but for King they fitted into a countryside — an English countryside — which he equated with beauty.

H. Blair Neatby, *MacKenzie King: Prism of Unity*, 1976

King and Tallulah Bankhead

I will never forget one occasion during the war when he asked me to accompany him to the theatre, where Tallulah Bankhead was starring in Noel Coward's *Private Lives*. During a posting at the US embassy in Ottawa, the actress's uncle, Colonel Bankhead, had become friendly with the prime minister and had invited him to opening night. Knowing that I too was attending as a friend of the colonel's, King offered to take me along. Sitting in his car on the way, King confided, "I couldn't offend Colonel Bankhead by refusing, but I don't think much of that woman." During the performance, things went from bad to worse as Coward's risqué dialogue set the prime minister to squirming. "Martin," he whispered, "this is so humiliating for people to see me here listening to that terrible woman in this off-colour play."

After the final curtain, King said that he would drop me off and not attend the reception at the colonel's apartment. But, as his car pulled up, he reconsidered and decided to make his apologies personally. When we stepped out of the elevator, the party had spilled over into the hallway; before King could duck, Tallulah, in a slinky dress, was standing right in front of him with a glass of champagne. Handing King the glass, she purred in her husky, almost narcotic, voice, "My favourite prime minister." Then as I watched, thunderstruck, she leaned over, knocking off King's hat in the process, and gave him a big smack on the cheek.

By now the prime minister was enthralled. A changed man drank his glass of champagne, and stayed late at the reception, chatting with the woman who was now his favourite actress — all the while sporting a ruby-red lipstick mark.

Paul Martin, *A Very Public Life*, II, 1985

King and Cabinet

Intellectually and physically King always dominated his cabinet. When he entered the council chamber small-talk ceased on the instant and members of the cabinet automatically straightened up in their chairs. King seemed to possess the initial advantage of expecting and receiving respect. He seldom joked with his ministers and when, occasionally, he did attempt a sally his colleagues had to think twice before deciding whether or not King was, indeed, trying to be funny.

Because King disliked tobacco smoke, ministers made a habit of knocking out their pipes and snuffing out their cigars and cigarettes when he entered the room.

But once settled in his chair King relaxed, addressed his ministers as "Humphrey", "Clarence", or "Chubby," and listened attentively while each said his piece.

"I never saw a man with such an even temper," one of his cabinet colleagues remarked towards the end of the war. "He is as bright mentally as when he was forty. He is the most considerate man I ever met. He respects the opinions of his ministers at all times, and I have yet to see him lose his temper."

But opinions varied.

"King may have had dinner with you at your home the night before," said another minister, "but when he meets you in council the next day it is as Prime Minister and not as a personal friend. You can expect no favours, you can make no mistakes. King can accept your hospitality one day and be perfectly ruthless with you the next."

"Don't let anyone tell you that King can't be tough," said one man who had been in the cabinet for many years.

"He knows how to wield the big stick when necessity arises."

King could always out-sit his colleagues. It was said that he sometimes adopted a deliberate policy of prolonging cabinet meetings until every one of his opponents was worn down to the point of exhaustion and ready to throw in the sponge. It is true that he would sometimes spend hours discussing relatively unimportant matters, leaving major problems to the end of the meeting. Finally, when the members of the cabinet were weary and spent, and weak from hunger, King would place the contentious question before them. Virtually starved into submission and acquiescence the dissenting ministers would give way and King would make his point.

H. Reginald Hardy, *Mackenzie King of Canada*, 1949

King Ruthless

By 1944 high casualties in the war and the lack of volunteers for overseas service led to prolonged and heated discussions in Cabinet over the need for conscription. King needed all of his Machiavellian talents to save Cabinet solidarity. James Layton Ralston (1881-1948) had been Mackenzie King's Minister of National Defence up to this point in the war.

Crerar had encountered Howe by accident in the Club and a few random words passed between them. Howe—that paradoxical man who could always decide any practical question on the instant but had wavered for weeks over a political decision in his view utterly impractical—had grasped the meaning of The Crisis at last. He said he intended to vote for conscription. If any further weight were needed, Howe's adherence to the conscriptionist wing of the Cabinet tipped the balance. King could not face the kind of mass resignation now impending.

As he was eating his lunch, Crerar was called to the telephone. The voice on the wire was King's, with an unusual note of strain in it. The Prime Minister said he had devised a solution of The Crisis. He would bring his plan to Cabinet that afternoon and he hoped that Crerar could support it. Crerar knew better than to ask a further explanation. He said he would consider King's recommendation on its merits. Meanwhile, he agreed to say nothing to anyone.

As Crerar returned to the dining room, he asked himself what King had in mind. The latest turn of events was the last thing he could have guessed. He knew, however, that King was working through him, the most determined ally of Ralston, to undermine the conscriptionist revolt. He would wait and see. The son of the prairie soil, who had nothing further to lose or gain in politics, would not be easily shaken. Or so he thought then.

Claxton was lunching with some trusted newspapermen in a Chateau bedroom. At King's request he was still busily contriving those endless compromises and diversions that would keep the Cabinet arguing, might somehow conciliate it, and at last would postpone a decision.

In the middle of the meal the telephone rang. Claxton answered it and went suddenly white. In that small room his companions could not fail to hear and recognize the voice of King. His words were few and rapid. A new complication had arisen, a new remedy had been devised, and Claxton need not continue his effort at conciliation.

With a puzzled look, Claxton hung up the receiver. What had happened? Like Crerar, he could not imagine. He was young then in politics and had been in the Cabinet only a fortnight but was destined for rapid advancement. He was a soldier like Ralston and, like Power, was a born politician, able to reckon The Crisis in terms of political adjustment. He trusted King as the only man who could adjust it.

With a few such preliminary warnings by telephone, when it was too late for the news to spread, King was preparing his intimates for the shock of the afternoon. It was essential to his strategy that Ralston should have no warning. He had none.

In midafternoon the Cabinet met as usual. On King's placid face at the head of the table no inkling of the previous night's bargain could be read. To all appearances this was to be another day of fruitless bickering. This dingy room, fronting on the river, had witnessed remarkable events, noble, tragic, and comic. It had heard many Canadian voices, from Macdonald's onward. But it had contained no personage remotely like King. It was about to witness an event unparalleled in daring, unspeakable in brutality, incredible in consequence, of which only King and McNaughton knew the secret. A few others had been told that something was under way, no more. The plan behind the placid face could have been conceived by no one except King and, if known, could hardly have been believed.

When Ralston began to speak in his quiet tone, King listened with every appearance of interest and respect. The hand which held the invisible razor already was twitching.

The time had come, said Ralston, for the Cabinet to accept or reject his recommendation. These were chilling words. They were followed immediately by a last offer of compromise. Ralston would agree to a final attempt at voluntary recruitment.

King listened with respect, knowing all the words to be irrelevant. He was acting the transcendent role of a long theatrical career.

After an hour of this play acting, King looked around the table and judged that his moment had come.

Still in the matter-of-fact tone of a man who discussed a purely routine affair, he remarked that some two years before Colonel Ralston had submitted his resignation. At this the dullest mind in the room could guess that a blow of some sort was to fall. The conscriptionists exchanged quick glances. Ralston sat motionless in his chair, regarding King with a steady eye. His expression did not change.

In the sudden silence following his first observation, King added that in view of Ralston's present attitude there appeared to be no change of agreement in the Cabinet. For this reason he had decided to accept the resignation submitted by Ralston in 1942. Ralston's place would be taken by General McNaughton, who was confident of securing voluntary reinforcements.

That was all. Ralston calmly thanked King and the Cabinet for their co-operation, picked up his papers, and walked around the table, shaking the hand of each man as he passed. When he reached King no word passed between them. The two shook hands and Ralston strode briskly from the room.

As the door closed, King, a little flustered at last, remarked that he deeply regretted this unfortunate occasion.

Bruce Hutchison, Incredible Canadian, 1952

Why King was Dull

During the 1945 Federal-Provincial Conference in Ottawa, the conference at which Mackenzie King announced that an atomic bomb had been dropped on Japan, Mr. King put on a dinner just for the premiers and the governor-general, who at that time was Lord Athlone. It was a very delightful evening. After we had finished dinner, everybody milled around chatting, and those who wanted to had a drink. Mr. King sat on the chesterfield holding court. He motioned for me to come over and sit beside him, and we chatted about a variety of things. That evening he made a very witty little speech to the premiers, completely off the cuff, and I told him, "I'm sure that ninety-nine percent of the people of Canada have no idea you have the capacity for suave and urbane witticisms as you demonstrated tonight." I've never forgotten what he said: "You know, Douglas, I made the great mistake when I started in public life of writing all my speeches. I have a terrible horror of being misquoted or saying something on impulse that could be held against me."

You and I know that he wrote his speeches with a back door in every sentence, so that he could back out of anything. Every sentence was qualified by another sentence, which gave him a perfect escape. But he said, "Most of my speeches have been formal; once started on a speech I have to go through to the end, even though I may recognize that the audience is not responsive, and that I'm not following a line which is interesting. This has really spoiled a lot of my public speaking. Don't ever get yourself tied down to it. It's such a crutch now that I really couldn't do in front of a large crowd what I did tonight in front of a small informal gathering." That was a good lesson, I thought.

T.C. Douglas, quoted in
Making of a Socialist, Lewis H. Thomas, ed., 1982

Ghosting for King

King found the ideal speechwriter in Jack Pickersgill who became Special Assistant to the Prime Minister in 1945 and mastered the chief's technique of construction and the intention behind it.

As King's main speech writer, private secretary and general confidant, Pickersgill grew closer to the Prime Minister than any other man in Ottawa. King, as he got older, found contact with new faces increasingly distasteful and learned to depend more and more on his trusted assistant to maintain touch with the political world. One reason Pickersgill's help was so acceptable to King was the younger man's instant realization of how useless it would be to attempt any alteration of the Prime Minister's style and vocabulary. "His language," Pickersgill said later, "appeared to have been frozen in the latter part of the nineteenth century. Mr. King didn't like flamboyant phrases. He detested the word 'challenge' and would never use the adjectives 'sober' or 'decent'." Pickersgill became such an expert in gauging King's reactions that he could point out to the other assistants who helped draft paragraphs for the Prime Minister's speeches exactly which words would be stroked out.

Peter C. Newman, *Distemper of Our Times*, 1968

Demanding Master

On one hot summer weekend he summoned members of his staff to Kingsmere and put them to work in a stifling upstairs room while he himself sat outside in the sunshine. A plea from the prisoners resulted in permission to set up a table in a distant corner of the garden, where they continued their work in silence. One of them, Jack Pickersgill, sneaked a cigarette, thinking the indiscretion would not be noticed as he was well downwind of King. But on Monday morning in the East Block office, when King was asked how he had enjoyed the glorious weather in the country, he frowned.

"Pickersgill," he said, eyeing the culprit, "Smoked!"

Charles Lynch, *You Can't Print That*, 1983

Shutterbug

Shortly after the war, King visited the ruins of Berlin.

King ended up by asking that his picture be taken on the site of the old house. A young army officer, a member of the Canadian Berlin mission, had been snapping pictures during the course of the drive around the city and King's companions beckoned to him to take a picture of the Prime Minister. As luck would have it, the officer had just run out of film. He was quite at a loss as to what he should do. There was the Prime Minister striking a pose in front of the heap of rubble and here he was without any film, having used it up on what King would probably consider far less important subjects. Completely flustered, he decided to go through the motions of taking a picture, hoping that King would never ask to see a print. With King posing in the midst of the ruin, the officer raised his camera, squinted through the sights, and clicked the shutter just as if the camera had been fully loaded.

Then, very indiscreetly, as it turned out, the photographer boasted to his friends of how he had fooled the Prime Minister. The story was too good to keep to himself and, apparently, some of those in whom he confided were of a like opinion. The story went the rounds and eventually reached King's ears.

Then the fat was in the fire. King was genuinely exasperated that the photographer had not only failed to get the picture but had then gone around bragging about his smartness. King reported the incident to General Pope, the head of the mission. Pope immediately wanted to dismiss the officer, but King said that he did not want to see such action taken. He did think, however, that the officer should be reprimanded. In the end, the matter was straightened out. The indiscreet photographer stayed on, but he was in disgrace for months afterwards.

H. Reginald Hardy, *Mackenzie King of Canada*, 1949

Tommy Douglas on Mackenzie King

For some reason King took a liking to me and always treated me well, both as a private member in Ottawa and when I was Premier of Saskatchewan. One time I came down for a federal-provincial conference but took ill and was admitted to the hospital. After being released I intended to take a taxi to the train station but found the Prime Minister's limousine waiting for me. He had me over for dinner and when we had finished I said, "You must be very busy, I'll be on my way." He insisted I come up to chat. He sat there in front of a blazing fireplace, feeding his dog. He proceeded to tell me what was going on behind the scenes in the war. He had an amazing proclivity for being reticent with his own friends but sometimes blabbing to anyone who came along. If I had talked to the press the next day I could have caused a national crisis.

T.C. Douglas, *Canadian Parliamentary Review*, Summer 1981

David Lewis on Mackenzie King

In the summer of 1947, Léon Blum, the great socialist leader of France, visited Ottawa. During his stay, he celebrated his seventy-fifth birthday and the French ambassador gave a small dinner in his honour. Those invited included Prime Minister King and a number of his ministers and their wives. Because of Blum's political position, the ambassador invited Coldwell and me as well. Mrs. Coldwell being an invalid, he came alone; Sophie accompanied me. During the evening King said to me in a private conversation that it was a pity I was wasting my time with the CCF. I should, he said, join the Liberal Party. He had no doubt that I would quickly enter Parliament and become a member of his cabinet. Needless to say, I was neither surprised nor impressed, because I knew he had made that sort of offer to Coldwell and others in the CCF, and the same kind of thing had been suggested to me by other Liberals. I thanked him for this generous flattery, but told him that his proposal did not offer even the slightest temptation. My words were chosen very deliberately. King's blue eyes grew cold and angry. I must admit that he had me momentarily apprehensive; I had a glimpse of the power which the man exuded when circumstances seemed to require it.

King was well known for his persistence. Later in the evening he asked Sophie to dance. She told me that he was an excellent dancer, even at his age, then seventy-three. She also told me that while they were dancing he referred to his conversation with me and argued that it was silly of her husband to reject off-hand the possibility of serving his country in a Liberal government.

Sophie's typical reply was that if her David had given any other answer, he would have had to look for another wife. Apparently King approved of her loyalty because he continued to be attentive and gracious, as he was reputed to be with all attractive women. Sophie thus experienced the considerable charm of which King was capable when his spirit moved him. A man of many contradictions.

David Lewis, *Good Fight*, 1981

King on Psychic Phenomena

Age deepened King's feeling of loneliness. He had a deep personal need for affection but he had never been able to sustain a close relationship which imposed any obligations or which required any concessions or sacrifices on his part. As a politician he attended many social functions and he did have some personal contacts outside of politics but none of these associations could fulfil his compulsive need to feel that people loved him. The need was always there but for King, who was determined not to let friendships interfere with his political decisions and who suspected that most people had ulterior motives, it was not easy to resolve his problem.

His solution was to find reassurance in another world. He had become intrigued and fascinated by psychic experiences. He recognized the political risks involved and also had some misgivings about the moral implications of communicating with the spirit world but he had come to depend on the solace of messages from the dear departed. He eased his conscience by keeping a record of his experiences and by telling himself that he was doing psychical research but his was a transparent rationalization. As he once explained to a woman who was deeply involved in psychical phenomena:

> The time I give to it, however, is rather by way of diversion and relaxation, and I should add, inspiration, than anything in the nature of serious study and research. I recognize that my real work is in Parliament and in dealing with present day affairs, and in particular, the problems of the people. Nothing, however, has helped me quite so much in the prosecution of my day to day work than what I have gained, and continue to gain, from the time I am able to give at odd moments to reading and reflection along psychical lines.

> H. Blair Neatby, *MacKenzie King: Prism of Unity*, 1976

King and Freud

King's diary was his psycho-therapist. In it he recorded everything, even his dreams.

Coincidences were more frequently recorded in his diary. His interest in his dreams was heightened; each dream was carefully recorded next day, together with his own interpretation. King was aware of the Freudian theory dreams are a form of wish-fulfillment, but he never applied this theory to his own dreams. Instead, he interpreted them as warnings of impending difficulties, as cautions against his own frailties, or as admonitions to take better care of himself. "This morning," he recorded for example, "I had a vision which clearly meant I was being shown I must rest"; he then described a dream in which he was receiving callers in bed. And always these dreams seemed proof that the heavenly spirits were still with him, giving him guidance and support.

King's use of the word "vision" to describe a dream was significant. He made a vague distinction between visions and dreams. Both came to him at night and were recorded next day; both required interpretation. The visions, however, were somehow of a higher order. Loosely defined, it was always a vision of his mother or some other guardian spirit appeared; it might be called a vision if he detected some appreciation or guidance which could only be attributed to the spiritual world. But, whether visions or dreams, all his nocturnal experiences were welcomed as evidence that he was not alone, and as proof that his rectitude and his selfless dedication were recognized and appreciated.

H. Blair Neatby, *MacKenzie King: Lonely Heights*, 1963

King's Visions

King believed that his dreams were messages from the other world. For him these messages had the advantage that there was no interlocutor and therefore no risk of evil intervention. He had frequent dreams, as many as two or three a week, which he carefully recorded the next morning. All of them seemed significant but those in which relatives or former friends appeared had a special meaning and were usually identified as visions. King had heard of Freud and knew of the significance he attached to dreams, but he remained naively unaware of what they could reveal about himself. When he interpreted his own dreams he ignored the possible psychological revelations and saw them as the voice of conscience or a confirmation that his motives and his actions were beyond reproach. Even when he could not interpret a vision, however, he was not disturbed. It was enough to have received a sign that he was not alone or forgotten.

His dreams do reveal the central place of his mother in his private world. It was not only that she appeared frequently; he often dreamed of Joan and other women as well. It was much more significant that these other women were sometimes explicitly identified with his mother. In one almost classic illustration of an Oedipus complex, King dreamt one night that he saw the face of Mrs. Wreidt change directly into the face of his mother. On another occasion he recorded that in his dream his mother had "the kind of look Joan had when I scolded her last night... a look that meant everything was understood." King, however, was blissfully unaware of the interpretation that might be placed on this transfer of identity. It was enough for him that his mother had appeared. For the first dream he recorded "a joy in my heart that was indescribable"; for the second, "a delight indescribable in my heart at being with her." He felt no need to probe more deeply into the meaning of such visions.

Mackenzie King, however, did more than record his dreams. He also interpreted them. He showed no awareness of the possible psychological explanations; for him his dreams were reminders of his obligations and duties, strengthening his resolve to catch up on his correspondence, to be more sociable, or to dedicate himself even more completely to the cause of humanity.

Dreams also provided confirmation for King's views on political leadership. He once found himself trying to board the engine of a train but somehow the engine was so crowded that he despaired of getting on until at last he found a place reserved for him. "It might mean," he concluded, "that I was party Leader, my business was to start the train moving, that also I should as Leader not get separated from the party but we should all keep together." King scarcely needed a dream to remind him of the importance of keeping the party united; as usual, the message he discovered was a confirmation of what he already believed.

The source, however, was more significant than the actual message. For this reason, he considered his dreams—or visions—to be the most reassuring form of contact with the spirit world. Dreams required no intermediary; he actually saw his loved ones and their spiritual presence was unmistakable. Any nocturnal message came to him directly, without any distortion and without the possible intervention of evil influences. And although King did not mention it, his dreams had the further advantage that they could mean what he wanted them to mean. His loved ones offered no specific advice or prophecies for the future; the message was what King drew from them. Even if subsequent events somehow contradicted his interpretation, he merely reinterpreted the dream without questioning the authenticity or the authority of the source. Whatever happened, nothing could shake his conviction that the dear departed had made their presence known.

H. Blair Neatby, *MacKenzie King: Prism of Unity*, 1976

Mr. King and Mrs. Patteson

Even table-rapping, however, had its hazards. There was nothing clandestine about his friendship with Joan — she even acted as hostess at some of his dinner parties — but it would have been unusual if King at times had not felt some physical attraction to Joan. He would never have admitted to such a natural feeling, even to himself, but on one occasion a session at the table gave some hint of what lay behind the self-control. One of the messages they received was in praise of love and King recorded that both he and Joan sensed they were being tempted by earthly passion. Joan wanted to end the session immediately but King persuaded her to go on "for scientific reasons." The messages then "became very personal and direct, so much so that I would not write down what was said." Both of them found it was a very disturbing experience but they could not resist the temptation to try again next evening. This time the messages restored stability by making it clear that the praise was for spiritual rather than physical love. According to King's diary, both he and Joan were much relieved and reassured.

H. Blair Neatby, *MacKenzie King: Prism of Unity*, 1976

Table-Rapping

Dr. Arthur Doughty, the dignified Dominion Archivist, had introduced him to the parlour-game of table-rapping in the winter of 1933. Many Canadians, at one time or another, had spent an evening seated around a table with hands touching and, if all went well, having the table leg tap out answers to their questions. For most of them it was no more than an intriguing experience but for King it was a confirmation of what he wanted to believe. "It was an amazing evening," he recorded. "The first time I have seen table-rapping and having messages come thro' to me from father, mother, Max and Bella. There can be no shadow of doubt as to their genuineness." This new form of contact with the spirit world had the added advantage that it did not require the presence of a medium. It was also fortunate that King's friend, Joan Patteson, shared his fascination for the occult and when he felt the urge he could drop in at the Pattesons and sit down at the table.

One of the frequent occasions when King felt the need to hear from the dear departed was on his fifty-ninth birthday, in December 1933. It was remarkable, if not uncanny, how responsive the loved ones were and how often they told King what he wanted to hear. On this particular evening he and Joan felt they were given amazing evidence of "the tenderness and love" which surrounded them. A long processing of King's relatives and ancestors sent messages of "love" or "happy birthday." The session ended when King, after three hours of greetings, was abruptly told to "go home." King commented in his diary that he was indeed very tired but by then he had also realized with some embarrassment that all the messages had been for him and that Joan had been ignored. He insisted on redressing the balance and Joan's dead daughter

Nancy did send her love. "I asked any other message—Answ. Go to bed." King thereupon yielded to this higher authority and went home.
H. Blair Neatby, *MacKenzie King: Prism of Unity*, 1976

The Princess Cantacuzene

Julia Grant, the wife of the Russian nobleman, Prince Cantacuzene, and the grand-daughter of President Ulysses S. Grant, had first met Mackenzie King at Newport during his Harvard student days. She later became a solace for King's loneliness.

King's fascination for probing into the unknown was not easily curbed by his innate caution. Julia encouraged him. She agreed "that in the world about us there are occult influences," and was ready to follow his lead. King warned her of the need for secrecy but could not resist taking the lead. By the end of May they were exchanging almost daily letters and telegrams, reporting each occasion on which they had sensed the presence of the other, to discover whether they were sharing similar experiences at the same time. After a month of this, King developed misgivings about the experiment. He reminded Julia that "this celestial fire is fire and could be devastating as well as revealing." He had almost overcome his temptation to play with any fire, however celestial. "I just gave way to my inclinations, which was a great mistake," he wrote in his diary. In his next letter he talked of Julia's presence in the past tense and went on to discuss his political activities. Julia took the hint. Rex, as she called him, would be no more than a close and dear friend.

The experiment was not so easily terminated. King might well comment in a letter to Julia on the strange fact "that in the many years we have known each other, we have been together alone not above the space of a quarter of an hour"; of course, he went on, "neither time nor space can separate us." Their correspondence continued because neither of them wanted to shatter the illusion that their friendship was unique. Politics replaced the occult as the main topic but the sentiments of friendship were repeated, and in each succeeding letter King outdid his previous assertions of undying affection. His letters sounded more and more like the love letters of an adolescent; by October he felt "the tenderest, the strongest, the purest, the most sacred feeling that a man can have towards the one he holds in reverence." But this feeling was almost too much for King; it would not be easy to surpass it the next time he wrote to her. He was already looking for an excuse to stop writing. In the same letter he referred to the danger of his correspondence falling into unfriendly hands and being misunderstood. He was soon reflecting in his diary on the examples of Salome and Delilah, who had turned men from the path of duty. He resolved to end the correspondence.

H. Blair Neatby, *MacKenzie King: Lonely Heights*, 1963

King's Séances

The séances were held with the appropriate air of mystery. According to King, there was a "small folding trumpet-shaped instrument in the centre of the room"; the audience sat around it in the dark. When the instrument fell towards one of the group, a voice from beyond became audible to all. If no voice materialized, Mr. Wreidt or a voice at the next séance might attribute this to the serious absorption of ectoplasm in the twilight or to the lack of the necessary receptivity by the audience. Mackenzie King was apparently a suitable recipient of spiritual communications. Members of his family, his grandfather, William Lyon Mackenzie, Peter Larkin, Madame and Sir Wilfrid Laurier regularly spoke to him on these occasions.

What kind of messages did King receive? In the main they were commendations or admonishments for which equivalents could easily be found in his own diary. Laurier, for example, emphasized two points: that King had been loyal and true to Sir Wilfrid, and that King should make more effort to learn French. Coming as it did at times when King was worried about his inability to speak French, the advice was not surprising. His mother was more likely to comment on his innate goodness and nobility, and to show that she, at least, appreciated the purity of his motives. "It would seem," wrote King, "as if those we loved know not only our behaviour, but our spiritual needs, our thoughts, and were seeking mostly to administer to them." It would seem, also, that they knew something of politics, for King's mother advised him not to try to convert others to spiritualism because they "might not understand it." This must have eased King's conscience. He was not eager to publicize his talks with the departed.

Occasionally, however, the messages went beyond this. King, for example, once asked the spirit of Peter Larkin if he was acquiring too much land at Kingsmere. Larkin's voice suggested he sell the lakeshore property. King was surprised by the advice. There is no suggestion, however, that he took it seriously; certainly he never parted with any of his land at Kingsmere. On a later occasion an unidentified spirit told King that Jesus Christ was a mythical person. King explained this away by deciding that this particular spirit was "still material in a way—the animal kingdom, not yet of the Kingdom of God."

H. Blair Neatby, *MacKenzie King: Lonely Heights*, 1963

Mrs. Gooch's Trunk

The trunk of Mrs. Gooch is not a weighty object in Canadian history, yet it had its own significance. It indicated the state of King's mind in this last active year of his life.

Mrs. Gooch had long been the superb cook of Laurier House. King, one of whose main pleasures was food, valued his cook highly. When he heard that she was traveling on the same ship with him to England on a holiday, he entertained her royally in his own cabin. When he learned on arrival in London that Mrs. Gooch had lost her trunk, he was as distracted as if he had lost a brother.

At the excited command of the Prime Minister, the whole resources of Canada House, the steamship companies, the Royal Canadian Mounted Police, and Scotland Yard were thrown into the search for the missing luggage. Even the sleuths who had uncovered the spy ring could not find Mrs. Gooch's trunk. King was in despair. If Mrs. Gooch did not recover her truck he was convinced that she would never return to Laurier House and cook his meals. The situation was critical.

The dollar crisis, the royal wedding, and all the business of the state were forgotten as King stood unhappily on the railway platform, waiting for the train to take him to Dover, for his tour of Europe. He turned to Norman Robertson, Canadian High Commissioner to Britain, and whispered anxiously, "Robertson, as soon as you locate the trunk cable me at once!" King stepped off his train in Paris to find a cable awaiting him. The trunk had been recovered. King's spirits soared, for the moment only. Yet another crisis, still worse, was ahead of him.

On the train carrying him to Brussels, King could not find his own trunks. They had been left behind in Paris. Mrs. Gooch's problem had been solved but her employer sat disconsolately in his private car, moodily observing the Belgian scenery and remarking, as a man who looks boldly into the teeth of disaster, that he supposed he would have to greet the Belgian Government looking like a scarecrow. He added pathetically that he had no other clothes, was dressed in his oldest suit, and wore a perfectly disreputable shirt. It was no matter, he repeated glumly at intervals, and let nobody worry about him. By the time the train reached Brussels he and his entourage felt practically naked.

King went stoically to bed, muttering that he would disgrace Canada by appearing at an official luncheon, and then accepting an honorary university degree, in his present costume. While he dozed, his invaluable valet, Nicol, and one his secretaries stole out to an establishment which rented clothes and there acquired, at weekly rates, a tail coat, striped trousers, and other accessories.

They hardly expected King, the sartorial dandy, to wear the apparel of other nameless and innumerable men. One of them recalled the occasion when he had been embarrassed by the sudden appearance of local dignitaries on his car during a prairie election tour before he could even brush his hair. On that occasion King had shaken hands with the visitors and never said as much as "hello." After they departed he explained his mortification—he had forgotten to insert his dentures. Would he now agree, in a foreign country, to wear secondhand garments of unknown origin?

The entourage waited breathless in the hall as Nicol entered the Prime Minister's room. Fifteen minutes later, to everyone's relief, King emerged, resplendent in borrowed raiment. Everything was all right, he said, a perfect fit, except that the collar of the shirt was far too tight. The imperturbable valet relieved the pressure by nicking the collar neatly with a razor blade, and King went happily about his public ceremonies. When he was finished with the rented finery he insisted that one of his secretaries wear it, because the rent had been paid for a week in advance.

Bruce Hutchison, *Incredible Canadian*, 1952

Power Shift

Mackenzie King's dominance of his cabinet persisted well into 1948. In May of that year, however, an incident occurred which to those of us close to the centre of power had major significance. The occasion was whether or not Canada should be represented on the United Nations commission to be set up to oversee elections and troop withdrawals in Korea. Ilsley, as head of the Canadian delegation, had agreed to Canadian membership on the commission and his decision had been backed unreservedly by St Laurent as secretary of state for external affairs. Increasingly concerned that, under Pearson and St Laurent, Canada was becoming much too deeply involved in dubious UN adventures, increasingly suspicious of the United Nations itself, King brought the matter to cabinet and bitterly opposed Canadian involvement. Ilsley, with St Laurent's backing, stood firm to the point of threatened resignation; King, in the end, gave way gracefully. Power was beginning to shift.

Arnold Heeney, *Things That Are Caesar's*, 1972

King and Byng

Byng's feelings about King may be gathered from a letter he wrote to his former aide-de-camp, Colonel H. Willis O'Connor after returning from London. He had been at the station when King arrived to attend the Imperial Conference and later a dinner had been given by the Canada Club in Byng's honour at the Savoy.

I went to the station to meet Mackenzie King—a beau geste of perfection. He fell into my arms and produced a Niagara of gush—"How noble," "How thoughtful," "He would ever remember it." There was a considerable crowd... Then, we had the Canada Club dinner. My speech may be said to have been an unqualified success owing to the enthusiastic applause of W.L.M.K. who cheered every utterance. It ran something like this: SELF: Your Royal Highnesses— KING: Hear! Hear! SELF: Mr. Chairman— KING: Trés bien! Good. Good! SELF: My Lords— KING: Attaboy... Buono Oratorio (Italian) SELF: And gentlemen— KING: Banzai... fine... clap, clap, clap, and so on until the end.

Roger Graham, *Arthur Meighen: And Fortune Fled*, 1963

King and Lady Byng

Lady Byng was much less reticent than her husband in discussing Canadian politics and politicians, even with the politicians themselves and their wives. In temperament she was volatile, her opinions were emphatic and she expressed them with an amply forthright vocabulary that left no room for misunderstanding. She made little or no effort while in Canada, especially after the crisis, to conceal her detestation of King and she did not forget or forgive. Some years later the Meighens received an arresting and laugh-provoking communication from the Byngs' estate, Thorpe Hall, Thorpe-le-Soken, Essex. Across the top of the page was pasted a small clipping, a social notice, from the columns of the Canadian Gazette:

> Mr. Mackenzie King received 3,500 Christmas cards and messages. The Prime Minister spent Christmas Day at Ottawa opening the messages.

Below this a few words were scrawled in Lady Byng's hand:

> I suppose you were both there helping our dear little roly poly friend.
>
> (sgd.) Evelyn Byng of Vimy, who did not send one of the 3,500 greetings.

Roger Graham, *Arthur Meighen: And Fortune Fled*, 1963

Ernest Lapointe

Ernest Lapointe (1876-1941) was Mackenzie King's trusted Quebec lieutenant for much of King's time in office. Lapointe served in various Ministerial posts from 1921 until his death.

I was driving down to one of the country parishes below Quebec with Ernest Lapointe. Lapointe was a man without any great prejudices, a kindly, good-hearted chap in every respect. It was a beautiful Sunday morning and I was watching the scenery as we proceeded. Turning to Lapointe, who I suppose had been preparing his speech for the day's performance, I said to him, "This is indeed a beautiful country and the scenery magnificent." Ernest, waking up from the consideration of his speech, turned to me and said, "Yes, too damn good a country to let Arthur Meighen run it." This to my mind was an indication of the feelings of the older members of the Liberal Party who had been meeting Meighen during the stormy days of conscription and afterwards.

The Memoirs of Chubby Power: A Party Politician, Norman Ward, ed., 1966

Calming Influence

From 1917 to 1938 Samuel William Jacobs (1871-1938), Member for the Montreal riding of Cartier, was recognized by common consent as the wit of the House. Even before becoming a member, he had earned the respect of the people of Cartier.

The estimation in which Sam was held by his own people, and indeed by all the foreign population of Montreal, is well illustrated by what happened on St. Catherine Street East in the spring of 1912. Early one morning a run had developed on the City and District Bank and it assumed such proportions that the authorities became alarmed and Sir Thomas White wired the Receiver General's office to release gold to stem the tide. But this was not effective and later that evening around one of the branches on St. Catherine Street East there gathered a mob of thousands upon thousands of these poor foreign people who believed that they were about to lose all their savings. Senator Dandurand pleaded with these people to disperse, assuring them that they had nothing to fear. This had no effect and the mob was becoming uglier all the time. As a last desperate measure, the Senator turned to Sam and asked him if he would not do something to calm the crowd.

He stood up and speaking first in English then in French and then in half-Yiddish, half-German, he assured them that they could go home to their beds, that he personally would guarantee that every cent of their deposits would be paid. The foreign population had such confidence in Mr. Jacobs that they accepted his statement without hesitancy and the crowd melted away, and a riot was narrowly averted.

Bernard Figler, *Sam Jacobs, Member of Parliament*, 1959

The Member for Coast to Coast

James Shaver Woodsworth (1874-1942) was first elected to Parliament in 1921 for the constituency of Winnipeg Centre. He later founded the CCF, and was its leader until the start of World War II.

He represented much more than the riding of Winnipeg North Centre. The people there had elected him, but somehow his boundaries widened out until the whole of Canada became his constituency. For twenty years he represented a growing section of the Canadian community from coast to coast, people who needed his help, and people who agreed with his basic ideas.

He kept in touch with his vast constituency through many channels. There were his speeches in the House of Commons which were widely reported by the press. Then he bought thousands of copies of Hansard reprints of them, sowing these broadcasts across Canada. He addressed the envelopes himself in longhand, pressing into service members of the family and any volunteers who could be found. He sent out the various papers, pamphlets, government reports, indeed anything that came to his desk, to every part of the country. He felt the loneliness of people in isolated districts, hungry for reading-matter and human contact. Sometimes he appeared to lack discrimination when he would send a bulletin of fisheries to some old lady he had met years before in a prairie town, or a periodical about an obscure Chinese college to a lumber-worker in the woods of northern Ontario. But often he would be rewarded by a grateful letter from someone who had been started on the road to community service by his mailed contributions, and the letters that often accompanied them, or by a visit from someone who had been encouraged to persevere in a worth-while task by reading reports of his speeches in the House of Commons. He had an abiding faith in the power of knowledge to bring reinforcements to his cause.

His correspondence was heavy. Many of the letters he answered himself, in longhand, though he was able to use the full service of an excellent stenographer during the session. He looked after his files himself, constantly clearing out letters as he finished with the matters involved, a process which destroyed a great volume of correspondence which would have been of intense interest to later readers.

Grace MacInnis, *Woodsworth: A Man to Remember*, 1953

Woodsworth in the House

Woodsworth is a small sized man of forty-eight with a short-cropped, tapering beard streaked with grey. He is thin and pale and ascetic, a little bit bald, built generally on delicate lines.... His countenance, while not dour, is rarely illumined with a smile...." The author noted that Woodsworth spoke splendidly, with a clear-cut, easy delivery; that his voice was rather of the staccato pitch, not unpleasant, and accompanied with energetic gestures: "He hasn't at all the method of the preacher, no ponderous solemnity.... The House appears to think well of him."

"D.C.L", quoted in Kenneth McNaught, *A Prophet in Politics*, 1959

Library Mountie

For a man who believed that the Mounties should be confined strictly to patrol duty in the unorganized territories of the northwest, it was a constant source of irritation to run across one of them every time he went into the Parliamentary Library to borrow a book. Everywhere else in the Parliament Buildings the regular protective officers were on duty, their sober dark uniforms relieved only by shining buttons. Here alone was one of the colourful riders of the plains, complete with wide-brimmed hat, scarlet tunic, riding breeches and boots, clinking spurs and even a riding crop.

One day J.S. Woodsworth questioned the Minister of Justice why this should be, and Mr. Lapointe promised to inquire. M.J. Coldwell, who heard the story later, recalls that a few days after his question J.S. Woodsworth was stopped in the corridor by Mr. Lapointe who urged him not to press for a public answer. It seems that the Minister's inquiry had revealed the fact that on the morning after the fire in the Parliament Buildings in 1916 a Mounted Policeman had been placed on guard outside the Parliamentary Library in order to prevent possible looting. No one, it appears, had ever countermanded the order—with the result that ten years later a Mountie was still doing patrol duty outside the Library door!

Grace MacInnis, *Woodsworth: A Man to Remember*, 1953

Frugal J.S.

Inherently frugal and disliking show or extravagance, he yet had no love for money as such but devoted such funds as he had to their most useful purpose. He never, even in his parliamentary days, received more than a modest income. Apart from his indemnity of $4,000 his extra income averaged about $400 from newspaper articles; the rent from the Vancouver house never offset the cost of living in Ottawa plus the Kitsilano mortgage. Yet by careful planning and the utmost of care in daily living he was able to achieve more than most men with several times his income. Following this rigorous domestic plan, he did more than his part, probably with some ill effect on his health, for by the end of the 1920's he was beginning to suffer from increasing blood pressure. While away from his home, which was the greater part of the time, he seldom ate in any but the cheapest restaurants. During boat or train trips he acted as his own porter, and in accommodation allowed himself only the minimum of comfort. But although his children were often refused pennies or nickels, they received money for bicycles; and none was denied instruction on violin or piano. Later, their father never asked for an accounting in their larger projects, knowing he could trust them to make the most of their opportunities.

Kenneth McNaught, *A Prophet in Politics*, 1959

Woodsworth Described

In the corridors of Parliament one may encounter at any hour of the day a little, thin man carrying a file bulging with papers under his left arm, who glides rather than walks over the marble floor-stones and who throws over you in passing, like a tender reproach, the gentle glance of his brown eyes. A very neat coat whose cut vaguely recalls the habit of a Protestant pastor covers his anaemic body without hiding the jut of the bones which seem, at the shoulders, ready to pierce the cloth.. The first impression is that one has come across some ruined gentleman who has kept from his former splendour the care for his appearance and the taste for clean linen....

"Claude", quoted in Grace MacInnis, *Woodsworth: A Man to Remember*, 1953

Woodsworth's Office

Once in Parliament, Woodsworth took to the new life with immense verve. Even after he had moved his family to Ottawa his office on the Hill was the centre of his existence. In one sense, the new work was not so very different from that of his earlier plunges in welfare activities; the gathering and dissemination of social information was still important, and his parliamentary office reflected this. Fitted with books, pamphlets, and steel filing cabinets which contained a growing mass of correspondence with people all across Canada and in all walks of life, the office also became a centre for anyone visiting Ottawa who wished to learn something of labour politics, unemployment, civil liberties—or just to meet and talk with the country's most dramatic spokesman of the Left. The office also gave evidence of some of Woodsworth's chief characteristics. There were no samples of modern art, but there were several books of sentimental poetry and a number of souvenirs of his travels and his boyhood home.

On top of one of the filing cabinets reposed three huge scrapbooks (newspaper size) and two smaller ones, in which he had pasted every printed item and many other documents concerning his activities from the time of the Winnipeg mission days. These volumes he was to keep up to date until 1939. The items on each side of each page were fitted in half underneath each other so that each volume, when complete, resembled a small barrel.

Kenneth McNaught, *A Prophet in Politics*, 1959

Brown Paper

Woodsworth led a study group which met once a week in his office in the Parliament Buildings, on the session-free Wednesday night when most M.P.s sought rest and relaxation. One participant recalls how they would carefully fasten great sheets of brown paper to the office walls, and then J.S. Woodsworth would lead discussion on the evolution of productive methods, of social institutions, of politics, of morals—until the brown sheets were covered with writing and the hour was late.

Grace MacInnis, *Woodsworth: A Man to Remember*, 1953

Sound Advice

He had the complexity of a Methodist minister. Strict with his family, but not tyrannical, strict with himself, he was quite a disciplinarian, but nevertheless very kindly. When I went to Parliament after I'd made my first speech, he took me up to the Hansard room to show me how to check my speech and make sure the quotations were correct and so on.

He advised me to make my first speech fairly early in the debate. He said, "Don't wait for months until you get such cold feet you never have the nerve to try it. And after you've made your first speech, don't get in too often until you know what you're talking about. Take time to find out how the House is run. The important thing is to gain the ear of the House. A lot of men make speeches almost every other day, but nobody listens to them, partly because they don't know what they're talking about, and partly because their material isn't well prepared. Once you have the ear of the House, then you can speak on almost anything that comes up and you'll get a hearing."

His advice was very useful to me throughout the years. As he got older and we got to know him better, he would take a little time out to talk. In the first years, he was so busy that he would read the newspaper standing up so he wouldn't waste any time. He only allowed himself so many minutes to read a newspaper. He wouldn't waste time reading a lot of nonsense. He was always working.

T.C. Douglas, quoted in *Making of a Socialist*, Lewis H. Thomas, ed., 1982

Work, Work, Work

Throughout the parliamentary sessions he was seldom absent from his seat in the Commons or the desk in his office; he insisted on answering personally the thousands of letters that came to him each year; and on the weekends he was usually to be found addressing meetings anywhere within the transportation radius of Ottawa.

A story is told of an occasion when he was persuaded to take a brief holiday weekend at Lake Simcoe in Ontario in the middle of a busy summer. His host suggested a drive to Orillia to see the famous Champlain Monument. On the way there they passed the road leading to Couchiching Park, and Woodsworth, without apparent guile, suggested that he would like to see it. Upon arrival it was discovered that the Couchiching conference on international affairs was in full swing; the rest of the day was spent in animated conversation with the delegates and included a speech by Woodsworth.

Kenneth McNaught, A Prophet in Politics, 1959

Conscience of Parliament

Woodsworth, then leader of the CCF, was one of the few Members to speak out against the declaration of war against Germany in 1939.

In one of the most moving scenes in Parliament, just before Woodsworth rose to his feet, Mr. King asked for permission to say a word. He said that in view of the fact that Mr. Coldwell had spoken, he took it for granted that Mr. Woodsworth was going to take a position different from the rest of the House. He hoped there would be no untoward demonstration, nothing said of an unkind nature, because Mr. Woodsworth had been the conscience of the Canadian Parliament for a quarter of a century; men of his calibre were an ornament to any Parliament and he hoped Mr. Woodsworth would be listened to accordingly. It was a magnanimous tribute from a political opponent, and showed us the depth of Mackenzie King's character in a time of great crisis.

When Mr. Woodsworth rose to speak, few people knew his physical condition. I moved down to sit beside him. Normally this seat was occupied by H.H. Stevens, who had left the Conservative party to become the Reconstruction party leader.

His wife had written out his notes with a crayon in great big letters, an inch or two inches high. He had several sheets of these notes, each with just a few words, to remind him of what he was going to say. He could hardly see them, and I passed them up to him one by one. I never admired him more than I did that day.

He made his great declaration of faith, that some day men would learn to settle their differences without resorting to force, and that in the long run, end determines means. When we take the wrong end, this destroys the means, and when we take the wrong means, this destroys the end that we have in view. While we might think we were fighting to preserve democracy, the fact that we were now going to engage in wholesale butchery would destroy the very democracy that we were seeking to preserve.

It was a fine speech. When he first started, two or three Conservative members shouted, "Shame!" I knew one or two of the men who were shouting. They had never seen a shot fired in anger in their lives, had never taken a stand for any unpopular issue, and were completely incapable of understanding a man like Mr. Woodsworth.

But in the main, the House gave him a most respectful hearing, and when he sat down I'm sure there was hardly a member in the House who didn't admire him.

T.C. Douglas, quoted in *Making of a Socialist*, Lewis H. Thomas, ed., 1982

Woodsworth's Stroke

Only a few people knew it then, and only a few have heard of it to this day. But a few days earlier Woodsworth had had a severe stroke. When he rose to speak he could scarcely see and one side was partly paralyzed. The night before Mrs. Woodsworth had made a few notes at his dictation—a cue word here and there—and put them on cards in thick crayon letters at least an inch high. I slipped into the seat beside him and handed the cards up to him one by one while he made his moving but hopeless plea for peace. I knew that in a few minutes I would be voting against him, but I never admired him more than I did that day.

T.C. Douglas, quoted in Doris French Shackleton, *Tommy Douglas*, 1975

Woodsworth Working Class

After Woodsworth's stroke of 1939, the people around him in the CCF tried to keep him from over taxing himself and his travelling during the 1940 election was kept to a minimum. To ease the strain of a trip that could not be avoided, David Lewis bought a first class compartment ticket for Woodsworth. Woodsworth cashed in the ticket and sent Lewis a cheque and the following letter.

"You must not think me lacking in appreciation of your great kindness in arranging this mode of transportation for me but when I told you that such arrangements were unnecessary I meant just what I said... I have usually travelled tourist, this not merely to save expense both in berth and meals but also because I meet the class of people with which our movement is most closely identified."

David Lewis, *Good Fight*, 1981

Taken Ill

In 1940 Woodsworth suffered a debilitating second stroke.

The House opened on a Thursday. Two days later there was a meeting of the CCF National Council which usually convenes as Parliament opens so that there may be an exchange of view with the M.P.s on matters likely to arise during the session. Wartime difficulties had cut down representation from distant points, and arrangements were made to hold the rather small meeting in a committee-room just off the Parliamentary Reading Room. Dim and airless, its gloom was a great contrast with the May sunshine outdoors.

M.J. Coldwell presided, my father on his right, while the Council members sat along three sides of the committee table. The session was quiet and constructive. David Lewis, National Secretary, was reading a letter from the Saskatchewan Provincial council when my father started to rise. Mr. Coldwell urged him to wait for the conclusion of the letter, but he said: "I must go," and again attempted to rise. He fell back into his chair, saying quietly: "I think I've had a stroke." Later we learned that Hugh Castleden had observed him a few seconds earlier trying to reach for a glass of water. His right hand fell to his side and he reached with his left. We learned too that Mother had been watching him apprehensively and waiting for the moment he would say that something was wrong. Her self-control and her determination to let him do things in his own way were always amazing, and never more so than at this moment.

The men carried him out to the elevator and then to his own office, remarking later on the calmness and control of his face. Dr. Gershaw, M.P. for Medicine Hat, arrived on the scene and bent over him as he lay on the couch, his eyes covered by a cloth. The waiting men in Mr. Coldwell's office learned that the right side was paralyzed. My father, still able to speak, was apologetic for having disrupted the meeting, and urged his colleagues to proceed. Mother, quiet and self-possessed, went off with him to the hospital.

Days of suspense followed. Father, who had lost his speech almost immediately, regained it after some days, but failed to move his arm and leg, in spite of continual and impatient efforts. Messages and flowers poured into his room from across Canada, and there were countless anxious enquiries at the Parliament Buildings.

Grace MacInnis, *Woodsworth: A Man to Remember*, 1953

The Chair

Abraham Albert Heaps (1885-1954) represented Winnipeg North in the Commons from 1925 to 1940.

MacKenzie King had invited Heaps on occasion into his office in the East Block to hear his views on the Unemployment Insurance Act as well as other legislation that he was urging upon the Government. It was on one of these visits that Heaps noted an old black leather chair in bad need of repair. His professional upholsterer's pride was challenged. The Prime Minister of Canada could not possibly sit in such a chair. Something should be done about it immediately. When King agreed, Heaps, to the amazement of the Prime Minister said he would have the chair taken to his office and he would re-upholster it himself. The old chair was a relic left by Sir Wilfrid Laurier and, rather than throw it out, King had kept it for sentimental reasons. Late in the year 1927, Heaps had the chair moved to his office in one of the garret rooms on the fifth floor of parliament and started to work on it in his spare time. When Parliament opened for its new Session in 1928, the chair was completely reupholstered, sprung, padded and polished. It was ready to be returned to the sentimental King, who was convinced that he had lost forever his cherished souvenir from his beloved Sir Wilfrid. King had never doubted Heaps' ability as a parliamentarian but, not knowing Heaps' upholstering background, had reservations concerning his technical skill as an upholsterer. Shortly after the new Session began, Heaps returned the magnificent new chair to the office of the Prime Minister. King was overwhelmed.

Leo Heaps, *Rebel in the House*, 1984

The House

The House of Commons in the 1930s as described by Charles Grant Mac-Niell, the then CCF member for Vancouver North.

The House of Commons of the 1930s was a much narrower and more provincial world. MacNeil recalls it as racist, anti-semitic, to an extent that would be unacceptable today. He said that one day he had two overseas visitors from India, and he asked them to go to lunch with him in the parliamentary dining room. He called Angus MacInnis, who said he was tied up, but Grace was free to join him. "Did I catch it afterwards! A very prominent Liberal was the worst. He said, 'The idea of taking a white woman in there with those Indians!'"

Sometimes it was rowdy, MacNeil said. "Tommy [Douglas] didn't drink, not compared to the rest. One time a big bunch of ex-servicemen met, a non-partisan group, and we came thundering down the stairs. I went into the Chamber just as Woodsworth led a terrific attack on this sort of thing going on in the House of Parliament."

Doris French Shackleton, *Tommy Douglas*, 1975

Bennett Ambitious

Richard Bedford Bennett (1870-1947) became Prime Minister in 1930, fulfilling a life-long ambition.

As a student at Dalhousie Law School, Bennett used to declare—and to himself the declaration was not so much a boast as the plain statement of an inevitable fact—that some day he would be Canada's First Minister. Mr. Justice W.H. Trueman, late of the Manitoba Court of Appeal, was one year his senior at Dalhousie. One day Bennett proposed to Trueman that they should attend together a political meeting to be addressed by Sir John A. Macdonald.

Trueman accepted his invitation and they drove several miles by horse and buggy to the meeting. On the return journey, Bennett was full of the speech they had heard. His mood was serious as he turned over Sir John's words, and he was silent with his thoughts, until he said suddenly, "I'm going to be Premier of Canada." At the time his companion treated this remark as one would expect such a remark to be treated.

In 1930, just after Bennett had been elected Prime Minister, when he was passing through Winnipeg on his way to Ottawa, Trueman called to see him at his hotel, and, as they were chatting over old times, Trueman asked, "Do you remember the night we heard Sir John A. Macdonald speak, the night you told me you would be Prime Minister? Well, you made it all right." "I said I would, didn't I?" replied Bennett, and his tone implied that he was disappointed that he had not been taken at his word forty years before.

Roy St. George Stubbs, *Prairie Portraits*, 1954

Honourary Colonels

Mr. Bennett took the [1914–18] war very seriously, even emotionally, and was disgusted at anything in the nature of trifling. He was especially critical of the policy of creating "Honorary Colonels", some of whom caused a good deal of public derision. On one occasion, Sir Sam Hughes went overseas, and left as Acting Minister Sir James Lougheed of Calgary. Mr. Bennett and Sir James had at one time been law partners, and in the subsequent dissolution of this partnership the elder man treated his brilliant associate rather badly. Under the circumstances the incumbency of Sir James in temporary control of military affairs did not tend to strengthen R. B.'s confidence in the manner in which Canada's effort was being handled at Ottawa. On one of his trips to the capital he made a stormy protest about the Honorary Colonels who, in his opinion, were making the country ridiculous.

After he had gone home Col. Daly (one of Bennett's friends) jocularly said to Sir James, "Why don't you make Bennett an Honorary Colonel himself?" "Fine!" said Sir James, "make out the necessary forms for gazetting his appointment and I'll sign them." The order was duly carried out and the Calgary member was advised by telegram of the honour that had been conferred on him. But they reckoned without their man. Mr. Bennett was in a towering rage, and raised such a storm that the appointment had to be cancelled.

Hector Charlesworth, *I'm Telling You*, 1937

Bennett at Work

He was impatient with the red tape of government. He was not afraid to cut it, and if he wanted information he did not hesitate to call up the humblest civil servant. The story goes that one day, impatient to obtain some information and without waiting for his secretary, he telephoned some minor department for information. A girl answered.

"This is R.B. Bennett speaking," came over the phone.

The last thing in the world she expected would be the Prime Minister telephoning her. She thought it was some boy friend kidding her.

"Oh yeah! This is Greta Garbo," was the reply the astonished Prime Minister heard over the telephone.

Arthur Ford, *As The World Wags On*, 1950

"Bonfire" Bennett

Bennett was all bluff and bounce. He was a powerful speaker, his speed of delivery in the House so rapid that he was known as Richard "Bonfire" Bennett.

Prickly, puffed up, and overbearing, he never bothered to hide his jealousy of Meighen, who surpassed him in so many of the things that touched Bennett's pride. At times, though, Bennett was capable of surprising and even endearing touches of frankness. "I'd have given anything," he told me one day, "to have Meighen's mind."

Grattan O'Leary, *Recollections of People, Press, and Politics*, 1977

A Day With R.B.

The Prime Minister, who had never owned a home of his own, now occupied a huge suite in the Chateau Laurier, rose at 7:30 a.m., dressed himself with foppish care (he did not employ a valet), and resplendent in top hat or bowler, cut-away coat, cane and gloves, walked up the Hill to his office (his only exercise) before nine o'clock.

Then he worked steadily for fifteen or sixteen hours, with a brief interruption for lunch and a leisurely dinner in his suite, where he usually consumed a pound of chocolates every night and occasionally, if he had guests, would stretch his principles to drink a thimbleful of crème de menthe since he considered it non-alcoholic. Several times a week expert massage would substitute for exercise. The Chateau barbers grew prosperous on his tips.

Radiant health and unquestioned faith in himself supported enough daily work to occupy the whole Cabinet, which he treated as a staff of servants.

Bruce Hutchison, *Mr. Prime Minister*, 1964

Bennett's Sweet Tooth

Few wealthy men use their riches as does R.B. Bennett; he lives always in a large suite in the Palliser Hotel at Calgary, or in the Chateau Laurier at Ottawa; he is fond of well-cooked common-sense foods; and, like many men who neither smoke nor drink, feels the need of no small amount of chocolate — which he consumes in surprising quantities; although of recent months his doctors have apparently advised against this.

Andrew MacLean, *R.B. Bennett*, 1934

Bennett's Memory

He has a prodigious memory for facts. During the first year of his regime when he was serving as his own Finance Minister, a friend of mine took a deputation interested in the hat industry, to see him. His visitors were amazed at the wealth of knowledge on all matters relating to their industry—materials, marketing problems and so on. One of them remarked afterwards, "I did not know Bennett had been in the hat business."

Shortly after he had relinquished the Finance portfolio I sought an interview with him on a very important matter. Unscrupulous attacks had been made on two leading insurance companies, with the result that thousands of persons carrying policies not only with these but all other Canadian companies became alarmed. The publication of which I was editor was receiving scores of letters daily from subscribers enquiring as to whether their policies were safe. It occurred to us that it might be advisable to publish a complete survey of all Canadian insurance companies and their assets, and by this means inform every insured person exactly what stood behind his policy. This could not be done without Governmental assistance in providing accurate information. I went to

Ottawa with this request, and submitted the idea to the Prime Minister. "It would not be advisable," he said, "and I'll tell you frankly why." Then without a note before him he recited the exact position of every company—what its investments were; and the condition of the investments themselves.

Hector Charlesworth, *I'm Telling You*, 1937

Tommy Douglas on R.B. Bennett

Bennett was quite brilliant—the Conservatives have produced some brilliant men. He had an amazing memory. I've seen him sitting in the House writing letters, but with one ear open. A minister was stumped when a question was thrown at him about the capacity of a certain harbour. Bennett growled out the answer— the size of the harbour, when it was built, the tonnage of the ships that could be accommodated. The press boys suspected he was bluffing and went and looked it up, and he was right.

Bennett had no capacity for making friends; neither had Meighen. Both would pass through the Members' Lobby and they might nod, or might not even speak.

T.C. Douglas, quoted in Doris French Shackleton, *Tommy Douglas*, 1975

Bennett's Presence

In appearance as in character the new Conservative leader was as much a contrast to King as Meighen had been. His face, round and smooth, with the glint of porcelain, his eyes gleaming through pince-nez of antiquated design, had a look of obvious power, courage, and honesty, qualities that no one could deny him. His figure was tall, rotund, and elegantly tailored in old-fashioned tail coats of varying hue, often changed several times a day. He took no exercise. He took no liquor or tobacco either, his sole vice being rich chocolates, which he consumed by the pound. With the aid of a daily massage he avoided all exercise and enjoyed robust health. Beside this handsome and glistening extrovert King appeared small and fragile.

Bruce Hutchison, *Incredible Canadian*, 1952

169

Bennett in the House

Bennett was a ferocious debater in the House. In fact he was somewhat of a bully. If he thought he could browbeat you he would. The very first time he interrupted me I gave him a tongue lashing. Afterwards he came over and shook hands. "That's what I like to see," he said, "I like a fellow who can talk back." Jimmy Gardiner, the Minister of Agriculture was one of the few Liberals not afraid to tangle with Bennett. One day Gardiner interrupted him. Bennett told him to remember that he was in the House of Commons and not back in Saskatchewan talking to a bunch of rural rustics. Gardiner decided to let it pass but the Liberal member for Moose Jaw, Jack Gordon Ross, rose on a point of order. "I wasn't talking to you" said Bennett. "No," said Ross, "but Mr. Speaker I am one of those rural rustics referred to by the Leader of the Opposition." Bennett looked at him and replied, "Yes but there is absolutely no need for you to get up and prove it."

T.C. Douglas, *Canadian Parliamentary Review*, Summer 1981

One Man Show

Ministers complained that Cabinet meetings were given over to registering their Prime Minister's decisions. He did not act on the British theory that the Prime Minister is "first among equals." He always regarded his Cabinet colleagues as subordinates, and often erring subordinates.

A popular story was told of Bennett sitting alone in his club, muttering to himself. A stranger asked: "What is he saying?" "He is holding a Cabinet meeting," was the reply.

Lord Beaverbrook, *Friends*, 1959

Pearson on King and Bennett

Lester Pearson began his Ottawa career as a public servant, and served both Bennett and King before entering politics in 1948.

I got to know Mr. Bennett better than I had known Mr. King. I was, indeed, given assignments that brought me into direct contact with him. He was also an easier man to get to know. He was more out-going, more straight-forward than his more subtle and complex predecessor. Both his virtues and his defects were more obvious. His reaction to the defects of others, when he detected them, was frank and expressive. I once was accused by Mr. Bennett of taking a decision as secretary of a Royal Commission on Grain Futures which resulted in the insertion into its report of a passage both inaccurate and misleading and, even worse, which got the government into trouble in the House of Commons. The Prime Minister gave me some stormy minutes in our discussion of the matter and let me know in no uncertain terms that I had not only exceeded my authority but had acted either stupidly or maliciously or both. When eventually I was allowed to get a word in, I was able to show that I was being most unfairly accused and that I was not responsible for the offending words and figures. Mr. Bennett at once apologized and directed his wrath elsewhere. His storms were rough, but they were usually of short duration and often cleared the air.

I do not recall that Mr. King ever stormed. When he felt that he had been badly used or not adequately or wisely served, the weather became sultry and overcast. For those around the presence at these times, a fan was more useful than an umbrella. Where, to change the metaphor, Mr. Bennett would burst into flames, Mr. King would smoulder. Where Mr. Bennett made a frontal attack, Mr. King would exercise an outflanking movement; he would reproach himself in your presence for expecting too much of a young officer. That, of course, made a junior feel more unhappy than any outright criticism; especially when the insinuation was quite unfair.

Lester B. Pearson, *Mike: Memoirs of Lester B. Pearson*,
Volume I, 1972

Bennett and King

Agnes Macphail said one night that she had sat in the House with two prime ministers, and they had somewhat different attitudes toward poor people: we had a lot of poor people in Canada in those days. She told us that one day Bennett, looking out from his office in the East Block, noticed some unemployed fellows sitting around on the parliamentary lawn. He ordered the RCMP to chase them off. He didn't want to look at them. King would never have done that, Agnes said. He would have gone over to the window and pulled down the blind.

Doris French Shackleton, Tommy Douglas, 1975

Bennett and the Strikers

By 1932, R.B. Bennett believed Canada was threatened by revolution. Mass delegations were interpreted as a potential attempt to intimidate or even to overthrow the government. In the summer of 1932, some two thousand farmers met in Ottawa to air their grievances. Delegates were chosen to present a petition to the government. Bennett had tried in advance to persuade the farmers not to assemble — he understood their problems and so the convention could only be interpreted as a show of force. He refused to meet the delegation when it came to his office.

A convention of unemployed labourers which met in Ottawa during the session of 1932 had seemed an even more serious threat of revolution. Bennett was asked to meet a small delegation from the convention. The Prime Minister decided to face the threat boldly. He would meet the men on the steps of Parliament and tell them bluntly that his government would not be coerced. But Bennett took no chances. The staid citizens of Ottawa had never before witnessed such elaborate preparations for receiving a delegation. An armoured car appeared on Parliament Hill that morning; city policemen paraded up and down Wellington Street in front of the Parliament buildings; armed detachments of the Royal Canadian Mounted Police were posted in front of the East and West Blocks; another detachment, on horseback, was hidden in reserve behind the Centre Block. Even the Conservative Ottawa Journals was moved to protest against "the almost craven and un-British things that went on on Parliament Hill yesterday; in this Chicago-like flaunting of firearms; in a scene that smacks more of fascism than of Canadian constitutional authority." It was an anticlimax when the delegation listened quietly to the Prime Minister's statement and then as quietly dispersed.

H. Blair Neatby, MacKenzie King: Lonely Heights, 1963

Pearson's OBE

Bennett took Pearson with him to a commonwealth conference in London in 1934, and on the ocean voyage the Prime Minister was at work on a list of names he planned to submit for the king's annual "honours list." Mackenzie King, who served his second term as head of government just prior to Bennett, had abolished the "honours-list" system but Bennett had restored it and was trying out names of worthy Canadians on Pearson and one of his secretaries.

One night on shipboard after he got the list completed he called Pearson to his cabin and informed him: "I've put you down for an OBE." It was intended as a reward for the work Pearson had done on the price-spreads commission.

Pearson was surprised. He knew it would cause comment in the external affairs department and that Skelton didn't believe in decorations for his officers. He wondered if Bennett would settle for a promotion instead of a decoration. With an attempt of jocularity he said, "Mr. Prime Minister, I would settle for twenty-five dollars more a week. I can't raise a family on a OBE." His pay was then about three hundred dollars a month. His allowances on such trips were only enough to cover the cost of his room at Claridge's, where he had to stay because Bennett did, and did not suffice for his other expenses.

Bennett was very annoyed by Pearson's attitude. He snapped: "If you make me change my list again, now that I have it all completed, not only will you not get an OBE, you will not even get a promotion." But he relented; and taking the hint, he saw to it eventually that Pearson got both the OBE and reclassification in grade that carried higher pay.

John Robinson Beal, *Pearson Phenomenon*, 1964

Surprise Appointment

Bennett selects Winnifred Kydd, president of the National Council of Women, as a delegate to the first World Conference on Disarmament, which opened at Geneva, Switzerland, in February 1932.

Dr. Skelton and I were in Mr. Bennett's office one day when he was considering possible members for the delegation. He felt it should include a lady delegate, but whom? He had a brilliant idea—"Let's appoint the president of the National Council of Women. After all, she is, in effect, the prime minister of the women of Canada!" So he sent for *Who's Who* to find out who the lady "prime minister" was. She turned out to be a Miss Kydd who was also Dean of Women at Queen's University. "Fine," said Mr. Bennett, "phone and ask if she could see me tomorrow or the next day."

Miss Kydd was no doubt surprised at this summons to Ottawa by the head of the government. But she could not have been more surprised than the Prime Minister when she arrived at his office. He naturally thought that the president of the National Council of Women and a dean of women to boot would be a lady of at least middle age with the maturity and even severity one might expect to attach to these two offices. Miss Kydd turned out to be a most attractive, smart, auburn-haired lady in her later twenties. I'm sure Mr. Bennett's surprise turned at once to delight. Like Mr. King, he was not unappreciative, except in the marrying sense, of feminine grace and charm.

Lester B. Pearson, *Mike: Memoirs of Lester B. Pearson,*
Volume I, 1972

Bennett's Questionable Humour

He is very fond of humour, and his infectious laugh is frequently heard resounding through his office. He is quite a practical joker! Once he called up his own secretary, and disguising his voice, complained bitterly that he had tried repeatedly to see the Prime Minister. He thoroughly enjoyed his secretary's explanation and discomfiture!

Late one Saturday night, he called up one of his stenographers, and asked if she would mind taking some dictation at nine-thirty on Sunday morning. As she readily agreed, he said: "You're a good girl — I was only joking."

Andrew MacLean, *R.B. Bennett*, 1934

Under the Mistletoe

Mr. Bennett always dressed in formal attire; morning coat, striped trousers, and a large, black waistcoat covering his well-developed paunch. He was not what in these days might be described as a "swinger." Nevertheless, there is a story about him, no doubt apocryphal, striding into the stenographers' pool in the East Block one Christmas Eve. There was some mistletoe over the door and coming the other way was a pretty young stenographer. According to the story, Bennett grabbed her and kissed her soundly on the lips. Then holding her off away from his ample paunch, he demanded, "What did you think of that, young lady?" To which the young typist is said to have replied, "More of an honour than a pleasure, Prime Minister."

Walter Gordon, *A Political Memoir*, 1977

Naked Women

Bennett had the reputation of being a dangerous man with the ladies. One day while he was still Leader of the Opposition, when the House was discussing a Doukhobor protest march in the Kootenays, a member launched at King the rhetorical question, what would the Prime Minister do if he came out on the porch at Kingsmere to find a group of naked women?

King replied quick as a flash, "I'd send for the Leader of the Opposition."

Bennett shot back the sharp reply that the Prime Minister was not known for sharing patronage with the other parties.

Bennett's lapses into heavy-footed humour were rather rare; he was noted for portentous solemnity. Before speaking he would glare round the Chamber from under straggly brows, pulling down sharply on the points of his waistcoat; then he would launch himself on a wave of bombastic prose, which members endured as best they might.

Grattan O'Leary, *Recollections of People, Press, and Politics*, 1977

R.B.'s Alberta Manager

Bennett was known and respected throughout Calgary, but it is hard to find that he was as generally liked. His closest, perhaps his one complete friend was George Robinson. Robinson was a real estate and insurance agent in Calgary, a man in complete contrast to Bennett. He was Bennett's political adviser and manager in Alberta. He knew the organizational side of politics instinctively and completely. He could fix anything that could be fixed. Equally instinctively, he knew how to handle Bennett himself. He never stood in awe of him, as so many did. When he went to see him, almost ostentatiously he kept his bowler hat on and continued to smoke his cigar, although he knew Bennett detested the smell of tobacco in his office. He could ignore Bennett's bursts of temper as though they had never happened, and Bennett knew it.

On one occasion he was travelling with Bennett on a speaking tour in the province and they arrived at nightfall in a small town with only one hotel. Robinson went to the desk to see about the room, and the proprietor, recognizing Bennett, thought it a suitable occasion to advance his asking price considerably.

"What?" roared Robinson when he heard the figure. "For that women must be included. Bring 'em out."

Bennett was not amused, but George was George.

Ernest Watkins, *R.B. Bennett: A Biography*, 1963

It Burns in the Soup

Throughout his career he had deplored drink and denounced drunken habit with passion and eloquence. If his custom of eating too much sugar was likened to the drinking excesses of his companions (me), his resentment was swift. Sugar, he declared, did not ruin innocent persons or bring family life down in despair. "Drink the Demon" was responsible for all such tragedies.

Now in his house at Mickleham to gave whisky and champagne to his guests and offered them cigars and cigarettes. The champagne was good—from my wine merchant.

Bennett was occasionally persuaded to take a glass of crème de menthe after meals, declaring that it was a "soft drink". He added sherry to his soup, saying that the heat of the soup burned up the alcohol. Cider from the West Country was to him a temperance drink and he liked it. When pressed to join in a glass of champagne, which would have been good for him in his old age, he said he had never taken alcoholic beverages "on principle" and he would "uphold that principle for life".

Lord Beaverbrook, *Friends*, 1959

Bennett's Constituents

Bennett's attacks on drink aroused some opposition in his constituency and he was damaged by a story that he had been asked in the East: "What is the West thinking?" and had replied: "The West is not thinking, the West is drinking."

Lord Beaverbook, *Friends*, 1959

Bennett Exiled

In 1938 Bennett moved to England. He was later appointed to the House of Lords and remained in the United Kingdom until his death in 1947.

The train left for Toronto very early. It was snowing. I had said goodbye to Bennett the night before; I felt very badly about his leaving. I happened to wake up early and I didn't want to think he might be leaving with no one there, so I went down to the station. Bennett just came down from the shadows and shook hands with us, didn't stay to talk. He felt he was being driven out of his native land. It wasn't the case, of course.

T.C. Douglas, quoted in Doris French Shackleton,
Tommy Douglas, 1975

"More Beer!"

The long and weary war worried him desperately. Want of transportation isolated him from friends and visitors. He spent many lonely hours in the great house he had prepared with such meticulous care. His dream of important week-end events was over. And he took little part in social occasions.

Nor did the end of the war bring relief although there was an evening when high spirits were recaptured. He was persuaded to appear at a dinner of the New Brunswick Regiment in London, when the troops were on their way home. His reception was enthusiastic and possibly on that account he made a thrilling speech, which gripped his audience.

Monsignor Hickey, the gentle priest from Newcastle, New Brunswick, pleased the company by singing 'Molly Malone'. The applause was tumultuous. Bennett, delighted and excited, asked: "What will you have next?" With a mighty roar the boys replied: "More beer!" Bennett, the teetotaler, amidst ever louder shouts of approval, called out to the waiters: "More beer!"

Lord Beaverbrook, *Friends*, 1959

Bennett the Recluse

In the New Year of 1947 he [Bennett] closed the Juniper Hill house and set out for the Fortfield Hotel in Sidmouth. Mr. Epps, his devoted butler, went with him, acting as a servant, secretary and companion.

Bennett attended the Methodist Church there and Epps went with him. This return to his early allegiance was the close of his long religious habit. His interest and pleasure in church never faltered. It was more than a habit or a duty; it was exaltation.

His health improved as the measure of his medicine was reduced, and he did not return to Juniper Hill until April.

He believed that his stay at the seaside had restored his health, saying: "Everybody at Sidmouth walked with two sticks — I now walk with one."

In spite of Sidmouth, his condition rapidly deteriorated; invitations were refused or neglected; letters went unanswered. He was continually feeling his own pulse, counting the heart beats.

His country house became a refuge, where he dwelt almost alone. He was behaving like a recluse.

The last year, though friends rallied to him, did not bring relief. His loneliness became more and more apparent.

Lord Beaverbrook, *Friends*, 1959

Bennett's Death

He dined alone in his large and spacious dining-room. Then he sat in his library, looking through the open window into the gathering darkness. As usual, at bedtime, half-past ten, he was carried by elevator to the next floor, Mr. Epps in attendance. In his room he took off his coat, then detached from the button-hole of his vest the heavy, ornamental gold chain with seal. The watch carried a mechanism which he touched off, releasing chimes giving forth the hour and all the minutes, one by one.

He placed on the 'Disraeli table' the watch, chain and money from his pocket. He signalled to the dog Bill to take up a place on his bed— as usual.

Bennett said he would not take a bath that night. He was tired. Epps therefore left the room, saying, "Good-night, my Lord," closing the door gently just as Bennett was turning to the Bible to read one chapter, as he always did.

Early in the morning of 27th June Epps called me by telephone, asking me to come at once to Juniper Hill. I expected trouble, but not the tragedy that was unfolded.

Bennett was dead. When Epps went to call his master at 7:30 in the morning he drew back the curtains to discover that the bed had not been slept in. At the foot of the empty bed, Bill, the short-haired terrier, was sleeping. Epps found Bennett in the bath-tub. The bathwater was running over. He may have fallen asleep in his bath, when death came to him.

Lord Beaverbrook, *Friends*, 1959

Sir George Perley

Sir George Halsey Perley (1857-1938) headed the Canadian delegation to the 1932 World Conference on Disarmament held at Geneva.

The head of our delegation, Sir George Perley, was an elderly veteran of the Conservative high command, having been High Commissioner in London during the First World War. He was a very serious, almost a dour, man and knew less about international affairs than about domestic politics or business. He was as insistent on an ordered routine as he was rigid in his views, by no means an extrovert, but conscientious and persistent in his work. Every morning after breakfast, I read to Sir George an impromptu translation of the editorial in the day's Journal de Genève, the Bible of the conference. Every evening at 8 PM, if there were no official engagements, I was also conscripted to make a fourth at bridge, which I do not enjoy. Precisely at 10 PM, regardless of score or anything else, the bridge ended and we were dismissed. Lady Perley was the exact opposite of Sir George in temperament; warm, sociable, bubbling over with good will and good humour. She was a great asset in maintaining Canadian morale and we were sad when she went off to Aix-la-Chapelle—as she often did—to take the waters.

Sir George was a man who liked his instructions to be carried out quickly and without question. I knew this, so I was the more disturbed one afternoon by an unusual order from him. We were sitting together at a plenary session listening to a speech. Sir George turned to me and asked if I knew the name of the League official sitting on the dais next to the Chairman. I did. It was Aghnides, head of the disarmament section of the Secretariat. "Has he lived in Geneva long and do you think he knows the place?" asked Sir George. I told him that he had been with the League from the beginning and undoubtedly knew Geneva perfectly. My curiosity about Sir George's interest in Aghnides was then satisfied. "I am having trouble with my teeth,'" explained my querulous chief, "so go up and ask him if he can give you the name of a good dentist." I was rather startled by this. The assembly was very quiet, hanging on the words of what seemed at the time a very important speech. I would have to walk up the aisle, make my way to the platform, walk across it (by now the centre of attention), and ask a surprised Mr. Aghnides for the name of a dentist. It seemed an unusual way, in the circumstances, to interrupt the attention being given to a speech on world disarmament. But an order was an order, especially from Sir George.

As it happened, I knew a way around the side of the hall to the platform. On the way, I met, fortunately, a Canadian friend who was on the Secretariat. From him I got the name and address of an excellent dentist. That was not enough, however. I had to be seen by Sir George getting that address from the man he had chosen for the purpose. So I moved up to and across the platform, in full view and with some embarrassment, and quietly asked Aghnides a perfectly normal question about the number of speakers on the list as the Canadian delegate might wish to speak. Sir George watched me, no doubt with interest, and was fully satisfied with the name and address of the dentist I gave him when I rejoined the delegation.

Lester B. Pearson, *Mike: Memoirs of Lester B. Pearson,*
Volume I, 1972

King and Massey

As President of the National Liberal Federation, Charles Vincent Massey (1887-1967), later Governor General of Canada from 1952 to 1959, came into frequent contact with Mackenzie King during the 1935 general election campaign.

The pressure on King to be more definite had no effect on his strategy but on one occasion he did show some signs of strain. He expected conflicting advice from Liberal candidates and always tried to be conciliatory. He was less tolerant of Vincent Massey, President of the National Liberal Federation, who was still arguing for a more dynamic approach. Massey was in a vulnerable position because his ambition was to become Canadian High Commissioner in London, an appointment which only a Prime Minister could make, and King took advantage of the situation to give vent to his resentment. When Massey came aboard King's private car in Toronto to suggest the line to take for the last week of the campaign, King lashed out:

> When he began telling me what to do etc. I let out at him very hard. Told him he had caused me more pain & concern than anyone or all else in the party besides, that I had never had my privacy invaded as he had, for years... it was always Rex must do this etc. also his talk about helping me & "the cause" was all nonsense, it was himself & London that alone kept him to the party, that I had to tell him, it was only in this way he could hope to get appointed.... It was a scathing review of his selfish actions including telling him frankly he had been quite wrong in his views on most things. He was quite crushed—perhaps I went too far but it was the "last straw." I told him when he was 60 he would come to see I was right—that I thought I knew something about political leadership or would not be where I have been for so long a time.

It was a humiliating experience for Massey, all the more so because Nicol, King's valet, was present during the tirade. King could be charming and conciliatory but he could be very unpleasant with people who relied on his favours.

H. Blair Neatby, *MacKenzie King: Prism of Unity*, 1976

CCF HQ

David Lewis (1909-1981) first ran for Parliament in 1940 and was defeated four times before finally winning a seat in 1962. He lost his seat in 1963 but regained it in 1965. He became Leader of the New Democratic Party in 1971 but retired from politics in 1975 when he lost his seat for the last time.

My term as an officer began on August 6, 1936, when, after the convention had elected me to the National Council, the Council elected me national secretary. The fact that I was to perform important duties while also working with a law firm did not worry me at the time, since I had already been doing it for many months, but I was much concerned about the fact that there was no national office. I knew that Russell Smart, my employer, owned some properties on Wellington Street, opposite the Parliament Buildings, and I also knew that he tended to be friendly toward the CCF and approved of my involvement, so long as it did not diminish my productivity with the firm. I was, of course, careful not to give reason for complaint and enjoyed a happy relationship with my seniors. None the less, it was with considerable trepidation that I knocked on the door of Mr. Smart's office a few days after my return from Toronto, to ask him to donate office space to the CCF. He was, as always, courteous and offered me a lean-to behind one of his buildings. Some of the M.P.s, Sophie, and I happily inspected the premises and were pleased to accept the space—for space, mostly open, was all we really had—but since the day was clear and warm, anything would have looked fine. All that mattered was that the CCF had a national office and an imposing address: 124 Wellington Street, Ottawa.

The lean-to was just that and nothing more. It had been used as a store-room for a restaurant some years earlier. There was no floor, only sand underfoot. The entrance was a battered door through which the winds blew unimpeded until we stuffed weather-stripping round the door-frame. A small window, also open to the winds, looked out on an unpaved parking-lot through which we had to walk in mud on rainy days and on icy patches in the winter. The ceiling was low, the walls were unpainted, and the washroom was inside the building, some distance away. On the whole, the place looked rather uninviting, but this did not deter us at all. What mattered was that we did not have to pay rent and there was ample space in what could be called two rooms, if one were not worried by verbal inexactitude.

When we had cleaned up the lean-to and made it habitable, we had to find the necessary furniture and equipment. This sent me on frequent scrounging expeditions. Fortunately, I had addressed numerous organizations in Ottawa during my first year in the city and had thus met many people. Shamelessly I exploited any little goodwill I had gained with my post-prandial oratory and eventually found here a usable desk and a couple of chairs, elsewhere a filing cabinet, a typewriter, and a desk lamp. To my surprise, someone offered us a couch which was useful as well as decorative. When winter approached we realized that there was no heat in the place and I set out again, this time to find a Quebec heater or stove. I found one which was adequate to warm the office comfortably and which we also used to make tea and sometimes to cook a simple meal. I remember saying proudly to a group in the office that the only thing standing there for which we had paid was the telephone. I can't remember who our benefactors were, except that they were all small-businessmen who were intrigued by the idea of helping to set up a national centre for a new party. For at least two years we worked in the lean-to with the obsolete equipment donated to us. Naturally, the opening of the first national office was announced proudly in the CCF papers. In view of the nature of the office space, the report in the Ontario New Commonwealth for October 10, 1936, still makes me blush. "The headquarters occupy ground floor rooms and are situated immediately in front of the main entrance of the Parliament Buildings.... There are two large rooms, one large enough for fair-sized meetings." All true as far as the mere words were concerned, but the total impression given by the words was much more uplifting than accurate. However, the mere fact that the party had a national headquarters was important, and under the circumstances, perhaps a little gloss was forgivable.

David Lewis, *Good Fight*, 1981

Voters in Cartier

David Lewis ran unsuccessfully in the Montreal constituency of Cartier in 1943.

The riding of Cartier's reputation for dishonesty in elections was demonstrated once again by the first set of voters' lists. As soon as we obtained them, workers were sent out to check small sections picked at random for about fifteen polls. We had suspected that the lists would be padded, but the extent astounded us: of a total of about 2,000 names checked, 650 were found to be false.

Some of the discrepancies which we found on the voters' lists were unbelievable to innocent CCF canvassers in 1943. Today they seem amusing as well. The following is a list of some as I set them out in a memorandum:

A baby seven weeks old listed as a bookkeeper. A number of non-existent addresses which would make the voters reside over an intersection. Seven voters listed for a United Cigar Store. Seven voters listed for the store which is now the Liberal Candidate's committee room. Eleven voters listed in a barber shop. Six voters listed at a restaurant. (The waiter at the restaurant laughingly told our canvasser that the enumerator took the names of the people sitting at the counter). There were names of people who are dead, people who had moved away a year or more before, fictitious names, fictitious addresses, and people not citizens. The most common occurrence was the enumeration of all members of a family without regard to age. As I have put it, they inscribed everybody from the cradle to the grave, inclusive.

David Lewis, *Good Fight*, 1981

Jimmy Gardiner

James Garfield Gardiner (1883-1962) was Minister of Agriculture from 1935 to 1957 in the cabinets of King and St. Laurent.

There are those with whom you can remain friends despite political differences. Then there are those who, if you attack them in the cut and thrust of debate, will go around nursing their wounds. Jimmy Gardiner was a fierce debater and a very courageous little man. But like so many persons, he did not like to get it back. I had some real battles with him. He would hardly speak to me unless he absolutely had to.

When I was Premier of Saskatchewan I had occasion to visit France to unveil a monument near Dieppe, where so many men of the South Saskatchewan Regiment were killed. I was about to leave on Sunday evening when someone told me Mr. Gardiner's son was buried about six miles from there. I wanted to visit his grave but it was very hard to get there. The military attaché at the Canadian embassy in Paris, Colonel Alan Chambers, was with me. He arranged for an airplane, some wreaths and a piper. At five o'clock the next morning we flew in, laid the wreaths and put on a bit of a military parade. Sometime later I was in Ottawa for a federal-provincial conference. I went for a haircut and there, sitting next to me, was Jimmy Gardiner. I nodded to him but he looked straight ahead. He finished first and paid his bill. I could see him standing at the door struggling. Finally he turned around and came over. He put out his hand and said, "I want to thank you for what you did for the boy." We eventually came to be quite good friends; but sometimes it takes a long while for the resentment of the debates to break down.

T.C. Douglas, *Canadian Parliamentary Review*, Summer 1981

R.B. Hanson

Richard Burpee Hanson (1879-1948), Minister of Trade and Commerce under Bennett, became Leader of the Opposition in 1938 when Bennett left the country.

On the day when Richard Burpee Hanson was welcomed in the House as Leader of the Opposition, King praised him. Coldwell praised him.

Blackmore praised him. The saccharine matter poured out. Now, Dick Hanson had a tremendous paunch. When he stood up, it served as a guide as to how long he was going to speak. If he just put his hands around his tummy, he was up for ten or fifteen minutes. But if he laid his stomach on his desk, you knew the House was in for a long speech. On the day in question, Hanson was just preparing to lay it on his desk to reply to his well-wishers when up jumped Jean-François Pouliot, the Liberal Member for Témiscouata. Pouliot was the parliamentary wit of his day, and the best that I have ever known. He could be nasty and irresponsible, but he had about him a way of expression and a manner of delivery that captivated the House. We knew when he got up that the impossible was about to be said. And Hanson he did not like. "There he sits, Leader of the Opposition. All he has is the initials [an allusion to R.B. Bennett]. Richard Burpee, R.B., he's got the initials. That's all. Nothing else. Mr. Speaker, the words of the poet come back, 'But O for the touch of a vanish'd hand, and the sound of a voice that is still!' R.B. Every time I look at the honourable gentleman, I think to myself of Ferdinand the bull with a flower in the mouth." Hanson was livid. It was obvious that the Speaker was going to ask Pouliot to withdraw. And Pouliot, without delay, said, "Mr. Speaker, I withdraw the bull, nothing else."

John Diefenbaker, *One Canada: Crusading Years*, 1975

Coldwell's Oratory

Major James William Coldwell (1888-1974) was Parliamentary leader of the CCF from 1940 to 1958.

He dresses well, but not too well, and suggests still a bit of the school teacher in his conservative clothes.

When he rises to speak, those old rehearsals in the classroom, those noisy meetings on the prairie, show they did their work well. Where King mumbles and others fumble, Coldwell's phrases float out clearly, each word neatly clipped off and flung into space in pleasant succession. No machine-gun deliverer of the King's English, Coldwell speaks as if he wanted every syllable to be heard, every sentence to count. You almost get the impression he was dictating to a man who took notes only in longhand, so deliberately do the words come.

Coldwell is not as extemporaneous as he seems. But he can read his manuscript and give the impression that it is all spontaneous. What helps to preserve this illusion, of course, is the fact that when he speaks without notes he is just as good as when he doesn't.

Only slight vestiges of his Devonshire youth linger. These are manifest when he says something like "nun" for noon and "sun" for soon.

The greatest handicap he suffers is his inability to conceal his anger. As soon as his ire is aroused, his face and neck get turkey red. Sometimes he tries to smile to hide it, but the pigments in his physiognomy spell the story.

Austin Cross, People's Mouths, 1943

Woodsworth's School

In the autumn of 1940 the Woodsworths were in Winnipeg to distribute the contents of their family home in preparation for a move to Vancouver. Would Stanley take the old washing machine? And would he take J.S. out to the two-room school that was named for him in the Brooklands area of his riding so that he could donate his dictionary? Knowles did so, speaking for Woodsworth and explaining to the pupils who the frail gentleman standing by the wall was.

A year or so after his election, in 1942, Knowles greeted Coldwell when the latter was passing through Winnipeg, and drove him around the city. He went by the tiny Woodsworth school and told him in minute detail (the way Knowles tells all his stories) of the last occasion he had been there with J.S. Woodsworth for the presentation of the dictionary. Coldwell absorbed it all, more thoroughly than Knowles realized at the time. Two years later Coldwell was once again in Winnipeg and this time accompanied Knowles into the school where the latter was to speak. Before doing so he introduced the leader of his party and asked him to say a few words. He could hardly contain his surprise as Coldwell launched into his remarks: "As I stand here today, I think of the last time I was here. I remember it very well. It was the last public appearance that Mr. Woodsworth made. I remember his coming into this room and standing back there while Mr. Knowles presented the dictionary on his behalf for he wasn't able to say a word."

The younger MP was startled and embarrassed. Here was his leader, a man whom he admired and respected, making up this story! Is that what politicians did after they had been in the game a while? Would he start doing the same thing? Whatever would the audience think? Knowles assumed the pupils might not know the difference—it had been at least three or four years since he was there with Woodsworth—but the principal was the same. He would know that Coldwell was concocting a story. What would he say?

Fortunately Coldwell also began looking a bit puzzled. As they were leaving the school in the company of the principal, Coldwell admitted his perplexity. "Stanley, I'm a bit puzzled about that occasion when Mr. Woodsworth's dictionary was presented. I don't see how I could be there at that time because I was in Europe at the meetings of the Commonwealth Parliamentary Association." Knowles tremendously relieved that he did not have to make Coldwell into a liar, explained that in fact he had not been there. Either Knowles' graphic description or Coldwell's own photographic retention of detail had made him think he had been present. Coldwell roared with laughter and continued to do so whenever Knowles retold the tale.

Susan Mann Trofimenkoff, *Stanley Knowles*, 1982

Coldwell Lost in the Mail

He [M.J. Coldwell] requested that Knowles and Tommy Douglas, the two preachers of the party, conduct his funeral service. The service was in Ottawa to be followed by cremation and the burial of the ashes in a cemetery in Regina. Would Stanley see to the details? It was fortunate that he did so, for there was almost a hitch that upset the Coldwell family but which Knowles is sure Coldwell would have enjoyed. Sometime before his death Coldwell had complained to Knowles about the inordinate length of time mail took to get from the House of Commons to his apartment just a few blocks down Metcalfe Street in Ottawa. Couldn't Stanley say a word about it to the postmaster general? He did so, only to receive the normal post office reply: regrets and the hope that it would not happen again. Apparently it didn't while Coldwell was alive. But then came the time to send his ashes by mail to Regina for burial on 10 September 1974. Ever attentive to detail, Knowles checked with the undertaker in Regina a few days before the scheduled ceremony.

Everything was in order except that there were no ashes. The Post office admitted that the parcel had gone astray but assured Knowles that it would be found and delivered on time. It was, and the family, annoyed but amused, agreed that their father would have enjoyed the story too.

Susan Mann Trofimenkoff, *Stanley Knowles*, 1982

Long-winded Bracken

John Bracken (1883-1969) was leader of the Tory party from 1942 to 1948. He was instrumental in re-naming it the Progressive Conservative party.

Bracken's first mistake was to speak for too long—anywhere up to two hours. What was worse he spent most of the initial time, when people were fresh and alert, outlining his own personal political history and the delights of his tours across Canada. After about forty-five minutes or an hour of this he would rush hurriedly through a few points of his farm platform and that would be that. Alice and Mel Jack were in despair at his stubborn refusal or sheer incapacity to change his tactics. The two resorted to a warning system. When Jack, placed at the back of the hall, detected gathering restlessness in the audience he would wave a handkerchief. Alice would then tug her husband's coat-tail. If he ignored her, as he usually did, she would tug harder and repeatedly. It usually had no effect. All Bracken would do was smile ruefully at his wife afterwards and say, "You almost tore my coat off my back." But at the next stop he would do exactly the same thing. His advisers were frustrated and his audiences departed dissatisfied.

John Kendle, *John Bracken: A Political Biography*, 1979

Speech Therapy

Bracken took instruction in speech and the use of the voice from Charles T. Harrell of the American Broadcasting Company.

Bracken had always been aware of his deficiencies as a speaker and his first session in the House of Commons had underlined them. Not only did he speak for too long and too diffusely but he still had the bad habit of mumbling into his waistcoat or of addressing the government front bench rather than the Speaker, either of which meant that he could not be heard properly in the Press Gallery. The result was a continuously poor coverage for his speeches and actions in the House.

   Bracken spent the second week of February in New York with Harrell receiving instruction in pitch, tone, pace, emphasis, and enunciation. It was a mark of John Bracken's character and his pragmatic approach to problems that he was prepared to accept such instruction. He found it rather a difficult experience but in his tough-minded manner he wrote himself a memorandum outlining his deficiencies: "Big trouble lack of colour—change of pitch, change of pace, more spontaneity, more emphasis, too fast, not enough pauses. Practice a style. Put life and emphasis into it—now too much reading. Too monotonous—practice pitch. Assume the importance you have. Give assumption of Confidence in what I say. Pitch dead. Voice dead. Breathing exercise. Open mouth. More air in lungs. Speak loudly."

   John Kendle, *John Bracken: A Political Biography*, 1979

Tempting Fate

Humphrey Mitchell (1894-1950) was Minister of Labour from 1941 to 1950.

Early in his career Humphrey Mitchell had made it a rule never to allow anything to interfere with his Sundays at home. He did no business over the telephone on that day nor saw anyone on a business matter, but devoted the entire day to his family.

   Thus one Sunday, early in the war, when the telephone in the Mitchell home rang it found the family gathered comfortably around the fireplace. Mr. Mitchell's young son answered the telephone.

   "There is a Mr. King on the telephone and he wants to talk with you, Daddy," reported the lad.

   "King? King?" mused Mitchell to himself, "Whom do I know by that name who would be calling me on Sunday?"

   When he went to the telephone he was surprised to find it was the Prime Minister. Mr. King said he would like to see him down at Laurier House that very afternoon.

   "I'm sorry," said Mitchell, probably more through force of habit than anything else, "but I never go out on Sunday, Mr. King."

"Well," said King, after a slight pause, "will you drop around to Laurier House tomorrow at nine?"

Mitchell "dropped around" the next morning and that night was Canada's new Minister of Labour.

H. Reginald Hardy, *Mackenzie King of Canada*, 1949

Arthur Beauchesne

Arthur Beauchesne (1876-1959) was Clerk of the House of Commons from 1925 to 1948.

Arthur Beauchesne was at the height of his career when I came to Ottawa. He ruled the House administration like an absolute monarch but he always encouraged members to come to see him if we had difficulty understanding the rules or if we wished to draft a motion. He had that marvelous ability to look down two roads at the same time. He could quote you chapter and verse from his own book or from Bourinot to prove that your motion was in order. Yet somehow he always managed to find other sections that proved you were not in order if the government did not want the measure to proceed.

T.C. Douglas, *Canadian Parliamentary Review*, Summer 1981

Norman McLarty

Norman Alexander McLarty (1889-1945) was the Member for Essex West from 1935 to 1945. He served in a number of portfolios in the King cabinet from 1939 to 1945.

Norman McLarty not only enjoyed socializing with the Windsor magnates but also loved the social life in Ottawa. I remember one afternoon he turned to me on the backbenches and commented on what a "delightful place" the national capital was, asking me why I made the long trip home every weekend. Some weeks later — on a quiet Thursday afternoon in the House — I saw Norman sitting at his place, probably thinking of his weekend social engagements. I called a page boy over and gave him a dollar to tell Norman that Lady Tweedsmuir wished to speak to him on the telephone. Naturally, when he got there the line was dead. A few minutes later, I asked my secretary to call McLarty, pretending that she was a member of the staff at Government House, and invite him to tea on Saturday. He returned with his "invitation," sat down beside me and said, "Paul, are you going home this weekend? You should stay here and sample Ottawa's social life. For instance, I'm going over to see Lady Tweedsmuir on Saturday." "Gosh, isn't that nice," I remarked, chuckling to myself.

I fully intended to "disinvite" Norman before I left for Windsor, but it went clean out of my mind. At mass the following Sunday, as I was contemplating "mes pèchés mortelles," I remembered my practical joke, but there was nothing to do. As soon as I returned to Ottawa, I went to see McLarty. "Well, Norm, did you have a busy weekend?" "Oh yes, Paul, I had a wonderful time at Government House. Lady Tweedsmuir was so gracious."

Stumped, I left his office, and for a couple of days could not figure out what had happened. After a few discreet inquiries, I found out that Lady Tweedsmuir had been holding a tea party for the Imperial Order of the Daughters of the Empire, when in walked Norman. Not knowing what to do with this misplaced member of parliament, the governor general's wife and her staff said nothing and served tea for him — the only thorn among the roses.

Paul Martin, A Very Public Life, I, 1983

Ilsley's Independence

James Lorimer Ilsley (1894-1967) served in Mackenzie King's Cabinet from 1935-1948, the last two years as Minister of Justice.

It has always intrigued me to think that the minister of justice, J.L. Ilsley, might well have become prime minister if his health had been better and if he had shown more understanding of French Canada. St. Laurent, I am sure, would not have run against him. Ilsley spoke his mind firmly and certainly had the strength of character necessary for a prime minister. This independence sometimes provoked Mackenzie King to a cold fury. In December 1947, the prime minister had returned from Princess Elizabeth's wedding in London to find that Canada had agreed to serve on a United Nations temporary commission that would observe free elections in Korea and also arrange for the withdrawal of foreign troops from that country. At cabinet on 18 December, Mackenzie King opposed this decision, taken in his absence by St. Laurent and Ilsley. King himself records that Ilsley was "dour, hard as a rock"; he had headed the Canadian delegation at the United Nations that had agreed to serve on the commission. The prime minister threatened to resign. As he had done during the conscription crisis, King said something like, "Well, I'm not going to carry on. You'll have to get another man. I'd like to know if any one of you is prepared to take on these onerous responsibilities; if any one of you is prepared to go through the agony that I go through and have gone through all these years. Mr. St. Laurent?"

"No."

"Mr. Howe?"

"No."

"Mr. Ilsley?"

There was complete silence. King said: "Well, would you, Ilsley?"

"I'm not sure," replied the minister.

Paul Martin, A Very Public Life, II, 1985

C.D. Howe

Clarence Decatur Howe (1886–1960), an engineer by profession, sat in the House from 1935 to 1957. The most powerful member of the wartime Cabinet, Howe became known as "Minister of Everything."

From the West Block in was only a quick stroll to cabinet meetings in the East Block, or to lunch in the parliamentary restaurant or, if Parliament was not in session, across Wellington Street to the Rideau Club. (All his life he refused to have working lunches in his office, or anywhere else.)

Howe enjoyed the club, and its members enjoyed their cheerful new associate. In his terse, utterly frank way, Howe liked to chat; and he loved political gossip: he eventually became one of the better retailers of cabinet secrets. Grant Dexter, the dean of Ottawa newsmen, and a regular inmate of the club, described Howe in 1936 as "good-natured, affable, with a ready sense of humor, but a mind that is razor-edged...."

Howe was good value among the members of the cabinet: more intelligent than most, and more talkative than some, he could always be relied on for an opinion or a story that would enliven the rest of his listener's day until the listener could get home and tell his wife the latest news. Howe never did: his gossiping was something he associated with the man's world at the office. The house and family were Alice's preserve, and the Howes made and kept a tacit agreement never to bring business matters home.

Robert Bothwell and William Kilbourn,
C.D. Howe: A Biography, 1979

Howe Do You Manage

Howe's administrative style was established early. When he had picked the man he wanted to run an enterprise, he delegated near total responsibility to him. He expected him to take the initiative and backed him up with absolute trust and support, unless and until he found his confidence misplaced. "Keep out of here and keep out of trouble," he would say. "But if you're in deep, tell me." If one of his people needed help, he learned to provide Howe with a concise summary of the issues and a clear recommendation. This was done verbally, in a brisk one-to-one meeting, or by a brief memo no more than two pages in length. Howe refused to read long policy papers unless absolutely necessary and he did not take patiently to elaborate discussions of principles and weighings of pros and cons. He particularly disliked and avoided departmental meetings or group consultations.

Robert Bothwell and William Kilbourn,
C.D. Howe: A Biography, 1979

Howe in 1940

C.D. Howe at fifty-four was at the height of his powers. Only his grizzled hair indicated the passage of time; the dark brown eyes still penetrated, and the abrupt bark still dominated any room he entered. The war made no difference to Howe's routines. Except on his House of Commons "duty days" his car picked him up at the office door and swept him away to Crescent Road where he presided, genially but obliviously, at the dinner table. After a few hours with a detective novel (the chauffeur was periodically sent out to buy them) Howe disappeared to bed and a full eight hours' sleep. He would, he reasoned, be no use to the war effort if he came to work exhausted. When he walked in the office door the next morning at nine, he was fresh and ready to tackle whatever problems the day might bring.

Robert Bothwell and William Kilbourn,
C.D. Howe: A Biography, 1979

Torpedoed

The Canadian party sailed in the liner Western Prince. On Saturday, December 14th, the ship was torpedoed in the Western Approaches. There was little time to abandon ship, but passengers and crew took to the boats with what Howe described later as "no panic and no milling around." A heavy sea was running, however, and Scott [Hon. Gordon, M.L.C.] lost his life when, after losing his footing, he fell into the sea and was crushed between a life-boat and the ship's side. The captain, second officer and the captain's steward went down with the ship.

Howe's boat was the last to leave the scene, standing off at a short distance as the Prince went down, in the hope of picking up survivors. All but one of six lifeboats were picked up by a rescue ship eight hours later, and it was not until then that Howe learned of Scott's death. The sixth overturned with the loss of several lives.

The Minister, who lost all his clothing and papers, made no reference to the torpedoing on his return to the House of Commons in February. In private conversation he sometimes credits Mrs. Howe with having saved his life by packing a special "torpedo kit" containing heavy trousers, sweaters, a windbreaker and a flask of brandy. He dilates on the seamanship of the men of the Western Prince and their rescuers who behaved "as if they did this sort of thing every day". The captain of the rescue ship gave up his cabin to Howe and nine other survivors. Others were bedded down in every available space on what was actually a grimy collier.

Leslie Roberts, *C.D.: Life and Times of Howe*, 1957

What's a Million?

A heated exchange between John Diefenbaker and C.D.Howe said much about Howe's attitudes and Diefenbaker's tactics.

The exchange arose from a 1945 debate on Howe's war estimates. The estimates debates had a tendency to drag along while the opposition probed for some politically useful weakness in the government's case. The estimates under discussion totalled $1,365 million. When replying to a question about that sum, Howe exclaimed to the House, "I dare say my honourable friend could cut a million dollars... but a million dollars from the War Appropriations Bill would not be a very important matter."

Diefenbaker spoke the next day. His version of Howe's remarks was different: "We may save a million dollars, but what of it?" Howe jumped to his feet. He had said no such thing; Diefenbaker was "a past master of distortion." Diefenbaker was incensed at the slur on his reputation. Howe was guilty of bad manners and must withdraw his remarks. Eventually, after much bellowing back and forth across the floor of the House, Howe retracted his epithet, which was promptly forgotten. But Diefenbaker's was refined and sharpened, until it finally emerged as "What's a million?" — the epitome of Liberal arrogance and condescension toward Parliament.

Robert Bothwell and William Kilbourn,
C.D. Howe: A Biography, 1979

C.D. in Cabinet

In 1949, Howe was presiding a cabinet two weeks after young Hugues Lapointe's appointment as solicitor-general; Lapointe's first recommendation to cabinet was for commutation of the death sentence for a young Sudbury man convicted of murder. A number of ministers, he knew, were strongly for hanging, in this as in almost every case, and they gave their new colleague a rough time. The pro-clemency members contested the matter hotly but it appeared they were losing, and Howe could be counted on to vote against them. After forty-five minutes of argument, Howe got restless and to everyone's surprise abruptly declared "As Mr. King would say 'the consensus of the meeting' is for clemency." Afterwards Howe took Lapointe aside and told him: "I wasn't going to see you lose your first case in cabinet," and then added "but you had better get up a better case next time."

Robert Bothwell and William Kilbourn,
C.D. Howe: A Biography, 1979

Ever the Engineer

One of the things that disturbed Pearson most was Howe's penchant for tearing down old buildings. With Howe's support, Public Works Minister Robert Winters proposed to tear down the magnificent but inefficient old West Block on Parliament Hill; it was all Pearson and his allies in cabinet could do to get the Prime Minister to overrule them. Similarly, when the Parliamentary Library was badly gutted by fire, Howe thought it should not be restored but rather replaced by a sleek new building on cheaper vacant land; books requested by members could be moved into the Parliament Buildings via tunnel and a conveyer belt. With respect to architecture and the arts Howe was a complete philistine, but he could be readily persuaded to support specific cultural policies by the right person and a well-put case. During a Rideau Hall state dinner, the voluble and charming Père Georges-Henri Lévesque of Laval was seated next to Howe by Governor General Massey, after Massey learned that Howe and St. Laurent were hesitant about backing the proposed $100 million endowment for a national arts council. Before the evening was over Howe was favourably impressed, and not long afterwards the Canada Council Act was put before Parliament. As for setting high standards in design, Donald Buchanan of the National Gallery got to Howe through his father the Liberal senator, and thereafter Howe was a firm supporter of the Gallery committee which eventually became the National Design Council.

Robert Bothwell and William Kilbourn,
C.D. Howe: A Biography, 1979

Howe Talkative

Early in 1958 I needed Mr. Howe's help with a business history I was writing. His friend and fellow engineer, Hugh Hilton of the Steel Company of Canada, spoke to him for me and I was promptly instructed to be at the Rideau Club in Ottawa at noon the next day. Standing alone waiting, he looked unspeakably old and haggard. In repose, the bronzed wrinkled reptilian skin, the heavy sepia patches under the eyes, gave him the mask of a sort of living monument. Animated suddenly, with a flash of the dark glittering eyes and a broad smile, his face shed fifty years. The flat Boston accent rang out: "How ah yuh!"

After the cordial little procession of old comrades to his table had subsided, Mr. Howe wrote out our "dinner" order in a sort of phonetic shorthand and proceeded to make short work of my prepared questions. He then turned to the topic of the day which was the Liberal leadership contest between Lester B. Pearson and Paul Martin. After various blunt personal remarks on that subject, he began gossiping about other things he probably shouldn't have, not at least to an inquisitive young stranger. To my astonishment we were quickly into 1957 cabinet debates or anything else I had the wit to ask about. His Privy Councillor's oath of secrecy, as I was to discover much later from others, never did extend to the premises of the Rideau Club. As we were about to leave, he told me there were several mountains of his papers out in Tunney's Pasture which I might like to look through some time, in fact some of his friends were after him to have them used for a book and would I be interested in doing that sort of thing? As I was already otherwise occupied, I did not pursue the matter.

William Kilbourn, quoted in Robert Bothwell and William Kilbourn,
C.D. Howe: A Biography, 1979

Mrs. Fisher

Election day in Port Arthur was cloudy and by the evening a light rain was falling. At 7:30, half an hour after the polls closed, it was obvious that Fisher had carried the city. Only an overwhelming surge for Howe in the outlying townships would save the day. Howe waited with a few faithful workers until the results came in from Terrace Bay and Nipigon. Howe had carried both polls, but by a slim margin. The other polls could not make up the difference and Fisher stood to win the seat by at least a thousand votes. Howe swore for five minutes, in a style that would have commended him to his lumberjack constituents. He then turned around and kicked a pile of beer cases, which had been set aside for the victory celebration. Then he turned around to his appalled supporters.

"Okay, where do we go to concede?" No one seemed to know. It was decided to drive to the local television station.

There once again Howe found his young nemesis waiting for him, this time in the company of his wife and his mother. The elder Mrs. Fisher was distressed. She herself had always voted for C.D. Howe, up until this election, and she was crushed to see her hero defeated, even though she was happy about her son's victory. "Oh, Mr. Howe," she mourned, "what will you do now?"

"Why, Mrs. Fisher," said Howe, comforting her, "there are so many things to do! The only thing that worries me is that I might not be around long enough to do them." He shook Fisher by the hand, and walked onto the set to make his concession.

Robert Bothwell and William Kilbourn, *C.D. Howe: A Biography*, 1979

Louis St. Laurent Takes Over

Louis St. Laurent (1882–1973) was Prime Minister from 1948 to 1957.

Postmaster General Ernest Bertrand marked the occasion by presenting the new Prime Minister with a cane that had once belonged to Sir Wilfrid Laurier; it was a symbolic gesture, for the Liberals were hoping for a second period of national unity and rapid economic development. Seated at the head of the table, St. Laurent drew out his silver cigarette case, fitted a cigarette into his holder, and lit it. Other ministers followed suit. That, too, was a symbolic move: under Mackenzie King, smoking had been forbidden in the Council Chamber. It was truly the end of an era.

The cabinet meeting was a short one. Louis St. Laurent announced the appointment of Walter Harris as parliamentary assistant to the Prime Minister, and obtained approval of a more extensive housing program, to be directed by Winters. Then he crossed the corridor of the East Block to his new second-floor office, with its Gothic windows opening onto the lawns in front of the Parliament Buildings, and the massive fireplace recalling the days when Sir John A. Macdonald and other predecessors had occupied the room. He sat at the huge desk for a long time, working his way through the documents before him and planning the days ahead. When at last he put on his hat and coat, picked up his well-filled brief-case, and made his way towards the stairway he found to his surprise that the elevator operator was still on duty. He asked the man why he had not gone home at the same time as the other members of the staff. Strict instructions had been given not to leave until the Prime Minister had been taken down to the main floor, he was told. St. Laurent shrugged his shoulders. "In the future, you go home with the others" he said; a prime minister could walk down a flight of stairs just the same as everyone else.

Dale C. Thomson, *Louis St. Laurent: Canadian*, 1967

King and St. Laurent

The organization of the Prime Minister's Office in the East Block was not changed after St Laurent became Prime Minister, but there was a great contrast between the working habits of the two Prime Ministers. Except on days when the Cabinet was meeting or Parliament was sitting, Mackenzie King usually worked at Laurier House or Kingsmere where he had a personal staff presided over by Edouard Handy. His hours of work were irregular and he did not hesitate to call his secretaries at any time. Unless there was an emergency, he did not like to be disturbed, and it sometimes took days or even weeks to get answers to questions his secretaries, or even ministers, considered urgent. It often took longer to arrange interviews.

St Laurent, on the other hand, came to the Office on every working day when he was in Ottawa, usually early in the morning, quite often before I did. He liked to leave his desk clear every night, though he often took official papers home to read in the evenings. He was always approachable and many matters which would have had to be cleared in writing with Mackenzie King could be disposed of orally with St Laurent in short order. This practice enabled him to deal with far more business every day than Mackenzie King did, but it had the disadvantage that often no record was kept of minor decisions.

While King liked to delay decisions until he had reflected on all their repercussions, St Laurent, especially in his early months as Prime Minister, usually made decisions immediately, and sometimes failed to foresee some of their implications.

Another difference between them was in their accessibility to Ministers and important visitors. Even Ministers often had difficulty seeing Mackenzie King. In St Laurent's early months as Prime Minister, the problem was to persuade him not to see everyone who asked for an interview, and he remained accessible to the end of his career.

There was a marked contrast in their attitude to publicity. Mackenzie King qualified almost every public statement he made to cover foreseen or even unforseen situations, and he instinctively avoided answering hypothetical questions. St Laurent, even after seven years in public life, usually made simple and unequivocal statements and too often replied frankly to hypothetical questions. Sometimes these answers proved politically embarrassing. On the other hand, his directness and frankness were attractive to the public, possibly because he did not conform to the conventional image of a politician.

Helping Mackenzie King to prepare a written speech was a tedious process of revisions, often continuing up to the moment the speech was delivered. He gave no thought to the preparation of a French version and a translation was rarely ready in time. For St Laurent, the French and English versions were equally important. The theme of his speech was usually settled orally and a draft was then prepared by one of the secretaries, generally me. St Laurent then read the draft by himself. Occasionally he rejected it entirely, indicating a different line he would like to take, and a new draft had to be prepared; but usually he made few changes. For the first month or two he occasionally told me my drafts sounded too much like Mackenzie King, but it did not take me long to change to his conversational style.

St Laurent insisted that he should say the same thing in both languages, but he did not want either English or French to be a literal translation of the other. To achieve this result, simplicity and clarity were essential in both languages.

The most exhausting feature of working for Mackenzie King was the difficulty his staff had in getting precise directions as to what was expected of them. We had to be prepared for unpredictable changes of intent and timing. In working for St Laurent, the most refreshing change was that his directions to the staff were clear and final and there was never any need for confirmation. As a result, for a time after he became Prime Minister I did not feel fully employed!

J.W. Pickersgill, *My Years with St Laurent*, 1975

Life in Ottawa

Jeanne St. Laurent was determined not to close the house on Grande Allée, even if it meant supervising two households. "My home," she told a newspaperman firmly, "is here in Quebec." In order to help her pass the time in the capital, friends furnished a basement room in the prime minister's residence as a card room, and a small sitting-room that formed part of the prime minister's suite in the Centre Block continued to be reserved for her as well. The only change in St. Laurent's life as a result of the move was that he had to be driven to and from work by a chauffeur instead of walking the short distance from his apartment building; his work schedule remained the same.

Dale C. Thomson, Louis St. Laurent: Canadian, 1967

St. Laurent in Cabinet

St. Laurent presided magisterially over the cabinet, and displayed an extraordinary capacity to master his brief. He usually knew each submission as well as the minister who was proposing it, but sometimes tended to show his hand too quickly. He loved the work of cabinet, particularly the intellectual exercise of meticulously arranging the details of a problem. Although he treated his ministers courteously and would never knowingly embarrass them, he would often anticipate their arguments and present them himself. There were rare times when he got fidgety with C.D. Howe, who wanted competence or silence. Louis St. Laurent was really not the "chairman of the board," as many have branded him. Rather, he was the "president" of the company.

The new prime minister was much more relaxed than his predecessor. King never allowed smoking in the cabinet room, but St. Laurent occasionally would puff on a cigarette. Unlike King, he would join his ministers for lunch at a common table in one of the alcoves of the parliamentary restaurant, to chat leisurely about our morning meeting. Sometimes he used to walk down from Parliament Hill to have a 10-cent plate of beans at Bowles lunch counter.

Paul Martin, A Very Public Life, II, 1985

"Wiggles"

Dressed in a bright sports shirt, pork-pie summer hat, and grey flannel trousers, St. Laurent spent many hours of the month of August on the St. Patrick golf course. Unlike President Eisenhower, he did not take the game seriously, keeping no score, moving the ball out of the rough for a more convenient shot, using any club that was at hand, and displaying an amateurish style that won him the somewhat disrespectful but affectionate nickname among the caddies of "Wiggles."

Dale C. Thomson, *Louis St. Laurent: Canadian*, 1967

The St. Laurent Routine

St. Laurent maintained his regular pace throughout the closing months of 1954. Rising shortly after 7 a.m., he read the *Montreal Gazette* while eating a hearty breakfast, then stepped in the front seat of his Chrysler limousine beside his chauffeur, Gordon McCartney, to be driven to Parliament Hill. By the time he arrived there, his confidential messenger, seventy-year-old Aldéric Groslouis, had aired and dusted his office, and Pierre Asselin had placed the morning mail on his desk; a staff of forty persons was busy answering routine correspondence, preparing material for statements and speeches, clipping items from two dozen newspapers for his attention, and preparing memoranda on a wide variety of topics. At one o'clock he returned to the official residence for a quiet lunch; from two-thirty to six o'clock he was back in the East Block. About two evenings a week he attended a reception on the way home, usually at the residence of some foreign diplomat observing his country's national anniversary or some similar occasion. His routine on such occasions was always the same; he arrived promptly, took one drink and smoked one cigarette, circulated among the guests until he had greeted everyone, then left in time to watch the 6.45 p.m. news on television at home. His evenings were spent in a small study on the second floor of the Prime Minister's residence, reading the documents he had brought home from the office, or playing cards with his wife. At eleven o'clock he watched the news again, and then went to bed.

Dale C. Thomson, *Louis St. Laurent: Canadian*, 1967

Uncle Louis at the Wheel

When Louis St. Laurent took the wheel himself, he started off invariably with a tremendous jerk, alarming all his passengers, and seemed so frozen to his seat that he could not adjust the speed or avoid objects in his path. Whenever the children became noisy, he would stop the car, turn around, and give them a lecture on the importance of remaining absolutely quiet so that he could concentrate on driving. The nerves of even the youngest became frayed, and they were all relieved when the outing was over. In Quebec City, he drove to work for a time, but proved something of a threat to other motorists and pedestrians. On one occasion, he struck a streetcar as he was pulling out of his driveway; another time, he gave himself a bad scare by narrowly missing a cyclist. Other members of the family urged him to leave the car at home or to let someone else drive. Finally, he hired a chauffeur, who doubled as handyman, but he persisted in trying to master the art of driving for several years, knocking down gate-posts and scraping fenders in the process.

Dale C. Thomson, *Louis St. Laurent: Canadian*, 1967

St. Laurent and Eisenhower

Eisenhower was spending a few days at a golf course near Atlanta, Georgia; it was arranged that St. Laurent should call there on his return journey to Canada so that he and the President could play a round together, and have a chat about matters of common interest.

The game was pleasant as well as fruitful. St. Laurent was paired with the local golf pro, while Eisenhower played with Madeleine O'Donnell, who had been holidaying with her father in Florida. If the Canadian Prime Minister was no match for the President as a sportsman, he could hold his own as they rode from tee to tee on a two-seater battery-powered golf cart. He commented later with amusement:

I found ...that a game of golf with one of those electric go-carts was about the best way to have an international conference, because you are getting off the go-cart quite frequently for only a couple of minutes but for time enough to reflect on what has been said up to that moment and... what is going to be said when you get back on....

Dale C. Thomson, *Louis St. Laurent: Canadian*, 1967

St. Laurent and Drew

St. Laurent liked George Drew. Occasionally after Sunday mass he would drop in at Stornoway for late breakfast. Part French, part Irish, something in St. Laurent responded to the fighter in Drew. I am sure St. Laurent would not have been greatly disturbed if George Drew had been Prime Minister of Canada.

When Drew became ill in the months following the Pipeline Debate, St. Laurent said to me, "I want to do something for George. If he should have to give up on account of his health, I want to name him High Commissioner to London." The offer was sincere and well meant, with no ulterior motive but to set Drew's mind at ease. At that moment Drew was a very ill man, far more so than he realized or would admit. At one point when Drew's health took a turn for the worse, St. Laurent called him personally and said, "George, I want you to work hard at your recovery. I would like very much to send you on an important assignment to London". Such was the breadth of St. Laurent's innate decency and honour.

Grattan O'Leary, *Recollections of People, Press, and Politics*, 1977

St. Laurent in Defeat

He sat with his grey head bowed forward, his heavy glasses standing out against his pale face. When occasion required it, he would rise slowly to his feet, make a brief statement and slump back into his seat. When the daily routine was over, he got up and left quietly, with only a polite nod to those nearby. Walking slowly to his office, he hardly noticed the respectful salutes from the protective staff and the whispered recognition of visitors. His world had fallen apart.

Gordon Aiken, *Backbencher*, 1974

The Resignation

Mr. St Laurent was in a low, depressed condition, without vigour or strength, and obviously quite unequal to the demands of leadership. His family had been trying hard to convince him that he should announce at once that he would not contest another election. St Laurent agreed with his family that he was unfit to carry on but was possessed with the idea that people would think he was running away from his duty after a defeat, that he could not take it. He knew that he had lost his energy and his interest in politics, and especially his skill in public relations, as certain recent contacts with the press had shown. But he could not take it. But he could not seem to make up his mind to take the final step and announce his withdrawal.

Renault was most anxious that we should tell his father that public opinion, far from criticizing, would fully understand and approve a decision to resign before, during, or immediately after the autumn session, the decision to be announced now. His father had seemed anxious, however, to get confirmation of the wisdom of this course from Chevrier and me, and for this reason they had sent for us with his full approval. They were all most grateful we had come. We realized, from what we had heard, that our visit was not going to be easy.

At five o'clock, in heavy rain, we reached the very pleasant guest house where we were to stay, opposite the St Laurent home, a lovely old white brick place with beautiful gardens sloping down to the river. At six we walked across, had a drink and then dinner. Madame St Laurent, very domestic and cordial, and Miss Lora, his sister, were also there. His sister impressed me as a very nice, sensible, and calm person who, I gathered, had been a strong influence for good while she was there. Mr. St Laurent was, I thought, in shocking condition, dejected, and looking much older.

After dinner, a very good meal, with talk mostly in French, we five men got together for the business of the evening. Mr. St Laurent made it easier by announcing at once that he agreed he was no longer physically fit to retain the leadership. But he had three worries. Would he be considered as letting the party down if he dropped out now? Should he not go to Ottawa, see his colleagues, and face the music there? How could he reconcile the announcement of his retirement now with the regrettable opposite impression he had given to the press, as recently as two days earlier? It was our task to reassure him on all these points and we made some progress in this, though the going was hard. He made it difficult to carry on the discussion by his lack of responsiveness; he seemed too tired to show much interest, the interest indeed which we knew he actually felt. It was a pathetic situation.

Renault finally suggested that I should try my hand at drafting a statement for the press, announcing the decision not to go through another election but willingness, if health permitted, to continue as leader until a new leader had been chosen. I agreed to try this, though only on the clear understanding that he had already made the decision and merely wanted me to put it into words. Mr. St Laurent seemed very relieved and grateful that I would take on the assignment and have a draft ready for him next morning.

I worked on a text in my room until after midnight. It was not easy to get it right. Next morning before breakfast I showed it to Chevrier, who was very pleased and suggested only one or two minor changes. At ten we met Mr. St Laurent, who looked even older and more tired than the previous night. He stared uneasily at the draft, at times reading, at other times merely brooding, for what must have been some minutes. This reaction seemed to suggest that he did not think much of my work or even of the decision it announced, and I rather expected him to throw it into the wastepaper basket. However, after two or three more readings, he looked up and said it was just right. Then there was more silence until we urged him into a discussion of the timing and manner of release. I had hoped that this could be postponed for a week, so that it would not be associated directly with our visit. Nasty people would say that Chevrier and I had gone to St Patrick and had pushed him into resignation for our own purposes. The others all felt, however, that it would be better to get the document out at once to prevent speculation and leaks; and we agreed to release it Friday evening.

Mr. St Laurent seemed to cheer up after the work had been finished and the decision taken. He thanked me privately, and in a very moving way, for my help. I do not think I have ever felt more sorry for anyone; but I know I would have felt even worse had he decided to try to carry on. To resign was sad, to continue would have been tragic. Madame St Laurent, meanwhile, had been busy in the kitchen showing her cook how to deal with an eleven-pound roast and apple pie. She was very happy. She felt that the danger was over and that her husband was safe. Renault and Mathieu were also pleased at the way everything had gone; indeed, they were much more than pleased.

We did full justice to an enormous meal; then, again through heavy rain, motored back to Quebec. We had tea there with the other members of the family anxious to hear the news. They were all relieved and happy and warmly thanked us for our help. We then got the 6:15 train to Montreal. It seemed only fitting that our journey should keep its depressing character to the end, for our train hit and killed a motorist on a level crossing.

After our return to Ottawa on Friday, 6 September, Mr. St Laurent issued the statement we had drafted:

"After carefully considering medical advice which I have now received, I have decided that I have no longer the energy and stamina required to lead the Party through another general election campaign.

From participation in four elections, I know the physical demands they make on one's strength and physical resources and I am convinced that I could not do full justice to those demands in another campaign.

Health permitting, however, I will be happy to continue to serve as Liberal Party Leader in the forthcoming session of Parliament until my successor has been chosen.

My regret at having to make this decision is equalled by my conviction that it is the right one and that any other would not be fair to the Party through whom I have had the honour—and there can be no greater one—to serve my country for so many years."

Mike: Memoirs of Lester B. Pearson, Volume 3, John A. Munro and
Alex. I. Inglis, eds., 1975

Where's My Hat

Throughout the convention, St. Laurent fulfilled his role with the thoroughness and punctuality that were part of his nature. Only after Pearson was chosen to succeed him did he allow himself to relax. Immediately, the signs of accumulated years of fatigue became evident. A winter rain was falling as he prepared to leave the Coliseum, late in the evening of January 16, to return to the hotel. He was helped into his coat, but his black Homburg had disappeared from the improvised cloakroom. Fretting to be off, he paced up and down, restless and bewildered, while friends and members of the family tried to dissuade him from going out bare-headed into the storm. Suddenly he was a helpless, spent, old man. After a few minutes, the missing hat was discovered and he was able to leave.

Dale C. Thomson, *Louis St. Laurent: Canadian*, 1967

Black Friday

On Friday, June 1, 1956, in the midst of already heated proceedings on the government's pipeline bill, Speaker Beaudoin reversed an important decision he had made the previous day on a question of privilege. The reversal outraged the opposition and led to an explosive scene in the House.

The House of Commons met at eleven o'clock the next morning, and the Speaker read the daily prayer in a tone of suppressed emotion. As soon as the Orders of the Day were called, Drew rose to continue his speech, but Beaudoin himself remained standing, not even giving the clerk, Léon Raymond, the opportunity to announce the resumption of the debate on Cameron's motion. He had read carefully the articles complained of, he stated, and had come to the conclusion that "because of the unprecedented circumstances surrounding this pipeline debate and because of the remarks that were made in the House by members themselves," they should not be considered as breaches of parliamentary privilege; had it not been for some of the "insinuations or attacks directed…to the occupants of the Chair," they might not have been written. In the circumstances, he did not consider that they went beyond "the bounds of fairness," and he ruled Cameron's motion out of order. "Do honourable members wish to appeal?" he asked. In the general consternation as members sought to grasp the new situation, Drew asked somewhat confusedly if the Speaker was "prepared to hear any discussion," since the debate of Cameron's motion had already begun. Beaudoin refused. "It is a matter of privilege," he stated, referring to Cameron's complaint, and ignoring the fact that he had already accepted a motion based upon it. "Whether it is privilege or not, it is my responsibility to decide." Once again, he asked if his ruling was being appealed. The Leader of the Opposition did appeal and the bells began to ring to announce the vote. The cries of protest from the opposition benches were answered with catcalls from the Liberals, despite Harris's attempts to calm them. "Why did you change overnight?" called Diefenbaker,"… Are you afraid today?" "What took place in the dark?" shouted Earl Rowe. Perspiration glistening on his cheeks, Beaudoin teetered on his feet, as if about to collapse. Dr. McCann left his seat on the cabinet benches and went up to him, amid opposition cries of protest; he prescribed a drink of water. Another Liberal member, John

MacDougall, who suffered from a chronic heart condition, offered him some of his pills. St. Laurent sat as if frozen to his chair, looking small and miserable. When the vote was taken, the members divided on the same lines as on so many previous occasions in recent day; the Speaker's ruling was upheld. While the counting was taking place, George Hees declared, "Mr. Speaker, I am voting against the dictatorship which you have imposed on Parliament."

Events continued to move swiftly, Stanley Knowles moved the adjournment of the House; the insults from the opposition benches continued. Beaudoin rose and, speaking slowly, announced the next step in his strategy. "I want to tell honourable members that I know what my responsibilities are," he stated, "and that I am fully conscious of every step that I am taking." "I wonder," interjected one member. He had "thought very seriously" about the happenings of the previous day, the Speaker went on, and he considered that he had "made a very serious mistake" when he had returned to the Chamber to hear the appeal from the chairman's ruling, "in allowing the point of order and the other dilatory motions." Since he felt that "the House should not suffer any prejudice or detriment" on his account, he proposed that it should "revert to the position where it was yesterday when I was brought back to the Chair to receive the chairman's report at five-fifteen." He called for a vote on "the situation which I take at the moment". Once again, cries of protest rose from the opposition benches. "What are you doing, Mr. Speaker?" Coldwell called out in disbelief. Raising his voice above the din, Drew moved that "in view of the unprecedented action of Mr. Speaker in improperly reversing his own decision," the House "no longer has any confidence in its president officer." Beaudoin pointed out that forty-eight hours' notice was required for the motion. Knowles succeeded in getting the floor, and began to argue that his own motion to adjourn the House was in order. The Speaker accepted it, a vote was taken, and it was defeated. With that matter disposed of, the president officer tried again to call a vote on his proposal to revert to the situation existing the previous afternoon, but Knowles and Fulton launched into a procedural discussion, arguing that he could not do so at that state of the proceedings. His strength and determination flagging, Beaudoin retreated and agreed to postpone his proposed action until after the question period. The shredded remnants of control were slipping from his hands.

Nearly an hour later, the unhappy Speaker tried again and, after a further series of exchanges, managed to call a vote. As the bells begin to ring once more, Drew, Coldwell, and other opposition members surged into the central aisle, shouting their protests. To drown their voices, Liberals broke into song, chanting "Hail, Hail the Gang's All Here" and "Onward, Christian Soldiers." "Parliament has ceased to function," proclaimed Coldwell above the din. "Where is the Prime Minister?" asked John Diefenbaker. "Is he silent in the face of this demonstration?" "This is the lowest moment in Canadian parliamentary history," declared Donald Fleming. "This is black Friday, boy," pronounced Thomas Bell. "Hitlerism," added Clayton Hodgson. "You did it; you brought it on yourself," called back Jean Lesage. Liberal backbenchers continued their demonstration with songs they had devised in recent days: "There'll always be a pipeline," and "I've been working on the pipeline"; attempts by Harris to silence them proved fruitless. St. Laurent and Beaudoin sat in their seats, the former flushed and fingering his moustache, the latter pale and perspiring, as chaos reigned about them. It was the low point in both their careers. After what seemed an eternity to observers, the vote was taken at last on the "course of action submitted by Mr. Speaker." The Progressive Conservative and C.C.F. members abstained on the grounds that there was no question properly before the House; the proposal was carried, and a luncheon recess was called.

Dale C. Thomson, Louis St. Laurent: Canadian, 1967

René Beaudoin

Many feared for the health of Speaker Louis-René Beaudoin (1912-1969) on the infamous "Black Friday" of the 1956 pipeline debate.

In the midst of the debate, when tension was very high on all sides, Beaudoin began to perspire and turned very pale, as if he were suffering from a heart attack. Dr. McCann, the Minister of National Revenue at the time, who was a medical doctor, got from me some nitroglycerine pills, wrapped them in a piece of paper and sent them to the Speaker with a note telling him to put them under his tongue. The next day it was widely reported that the government had been sending notes to the Speaker telling him what to do, and that the Speaker was following them. That indicated the tension that had built up in the House, and the state of emotion in which the debate was being held.

George Drew

George Alexander Drew (1894-1973) was Leader of the Opposition from 1948 to 1956.

Drew had a deformed left hand, injured in war, which he habitually concealed, perhaps unconsciously, in the pocket of his suit coat. When he was standing to speak, the damaged hand thrust in his pocket, he gestured only with his right hand, his large, square body erect, shoulders back, the athletic chest and slightly protruding stomach thrust forward, all lending his figure an exaggerated corpulence, giving his physical mannerisms an unnatural stiffness, and creating a general impression of stuffiness.

In repose the muscles twitched in his cheek and occasionally, when he blinked, his eyes would close like a boxer anticipating a blow, almost a flinch. When he was listening, his tongue would play against the cheek inside his mouth, as he measured his pauses, censoring his thoughts. This impression was further confirmed by his manner of speaking, which included a frequent stammer and numerous audible hems and haws.

Dalton Camp, *Gentlemen, Players and Politicians*, 1970

Drew's Resignation

I don't think I've told anyone publicly before, but it was I who typed George Drew's resignation. We met in a bedroom in the Royal York Hotel. There was Grattan O'Leary and Jim Macdonnell and Earl Rowe and Bill Rowe and Fiorenza and myself. Fiorenza had come from the hospital. We were perched on beds and chairs. She sat beside me on one of the beds and she told us what the doctor had said about George.

She said, "I have ruined his life. I have urged him to go on when he shouldn't have gone on." I never saw a woman weep as she did—the tears didn't roll down her cheeks, they spurted from her eyes. They went straight out. I never saw anything like it, it was just like a shower. She was very much upset.

She said, "Now I have the hardest job of all, I have to go back and get him to sign his resignation." Of course we all reassured her, particularly Jim Macdonnell and Grattan O'Leary, of whom she was very fond. They said, "Now how are we going to do this so that no one will know?" And I said, "Well, have you got a typewriter?" Bill said, "No," So I said, "where can we get one?" Bill said, "I know, we can go over to the Albany Club and type it there," I said, "Well, I can type."

So we drafted it as well as we could, the bunch of us in the room. Bill and I hopped into a taxi and ran over to the Albany. I typed it and I made three or four copies for my scrapbook, signed by all the people in that room. Not George's signature because he was too sick at that time to realize what had happened. But he signed his resignation.

I know that one of the things that the doctor had said to Fiorenza was, "Sure he can go back, he can recover and he can go back, but one day you will be sitting in an audience or on the platform and you will see him start to grope for words and he will just disintegrate right before your eyes. Now is that what you want?"

Which is pretty cruel, you know, but I remember Fiorenza saying this. She said, "Oh no, I want George, I don't want him to be prime minister of Canada, I want George for my husband."

Ellen Fairclough, quoted in
Peter Stursberg, *Diefenbaker: Leadership Gained*, 1975

Stanley Knowles

Stanley Howard Knowles (1908-   ) was first elected to Parliament in a 1942 by-election. He was the Member for Winnipeg North Centre from then until 1958 and from 1962 to 1984.

Stanley Knowles scrutinized my every move and fought hard to get improvements in social welfare legislation. Day in and day out, he would go after me in the House. "Why are you doing this?" I asked him privately; "it only gives me a chance to make a smart answer, outlining our achievements, and this delights the Liberal backbenchers." Stanley understood, but said that no progress would take place unless he kept at me. His constant harping used to irritate some members of his own party. During one of the pension debates, while Stanley was speaking, I received a package from one of the House page boys. Opening it, I found a set of teeth that, when wound up, would chatter merrily away. To the great delight of the donor, a CCF member, I set them going on my desk during one of Stanley's homilies.

Paul Martin, *A Very Public Life*, II, 1985

The Speakership

During the summer of 1957, rumour had it that Knowles was to be named Speaker of the House of Commons. The press, noting his mid-summer appearance in town, jumped immediately: "We know what you're here for! When are you getting it?"

He denied it all. He was, he insisted, in town on party business. Moreover, he was not interested in the position and he doubted if Diefenbaker was either, given the late date. The press pointed out that Diefenbaker was still putting his cabinet together: anything could happen. Knowles left them to their speculating and went on about his business.

Later in the day he was walking from the Centre Block of the parliament buildings to the old Union Station (now the Conference Centre) to locate and organize some of his baggage. Passing the East Block which houses the office of the prime minister, he thought of dropping in to congratulate Diefenbaker on his surprising election victory. It was the proper thing to do. He therefore started into the building and up the stairs, only to see a crowd of reporters and television cameras waiting for the prime minister to appear and announce cabinet appointments. Knowles ducked out of the way as quickly as possible; if members of the press spied him here they would think he had been misleading them earlier. He vanished.

Nonetheless, the niceties had to be observed. Later in the day he returned to the East Block. This time there was no press hanging about and none of the security that has since come to surround the prime minister's office. It was therefore easy enough to gain access. Diefenbaker himself was out in the hall and saw Knowles coming. "Glad to see you, Stanley. I've just written you a letter. Come on in." Once in the office the prime minister started to hand him a letter but then glanced at it, muttered something about the secretaries, and sent if off to be re-typed. The words personal and confidential were not to be on the letter; would the secretaries please redo it. Meanwhile Diefenbaker told his visitor the contents of the letter. Just as the press expected, the letter contained a proposal from Diefenbaker that Knowles take the position of Speaker of the forthcoming parliament.

The letter offering the Speakership was being typed in the next office and he had to give some reply. The offer was, he recognized, a great honour. His own fascination and love for parliament centre as much on the workings as on the accomplishments of the institution and those workings only run smoothly under a master's touch; it is the Speaker who has, or should have, that touch. That other people thought he might have the required talent was high praise indeed. Moreover, as he mentioned to the prime minister, rumours about such an offer had already spread and he had given the matter some thought. Now, however, he had the prime minister's letter; he would give it serious consideration and tell Diefenbaker within a week. His answer, he added, might be yes or might be no.

Diefenbaker was shocked. Here he was, the prime minister, handing out plums; indeed, he had been spending weeks at the task, all the while listening to importunate demands for those very plums.

He also enjoyed the look of delight on the face of the chosen recipient. But here was that sombre member from an opposition party being offered the most prestigious plum there was—with a commensurate salary—and blandly remarking that the answer might be yes or might be no. Diefenbaker let his annoyance show. "You'll never get another offer like this." Then it was Knowles' turn to be shocked. He was tempted to give the letter back immediately, so appalled was he by the crudity of the remark.

In the meantime, he put the prime minister's letter, no longer marked personal and confidential, into his pocket and recrossed Parliament Hill to his own office in the Centre Block. On the way he noticed the same reporters who had told him with such certainty earlier in the day why he was in town. What could he say to them now that he had the actual offer in his pocket? And what would they think of him after his remarks that morning? The reporters, however, were already onto the scent of some other rumour and they were no longer interested in him.

Knowles was therefore left to ponder. Eventually, he decided he would say no.

Susan Mann Trofimenkoff, *Stanley Knowles*, 1982

Knowles' Illness

In the election of 1963, he came down with a vestigial illness. Only one person in a hundred still has two appendices; evolution has sloughed the second one off. But Knowles retained his, a Meckel's diverticulum. With a lining similar to that of the stomach, a misbehaving diverticulum displays all the symptoms of stomach ulcers. He therefore bled internally for days without being aware of it. He knew that something was wrong but he could not and would not give in in the midst of a campaign. Eight days before voting day, however, he was increasingly feeble and began curtailing his activities. He called off one meeting, cancelled an out-of-town speaking engagement in Saskatchewan that would have had him on the train in the middle of the night, and planned to spend the next day in bed. In the meantime, he could just manage a drive to the printers to leave some material and perhaps a tea out in Brooklands in the far west end of his riding. But the effort was too much and he startled passers-by on the street when he simply had to sit down on the curb to regain enough energy to continue. The following morning his family found him in a dead faint in the bathroom.

It was April fool's day and he thought the end of the world had come. Alone in the ambulance on the way to the hospital, he was exhausted and thoroughly dispirited. His iron will had conquered every other hurdle in his life, but even it seemed bone weary now.

He did not even have his medical cards for admission to the hospital, "That's all right, Mr. Knowles," the attendants remarked, "we know who you are." But it took sixteen pints of blood before he knew quite who he was. The blood count had been dangerously low and the doctors marvelled at his stamina. They tested for ulcers and pondered an operation, but there were no ulcers and eventually no operations. Instead, the Meckel's diverticulum showed up as the source of the bleeding. It gradually healed itself and the doctors simply removed a few more items from Knowles' already frugal diet. From then on he approached election campaigns with even more trepidation.

Susan Mann Trofimenkoff, *Stanley Knowles*, 1982

Dief the Chief

John George Diefenbaker (1895–1979) was first elected to Parliament in 1940. He became Leader of the Progressive Conservatives in 1956 and Prime Minister the following year. After losing the Prime Ministership to Lester Pearson in 1963, Diefenbaker's leadership increasingly came into question and he was finally ousted in 1967. He remained a Member of the House until his death.

Transcripts of Diefenbaker's speeches abound, but they convey nothing of the flavour or the mannerisms or the vocal effects—from falsetto to basso profundo, with the occasional horselike whinnies and the pauses for effect. He would point the avenging finger, and he would flap his arms like a pelican venting its wings prior to takeoff. The eyes would burn and the tightly waved hair would fly and, at the height of his powers, the crowds would roar and people would clutch at his garments.

Charles Lynch, *You Can't Print That*, 1983

It's All in the Delivery

Very often the Chief didn't know whether he was going to speak until the last moment. Sometimes whether he spoke or not depended on the kind of material we could gather for him. If it were not up to standard there would be no speech. Sometimes he would go down to the House with a pile of material in a folder and wait until someone gave him an opportunity to make use of it. Often it would sit on his desk for weeks before being used.

In delivery, the material underwent unanticipated metamorphoses. Speaking in the Commons Chamber, the Chief placed the notes on his desk. As he spoke, he picked them up and put them down. An interruption might generate a tangential excursion outside the theme of his speech. Back he would come, swooping, fumbling, perhaps dropping a sheet on the floor, talking all the while, rising triumphantly with the precise note he wanted at the precise moment he needed it. Each Parliamentary speech was unique—tailored to the circumstances, the mood of the House, sometimes even the smile on a ministerial face.

His notes might start a train of thought; or audience reaction might stimulate a performance both spontaneous and fascinating as the Chief threaded his thoughts together in mid-air. To those listening the speech was coherent and impressive; a study of the text compiled from a tape was often utterly confusing. The Chief didn't believe in making a carefully structured argument, moving from premises to conclusion. He left that sort of thing to academics. He believed in making an impact, a word-impression. The words, the gestures, the stabbing finger, the accusatory stance, the pushed-back lock of hair, the flaming eyes, the buglelike tones, everything contributed to a symphonic performance. The Chief could do more with a significant pause and a lifted eyebrow than most speakers with pages of text.

Thomas Van Dusen, *The Chief*, 1968

Dief in the House

Until his death, it was transparent that he was the beneficiary of special treatment as far as I was concerned. It was obvious that he could not go through the rigours of hopping up and down like a new Member and so, either through his party Whip or through a seat-mate, he would give me an indication of any Question Period in which he wanted to participate. In this way, I was able to recognize him on virtually every occasion he wanted, and I never had the impression that he sought the floor more often than he should have. However, during Question Period, he often went on longer than I would have normally permitted any other Member, but none of his caucus ever complained and I was always very careful to make sure that his time wasn't at the expense of the other Opposition parties.

But if I create the impression that John Diefenbaker had somehow been purified in his later years, let me quickly disabuse you of that notion. I could always tell when he was going to tread on the rules. Instead of facing the Chair, he would look down toward the other end of the Chamber, while he reached in his desk for newspaper clippings or some other prop to mount an attack or to otherwise enrage the Government Members. At times, he wasn't above a convenient hearing difficulty if I attempted to interrupt him from over his shoulder.

James Jerome, *Mr. Speaker*, 1985

Bitter Diefenbaker

A childless man with a strong sense of lineage, Diefenbaker sought his fulfilment in a lifetime of service to Canada's Conservative Party. Yet his deepest feelings of personal bitterness were directed at his own political cohorts for choosing George Drew over him at the Party's 1948 leadership convention. In Fredericton, N.B., where he was accorded the wildest welcome of the 1958 campaign, with women clutching at his coat and gasping: "I touched him!", Diefenbaker reacted by turning to a friend and saying bitterly: "I could have had all this in 1948, but for them."

Peter C. Newman, *Renegade in Power*, 1963

Dief's Idolatry

At his office in Parliament Hill's East Block, Diefenbaker worked under a portrait and beside a full-figure statuette of Macdonald. His inkwell had once belonged to Sir John A. In the Privy Council chamber, Diefenbaker sat in Macdonald's original chair, and dried the signature on his instructions with Sir John's spring blotter. One of Macdonald's mantel clocks timed his movements and had to be carted to whichever of his three Parliament Hill offices Diefenbaker was occupying. In his official residence, at 24 Sussex Drive, Diefenbaker encircled himself even more liberally with Macdonald relics, including parts of his library, many portraits of him, his easy chair, another clock, and a medallion given to a barber who had once shaved Sir John. The most valuable item in the collection was a copy, in Macdonald's own handwriting, of the original National Policy, drawn up on January 16, 1878, at a political meeting in Toronto's Shaftesbury Hall.

During his years in office, Diefenbaker was surrounded by these trappings of another age, but his homage to Macdonald went far beyond the accumulation of physical objects. Every January 11 he commemorated Sir John A.'s birth by leading a pilgrimage of Tory parliamentarians to lay a wreath at the foot of Macdonald's statue on Parliament Hill.

Allister Grosart's party machine capitalized on the Diefenbaker-Macdonald myth by issuing large, Tory-blue posters during the 1958 election which showed the Prime Minister standing before a framed portrait of Macdonald. The only text on the poster was:

TWO GREAT CONSERVATIVES: SIR JOHN A. — RT. HON. JOHN D.

Diefenbaker's Macdonald cult probably reached its climax during a small election meeting at St Boniface, Manitoba, in the 1962 campaign. Laurier Regnier, a local lawyer who had been elected as the Tory M.P. in 1958 after five previous defeats at the polls (he lost again in 1962), introduced Diefenbaker as the man who put Macdonald in the shade. "When history is written and the new generations read it, it probably will say that Sir John A. Macdonald was only the precursor of the Rt. Hon. John G. Diefenbaker," he told the audience of 150.

Peter C. Newman, *Renegade in Power*, 1963

The Diefenbaker Temper

There was one aspect of the Conservative Chief that was intolerable and a source of many miseries. This was his lack of control over his temper, which frequently led him to violent fits of anger. The Diefenbaker rages were something to see. I had had a preview of such a scene in December of 1956, after I had made a last-ditch appeal for the appointment of a French-speaking seconder. I was to witness many more scenes, some tragic, some only serious, some futile, but none of them very amusing. There was seldom a warning. The outbursts would start suddenly and end quickly, but they were startling while they lasted. The voice would rise to a top pitch, as the words poured out in ever faster succession, and the eyes would blaze, the head would shake, and the face would become deathly pale. The surprised listeners would stare in silence or protest with vigour, depending on individual temperaments, but few remained unmoved. The Leader never worried too much about the presence of witnesses, an unfortunate trait which led him to lose good friends and strong supporters. This permitted a particular wit on a particular day to paraphrase the great Talleyrand who, after a stormy session with Napoleon, had come out of the Emperor's chamber and said, "What a shame that such a great man must have such bad manners." John Diefenbaker was not Napoleon, nor were his manners bad, but we all would have been much happier without such explosions.

One French-speaking colleague, never too conversant with the intricacies of the English language, was once submitted to a strong, ten-minute tongue-lashing well within the hearing of the crowded anteroom. I happened to be among the listeners, and as the unfortunate man walked out, looking somewhat sheepish and much the worse for wear, I asked him what all the noise was about. He lifted his hands, shook his head in distress, and answered in his best French, "I cannot say, I did not understand what he said." There were times when I myself felt jealous of my friend, and deplored my adequate understanding of the two official languages of Canada.

Pierre Sévigny, This Game of Politics, 1965

The Chief's Vanity

Although he enjoyed the attention of photographers, he went to some length to prevent himself from being photographed in embarrassing poses. On March 4, 1958, during a campaign reception at Scarborough, Ontario, a middle-aged woman expressed her admiration of the Conservative leader by bussing him firmly on the right cheek. The Prime Minister, who had been chuckling affably a moment before, turned pale with fury and snapped at a photographer who had captured the kiss: "I won't have that used!"

Shortly after Diefenbaker assumed office, a reporter walked with him from his East Block office to a noon-hour banquet at the Chateau Laurier Hotel. As they made their way through Confederation Square jammed with summer tourists, the newsman noticed that the Prime Minister managed to spot every amateur camera pointed at him and contrived to give each of them his favourite angle—just off full face. It was a calculated response, yet grown so instinctive that all the way to the Hotel, he continued answering the reporter's questions without a pause.

Peter C. Newman, Renegade in Power, 1963

Diefenbaker's Books

Among the books in the private library that Diefenbaker treasured most was a ten-volume edition of the works of Molière. The books, published in 1739, had once been in Sir John A. Macdonald's library and still bore his bookmark. They had been presented to Diefenbaker in 1958 by

Henri Laurier, Sir Wilfrid's great-nephew, a Montreal lawyer who campaigned for the Conservatives in the 1957 and 1958 elections.

As well as his Macdonald collection, Diefenbaker's private library contained nearly all the works of Sir Winston Churchill, many of them autographed. While his reading consisted mostly of history and political biography, the books in Diefenbaker's study also included Kate Aitken's *Travel Alone and Love It* and Dale Carnegie's *How to Stop Worrying and Start Living* as well as such titles as *Tom Brown's School Days, The Black Deeds of the Kremlin, The Red Fog Over America, Crime and Punishment, and The Essentials of Descriptive Geometry.*

The overflow of books, including Diefenbaker's law texts, was kept in a downstairs recreation room which also contained a kennel for Happy, the Diefenbaker's Labrador pup. The panelled walls of the room were decorated with Diefenbaker's thirty-one honorary degrees and various other plaques, sometimes incongruously placed. A tablet from the Knights of Columbus hung beside Diefenbaker's 33rd Degree Masonic Order, and a satirical notice declaring him to be an honorary Yukon Pioneer was next to the august declaration making him a member of Great Britain's Privy Council.

Peter C. Newman, *Renegade in Power*, 1963

A Powerful Interest in Sharks

Mr. Diefenbaker travelled with a despatch case crammed with notes, stationery, pencils, erasers, rubber bands, socks, newspaper clippings and straight pins to hold notes together. We would have preferred paper clips, but the Chief insisted on pins, with the result that in handling the material there was a definite risk of punctured fingers. This preference would have been regarded by some as an interesting psychological phenomenon; more probably it was another lawyer's habit. In the air, the despatch case would appear on his knees, the notes would emerge and he would convey an air of busy involvement. With a lawyer's preoccupation with papers, the Chief never discarded anything, on the assumption, no doubt, that it might later turn up in evidence. He seemed to be under the impression that his travelling companions were provided with bottomless briefcases and saddlebags to boot, for Guthrie and I ended each flight with bags and pockets bulging.

Once he had his papers in order, the Chief would talk or sleep.

He had a phenomenal capacity to snatch forty winks almost anywhere, one of the secrets of his staying power. Rarely, he would read for pleasure. Once coming up from New York, he leaned over to ask, "What are you reading?" It was a rather interesting book on man-eating sharks. It gravitated into his hands.

Thomas Van Dusen, *The Chief*, 1968

Olive Diefenbaker

Olive Diefenbaker as an omnivorous reader of English and French literature. She had been a teacher of French and spoke the language flawlessly. Years later, she recalled how she would sit for hours when her husband was Prime Minister, knitting and reading on the bed while Mr. Diefenbaker worked into the night. Mrs. Diefenbaker was, by nature, a night person, "an owl" as she called herself, and was never keen to get up early in the morning. Her husband, up with the larks, was always out for his thirty-minute walk shortly after first light. On his return, she would join him for breakfast—he "so cheerful it would kill you." She had a delightful sense of humour. Mr. Diefenbaker enjoys telling of the time he asked his wife to say grace before dinner. She said it in her soft tone and Mr. Diefenbaker said to her, "I didn't hear you." To which she replied, "I wasn't talking to you." On another occasion her husband remarked, "Now you read faster than I do." "I always did!" was her reply.

John Diefenbaker, *One Canada: Tumultuous Years*, 1977

Epicurean Delights

Aside from his fascination with TV wrestling, circuses, and fishing, Diefenbaker had few diversions. He had no interest at all in music, art, literature, ballet, the theatre, or gourmet food. In New York, he fell asleep during the musical My Fair Lady and, when reporters badgered Mrs. Diefenbaker to tell them her husband's favourite food, she had no answer. Later, when she asked him, he hesitated for a while, then replied, "Oh yes, I know. Potatoes."

Peter C. Newman, *Renegade in Power*, 1963

Camp and Diefenbaker

I was concluding another productive week in Ottawa. It was Thursday and I had left Nowlan's office to go to the parliamentary cafeteria, fifth floor, Centre Block. It was during the afternoon coffee break, and when I came in I saw some of the gallery press sitting at the long table near the coffee urns and the cash register. I decided to take my coffee with them.

"Mr. Camp," a sweet voice called.

It was Olive Diefenbaker, smiling, with John; they were sitting alone, near the door. I returned the smile, saying hello, but I had seen Arthur Blakely and wanted to talk to him.

"Sit down," Diefenbaker said. "I want to tell you something."

Well, it had been a good week and perhaps he would make it even better.

I had not seen him since a dinner in Winnipeg, and never in my life before that, and when I sat down, it occurred to me that our last conversation had been ridiculous. Maybe he remembered it, and maybe we would do something to repair it.

"I don't want my wife to be insulted again, you understand?"

He was looking at me, or through me, but I was almost certain I had heard him right. Frantically, the mind raced ahead of the tongue in search of clues to the insult to Olive Diefenbaker.

I looked at Olive who looked down into her teacup, half smiling.

"I don't understand," I said, and I could not have been more truthful.

"I don't blame you," Diefenbaker said. "I know how they do these things, but I want you to know."

"Yes, sir," I said, feeling myself slipping into an abyss of incomprehension.

"I want you to know that wherever I go, my wife goes." His voice was low, quavering, menacing.

"I don't understand," I said, looking at him. Olive said, "Now, John, he doesn't understand."

"I mean Winnipeg," he said. "If I'm asked to sit at the head table, my wife sits with me. You see, that's the way it is with me. My wife does not sit below the salt."

Ah, the head table at Winnipeg! Relieved, I began to explain. "The trouble was," I said, "there were too many people for the head table. We had to ask all the wives to sit together at another table."

"I believe Mrs. Drew was at the head table," Diefenbaker said, a debater's note of triumph in his voice.

"She was the only exception," I said. "Except the mayor's wife."

"John," Mrs. Diefenbaker said, smiling at me, "Mr. Camp has explained it couldn't be helped. Let's not talk about it."

"Just a minute," he said. "I know how these things happen. But I want you to know, you see, there will never be a next time. That's all. If my wife can't be there, then I won't be there. Is that clear?"

"All right, John," his wife said.

"I'm sorry," I said.

"I just want you to know," he said.

"Nice to see you again," I lied to them, getting up from the table, going out the door.

What a strange man, I thought.

Dalton Camp, *Gentlemen, Players and Politicians*, 1970

Early Riser

On a normal morning, as Prime Minister, I would get up at half past five or a quarter to six. On first rising, I would have half a grapefruit or an orange and coffee. Then I would dictate memoranda, letters, etc., for an hour or so before I set off on my morning walk. I did not have security guards to follow me wherever I went; I've never had them. I did take the obvious precaution of not always walking the same route, and thereby inviting trouble. Often I would walk along Sussex Drive as far as the Mint and back, or across the Rideau Hall Park, or up John Street, or into Eastview (now Vanier), or in the general direction of the Japanese Embassy in Rockcliffe. I would try for a mile and a half each day, at about 140 to 160 paces a minute. When I returned home, my wife would join me at breakfast. I arrived at the office, ready for the day ahead, by eight o'clock.

John Diefenbaker, *One Canada: Years of Achievement*, 1976

From John to PM

All of a sudden he tasted power. He became much more the leader. He gained a certain assurance. He spoke with strength. He could feel from the press and what was said about him that he had the wind in his sails. He demanded that even his closest friends stop calling him John and call him Mr. Prime Minister. I remember one day I dared to tell him that he needed a good tailor, and he called me up, much to my surprise, and said. "Take me to a good one." And I took him to a man who made him many suits. From a shabby dresser, Diefenbaker became a tailor's dummy straight from Savile Row, and the image of the man changed completely for the better.

Pierre Sévigny, quoted in Peter Stursberg, *Diefenbaker: Leadership Gained*, 1975

Dief the Gardener

The Chief had a number of drivers, due to the fact that he was constitutionally unable to drive and converse at the same time, and he had no intention of giving up conversation. For a while Mrs. Diefenbaker drove.

One of the Chief's drivers was a Czech gentleman named Klementi Vocun, who later went to work for Paul Martin. The Chief liked his driving but didn't think much of his gardening—Klem had his own way of planting tomatoes, corn and wax beans. It was not the Chief's way. Klem had his own method of cutting the grass, and the Chief never thought Klem had the hang of the automatic lawn mower. He decided to show him and charged into the shrubbery to the accompaniment of metallic clanks and rocks whizzing in the air. Philosophically, Klem took the machine to be repaired.

"But why did you give it to him?" I asked Klem.

"Ven he say, 'I vant,' I give."

Mr. Diefenbaker did not like being alone on weekends and generally made arrangements for people to drop down. He usually phoned on Saturdays. "News?" That was his first question. Sometimes he varied it. "News, views, interviews?" I never had much news on Saturday mornings. I was happy to free my mind of politics whenever the occasion offered. One Saturday when the Chief called, I was shingling the roof.

"Remember to leave four inches to the weather," he said, quick-as-a-flash. Remarks of this kind endeared him to my father whose unvarying test of politicians was whether or not they knew how many pounds there were in a bushel of oats. The Chief passed with flying colours.

Thomas Van Dusen, *The Chief*, 1968

Mechanically Disinclined

I was appalled to find that there was no lock on the door into his office. Any crank with a gun could just push someone aside and walk right in and mow him down. I thought that there should be one of those electric locks that he could control from his own desk. I asked him about it, but I don't think he knew what I was saying. Anyway, we had it installed, because there was a guy sending threatening letters to him and I saw him a few times out on the lawn. I was getting a little apprehensive, and so were other members of the staff.

We had this electric lock installed. Someone important like Senator Brunt would come, and we would then press the buzzer outside for Mr. Diefenbaker to press his buzzer, which would release the lock. He'd always get mixed up, and he'd think it was the telephone ringing, and he'd grab the red phone to Moscow or Washington, and he'd knock over pens and everything. He never could seem to get on to this mechanical lock. It would make him furious. Finally we'd have to bang on the doors. And we had another secret—we could unlock it from our side. So that only lasted a few days, and it was out.

Mechanics really troubled him. We tried to get him to use the hearing aid so he wouldn't miss things, but he would either turn up the volume too high, and it would nearly drive his brains in, or he wouldn't use it at all, or he didn't have it in right. It was just a waste of money—anything mechanical.

John Fisher, quoted in Peter Stursberg, *Diefenbaker: Leadership Gained*, 1975

Some Crackpot is Using Your Name

Mr. Diefenbaker kept half a dozen secretaries busy with his correspondence, dictating every reply personally, going into considerable detail, elaborating on the issues of the day and the state of the nation. Correspondence to him was not routine but a link with people. He frequently referred in his public statements to his mail; he asked people to write to him and he religiously read every letter he received. Frequently in the office, he would read extracts to whoever happened to be there. In his replies to correspondents, the Chief put forward his views with vigour and sharpness, in a way, which if made public, would have resulted in headlines; but I have never heard of his correspondents betraying him by forwarding the contents of his letters to the press.

His letter writers were humble people, ordinary men and women in every walk of life, including the poor, the ill, the handicapped and the aged; among them were women whose husbands were in prison; young boys who had gone wrong; people who could not help him in any way but wished to assure him of their support. They felt they knew him personally because he had been a feature of the political landscape for as long as many could remember. To the Chief, his correspondents were more than mere signatures. Some amused him; others annoyed him immensely. Nothing annoyed him more than to have a clergyman adopt a high moral tone. He had a short way with correspondents who displeased him.

> Dear Sir:
> This is to inform you that some crackpot is using your name and has recently written to me over your signature putting forward views so eccentric in nature and so much at variance with your usual logical style that the letter could not possibly be from you. I felt I owed it to you to bring this to your attention.

That usually ended the discussion.

Thomas Van Dusen, *The Chief*, 1968

Dief's Dictaphone

The Chief's working habits, even as a private member, were such that he had difficulty keeping secretaries. Not many girls are interested in working nights, weekends and sometimes holidays. The Chief's only capacity to relax came when he was fishing, walking with his dog, Happy I or Happy II, or watching a sporting event on television. The girls in the office got the bright idea of eliminating weekend work by providing the Chief with a dictating machine to take home with him. After a few false starts, he became quite proficient. The drawback was that the Chief never, under any circumstances, shut off the machine, so some strange conversations were picked up by the girls on Monday mornings: long-distance calls, chats with visitors, instructions to Happy, even important and confidential discussions. He took the machine on plane trips and mailed back the belts. His dictation was overlaid by the roar of the motor, conversations with stewardesses and chats with other passengers. Returning to Ottawa following the leadership convention, he sent in some belts to a new secretary. She listened with interest. "What is it," she asked, "Russian?"

Thomas Van Dusen, *The Chief*, 1968

Body Cast

Diefenbaker had slipped on a pebble and strained a muscle in his back while crossing from his East Block office to the Centre Block of Parliament. The doctors ordered him to rest, and soon the rumours were spreading that he had injured himself more seriously than we were being told, that he would be laid up for weeks or months, and that he had a body cast that extended from his hips right up to his neck.

I put in a call to the official residence at 24 Sussex Drive and got him on the phone, things being simpler in Ottawa then than they have since become.

"John?" (A few of us still called him that, not yet fully adjusted to the fact of his being prime minister.) "Yes, Charles." "They are saying you are hurt worse than we've been told." "Who says that?" "Grits." "What are they saying?" "They are saying you will be laid up for a long time and that you have a body cast, and that you won't be able to work, much less lead the party in an election." Short pause. Then: "You get right out here!"

I jumped in my car and drove around to the residence and rang the doorbell, there being no guards in those times. A maid answered and told me to go right upstairs, that the prime minister was expecting me.

Diefenbaker greeted me at the door to his bedroom and beckoned me inside, dismissing the two stenographers who had been taking dictation there. He was dressed in his pyjamas and was wearing a blue silk dressing-gown with gold brocaded squares on it.

When we were alone, he chuckled. "Now," he said, "let's hear all that stuff again."

I told him about the severity of his injuries, and the body cast and the rest of it.

He untied the sash of his dressing-gown and threw the garment on the floor. He unbuttoned the top of his pyjamas and threw that on the bed. He pulled the string on his pyjama pants and they fell to the ground, and I found myself in the full and complete presence of the Prime Minister of Canada.

"Do you see anything?" he demanded. "Well, sir...." "Do you see any body cast?" "No." He faced away from me and put his hands on his hips. "Do you see any swelling back there?" "No." "You see that chair there?" "Yes, sir." "Well," he said, "I'd jump over that chair for you, just to show I'm fine, but I can't , because I've got an awfully sore back."

He then asked if I was satisfied. I said I was and that I couldn't help remarking that this method of dealing with his medical problem was somewhat different from the way they were going about it in Washington, where President Eisenhower was ailing and medical bulletins were being issued almost hourly, with great diagrams of Eisenhower's insides splashed over all the magazines and newspapers.

"There will be none of that Hagerty nonsense here," said Diefenbaker, a reference to Eisenhower's press secretary James Hagerty, who had become a media hero during the president's illness.

While Diefenbaker was pulling his pyjamas back on, I remarked that I hoped he realized I would be reporting on this encounter in full detail, and he chortled.

"Of course you will, why do you think I asked you out here?"

Charles Lynch, *You Can't Print That*, 1983

The Tea Party

The members of the Parliamentary Press Gallery and others had received invitations to a reception held on one of the hottest days of the summer of 1958.

This reception was at a time in the afternoon when everybody expected to be getting a nice, cool gin and tonic. It was a sweltering hot day, in the middle of a heat wave in the summer, and I remember going home to pick up my wife. I changed into a lighter suit because I was terribly hot, and as I came out of the house my neighbour was sitting on his lawn, relaxing with a cool gin and tonic in his hand. He said, "Have a drink." I said, "Oh no. I'm going over to 24 Sussex and I'm going to be having drinks there." When my wife and I arrived, George Nowlan was behind us. He was then minister of national revenue. George quipped about the terrible heat and what a heck of a day it was. Olive and Diefenbaker were standing in the receiving line. I commented on the heat, and John had a big smile on his face and he said, "Yes, isn't it a terrible day?"

We moved on and, as soon as we passed through, Nowlan, who was a very abrupt man, said, "Well now, let's have a good cool drink, Vic." He saw a chap in a white jacket, carrying a tray, and he said, "Bring me a long, tall, cool one—gin and tonic." The fellow said, "I'm sorry sir, there's only hot tea." Nowlan said, "What?" He said, "We're serving hot tea, that's all, sir, or lemonade." I'll never forget to my dying day: Nowlan turned to me and said: "To hell with this," and he turned on his heel and walked out. I didn't have the guts to do that. I stayed with my wife. I had a cup of hot tea with the perspiration rolling off my forehead. Then we beat a retreat.

I've often wondered why John did that. He did it as a lark, I think. This was his way with the press. He liked to play jokes. But he didn't realize that there were a lot of newcomers. This is the thing about the Gallery: it's ever-changing. New faces appear, and new people who don't know the man, and they react differently. I knew Diefenbaker and I knew this was a typical kind of thing Diefenbaker would do. He'd say, "Oh, you fellows have got a reputation of being heavy drinkers. Well, we'll make sure that we protect your liver on this occasion."

Senator Grosart said this was not his idea. He said, "I knew we were in trouble over that, and I tried to talk him out of it, but there was no way. The Old Chief's eyes twinkled, 'Give them hot tea; it will be good for them.'"

The tea party was one of the contributing factors to the growing rift between him and the press because most reporters felt this was one more indication of Diefenbaker saying, "Well, the press don't really matter to me; I don't have to worry about whether you like me or don't like me."

Victor Mackie, quoted in Peter Stursberg, *Diefenbaker: Leadership Gained*, 1975

Dief Intimidating

A most unpleasant habit of the Leader was his reading of various papers or documents during the course of a private conversation while the person in his presence was laboriously trying to explain some point or develop an argument. This usually led the person to forget what he wanted to say and to become thoroughly confused. Some colleagues could not take this treatment and considered a private meeting with the Leader an ordeal to be avoided whenever possible. I knew at least one minister who used strong tranquilizers before such audiences and regained his fortitude with stiff drinks when the session was over.

Pierre Sévigny, *This Game of Politics*, 1965

Unusual Channels

He'd receive confidential letters that would come from President Kennedy by special courier from Washington. They wouldn't go through the US embassy or the Canadian External Affairs Department. They would come straight to the prime minister's office and right in to him. He'd open them, look very mysterious, and usually shove the letter into his pocket, or under the blotter, or in a drawer. A few days later, the US State Department, through the embassy, would start to make some enquiries. The embassy people would be shocked too that there were such letters. They'd enquire of External—I guess that's the way protocol goes—and External had never heard of these letters. And there'd be all hell breaking loose.

The girls got used to this, and they were very smart about it. Usually they'd say, "Well, they're either between his mattresses at home or they're in one of these deep drawers, or they're in a pocket in a clothes cupboard somewhere, or under the blotter." Sure enough, we'd usually find the notes in one of those places.

That was a real hang-up with him. He did the same with Macmillan. He wouldn't answer these letters. Now, why? Who knows? Whether he didn't want to touch the problem, whether he was snubbing them—I don't know what reason he had, but he would avoid answering those special letters by courier. It was a great joke around the prime minister's office. Whenever the pressure was on, we knew where to go—even had the maids briefed. We would phone to 24 Sussex and get the maid to go up and do a little feeling in between the mattresses and usually pull out some secret documents.

John Fisher, quoted in Peter Stursberg, *Diefenbaker: Leadership Gained*, 1975

Champagne

Prime Minister Diefenbaker and his entourage visited Ireland in 1961.

The day before our departure from Ottawa, I was chatting with my confidential messenger, Gilbert Champagne. I asked him if he wouldn't like to accompany us to Ireland. He was astounded; he had never before been invited to travel anywhere. Of course he agreed. In order to make our hosts in Belfast aware of this addition to my party, a telegram was sent by External Affairs to this effect: "Prime Minister will be bringing champagne." I gather that this caused some annoyance among the officials responsible for our welcome in Belfast. Their reaction was that I was bringing my own because I feared the champagne in Ulster inferior. It was a case of "B.Y.O.L."; it appeared to them that I was initiating the practice internationally of bringing your own liquor. But they rose to the occasion. When our airplane landed, a panel truck equipped with wine racks wheeled onto the tarmac to accommodate our Champagne. Brookeborough was most amused. He personally directed that a special table be set in an alcove for Gilbert at the state luncheon in my honour, and that several bottles of champagne be within his reach.

John Diefenbaker, *One Canada: Years of Achievement*, 1976

Third Rate Fighter

I have yet to see a speech that he was to give—that is one that was not impromptu, a formal one that he was committed to make—when he wasn't extremely difficult for some hours before. Pettish about this and that, and complaining about his stomach and he couldn't eat, and feeling as if he was going to be sick. It was rather like accounts I'd read of great performers who are temperamental and have problems with their stomachs before they go on to give their Shakespearean role or whatever. He told me that he always felt this way, nervous.

Another manifestation was that he'd keep asking for reassurance that there were going to be enough people there. His favourite expression was, "I haven't got any material, I haven't got any material," and sometimes he'd say, "You haven't given me any material." This became a joke between Tommy Van Dusen and me because we'd have given him about twenty-five pounds of assorted material, and he had it, and he had his notes, but he was always tremulous on the eve of making a speech. His great fear was that he'd go to a hall and it would be half full.

Then this remarkable change would come over him when he got on the platform and saw that they were hanging on the rafters, and you could see him picking up steam. He'd get out his notes and start making incomprehensible pencilled notes on top of the pencilled notes that were on top of the original notes. How he ever read them I don't know. But knowing his memory, I think that as a result of the act of writing them down, he didn't have to refer to them again. He would get up and start speaking, and it was fantastic to watch him. He was like a man fishing a trout pond. He would cast a fly out in different places and when he got some action he would come back to that place all the time. He was a master of oral communication. You know, people don't hear the way they read. It's one thing to read a prepared speech and digest what's in it, but if you listen to it you get very little out of it because you don't listen logically or in sequence. He knew that all you could ever hope for was that the audience would carry away one, or at best two, main ideas or impressions. For that reason he would continually come back to his main point. He'd touch them up with a little humour, and then he'd be serious, and then he'd come back and rephrase the main idea he was trying to get over. This is why I always thought he was a very effective speaker.

He was a great performer. He had a great sense of timing and emphasis and a feel for his audience, and in the early parts of his speeches he would feel out the audience, see what interested them, and then he would go for it, and he could get them with him. At the end, he would come off, and I would think he'd lose two to three pounds making a speech. He'd be absolutely soaking wet. In the campaign when we spoke in some rather primitive surroundings—in the Cow Palace in Charlottetown, for instance—we would be in a rather drafty room, a dingy little room with drafts and one naked bulb, and we'd have to strip the Chief and rub him down with a towel.

We finally found out that the best thing to do was to give him a black sweatshirt that came up tight around his throat. He would take off his shirt, which was wringing wet, and hopefully his coat would dry out in the interim, and we'd sponge him off with a towel and put on this sweatshirt. Then he would put his coat back on and he couldn't wait to get back on the stage to shake hands with people, and hear how great the performance was. His first question when you'd be going out to get his clothes changed was "How do you think it went?"

I remember in Winnipeg, during the '65 campaign, they had a terrible arrangement whereby there was a stage in a great auditorium. At the end they lifted the back curtain so that people came up on the stage from both sides. The Chief's instinct was to head to the heart of the crowd rather than towards the exit. We were trying to get him out, and to cut him out of the herd was really a difficult thing because people were clutching his hands and his coat. Sometimes we had to be quite peremptory, and in this particular case I remember bodily picking him up and changing directions and guiding him towards the door and then rather rudely having to push him into the car and slam the door. He looked pathetic staring out of the window, looking at people still reaching out their hands. I could see him saying to himself, "All those hands and I can't shake them!"

But sometimes you had to take direct action. Often it was Mrs. Diefenbaker's suggestion that we should get him out because he perspired buckets, and if we hung around too much in these corridors backstage where there's usually no heat, he might have taken pneumonia very easily. But I used to laugh. I told him it was like managing a third-rate fighter.

Greg Guthrie, quoted in Peter Stursberg, *Diefenbaker: Leadership Lost*, 1976

Whistlestopper

Diefenbaker's advisers had warned him that campaigning by train could prove disastrous, because in the age of the automobile, railway stations were no longer a factor in most people's lives. During the first leg of his journey, from Halifax to Montreal, it looked as if his advisers had been right. At Matapédia, Quebec, only five off-duty trainmen and three stray dogs turned out to meet the Chief. At Rimouski, where seven lonely Tories were waiting on the platform, Diefenbaker asked one of them: "Who's the candidate here?" He replied: "I am, sir. My name is Gérard Ouellette." At Amqui, the Conservative leader was introduced to a Monsieur Legris, who in turn presented the young man beside him as "mon fils." Diefenbaker smiled and said: "Bonjour, Monseer Monfils."

Peter C. Newman, *Home Country*, 1973

Mount Fujiyama

The Chief set great store by a large picture of Mount Fujiyama that Emperor Hirohito had given to him on his visit to Japan. It hung in the reception room, looking like a giant ice-cream sundae. In 1967 the Chief decided that the 150-pound stuffed marlin he had caught off Jamaica in 1961, which was moldering in the basement at Stornoway, belonged in the House of Commons. Up it came, gracing the wall of the reception room, to the awe of casual passersby. Down went Fujiyama, to be placed on the floor of the Chief's office until such time as it could be re-hung. One day Bunny Pound, the Chief's private secretary, looked up to see the Japanese Ambassador sitting in front of her. A vision of Fujiyama on the floor in the chief's office flashed through her mind, and she rushed in, took down a view of Quebec city in 1868 and put up Fujiyama. The Chief went calmly about his work.

"Is anyone waiting outside?" he asked idly.

"The Japanese Ambassador."

"I gollies! Why didn't you tell me?" The Chief came out from behind the desk and started for the door. "Really, Miss Pound, you must learn not to keep people waiting." He ushered the Ambassador in personally, while Miss Pound, properly rebuked, returned to her work.

Thomas Van Dusen, *The Chief*, 1968

"For Those not Bilingual..."

When he spoke French, he frequently said every English-speaking person from St. John's to Victoria understood. He never failed to produce laughter when, after speaking for a few moments, he stopped and "for the benefit of those who are not bilingual," turned to English. The Chief's use of French was in a class with Blondin's crossing Niagara Falls on a tightrope, and the reaction of French-Canadian audiences was compounded of horror at the Chief's brand of French and awe that he was even attempting it. The Chief seemed to share some of the horror as he struggled along; and eventually Quebec audiences accepted his French as a strange but impressive convulsion of nature, part of the national landscape, like Montmorency Falls. Some of his early difficulties were caused by the literacy of his advisers, who provided him with exquisite and complex sentences studded with words he could not possibly pronounce, material which would have tripped up Maurice Chevalier. When this was overcome by short sentences and easily mastered words, the Chief's delivery improved.

Thomas Van Dusen, *The Chief*, 1968

"En Français"

John Diefenbaker told us that he understood and could read French, but that he had some difficulty with vocabulary. This was without a doubt the understatement of his long and complicated career. At his request I tried to teach him in the correct pronunciation of a few simple words. But it was hopeless, and I almost felt like telling him to forget the whole thing, or to follow Mackenzie King's example and limit his Gallic efforts to the initial words mes chers amis and a final au revoir. This would have been useless. My candidate was determined to speak French, and nothing would convince him that he could hardly be considered a linguist. I therefore prepared the simplest of texts, which he laboriously delivered the following day. On countless occasions during the next six years, I was asked like many others to prepare his French speeches. I worked hard at this thankless function, and I must say that some progress was achieved in his dedicated desire to be bilingual. He eventually realized that he would never speak good French, and he could be quite amusing about his harmless admission. I remember his saying, after a particulary lengthy and difficult bout with the language of Victor Hugo, "In order to prove to you that I can also speak the other language of the country, I shall now address you in English." Upon his arrival in Mexico on a state visit, he was greeted by President Lopez Mateos, and John Diefenbaker answered his friendly greetings with a short speech which he delivered in Spanish as well as in English. He then asked the President if he had understood. Lopez Mateos, who spoke good English, answered that Mexicans could understand Spanish but not Portuguese.

Pierre Sévigny, This Game of Politics, 1965

Name that Dog

Somebody gave Mr. Diefenbaker a new dog and he came into the office one morning and told us about it. He said, "Now, I want a name for that dog. Get your brains together and see what you can come up with."

I said, "Mr. Diefenbaker, first of all, I think it should have a bilingual name that is pronounceable and understandable in both languages of this country." He kind of looked at me a bit and he didn't say anything. I went home that night and I whipped out, on my typewriter, thirty different suggested names for this darned dog. The next morning, I handed the list to him. He was a bit grumpy, and he just scanned it. Of course he could scan very rapidly—he can read a page in just a flash. He put it down on his desk, and reared back in his chair, and said, "I have decided to name the dog Prince."

I said, "Prince! Mr. Diefenbaker! Royalty isn't too popular right now, and in Quebec that won't go." He said, "You wanted a bilingual word." I said, "Yes but what you gain on the bilingualism you lose on the royalty aspect of 'Prince.'" He said, "Prince" (using the French pronunciation). I said, "Well, they'll think that's Prince Albert." He said, "That's what it is." I said, "I don't know. My recommendation would be that you could do better than that." "Well, you're so bright, give me some more names." I said I would bring in some more names in the morning, because he was busy all that day.

That night I prepared another list of names. I really worked hard at it too. I came in and I gave him the list; he scanned it and refused to comment. He said, "I have a name that Allister Grosart has given me." I said, "What's that?" He said, "Tory." I said, "Oh, Mr. Diefenbaker, you must have lost your senses! Tory for a dog? Can't you picture every cartoonist in this country. They'll say the Conservatives are so convinced that they've chosen a dog and they've gone to the dogs." He looked a little alarmed. I said, "No, that's the last name you should have for a friendly dog." He looked at me again as if I'd taken leave of my senses. I said, "If you don't believe me, ask your dear faithful courier out here, Gilbert Champagne. Ask him."

So he pushed the buzzer, and he never could remember which buzz-er he was supposed to push, because mechanics troubled him. Anyway, Gilbert was summoned to the throne, and he came in and he stood at attention, because I think he was always a bit intimidated by the Chief. The Chief said, "Gilbert, what does the word Tory mean to you?" Old Gilbert said, "That means George Drew. It means the striped pants, something what you in English call 'stuffy.'" Dief thought that was great and he had a roar of laughter. He said, "That's what you think it is, eh?" Gilbert said, "I would not be happy with that word." Dief said, "That's it! 'Happy!' You said it. Thanks, Gilbert."

And that's how the dog was named "Happy."

John Fisher, quoted in Peter Stursberg, *Diefenbaker: Leadership Gained*, 1975

Fight to the Last

In 1967 the question of John Diefenbaker's continued leadership of the Progressive Conservative party came to a head. He made an eloquent appeal to his remaining loyal supporters.

This was John Diefenbaker's private army, their violent loyalty tempered by an animal shyness that now burst its tolerance as women wept openly and men dabbed their eyes. They clustered in front of him—two hundred strong—chanting, cheering, yearning for his march-ing orders.

"My friends, I deeply appreciate this," Diefenbaker began, his head bowed, voice breaking with emotion. "I read in the press that the old magic has waned. But I don't know how one could practise that with the trained seals that stood in front of me the other night and were placed there in advance."

He had come down he said, to see his friends for one more time "be-cause this may be the last opportunity that I'll have the privilege of speaking to you."

"No. We want you. You're the only honest man we've got!"

The crowd quivered, hanging on his every breath. The restorative potion of their response made his whole being swell, his shoulders squared, the gooseberry eyes found their focus again. His sense of timing returned, so that he began to play the chants of homage as a counterpoint to this theme: "All through the years..." "We need you..." "I've fought on behalf of principle for this Party..." "You're an honest man, John..."

"What comes to mind are the immortal words of one of the great ballads of the other Elizabethan era. In that era there were men who stood. One of them was Sir Richard Barton. His words have been, through the years, a constant source of inspiration to me. 'Fight on, my man,' quoth Sir Richard Barton..." "Attaboy, John!" "'I am wounded, but I am not slain...'" "Three cheers for John!" "'I'll lay me down and rest a while and then I'll rise to fight again.'" Three cheers and a tiger resounded through the drawing room, interrupting only momentarily the serious enterprise being concluded across the hall. "We've marched together," Diefenbaker went on, "we've won over and over again. The reason is the rank and file, you men and women in the constituencies. And as long as you remain true to the faith, this party, even though predictions are made to the contrary, shall not die." "You'll never die, John."

Peter C. Newman, Distemper of Our Times, 1968

The Value of an Autograph

A lad of about seven or eight years of age tried to get through the crowd at the Simpson's store in Toronto where I was autographing the first volume of my memoirs. I arranged that he be allowed through. He didn't have a book, just a piece of paper for me to autograph. I signed it; he thanked me and left. Apparently, a member of the press stopped him to ask what he was up to. He replied that it took five John Diefenbakers to get one Bobby Hull, and he had only had four!

John Diefenbaker, One Canada: Years of Achievement, 1976

Congratulations

As keen an observer of Canadian affairs as Dief was, he most liked it when all eyes were on him. He regarded himself as something akin to a national shrine. And if you cared anything about him at all, he expected your homage always, but particularly on two days: his birthday, September 18, and the anniversary of his election to Parliament, March 26. In Ottawa, where national days, independence celebrations, and feast times were part of everyday life, for Dief and all who loved him these two occasions were especially to be honoured. Each year, both days would begin with him pretending they were nothing special. When the prime minister rose in his place in Parliament to pay tribute, Dief would feign surprise at achieving yet another milestone of age or gaining more lustre as the dean of the House of Commons. The ritual would continue later in his crowded office as he received personal greetings from MPs, staff and all sorts of people connected with the Hill. He paid close attention to who showed up and who stayed away. For days after, he'd pester staff and friends, saying: "Where was Mr. X? Why didn't Y show up?"

Knowing the command-performance level that each of these days had reached, I was fully aware I would be counted among the missing and presumed dead in March of 1977 when I was travelling with a parliamentary delegation in the Middle East. In order to stay in Dief's good graces, Claude Wagner, his wife, Gisèle, and I sent a joint telegram from Tel Aviv saying: "CONGRATULATIONS UPON ANNIVERSARY OF YOUR FIRST ELECTION." Feeling I had covered myself appropriately, I thought nothing more about it until I returned to Ottawa. Whenever one of his loyalists had been away, Dief expected to be first on the agenda upon your return, so I showed up at his office feeling jaunty and ready to flatter him with reports of how highly the Israelis thought of him. Before I opened my mouth he lit into me.

"Were you drunk?" he snarled.

"Sir?"

"Were you drunk? That is the only possible explanation."

I had no idea what he was going on about and could only repeat another dumbfounded, "Sir?"

"Don't play cutesy with me. This is the most damnable thing I've ever seen. And from you, of all people, I never...."

Finally, I was able to say: "I don't know what you're talking about."

"This is what I'm talking about." And he flung my telegram across his desk toward me. I picked it up and read the message: "CONGRATULATIONS UPON ANNIVERSARY OF YOUR FIRST ERECTION." I never was able to convince him that the mistake was unintentional.

Sean O'Sullivan, *Both My Houses*, 1986

Me-me-me-me-me!

Throughout, the man I went to Ottawa to serve was demanding. I was never an early riser, but I tried to be there for 9:00 a.m., knowing full well he'd been lashed in the harness for hours. If his mood were expansive, he would look up and greet me with one of his favourite salutations: "News, views, interviews?" That signalled he wanted to hear all the gossip that hadn't made the newspapers or the morning broadcasts. You could also tell where your information fell on his Richter scale of interest by his response. When he was pleasantly surprised by something, he'd utter, "I gollies"; if the news was bad, it was "What the hell."

My most important function, I quickly discovered, as it had been with my predecessors, was to provide political intelligence. The more it served to feed his ego at the expense of the party and those who followed his nemesis, Dalton Camp, the better.

His reaction to information was, by any measure, bizarre. If you told him about some minor feuding in the party, he would clench his left hand into a fist at his waist, slap it lightly with his right hand and say, very quickly: "Me-me-me-me-me-me-me." If the report were particularly salacious, the singsong would be the same but with a faster tempo and a slightly higher pitch. It was an incredible sight-and-sound show, and the only explanation I could ever come up with was that it was an absolutely unquotable response. If anyone ever said, "How did Dief react when you told him?" you couldn't possibly say. There was no response, only this indescribable sound. As a politician he was safe and couldn't possibly have his views come back to haunt him.

He would take such juicy news and spread it like the seeds of a thistle in the hopes that they would spring up and choke those who had once done him in. He would wave a memo he'd been handed or collar the information he'd just heard and shout: "Where's the list?" meaning the list of friends and supporters who received his regular calls and mailings. Often he'd phone Olive first, and his opening line was always the same: "It's everywhere." With the memo in front of him he'd begin: "What I'm hearing, you see, is this." And then he'd quote the best bits, sprinkling them with his own additions, such as "They're fighting and feuding."

After Dief had spoken to Olive, he'd start phoning the names on the list at random.

Sean O'Sullivan, *Both My Houses*, 1986

Hearing Problems

Another factor complicating the Chief's personal relations was that with passing time he became bothered by deafness. It was not a serious disability, but very often people who felt they had been hardly dealt with by the Chief had simply not been able to get through to him because of his hearing problem. He wore a hearing aid more and more frequently, but sometimes, for reasons known to himself, would leave it off. His disability made it difficult for him to converse with people who did not speak up or didn't speak clearly. Sometimes in a press conference, when there was a crossfire of comment or questioning, the Chief would lose the thread of the discussion. He usually kept one of us at his side to repeat the questions he couldn't hear. On the other hand, he sometimes showed an uncanny ability, in a crowded House of Commons in the middle of a heated debate, to pick out an interjection from a back bencher and shoot forth a sizzling reply. Sometimes we suspected his hearing problem was a political, not a health matter. While he had trouble hearing questions he didn't want to answer, or needed time to think about, he seemed to grasp the easy ones very quickly.

Thomas Van Dusen, *The Chief*, 1968

The Douglas Parables

Thomas Clement Douglas (1904-1986) was the pioneering Premier of Saskatchewan from 1944 to 1961 before becoming the first leader of the federal New Democratic Party in 1961, a post he held until 1971.

The stories he [Tommy Douglas] told were parables, delighting his listeners.

He talked of the white cats and the black cats. Every four years in Mouseland, it being a democratic country, the mice held an election. One year they would elect the black cats. And conditions—for mice—were terrible. So after four years they rose up in protest, threw out the black cats, and—elected white cats. The white cats preyed on the mice even more terribly than their predecessors had. So next time—back in went the black ones.

Until one day, a small mouse stood up in his corner and proposed "Let us elect mice." They called him a radical, a Communist, a National Socialist. But the idea spread. Mice got the message. The day came....

The story of the cream separator was even more beautifully apt. What Douglas did with this story is a perfect example of his skills for it was apparently derived from a paragraph by Lewis Mumford:

"During the age of expansion, capitalism gave cream to the few, whole milk to the middle classes, and a blue watery residue to the majority of farmers and industrial workers, agricultural labourers and slaves. The highest hope of capitalism, its most sacred incentive, was the hope that a fractional few of the skimmed-milk drinkers might, by elbowing and pushing, claim a place for themselves among the cream drinkers. In an age of economic balance, on the other hand, we must look forward to a widespread distribution of whole milk for everybody."

Doris French Shackleton, *Tommy Douglas*, 1975

Saskatchewan Campaigns

The campaign was rough. Douglas put a lock on his gasoline tank after several experiences with sand or sugar poured into it. After arriving home one night he examined his car and found that all the nuts on the back wheels had been loosened. Another night an opposition gang broke into his meeting, shouting and jostling, elbowing their way to the stage. Douglas realized, first, that there was no rear door, and they were going to have to stay where they were and meet the fracas on. He realized next, that his Baptist deacon and campaign manager, Ted Stinson, had taken off his coat and was rolling up his sleeves. Douglas grabbed the nearest weapon, the water jug, smashed it, brandished it, and said, "If you come up here you're going to get hurt!" But through the door at the opportune time came a group of CCF supporters from Montmartre, marching in and up to the stage. "'Having any trouble, Tommy?' they said. I said, 'Not now'".

Doris French Shackleton, *Tommy Douglas*, 1975

The Douglas Wit

At a federal council meeting there was discussion about having the next convention in Toronto, and how to dramatize it. One of the M.P.s said

"Well, we could have a nude woman riding down Yonge Street on a horse." And Douglas said, "What a great idea! It must be a long time since the people of Toronto have seen a horse."

Doris French Shackleton, *Tommy Douglas*, 1975

Douglas at Work

He wanted everything very precise. He was always working like the devil. He had two Christmases in Jamaica, other than that maybe two weekends off in the whole two years.

He worked at a ferocious pace and he liked to be sure that everybody else was working ferociously too. When I started, he went down to the U.N. for two weeks. My idea was to sign all his mail and get it all done so there'd be nothing when he came back. He was not pleased! So the next time he was away for a week we piled up all his mail, done and ready for his signature, on his desk, a tremendous stack. He sat down, obviously pleased, pulled over the stack and started going through it. It was tangible proof that we'd been working hard while he was gone. Then he bounded in with all the signed letters. He read almost everything that went out of the office.

Hans Brown, quoted in Doris French Shackleton, *Tommy Douglas*, 1975

Gardiner and Douglas

From 1935 to 1944 Douglas and Gardiner gave Saskatchewan two very able voices in the House of Commons.

Sparring between the two diminutive men—Gardiner and Douglas—was a special feature of the Commons. Gardiner was an inch or so shorter, barrel-chested and no mean speaker. Douglas was lighter, faster, always poised for a quick jab. When the Agriculture Department's estimates were before the House Douglas attacked government policy and was continually interrupted by Liberal hecklers, led by Gardiner. Douglas stopped short, turned and said, "If the minister will get back up on his chair and dangle his legs for a while, I'll get on with what I was about to say."

Gardiner scoffed at Douglas' championship of the farmer. "What does my honourable friend know about it?" he demanded. "He's not a farmer."

"No," Douglas retorted, "And I never laid an egg either, but I know more about omelets than most hens."

Doris French Shackleton, Tommy Douglas, 1975

Michener and the Chief

Daniel Roland Michener (1900-   ) was Speaker of the House of Commons from 1957 to 1962. He became Governor General in 1967.

Daniel Roland Michener was one of the best Speakers Canada's Commons had since Confederation. A thoroughly civilized man, he ruled the Commons with an easy grace that added to the dignity on which his office depends. Nevertheless the Prime Minister grew to dislike Michener so intensely that at a cabinet meeting, shortly after the Speaker had ruled against one of his breaches of protocol, Diefenbaker actually polled every minister, to see which of them had recommended that Michener be made Speaker, and then launched into a tirade against the man whose job it was to protect the rights of Parliament, which Diefenbaker the campaigner had pledged to uphold. Although Diefenbaker had in the 1957 election suggested that the Commons should have a permanent Speaker who would not have to stand for re-election, and although politicians of every party agreed that Michener would be the ideal candidate for the job, the Prime Minister did not fulfil his promise and Michener was beaten in the 1962 campaign. Then, instead of following the usual practice of appointing a former Commons Speaker to the Senate, Diefenbaker named Michener only to the Privy-Council—an empty honour that allowed him to place the prefix "Honourable" before his name and nothing else.

Peter C. Newman, Renegade in Power, 1963

After Howe

Gordon Churchill (1898-   ) became Minister of Trade and Commerce following the Conservative victory in the 1957 general election.

One of the strange things about my appointment as minister of trade and commerce was that Mitchell Sharp phoned me and said that the department offices in the temporary buildings would not be available for ten days because they were redecorating. Actually, they were getting rid of the files. But that was all right. I sat up in the House of Commons. Then I moved down with a small staff of four or five to the coldest reception that I have ever received in my life. It affected the staff as well. C.D. Howe was gone and here was an unknown, insignificant person coming down to take his place. The Conservatives were in power and the department was completely upset.

Later on, when Sharp left in 1958 and I got John English appointed as deputy minister, he told me quite frankly, "When you first came down here you were hated by everybody in the department, right down to the most junior office boy." But John English fixed it up. He was a very diplomatic chap, and I liked him very much.

That was my introduction to trade and commerce. What an experience!

Gordon Churchill, quoted in Peter Stursberg, *Diefenbaker Leadership Gained*, 1975

George Nowlan and the Princess

George Clyde Nowlan (1898-1965) was Minister of National Revenue from 1957 to 1962 and Minister of Finance from 1962 to 1963.

One of the highlights of the Diefenbaker years was the Canadian tour undertaken by Her Royal Highness Princess Margaret.

Margaret was the glamour item in the Royal Family at the time and people still referred to her as Margaret Rose. But she was showing signs of having a mind of her own and not wanting to be led around with a ring in her nose while on tour. She became more and more cranky as the tour progressed, and by the time she reached Nova Scotia she was fed to the royal teeth with the whole business.

Her host for the Nova Scotia segment of the tour was George Nowlan, in his role as the senior federal cabinet minister from the province. Nowlan was a tall, ambling figure of a man who had been a country lawyer all his life and had an easy way with people, not to mention an even easier way with the bottle. He was one of those unusual people on whom strong drink had a beneficial effect, heightening his good nature and sharpening his wits.

When Princess Margaret boarded the Royal Train at Digby, Nova Scotia, for the trip through the Annapolis Valley on the way to Halifax, Nowlan greeted her warmly and joined her in acknowledging the cheers of the Digby multitude. Then the train set off through Nowlan's riding, slowing down at each level crossing so that the people assembled could get a look at the Royal Person. It was drizzling rain and it was cold, and after three level crossings Princess Margaret informed Nowlan that she was too tired to go out on the observation platform any more and that she proposed to lie down and rest.

"But Ma'am," said Nowlan, as he himself recounted the story later, "these people have been waiting for hours in the rain to see you." "I don't care, I'm not going out." "But you owe it to them." "I do not." "Well then, consider that these are my people and you owe it to me." "I'm not going." Short pause while Nowlan took a deep breath. "Well then, Ma'am," he said, "in that case, it is my painful duty to inform you that if you don't go out and wave at the people I am going to take you over my knee and whale the bejesus out of you." Shocked silence. "You wouldn't dare!" "Wouldn't I," said Nowlan, flexing his big hands. "Here's another crossing, and if you don't go out you're going to get it!" She went, and the crowd cheered, as did all the crowds, all the way to Halifax.

Charles Lynch, You Can't Print That, 1983

The Plot

I spent a lot of time with George Nowlan, and my instinct told me that I should spend a lot of time with him if I wanted to know what was going on. One night, perhaps ten o'clock at night, I went in to George's office (he was the minister of finance at the time), and he was sitting in this big office in the Centre Block. All the lights were off except for the lamp over his desk. It looked eerie. I went in there in almost total darkness and sat down in a chair across from his desk. He was agitated. He said, "There's a meeting going on, and I'm not going to go." I said, "What's the meeting about." He said, "It's Fulton and these fellows, the damned fools. They're in a plot." Then the phone rang, George said, "No, no, no."

There was a knock on the door. I opened the door. Into the darkness, limping on a cane, came Pierre Sévigny. Black, all-black suit. I stood behind the door, and when he came in he saw George, and when he got past me I closed the door. He turned around—it startled him. He limped over and sat down and said, "George, you've got to come down. Come on, George." George said, "No, I'm not going to go down."

The meeting was in an office on the ground floor near the door on the west side. Sévigny left, and Nowlan said, "Well, I think I'll go home." I said, "It's a hell of a good idea, George. Let's go."

I was going to see him out. We walked down the stairs, and he said, "I think I'd better drop in here a minute." I said to him, "George, it's a mistake." "Well," he said, "I think it's all right just to drop in, say hello." So he went to the meeting.

Dalton Camp, quoted in Peter Stursberg, *Diefenbaker: Leadership Lost*, 1976

Ellen and Lumumba

Ellen Louks Fairclough (1905-) was Canada's first woman Cabinet Minister. She served in a variety of portfolios throughout the Diefenbaker years.

Canadian cabinet ministers tend to be tightwads, and no matter how often their pay and expense allowances go up, they can't be persuaded to pick up a tab and they hardly ever reciprocate all the diplomatic hospitality that comes their way in the Ottawa whirl. As for giving parties, they are poopers. The result is that whatever entertaining is done for diplomats or visiting dignitaries falls to the Governor General or to the speaker of the House of Commons, and the cabinet ministers get off scot free.

A notable exception to this pattern was Canada's first woman federal cabinet minister, Ellen Fairclough, who loved going to parties and loved giving them, even if she had to cough up some of the cost out of her own ample purse. Ellen was Diefenbaker's secretary of state, a job that gave her a special responsibility for visiting dignitaries, and she was on deck when Patrice Lumumba came flying into Ottawa.

Lumumba was prime minister of the Congo, and a strutter, and a stud. His memory is revered in revolutionary circles in various parts of the world, and there is a vast university in Moscow that bears his name where foreign students are indoctrinated into the gospel according to Marx. He brought an entourage of thirty to Ottawa, and no sooner were they ensconced in suites in the Chateau Laurier than they sent a message to Howard Green, the austere secretary of state for external affairs, asking, "Where are the women?"

Green, a prim and proper man with a minimal knowledge of the world outside Canada and no knowledge at all of Africa, sent back word that the Canadian government did not deal in such matters. One of Green's aides, in delivering the reply, let slip on the sly that maybe the distinguished guests could try the By Ward Market, the hangout for hookers, just two blocks down the street.

Upon receipt of these tidings, Lumumba went into a snit, and when it came time for the welcoming reception in the hotel that evening, with Howard Green as the host, he refused to show up. Finally he was persuaded to come, but the party had all the makings of a major fizzle, with Congolese and Canadian men standing around in surly silence and Howard Green frowning into his perpetual glass of orange juice, of which he consumed hundreds of barrels during his years at the diplomatic trough.

Enter Ellen Fairclough. With one twitch of her finely sculptured nose, she detected that the party was dead on its feet. "Whoop-de-doo!" she shouted, "let's get this thing on the road!" And she sashayed up to the prime minister of the Congo and told him to cheer up and enjoy himself.

Ellen did everything but chuck Lumumba under the chin. She led the assemblage in song and flounced up and down the room, and she got Lumumba laughing, and the rest of the Congolese loosened up too. The liquor flowed more copiously than Howard Green would have liked it to, either in the interest of temperance or the government's purse strings, it being well known that John Diefenbaker frowned on drinking at the public's expense. But Ellen's silver hair was flying and her arms were waving like wings, and the evening was a great success, and the Lumumba visit was off to a flying start.

After the party was over, Ellen returned to her suite upstairs in the hotel, exhausted but happy, having done her duty for Queen, country, and Howard Green. She changed into her nightdress and was about to flop into bed when there came a hammering on her door. She threw the security chain into place and opened the door a crack, revealing two of Lumumba's burly henchmen standing in the hall.

"Yes?" quavered Canada's first woman federal cabinet minister.

"The prime minister thanks you for the lovely party," said the larger of the two envoys. "He wishes you to know that he finds you charming and that he will receive you now in his quarters."

"The hell he will!" said the proud Ellen, and she moved to slam the door, but one of the callers blocked it with his booted foot.

There ensued a scene in which the two men tried to unhook the chain, and when that proved impossible they tried to break it, but fortunately for Ellen's honour, and Canada's, the Chateau Laurier has strong doors and everything held against the Congolese onslaughts. The men went away, and Canada's first woman federal cabinet minister rested in peace.

Charles Lynch, You Can't Print That, 1983

Dief and Hees

Toward the end of Diefenbaker's last administration the air was thick with plots and counter-plots, and numerous Cabinet Ministers, including the then Minister of Trade and Commerce, George Harris Hees (1910-   ) had privately vowed to resign.

Hees was the chairman of caucus and was in the centre of the table. To his right was Diefenbaker, and most of the cabinet were scattered among the members of the caucus. I deliberately put my chair just about four feet away from Diefenbaker because by this time my Irish was aroused and there was going to be some blood spilled if I had a chance. Hees starts out reading this paper and again the howls came up and Diefenbaker then just shushed me up. I wanted to move in but he just put his hand down, and I said when the old master himself wants to move in why should a second stringer move in.

So he began asking Hees a lot of questions, didn't you, didn't you, didn't you, he was destroying Hees and Hees began to cry. Great big tears dropped down and bounced off the table and then I got up and walked over into the corner. Terry Nugent came up to me and said, "Why are you standing over here?" I said, "I hate to see a grown man cry." "You never saw such a revival meeting," that's what Senator McCutcheon said. All these guys who had been plotting against Diefenbaker were up giving testimony—they were all for him.

Alvin Hamilton, quoted in Peter Stursberg, *Diefenbaker: Leadership Lost*, 1976

Instant Bagman

There was little money for the Conservative campaign of 1957 and the little there was came in very slowly — a clear sign that the business community thought the party's chances were poor. Indeed, the Ontario campaign might have collapsed before it began had George Hees not come to the rescue. The opening meeting in Massey Hall, attended by the province's eighty-five candidates, proved such a success that Diefenbaker described it as the turning point of the campaign.

It is so extraordinary how things happen. I was having lunch with somebody, I don't remember who, downtown on that day. I had been out in my riding, and was driving downtown. I had a few minutes to spare so I dropped in at the office of Harry Willis, the Ontario organizer, just to say "Hello, Harry. How are you doing? How are things going?" not thinking that things weren't going well at all. He was sitting in his office and he looked like a condemned man.

I said "Harry, what the hell is the matter with you?" He said, "We are never going to get going, never going to get going." I said, "Why not?"

"Well," he said, "these people are coming in from around the province tonight to be on the platform. I have to give each one of them $1000 to get the campaign going." This was only five weeks before the votes went into ballot boxes, and they hadn't gotten any money yet. He said, "Bev Matthews," who was our chief collector, "tells me," think of this, "that he can only give me about half the amount, about $45,000. At least half of these candidates have told me that if they don't get $1000 tonight, they won't run. They're not going to bankrupt themselves if we are in such bad shape that I can't give them $1000 to start their campaigns five weeks before election day. We are in terrible shape and they're not going to bankrupt themselves by going head over heels into debt. What am I going to do? There is nowhere I can get it. Bev Matthews says that we may get it sometime later but not now. He hasn't got it." Business didn't have any confidence in us at all.

So I said to Harry, "I can get some money for you." Of course, he looked at me with complete disbelief.

I went down to the Royal Bank. I bank at the Royal Bank, and our firm has always banked with the Royal Bank, which was the main thing, and therefore my credit was pretty good because the firm's credit was pretty good. My uncle had been a vice president of the bank. I went to the bank manager and said, "I will come back here in an hour and I want eighty-five packets, and in each packet, done up with an elastic, ten $100 bills. I want eight-five such packets, and I will be back in about an hour. Can you get it?" Well, he just about gagged, you know. This was the damndest thing he had ever heard. I said I would sign a note for it.

He said, "What do you want this for?"

I said, "Never you mind what I want it for, I want it, and I will be back in an hour. Will you get it?" Luckily it was the main branch. I came back in an hour, and he handed me this brown parcel of eight-five $1000 packages, all in negotiable money, and I called a taxi. If that taxi driver had ever known what he was driving uptown, I think he would have fainted.

I got to Harry Willis' office. I will never forget it. He was still, unbelieving, sitting behind his desk, like a man who had been condemned to the electric chair. I said, "Harry, here is your dough." He was just like a child on Christmas morning. He nearly wept he was so happy.

George Hees, quoted in Peter Stursberg, *Diefenbaker: Leadership Gained*, 1975

Busy Man

In October 1957 he [Hees] was on his way to speak at a meeting for Sidney E. Smith, the University of Toronto president who had just been appointed Secretary of State for External Affairs. At that time, George was federal Minister of Transport, in charge of air, rail and land transportation in Canada. As he was snoozing in the back seat, his driver stopped at a service station to go the wash room. George woke up when the driver was gone, and decided to go for a little walk. The driver returned and assuming that his passenger was still sleeping, drove off without him.

Time being short, Canada's number one transport man decided to hitch-hike. A car stopped and asked him where he was going. "I'm George Hees, and I'm trying to hitch a ride to Norwood to speak at a meeting for the Foreign Minister," he explained.

Assuming the man was either drunk or crazy, the driver took off into the night without opening the door. After several cars passed, a truck driver finally recognized him and drove him to the meeting. Arriving at Norwood an hour late, George was telling what happened to the people standing around. They couldn't believe him either. "We know you're a busy man, Mr. Hees, and we're awfully glad you came," said one old-timer, "you don't have to make up a story for us."

Gordon Aiken, Backbencher, 1974

The Multitudes

One of Hees's journeys into Saskatchewan won him the dubious distinction of having addressed the smallest public meeting in Canadian history. On a trip through Saskatchewan with Alvin Hamilton, then the Progressive Conservative leader for that province, Hees gave advance copies of his speeches to the *Saskatoon Star-Phoenix*, marked with dates of delivery. When Hees and Hamilton arrived at Star City, 120 miles northeast of Saskatoon, they were told by Jim Hill, the local organizer, that no hall had been hired because no other Conservative could be found in the district. Hees insisted that he had to make the speech, because the Saskatoon paper might run its report. Hill rounded up his brother George, and the two men sat in the back of Hamilton's car while Hees loudly intoned his address to them.

Peter C. Newman, Renegade in Power, 1963

Hee's Reputation

In Ottawa, he quickly gained the reputation of a parliamentary light-weight: Liberal backbenchers goaded him with the chant "Good suit—no brains," whenever he rose to speak.

He was labelled "the malarkey man in the House" by Jimmy Sinclair, the Liberal Minister of Fisheries, who called him "very charming, but better endowed physically than mentally." Even when Hees's attacks on government policies were well documented—such as his speeches on national defence and housing—Liberal cabinet ministers brushed them off as "nothing but Heesteria."

Peter C. Newman, Renegade in Power, 1963

Paul Martin and Mackenzie King

First elected a Member of the House of Commons in 1935, Paul Joseph Martin (1903-   ) was appointed to Mackenzie King's Cabinet in 1945. He went on to serve in the St. Laurent, Pearson, and (as a Senator) Trudeau Cabinets. He resigned his seat in the Senate in 1974 to become the Canadian High Commissioner in London.

I did not downplay Mackenzie King's importance and pointed out in most of my speeches that Canada needed his experience nationally and in the international arena. When the party was gearing up for the vote, my defence of Mackenzie King led to a curious situation. I was called to the prime minister's office; when I got there, Jack Pickersgill, fairly bouncing with excitement, said, "This is going to be an interesting session, Paul." I asked why, and he mysteriously replied, "You are going to become an author." Then I went in to see the prime minister. King was ensconced at the end of a long table; Ray Lawson, a prominent Liberal from London, was seated at his left. Making no bones about it, King began: "Martin, Mr. Lawson has prepared a book on me. I think that it would be an advantage if you were the author." I knew that King regarded me as a serious-minded man ("lugubrious" is the word he is reported to have used). He probably felt that it would be to his political advantage for the book, eulogizing the prime minister as a great social reformer, to appear with my name on it. I was flabbergasted but when I finally found my tongue, I hesitatingly asked if I could at least read the manuscript. King gave the distinct impression that he did not like my delay in giving an affirmative answer. To satisfy my conscience, I took the manuscript and made some changes in it before it appeared as an election document.

Paul Martin, *A Very Public Life*, I, 1983

Martin Versatile

He knew every trick of the parliamentary trade and was able to intervene with effect and without notice in any parliamentary imbroglio. Once, after the 1958 electoral débâcle, we had so few members that Paul found himself acting as the Liberal agricultural critic, a duty which he performed with aplomb. On yet another occasion when I rose as Leader of the Opposition, the Speaker betrayed our old friendship and strengthened his reputation for expertise and objectivity by ruling me out-of-order on some technicality. While the point was being argued, I told Paul to get the Speaker's eye at the first opportunity and give my speech, which we wished to get into Hansard that day—and into the press. I had a full typed text—those 'notes' which, under the rules, we were not allowed to read but could 'consult'—so as soon as he got on his feet I fed him the script, page by page, underlining what I wished him to emphasize. He performed magnificently, as if he had spent hours writing and memorizing the speech, and even the 'ranks of Tuscany,' who could see, naturally, what was going on, could 'scarce forbear to cheer.'

Mike: Memoirs of Lester B. Pearson,
Volume 3, John A. Munro and Alex. I. Inglis, eds., 1975

Martin at Work

When I arrived in Windsor I was surprised to find Paul Martin there to meet me. I thought he would have been in Ottawa but I should have known better. He had not remained the Member for Essex East since 1935 without maintaining a firm grip on everything that happened in his suzerainty. I should not have expected to meet with the local Liberal associations without Paul being there to supervise. It turned out to be a dinner meeting of about two hundred party workers held in a roadhouse on the outskirts of Windsor. A dance band played all the time in the next room, separated only by a temporary partition. The noise was deafening; one could hardly hear oneself think, and speaking over the din was an ordeal—but not, of course, to Paul.

He introduced me in the most superlative terms, and his compliments were so exaggerated and so prolonged that after ten or fifteen minutes everyone was laughing. I had no choice but to abandon my prepared speech and talk about Paul in kind, always a good thing to do in Windsor. Compliments about Paul, no matter how embellished, were accepted as the gospel truth by the faithful in that area.

Paul had shaken everybody's hand before dinner, and as soon as the speeches were over we both went around the room and shook hands with everyone again. When we had finished, he told me we might as well leave as there was nothing more to be accomplished. As we stepped outside onto a kind of porch, Paul pointed rather dramatically to a dark corner. In an obvious reference to the prohibition era, he whispered, "I saw a man shot there one evening." I replied, "Paul, I hope it was not your finger on the trigger." His reaction made it clear that I had passed the test.

Walter Gordon, *A Political Memoir*, 1977

Martin's Sense of Humour

Once when I was in Toronto with the Pearsons, I left their room in the Park Plaza and bumped into comedians Wayne and Shuster in the lobby. "Have you ever met Mike Pearson?" I asked. When they told me that they had not, I decided to take them up and introduce them. We rehearsed a little skit: they were to pretend to be recently arrived immigrants to Canada, who had asked me to see if Pearson could help bring their families into the country. Mike, working at a table in his dressing gown, did not recognize the two comics and was a little annoyed at being disturbed. Then Maryon came into the sitting room and shot me a look that said, "Why are you bothering us with this!" She, too, did not catch on at first, but then her eyes lit up: "You're Wayne and Shuster!" She and Mike got a great kick out of the prank. It was the beginning of a long friendship.

Paul Martin, *A Very Public Life*, II, 1985

Martin for Pope

During that first session, after the death of Pope John XXIII, I received a copy of the *Windsor Star* from a House of Commons pageboy. Its banner headline read LIBERAL FAVOURED FOR PAPACY; underneath were photographs of the five cardinals regarded as the most likely to become the new pontiff. Next to them, someone had carefully pasted a picture of me! Clipped to the paper was a note, purporting to come from the South Carleton Orange Lodge. It read, "Better Luck, Paul, than in '58." I must have been a sight to behold for those Tories who had concocted the ruse. Solemn-faced, I handed the paper to Mike Pearson, who laughed fit to die.

Paul Martin, *A Very Public Life*, II, 1985

Whelan on Martin

In those early years, when I was still a new boy on Parliament Hill, I used to have breakfast regularly with a group of other first-time MPs. We'd meet almost every morning in the parliamentary restaurant. We liked it because it's much quieter than the cafeteria and we could sit in a nice alcove all by ourselves.

Some mornings Paul Martin used to join us for a cup of coffee. As well as being a renowned parliamentarian he was quite famous as a cheapskate and by sitting with us he could always get away without paying for his coffee. When the waitress came by to take his order he'd always say, "Oh, just a cup of coffee, please." They all knew him and they wouldn't bother making out a new bill; they'd just laugh and let old Paul have a free cup. If he'd sat by himself he would have had to pay. Some of them told us afterwards that when Paul had first been elected in 1935 he used to leave a ten-cent tip and he was still leaving the same tip thirty years later.

Eugene Whelan, *Whelan*, 1986

Martin's Sense of Humour, II

I attended a three-day joint ministerial meeting with our Japanese opposite numbers, at which Paul Martin and the Japanese Foreign Minister acted as joint chairmen. We were entertained extensively and most generously, and at the conclusion of the meeting the Prime Minister of Japan, the late Hayato Ikeda, came out of hospital to preside at a luncheon in honour of the Canadian delegation. It was a lavish affair, and we were all relaxed and enjoying ourselves, especially Paul Martin who was relieved the meeting had gone off well. When the meal was over, the Prime Minister made a serious speech for half an hour or so on trade, finances, and economics. But as he spoke in Japanese, it was necessary at the conclusion of his remarks for an interpreter to repeat the whole thing over again in English. I remember smiling to myself about how Paul was going to handle these subjects in his reply, especially as neither of us appeared to have followed the Prime Minister's speech too closely. But I had underestimated Paul's dead-pan sense of humour. After thanking the Prime Minister for his hospitality, Paul stated, without a single muscle twitching to give himself away, that the Canadian delegation had met before the luncheon and decided that the Canadian Minister of Finance would reply to the Prime Minister's important speech. He then sat down leaving me no option but to rise and do the best I could do in the unexpected circumstances. In the presence of the Japanese Prime Minister and all his principal colleagues, I could not very well accuse my colleague, the Canadian Secretary of State for External Affairs, of being a practical joker.

Walter Gordon, *A Political Memoir*, 1977

I Have to Go

As Howard Green began his maiden speech as minister of external affairs, Pearson and I took our places side by side on the opposition front benches. Most members are not too interested in foreign affairs, and the House had emptied; even the prime minister was not in his seat, but Mike and I liked Green and wanted to show our goodwill. During the very long speech, I had to go to the bathroom in the worst way. But I did not want to show discourtesy to the new minister by leaving so conspicuously. In a whisper, I told Mike of my dilemma and he began to chortle; the more I squirmed the harder he laughed. By this time, our antics had disturbed Howard, so I decided to make a hurried trip to a small washroom that was in an office reserved for the prime minister, right behind the Speaker's chair. Making a hasty exist, I rushed into the office to find Diefenbaker relaxing, his feet up on the desk. The prime

ministerial jaw dropped when he saw me. Not having the time to explain my sudden presence, I dashed into his private bathroom. My business complete, I tore back into the chamber to hear Howard, calling
over my shoulder to Diefenbaker, "Why aren't you in the House listening to your new minister?" When I slipped into my seat again, Green
was still expostulating on war and peace, but Diefenbaker appeared behind the curtain, chuckling away and beckoning me to come over. I did
not want to leave my desk for a second time, but I felt like saying to Dief,
as one of the sentinels says to his companion in the opening scene of
Hamlet: "For this relief much thanks."

Paul Martin, *A Very Public Life*, II, 1985

Sinking Diplomat

I tried to go for a swim every day; but this was never allowed to interfere with business. On one occasion, an ambassador who had completed
his tour of duty insisted on seeing me — to pay his respects for a second
time. Since he had given me such short notice, I told him that our meeting would take place at Mooney's Bay beach, where I would be having
my daily dip. Out he came, but the minute he put his foot in the water,
I knew he was a non-swimmer. As I paddled around him, he tried to
have a serious conversation, all the while gurgling and swallowing water.
But when I turned my back for a moment, the poor man went under.
With some help, I hauled a very shaken diplomat to dry land, where we
finished our entente.

Paul Martin, *A Very Public Life*, II, 1985

Texas Style

*In 1965 Pearson and Martin journeyed to Texas to sign the Auto Pact with
President Johnson.*

Pearson and I signed the agreement with Lyndon Johnson and Dean
Rusk at the president's ranch in Texas in mid-January 1965. After a
night with Charles Ritchie, our ambassador in Washington, I flew to
Texas with Rusk on his government plane. We got there before Mike,
who was coming in from Miami. After the president and Lady Bird met
us at the airfield, we piled into a jeep; Johnson took the wheel and gave

us a tour of his enormous property. We had been driving for well over half-an-hour, when the telephone in the jeep rang; with one hand on the wheel and the other grasping the phone, the president announced that Mike's plane would be touching down at any minute. We drove back to the landing strip to meet the prime minister's jetstar and then walked over to a specially prepared stand in front of the television cameras, where the president welcomed us to Texas. He referred to his friend "Drew Pearson," the prime minister of Canada. I winced inwardly at his dreadful faux pas.

The formalities complete, we all got into a limousine, and again the president acted as chauffeur and cicerone. McGeorge Bundy, who had jointed our little party, sat up front with the president, while Pearson, Rusk and I scrunched into the back seat. For about an hour-and-a-half we drove over the scrubby Texas landscape. Somewhere in the middle of nowhere, a big helicopter came down on the road. Johnson pulled over, we all climbed into the helicopter and were whisked off to another portion of the presidential ranch. Then we had another ninety-minute drive. Up to this time, there had been hardly any discussion of Canada-US affairs. LBJ was full of his upcoming inauguration, and dwelt enthusiastically on his proposals for improving civil rights in the United States and rounding out his omnibus federal Education Act. At one point, he gave us a succinct lesson in presidential politics. Cocking his head towards the back seat, he asked: "Dean, has Senator so and so who had been defeated in the November elections ever asked to be made an ambassador?" Rusk replied that this was indeed the case. "Well, Dean, once in a tight vote in the Senate, I called him to say that I needed his vote. He told me, 'Lyndon, you can't have it'. Dean, he can't have an ambassadorship."

While all this was going on, my usual problem beset me — I had to go to the bathroom urgently. I whispered to Rusk about my discomfort, but the president overheard me and said, "So do I." Mike's dignity was a trifle ruffled! Johnson pulled the car over to the side of the road and the two of us stepped out and went about our affairs. As we stood there, the president began to rhapsodize about the Texan countryside, which did not excite me one bit. When we got back into the car, he called his wife on the phone to see if John Connolly, the governor of Texas, would have dinner with us that night. Then, to make sure that Connolly would come, he raised him on the limousine phone. Johnson offered to send a helicopter to Austin to bring Connolly over to dinner. Throughout all of this hugger mugger, Mike, who had expected our visit to be a bit more formal, was getting quite uncomfortable.

After settling the dinner invitation, the president phoned yet again and in short order a car pulled up beside us with a complete bar set up in its trunk. Everyone had a drink, we drove back to the helicopter, picked up the original car and went on to the president's home. We passed through a big entrance hall, full of the president's cowboy hats and boots, and were shown up to our rooms. Later, over drinks and dinner around a large oak table, LBJ again said not a word about affairs of state. Although a telephone sat right on the table in front of the president, he did not use it; instead, he kept popping up to go out to the hall to make his calls. The coming and going continued as we all sat around later, chatting over coffee, but Johnson finally did tell Mike how embarrassed he was for having called him "Drew." When the late news came on the television, we and millions more saw the president putting his foot in it all over again.

Next morning I got up early, as I usually do. Creeping downstairs in my pyjamas, I found one of the housekeeping staff in the kitchen, and she offered me a cup of coffee. On my way back up to read, I bumped into the president, coming down on an identical errand. He got his coffee and suggested that we sit with our cups in the living room. We spent the next hour deep in conversation about Vietnam, the Auto Pact, NATO, and a slew of other issues. This was the only sustained talk I had while we were Lyndon Johnson's guests. As the president spoke, he scanned his cables. The day before, American fighter aircraft in Vietnam had mistakenly bombed some of their own forces. He read me the cable and then called Robert McNamara. The president listened very quietly as the secretary of defence filled him in. Afterwards, we joined the others for breakfast, and then went outside and signed the Auto Pact on some rough benches that had been set up for the ceremony. Mike and I took our leave early in the afternoon. It had all been quite an experience.

Paul Martin, A Very Public Life, II, 1985

The Martin Style

He was a past master at handling the Speaker. Paul would smile — and then completely ignore the Speaker or turn his back on him. Everyone would be hollering, Mr. Speaker would be standing... and Paul would be coming on, making his points one by one, seemingly oblivious to the uproar. In those days, the Speaker couldn't kill your microphone to prevent you being heard, and Paul took full advantage of this. He could talk on any subject. Paul Martin talking about wheat made about as much sense as Jack Horner speaking on fish, but Paul could do it. Even if he didn't know a subject, he knew its political implications. One may not have liked his style or the way he went about things, but as a politician he was superb.

Jack Horner, My Own Brand, 1980

Bitter End

For a backbencher, the big thing, of course, was which candidate you were going to support. Most of them came courting and making the wildest promises—you'd be minister of this and minister of that. Paul Martin wanted my support—he expected it, because we'd known each other so long, we were old friends, and our ridings were next to one another. I'll say one thing for Paul: he didn't try to bribe me with a Cabinet post or some other plum. But I'd made up my mind I was going to support Trudeau, and when I told Paul to his face he was none too happy.

I delayed going to see him about it because I knew it would be unpleasant. But he called me four or five times and finally I said I'd come over and see him. When I got to his office I didn't beat around the bush. I said, "You know who I'm going to support, anyway. I'm supporting Trudeau and I've made up my mind." So he asked me why and I said, "Because Pierre Trudeau can lead us to a majority government and I don't think you can. I don't think you have enough support from Quebec." Just like that. That remark about Quebec would have hurt him, too, because he was bilingual and from a French Canadian family and he claimed during his campaign that if he won we could still say that we'd kept the principle of alternation going—that an English leader should be followed by a French leader.

As you can imagine, old Paul wasn't too happy when I said these things to him. And he tried to argue with me. He said, "Gene, out of the caucus I've got thirty-two members supporting me and a number of those are from Quebec." He was wrong and I told him so: "Paul you don't have any thirty-two. You've got five." I even told him who they were; I gave him the names, but he didn't believe me. Then I said, "Does this mean you were lying those times when you told me I was the wisest politician in the caucus?" "No," he said, "I meant what I said then and I mean what I say to you now. I want your support." Then I said, "You don't have a hope in hell of winning and I'm going to throw my support where it will do some good. I'm going to support Trudeau and I'm going to make a public announcement." Then he kind of begged me. He reminded me that we were both from Windsor and of how it would look if his own neighbour didn't support him. He cried at the end. It was a hard meeting.

Eugene Whelan, Whelan, 1986

Black Bart

John Whitney Pickersgill (1905-   ) served as an aide to MacKenzie King and St. Laurent before becoming Clerk of the Privy Council in 1952. He entered the St Laurent Cabinet as Secretary of State the following year and held various other portfolios under both St. Laurent and Pearson before leaving politics in 1967.

Pickersgill's way of dressing added to his reputation as a crafty figure. He wore a sort of a coat that hung loose—it looked something like a cape—and this wide brimmed black hat. He reminded me of Black Bart, a bandit in the silent movies I saw as a kid. In the House they used to say he only wore one blue serge suit that got shiny with use. He probably had three or four the same, but it seemed like he had only one.

He always wore suspenders and he'd hook his thumbs under them and stretch them out so far we were sure they'd break. In the House, when he made a real good hit against Mr. Diefenbaker, or when he asked a zinger question, he'd snap his braces and slide down under his desk until he'd pretty near disappear under the table he'd get laughing so much—all you could see was his head.

Eugene Whelan, Whelan, 1986

Jack's Purse

Though Pickersgill's influence was exercised in the hush of his office and the privacy of the cabinet chamber, he was best known for the displays he put on in the House of Commons. His penguin shape was constantly bobbing up and down during the excitement of debates. Physically clumsy, he was utterly incapable of sitting still. When he was a youngster, his grandmother had made him a standing offer of five cents for every five minutes he could keep quiet. "I needed the money badly, but I never earned a penny of it," he recalled.

The thrift he learned growing up on a prairie homestead dominated his life in the expenditure of both time and money. He never parted easily with the coins he carried in a woman's black, clasp-type change purse stuffed into his right hip pocket. He used pencils until they were inch-long stubs that could barely be gripped. He once complained at length in the House of Commons about the fifteen cents he had lost in an airport stamp-vending machine. On a twelve-day trip to British Columbia in 1952, as Clerk of the Privy Council, he submitted an expense account of $30.35. He wore only two kinds of tie—his Oxford New College brown-and-silver stripe and a blue-and-white polka dot—depending on friends to notice when the ties became frayed and send him new ones.

Peter C. Newman, *Distemper of Our Times*, 1968

Pickersgill and St. Laurent

The obscure fixer of the King era became the true grey eminence of Canadian politics under King's successor. When he was sworn into office on November 15, 1948, St Laurent had spent most of the preceding two years in the politically insulated External Affairs portfolio. He depended on the "special assistant" he had inherited from King for direction on how to operate the prime minister's office. Political observers in Ottawa insisted that for the first three months of St Laurent's term at least, the country was to an astonishing degree run by Jack Pickersgill. "I had a very great influence on Mr. St Laurent," Pickersgill admitted. "He had more confidence in me than in any cabinet minister or anyone else." During the 1949 election St Laurent made a pact that he would commit himself to no appointments or public appearances that weren't "cleared with Jack."

Peter C. Newman, *Distemper of Our Times*, 1968

Pickersgillian

John Whitney Pickersgill's approach to government was so uniquely his own that his name found a place in Canada's political dictionary. The expression "Pickersgillian" came to signify any partisan ploy that was too clever by half. His strong personality, encyclopaedic knowledge of Ottawa and its ways, his mastery of Commons rules and intense loyalty to Lester Pearson allowed him to exercise a decisive and not always benign leverage on the course of federal events. But his violent partisanship, dated view of Canadian society and erratic political judgement made him a doubtful asset to the hard-pressed government.

"Jack is so firmly hooked on the past that I sometimes think he's wearing cement boots," commented one of his colleagues. Another minister swore that rare indeed were the meetings of the Pearson Cabinet during which Pickersgill failed to mention the way Mackenzie King used to solve the crises of his day. Pickersgill readily billowed forth irrelevant historical date (such as the fact that John Bracken's Manitoba cabinet of 1922 was composed entirely of Presbyterians) but had little feeling for contemporary events.

Peter C. Newman, *Distemper of Our Times*, 1968

Job Creation

His world was vanishing but Pickersgill was shrewd enough to recognize it and proceeded to plan himself a new career. In the summer of 1967 Pickersgill as the minister of transport was busy piloting through the Commons the National Transportation Act, designed to regionalize Canada's obsolete railway system. Few MPs noticed that the presidency of the new Canadian Transport Commission set up by the legislation was made particularly attractive. The annual salary was set at $40,000 a year and the retirement age (Pickersgill was then sixty-two) was not the usual sixty-five, but seventy. The position was never advertised by the Civil Service Commission. Having written himself a job description, Pickersgill resigned from cabinet and recommended himself for the opening. Pearson accepted and "Sailor Jack" launched himself on his new career.

The circumstances that allowed Jack Pickersgill to flourish were part of a cynical old-style approach to Canadian politics. But even in that context he was one of a kind.

Peter C. Newman, Home Country, 1973

Jack Pickersgill's Judgement

His party affiliation seemed so close to a religion that one wondered whether faith alone and not reason informed him. Questioned by a reporter about the characteristics of Liberal prime ministers he replied: "They never, any of them, ever told a conscious lie or allowed anything that was calculated to give a false impression. Mackenzie King, for instance, was meticulous to the point of being tiresome about it, putting in all sorts of qualifications so that nobody in any conceivable circumstances could ever show that there was anything about his statements that was untrue."

If the Liberals were lily white in the Pickersgillian lexicon, the Tories were jet black. "The real trouble with the Conservative party," he once said, "is that basically it has been a party of Anglo-Saxon racists. They really don't believe in the equality of all Canadians. They really don't believe the French have any rights in this country, unless they act like a conquered people." On another occasion he remarked that Conservative governments are "like having mumps—something you have to endure once in your lifetime, but when it's over you don't ever want it again."

Peter C. Newman, Home Country, 1973

Native Son

"Mr. Pickersgill," asked a reporter, "now that you are leaving public life, have you any plans to live in Newfoundland?"

"Oh, no," replied the long time cabinet minister, "if I got elected six times without living there, I see no reason to live there now."

Gordon Aiken, Backbencher, 1974

Lester Pearson

Lester Bowles Pearson (1897-1972) entered politics in 1948 after twenty years with external affairs. He became Leader of the Opposition in 1958 and Prime Minister in 1963, a post he resigned in 1968.

Lester B. Pearson is a man of average size at 5 feet 9 inches and 173 pounds, with hazel eyes, thinning gray hair that tends to drift down over his forehead when he speaks, and a pleasant Irish face. During his op-position years newspaper cartoonists despaired of his lack of features distinctive enough to caricature and did what they could with his addic-tion to bow ties, even after he took to wearing four-in-hands. He ha-bitually wears dark suits, chosen for him by Mrs. Pearson. His speaking style is more suited to the lecture platform that the political stump. In the House of Commons, his favorite stance for a major address is to stand with a sheaf of notes in his left hand and his right hand in his trouser pocket. He is more inclined to emphasize sentences with mo-tions of his body and head than with manual gestures, and when he uses his hands to stress a point he tends to use short, chopping motions. With small groups of specialized audiences he conveys an air of sincerity and reasoned intelligence. As a political debater his strongest feature is the Adlai Stevenson type of spontaneous quip.

John Robinson Beal, *Pearson Phenomenon*, 1964

Isn't it Awful?

During the early part of the second World War Pearson remained in Ot-tawa. Norman Robertson directed Canadian diplomacy throughout the war.

He was still Robertson's assistant at the time of Pearl Harbor. Though it was Sunday, he was at the office when he got the news, from some-one who had heard the radio. He recalls he felt a tremendous relief, thinking that now there was no doubt who would win the war; although he had never believed Britain would give in and lose the war, it was dif-ficult at that stage to see how she could win. At home Mrs. Pearson and twelve-year-old Patsy had heard the radio reports of the Japanese at-tack, too. Shortly afterward a caller stopped at the house: General

Crerar, who was by then chief of the general staff, and who had been out for a Sunday afternoon walk in Rockcliffe Park, unaware of the tremendous turn the war had taken. Mrs. Pearson sent Patsy downstairs to talk to the General until she could come down. After exhausting the weather as a topic, Patsy remarked: "Isn't it awful about the Japanese bombing Pearl Harbor?"

"What!" exploded the General. "They haven't!"

"Oh, yes, they have," Patsy told him.

Crerar paced the floor, muttering, "I don't believe it!" and then walked out the front door without further ado.

John Robinson Beal, *Pearson Phenomenon*, 1964

Minister of the Crown

Pearson makes the transition from bureaucrat to politician.

I discussed all the pros and cons with my wife. She knew that my mind was moving toward one decision. She did not disagree with it, though she would have preferred the other one. In any event, the matter was put with characteristic clarity by our son at a family conference. After I had been engaged in "on the one hand" and "on the other hand" exercise for some time, he broke in: "Why are you wasting so much time, Dad? You know that by now you have made up your mind and all you want is for the three of us to tell you that this is the right decision and to confirm your judgment. It's OK." So I told Mr. King and Mr. St Laurent that I was available for new duties.

I recall so well Mr. King's remark on hearing this. "Now, St Laurent, we're going to have to get him elected." I suddenly realized, almost with a shock, that there was more to politics than being made Secretary of State for External Affairs. A few constituencies were mentioned and discarded as a possible political home. Then Mr. King decided that the member for Algoma East, who was marked for elevation to the Senate before the next election, should be given that honour at once. This would mean a vacancy in the Commons. Mr. King asked me whether I had any connection with Algoma East. My reply was so negative that he had to show me where it was on the electoral map. I did, however, agree to take my chances there if a constituency convention would accept me. It was a choice I never regretted, either politically or personally.

On 10 September Mr. King told his Cabinet that they were to have a new colleague. He then had the necessary Order-in-Council passed, took me to be sworn in, presented me with the Bible on which this was done, and, finally, with Mr. St. Laurent, exposed me for the first time as a Minister and a politician to the gentlemen of the press. This one was an easy and friendly conference, only slightly marred by my quip in reply to the question: "How long, Mr. Pearson, have you been a member of the Liberal party." " Since I was sworn in as a Minister a couple of hours ago." I should have learned by now that, while quips can get a politician headlines, they can also get him more easily into trouble than more serious observations.

At the end of the day, one so momentous for me, I called my aged mother in Toronto to tell her that I was now the Minister for External Affairs in the government of Canada. She had once hoped that I would be a Minister of the Gospel, so could not refrain from sending me her congratulations, her love and best wishes in these words: "Well, I am glad you have at last become a Minister, if only a second-class one."

Mike: Memoirs of Lester B. Pearson, Volume 2, John A. Munro and
Alex. I. Inglis, eds., 1973

Coffee and Doughnuts

From 1948 to 1968, Pearson represented the constituency of Algoma East.

In Algoma East politics and elections were taken seriously. Particularly on Manitoulin Island, meetings, however small, were conducted with due dignity and formality. On occasion, in some little red schoolhouse, there might be no more than a dozen or so present, half of whom would be on the platform and on the programme. Once, in my early days, when the audience and the performers were about equally divided, I ventured to suggest to the chairman that it might be more sensible if we just sat around and talked informally. "Not at all. This is a meeting and we have a programme." So we went through the prescribed ritual, as if I were addressing a large rally in a coliseum. At the beginning we sang "O Canada." At the end there was "God Save the Queen." In between, I was formally introduced, along with other platform guests. I spoke. I was thanked. The meeting adjourned.

At one of my smallest gatherings I was once thanked by a gentleman whose passion was not politics but monetary theory. This was his great opportunity to explain his views on the subject in public to a Cabinet Minister, and this he did for thirty minutes. I felt I should now get up and thank him in turn.

Introductions were usually shorter than this, but not always. The shortest and best I have ever experienced was at a constituency meeting when the chairman, a taciturn and weather-beaten farmer, spoke: "I have been asked to introduce Mr. Pearson, who has been asked to speak to us. He will." Each visit to a community at any hour of the day called at the very least for "coffee and doughnuts." During a campaign this might mean eating every hour or two. Once at the end of a day of travelling and speaking, greeting and eating, my wife and I found ourselves at a meeting of party officials from the various sections of the constituency. The survey of campaign progress was over by ten o'clock or so, and the moment for another snack had arrived, when the chairman said: "Is there anything else to bring up?" My wife who, as was her custom, had been attentive but silent all day, spoke up, to general surprise and pleasure: "Yes, I would like to bring something up." "What is it?" asked the chairman with respectful interest. "Twelve cups of coffee and eight doughnuts!" That remark got greater publicity than any of the wise and weighty political observations I had made during the day.

Mike: Memoirs of Lester B. Pearson, Volume 2, John A. Munro and
Alex. I. Inglis, eds., 1973

Beyond the Line of Duty

In 1955 Pearson visited the Soviet Union—the first time a Canadian foreign minister had visited that country. Toward the end of the visit he and the other members of the Canadian delegation were entertained by Nikita Khrushchev.

Some time after 10 PM Khrushchev suggested that we eat, and we followed him down the hall to a great dining room. He carefully pointed out to us three bathrooms off the dining room, the significance of which, at least in his mind, became apparent later during the "vodka" part of the evening. After sitting down to a table groaning with every kind of Russian food and drink, Khrushchev asked if we minded if the family joined us for dinner, as "they are hungry too." We thought this was fine, so he waddled away, returning with Mrs. Khrushchev, who turned out to be a plainly dressed, sturdy peasant type, with a strong, weather-beaten, but not unpleasant face. Their daughter had tired of waiting for dinner and had gone to the cinema.

Khrushchev was intensely interested in Ignatieff, "the Count" as he kept calling him, in tones which were half way between insult and re-spect. Mrs. Khrushchev, who sat next to him, was all respect. It soon became apparent that Khrushchev was determined, ably seconded by Bulganin, to put us all "under the table." He and Bulganin proposed toast after toast in "pepper vodka" and they kept eagle eyes on us, espe-cially on George and Ray Crépault (the "wily French boy," as they called him) to make sure that it was "bottoms up" each time. Someone said we drank eighteen toasts, but I wouldn't know. I do remember we even drank to the Canadian wheat surplus. "Drink up like a Russian," Khrushchev kept warning George. The conversation and the toasts were pretty general and Khrushchev did most of the talking, though Bul-ganin did not hesitate to pull him up once or twice. Once Bulganin pro-posed a toast to our Prime Minister, with whom he knew, so he said, I was on very close and friendly terms. This gave him a cue to emphasize that he and "Nikita" were on the same terms, had worked together as the closest of friends for years, and would continue to do so and with their colleagues. This was not the first time that it had been strongly suggested to me that the government was a "collective" or a "group" one, the inference being that there was no Stalin and hence no Stalin-ism.

We also toasted President Eisenhower's recovery from his illness and both Bulganin and Khrushchev said, and it sounded genuine, how much they had been impressed by him at Geneva, and that he was a good and "peace-loving" man. Khrushchev even went further and as the eve-ning went on, the atmosphere became mellower and mellower. John Watkins, however, looked less and less happy, and the rest of us also found the going pretty tough, except the two Russians, Watkins' friends "Aloysha" and Chuvakhin, who were not pressed to drink anything, and Troyanovsky, who couldn't possibly drink and translate. The latter he did magnificently and, according to our own two Russian speakers, fairly and accurately.

If Khrushchev had had his way, we would have been there, in one way or another, all night, but Bulganin finally assisted us in breaking up the party. About 12:30 the four Canadians marched straightly, heads up, with fixed determination and without any assistance, to our car, after a very spirited leave taking. We left our two Russian hosts in worse condition than we were, and we felt that we had not done too badly, either socially or diplomatically. I would like to think that we had earned medals that night for conviviality beyond the line of duty! But "once in a lifetime" only!

The sky was blue, the sun clear and bright, the prospect fair on the morning of 12 October. The four Canadians were not quite so fair and bright. After sunning ourselves for an hour the next morning we left by motor for a 148 kilometre drive to the airport.

Half the drive was along the Black Sea coast, with the roads, the curves, and the cliffs even more spectacular and, in view of the night before, far more disturbing than they had been the previous afternoon. It really was a very trying experience, as we screeched around the bends. At one point I stopped the car on the pretence of looking at the view. Then, about five miles down the road, we stopped to see a monument to Marshal Kutusov. "At this very point," said Chuvakhin with pride, "the Marshal lost an eye defeating the Turks." My sour reply was that you had better raise a monument to me some miles back at that place where I lost my stomach!

Mike: Memoirs of Lester B. Pearson,
Volume 2, John A. Munro and Alex. I. Inglis, eds., 1973

Where the Hell is Sharm el Sheihk?

I have a vivid recollection of him kicking off his shoes and putting his stockinged feet up on the coffee table during the Suez Crisis of 1956. When he noticed that the table had a map of the world inlaid into it, he leaned forward and pointed to the Middle East. "Where the hell," he asked, "is Sharm el Sheikh?" He had been engaged in furious negotiations all that day about the disposition of that port on the Gulf of Aqaba, without knowing where it was, though he had a vague memory of having flown over it years before.

Charles Lynch, *You Can't Print That*, 1983

Heard the News?

In 1957 Pearson was awarded the Nobel peace prize for his role in the Suez crisis.

Pearson learned from the press that he had won the Nobel peace prize. It was on the day Prime Minister John Diefenbaker was facing his first parliament, in October, 1957. Pearson was in his first-floor office in the centre block of the parliament buildings, reflecting gloomily that it was Mr. St. Laurent and he who had originally invited the queen to come to Ottawa for the ceremony of opening, which is usually performed by her representative in Canada, the governor general. Now, as a result of the 1957 election, another government was in charge.

The telephone rang. It was a call from Canadian Press.

"What comment do you have on winning the Nobel peace prize?" the reporter asked. "What!" Pearson exploded. "You must be mistaken. It must be that I have been nominated for the prize. I've been nominated before." "Just a minute, I'll check," said the reporter. "No, that's right, you've been awarded the prize." "Gosh!" said Pearson. "I'll have to call my wife and let her know."

John Robinson Beal, *Pearson Phenomenon*, 1964

Pearson and Smallwood

Whenever Pearson campaigned in Newfoundland, the inimitable Joey Smallwood was at his side.

Smallwood was totally committed to politics, and knew everything about political tactics—especially, his envious opponents would say, the trickier kind. He used to smile at these accusations and put them down to jealousy. Never did I campaign in Newfoundland without a motorcade from the airport at St John's to the hotel with, naturally, many more cars than there were in the welcome for the Tory leader the week before. Then there would be a drive through the streets in an open car. On one occasion the weather was so atrocious, with cold and sleeting rain pelting down, that I assumed the drive would be called off. My mistake. We started at the appointed time with the leaders in the lead in an open car. Joey insisted that I sit up with him at the back so that everybody could look at me. So far as I could see "everybody" was "nobody" because the streets were empty. He assured me, however, that faces were pressed against every pane of glass and that I should wave and smile enthusiastically for their benefit. I felt foolish, and was miserably soaked and cold. At one point our road went through a cemetery and I thought that here, at least, I would be able to get down and crouch from the elements for a few moments. "No, no," said Joey, "stay up there and wave. Some of your most faithful voters are in there."

Mike: Memoirs of Lester B. Pearson, Volume 2, John A. Munro and
Alex. I. Inglis, eds., 1973

Ghosting for Pearson

Pearson worked and re-worked the drafts of speeches supplied by his assistants, favouring strings of carefully shaded adjectives and complex sentences with triple subjects and triple predicates. While he put a great deal of energy into polishing his texts, he delivered most of his addresses as if they had been written by someone else in another language that he barely spoke or understood. Only before small groups, preferably in university common rooms, did he speak with feeling and style, without the self-consciousness that was so punishing to him on television or before large audiences.

A senior aide recalled taking the draft of a speech to the PM at his summer residence where, to his horror, the Pearson's poodle started to play with it, tearing a page or two. When he tried to rescue the manuscript, Pearson tiredly waved him away with the comment: "Oh, let him have it; he'll have more fun with it than I will."

Peter C. Newman, *Distemper of Our Times*, 1968

Washington Calling

The Pearson campaign of 1963.

I was visiting Northern Alberta on 28 March and had three separate meetings scheduled for Edmonton that evening, at 7, 8 and 9 p.m. I had just reached the last one, in a Legion Hall, had taken my place on the platform amidst the cheers of the faithful, and was about to be introduced when the chairman whispered that there was a long-distance call for me from Washington, urgent. Would I take it in the basement room where the phone was? Mystified, I said, 'of course' and was taken to the phone by the janitor of the hall who was much impressed, he told me. He had answered the call and it was from the White House. My mystification turned to alarm, as one of Mr. Diefenbaker's most strident criticisms of me in the campaign was that I was a tool of the Americans and, if the Liberals were elected, the country would be dominated by Washington. I could see without effort what he would do with the news that, so anxious was President Kennedy to get me elected, he had phoned me from the White House with advice, assistance, and comfort. When I reached the phone, I found that it was a Canadian journalist friend of mine stationed in Washington phoning from the White House Press Room, where he had been discussing the Canadian election. So he thought he would call to see how we were doing. The switchboard in Ottawa, with great and dangerous efficiency, found out, from our central organization, where I was supposed to be and switched the Washington call to Edmonton. This was a narrow escape since I knew that there were people abroad in the land who would never believe my explanation of the incident and insist that it was a deep dark American plot to take over the country via Pearson and the liberals. To my relief, it never was reported; the janitor said nothing about the call.

Mike: Memoirs of Lester B. Pearson,
Volume 3, John A. Munro and Alex. I. Inglis, eds., 1975

A Day in the Life

Becoming Prime Minister changed Mike Pearson very little. His personal tastes remained simple and surprisingly unsophisticated considering the number of years he had spent in the supercivilized environment of the diplomatic circuit. After a breakfast of toast with cheese and marmalade he would be driven to the office in his Buick Wildcat, arriving about 8:15. He'd work alone until nine, then see his main advisers to scan the day ahead. This daily session, known to his personal staff as "the prayer meeting," was the most important element in planning the Pearson Government's initiatives, deferring its decisions, and trying to react to the various events that were always threatening to overwhelm it.

Pearson would usually eat lunch (oyster or clam chowder, poached eggs and apple pie) in his office and leave at six with at least three hours of work in his briefcase. He could master complicated briefs and memos very quickly, signing most of his comments with the initials PM (for Prime Minister) instead of a plain LBP. He could be tough in dealing with the advice proffered in some memos, dismissing it with the marginal comment "This won't do," but more often he left the memo writer puzzled about his intentions. One senior adviser recalled ending his memorandum on an important political problem by suggesting alternative courses of action. Pearson sent it back, with a notation beside the two suggested options that merely read: "I agree."

Pearson rarely attended (or gave) cocktail parties and when he did go, he usually lingered briefly, sipping a weak rye and ginger ale. His official residence in no way became the capital's social or cultural centre. He liked listening to Brahms, occasionally tinkled on the piano, and went to view the offerings of touring theatrical companies that came irregularly to Ottawa, but his great relaxations were watching television westerns and sports.

Peter C. Newman, *Distemper of Our Times*, 1968

Pearson, Diefenbaker and the Fish

The rivalry between Lester Pearson and John Diefenbaker even intruded into sport. They both enjoyed fishing but neither had much luck at Harrington Lake, the official summer residence of Canadian prime ministers. Pearson kept hearing rumours that Diefenbaker had fished a 4 pound trout out of the lake. Unable to match this record, he tracked the story down by talking to a farmer who lived nearby and was delighted to discover that while Diefenbaker had hooked such a fish, he had never got it into his boat.

Peter C. Newman, Distemper of Our Times, 1968

Setting the Tone

At our first meeting around the Cabinet table in the historic room in the East Block we were a highly confident and cheerful group, looking ahead to a bright and productive future. Presiding from the high-backed, velvet-seated, awe-inspiring chair, more like a throne, on which prime ministers had perched, or sat, or lounged since 1867, I made one innovation. I asked Mr. Chevrier in French what he thought about something or other. He replied in French. I was anxious to establish at once that every French-speaking member had the right to use his own language in Cabinet if he so desired. There remained, of course, the old difficulty of converting desire into practice; if someone spoke French, only a few of the English-speaking members would understand; we certainly did not want translators for Cabinet discussions, even if this had been constitutionally permissible. Hence, though French was used more frequently in my Cabinets than before, English remained the normal language for our meetings.

Mike: Memoirs of Lester B. Pearson,
Volume 3, John A. Munro and Alex. I. Inglis, eds., 1975

An Urgent Matter of State

He [Pearson] rose and did his ablutions, and while he was looking in the mirror adjusting his polka-dot bow tie, wondering what the first challenge of high office would be, the telephone rang. It was a message from Governor General Vanier from his sick bed in Government House. Would Pearson come to Vanier's bedside with all speed to attend to an urgent matter of state?

Ah, thought Pearson with relish, this was it. The summit. The first big problem and the first big decision. He hastened to Rideau Hall and was ushered into the bedroom of his old friend.

"Thank God, Mike you are here. We have this awful problem to settle." "Ready, sir!" said the eager Pearson, "What is it?" "It's Vincent." "Vincent?" "Vincent Massey, he's been driving me crazy!" Vanier indicated a pile of correspondence on a bedside table. "He's been flooding me with letters for months, and I've been passing copies to that man, but he won't do anything." "That man?" "Diefenbaker. He hates Vincent, you know." "Yes, I know," said the crestfallen Pearson. "But what's the problem?" Vanier sighed. "Vincent is building Massey College at the University of Toronto and he wants his coat of arms over the archway." "So?" "So the Massey coat of arms contains nothing to indicate that Vincent was Governor General. It's all ploughs and pitchforks and threshing machines. He wants the coat of arms amended." "So?" "So the application can't go forward without the government's endorsation, and Diefenbaker wouldn't give it, and Vincent is enraged." "Is that all?" asked Pearson, deflated. "All!" fumed Vanier. "Nothing has caused me more trouble." "Well," said Pearson, "it need trouble you no more. I agree to whatever it is Vincent wants." "It's not that simple," said Vanier. "It needs the approval of your secretary of state." "Who is my secretary of state?" "I believe it's Jack Pickersgill, Prime Minister." "Well then, Pickersgill agrees." "No," said Vanier, "it's not that simple. It has to be stamped with the Great Seal of Canada." "Where is the wretched thing, then?" "It is in the custody of Pickersgill."

Pearson picked up the phone and demanded to be put in touch with Pickersgill, and when contact was made he instructed his secretary of state to round up the Great Seal with all speed and get it over to Government House in his own hands. Pickersgill got busy and arrived with the Great Seal, and the documents were processed on the spot and dispatched to London, and the Massey coat of arms was properly amended before being inserted into the wall of Massey College. Pearson said that, after that episode, he never did take affairs of state too seriously, using the Massey incident as his measuring stick.

Charles Lynch, *You Can't Print That*, 1983

Baseball Expert

The President had been told by the American Ambassador, Walton Butterworth, that baseball was a great hobby of mine. The President may have treated this information skeptically, knowing as he did that politicians must throw out ceremonial balls from time to time. Perhaps my hobby was "political" baseball rather than the real thing. In any event, he had on his staff a personal confidant, a shrewd Boston Irishman named Powers. Powers was famous not only for his statistical infallibility on past election returns but also on baseball. I suspect that John Kennedy must have primed him to bring up the subject at dinner on our first night at Hyannis Port. I love to talk baseball and so we tossed batting and earned run averages back and forth, with Powers throwing a few curves at me and my answers showing that I knew something about the sport. Then he mentioned a game played in Detroit the year before in which, he claimed, the pitcher had thrown a no-hitter and nonetheless lost, an almost unheard of event. I was able to fill in some of the details: the pitcher had not allowed any hits but he was pulled in the seventh inning, and the relief pitcher had let in the winning run in the tenth. I was able to add: "As a matter of fact, the reliever was Ken MacKenzie." Powers was somewhat incredulous, so at my invitation he sent someone to check it. I was proved right and my reputation was established once and for all in that group, although the only reason I knew this particularly obscure fact was that Ken MacKenzie was a Canadian who lived in Gore Bay on Manitoulin Island in my constituency. Indeed, I had helped to get him into professional baseball. I am not sure whether or not President Kennedy was impressed by my grasp of North American and international affairs, but I certainly know that Powers was impressed by my knowledge of baseball.

Mike: Memoirs of Lester B. Pearson,
Volume 3, John A. Munro and Alex. I. Inglis, eds., 1975

Sports Nut

Pearson's passion for baseball, hockey and football was intense. On one occasion when he met two Ottawa Rough Riders in mufti, walking along a Chateau Laurier corridor, he not only recognized them but knew what positions they played and what their records were. After a crucial game in the 1965 Stanley Cup play-offs, he was taken to visit the Maple Leaf dressing room. Even though the exhausted players were sitting around in sweaty underwear with their numbers off, he knew each man's name and could discuss his scoring history.

Earlier, during a dismal political journey into rural Saskatchewan in 1958, Pearson was slumped in the back of a car, listening to the rasping tones of an old political colleague, Jimmy Gardiner, as he held forth on the iniquities of Tory agricultural policies. Pearson said nothing for mile after dusty mile, but as they drove through a small elevator town he suddenly came to life and interrupted Gardiner by abruptly exclaiming "Hey, that was Floral we just passed through. That's where Gordie Howe was born."

Peter C. Newman, *Distemper of Our Times*, 1968

Pearson in Caucus

Pearson used to let the caucus be so free that sometimes they'd pretty near come to fisticuffs. There was the time when Judy LaMarsh had done something or other—she was Minister of National Health and Welfare—and the caucus was fighting mad. They wanted Pearson to fire her and they really made a hell of a fuss that day. Even the senators were aroused. I'll never forget Senator David Croll, with his great shock of grey hair, holding up his hand with his thumb sticking out and his two fingers bent back and lecturing Pearson. He said, "Mike, you're not enough of a son of a bitch to be Prime Minister." He meant that Pearson didn't have the toughness to fire someone when he or she needed to be fired.

Eugene Whelan, *Whelan*, 1986

Hotline

Pearson's amiable and irrelevant lack of pretension was noticeable even in the trivia of his office arrangements. John Diefenbaker had always kept in full view as a symbol of his power the red NORAD emergency telephone that connects the Prime Minister of Canada directly to the President of the United States. "I can get Ike any time," he would boast to visitors. Pearson not only removed the instrument from his desk, but hid it so carelessly that one morning during the winter of 1964 when it rang, he couldn't find it. Paul Martin, the External Affairs Secretary, was in the PM's office at the time. The two men heard the NORAD phone buzzing, couldn't locate it and began to chase each other around the room like a pair of Keystone Kops.

"My God, Mike," said Martin, "do you realize this could mean war?"

"No," Pearson puffed, "they can't start a war if we don't answer that phone."

The instrument was finally located behind a curtain and the caller—who wanted to know if "Charlie" was there—turned out, by incredible coincidence, to have both the wrong number and accidental access to one of the world's most private hot-lines.

Peter C. Newman, *Distemper of Our Times*, 1968

Pearson Angry

Something, I forget exactly what, was leaked during the last six weeks or so of Pearson's tenure. He was furious. (He really only became angry half a dozen times in five years of Cabinet and perhaps fewer in the House, and I was always concerned for his health when he did.) His face became suffused with blood, the veins in his neck and forehead bulged, and he had to restrain himself with effort. This time he made it clear he was mad and had had enough. We all had.

Judy LaMarsh, *Bird in a Gilded Cage*, 1968

Plugging Leaks

In 1965, the Prime Minister was talking to us about leaks. They bothered us so much that the latest was often the topic wherever a group of ministers congregated. The Prime Minister had just informed us that he was making new appointments to the Cabinet. There had been plenty of press speculation as to whom it might be, but none of us at the table knew whom it was he had in mind. He had just revealed the name of our new colleague and no Minister had left the room when a message was brought in to George McIlraith. He started visibly, and then broke into the discussion to tell us that the local newspapers had just hit the street naming the new appointee. (It was, if I remember correctly, Leo Cadieux.) The Prime minister was very upset. He had scheduled a press conference for later in that day to make his announcement, and the Governor General had not, as yet, been informed. He glared angrily around, but nothing but innocent faces answered his look. It was a puzzle to us all. Later it was explained that someone in the Prime Minister's office had telephoned the Liberal Federation to get background material for the Prime Minister's press conference statement on Cadieux, and someone there had mentioned the name, in all innocence, to one of the press corps. Would that all leaks had been so easily traced, or were so innocent!

Judy LaMarsh, *Bird in a Gilded Cage*, 1968

Dynamite

Perhaps the most violent expression (whatever the precise cause) of popular feeling was the action of the man who, in May 1966, tried to dynamite us in the House. It was during the question period. An explosion was heard but we continued in debate (I thought perhaps an elevator had collapsed) until I was handed a note that a man had killed himself in the washroom with a bomb. He had been seated in the Gallery with the device under his coat when he got permission to leave his seat and go to the washroom. There he tried to do whatever you do with a dynamite bomb that will set it off; he apparently mistimed the fuse and blew himself up. Had he been a little more accurate in his timing he would have blown up most of the members of the government (I assume he would have thrown the bomb in our direction). It was a terribly dramatic, terribly distressing afternoon.

One aspect of this tragedy was not generally known. The night before, while my wife and I were having dinner at Sussex Drive, the man had come to see me. (This was before the days of high security.) The maid sent him away with the advice: "If you have anything important to tell Mr. Pearson, you can go to his office tomorrow morning and the staff there will take your message to him and, if necessary, you can see the Prime Minister then." He said: "Tomorrow will be too late."

Mike: Memoirs of Lester B. Pearson,
Volume 3, John A. Munro and Alex. I. Inglis, eds., 1975

Vive le Québec Libre

The arrival of the French President passed without incident. The next day General de Gaulle made his historic progress and triumphant cavalcade from Quebec to Montreal. The special feeling and attention which he was receiving in Quebec was natural enough, and this did not worry me. But it was quite different when he reached Montreal. I was sitting in the small drawing-room upstairs at Sussex Drive watching him on television when he began his balcony speech. I could hardly believe my ears when I heard the words he uttered: "Vive le Québec libre." This was the slogan of separatists dedicated to the dismemberment of that Canada whose independence de Gaulle had wished to see assured only a few years before, when he proposed my health in Paris. This was a reflection on and almost an insult to the federal government. I have often been asked whether that phrase might perhaps have slipped out in the excitement of the moment. It is conceivable. No doubt this was a very emotional occasion for General de Gaulle. But he was not the sort of man to do or say things without careful thought. In any case, this phrase was impossible for any federal government to accept in the circumstances and in the atmosphere of the time. Nonetheless, I was not as distressed about that remark as I was about the analogy he made comparing his procession on that day to his march into Paris during the liberation of 1944. That I found infuriating. That his entry into Montreal should be compared in any way, shape, or form with his entry into Paris following the Nazi occupation was entirely unacceptable. I grabbed a pencil and started to write a reply. (It is always good to get something down on paper that can be torn up later.) Then my phone began to ring.

I called a Cabinet meeting for the next morning and told my colleagues that a statement would have to be issued very promptly. I undertook to prepare a draft. We knew what would happen if we did not take quick action. Public opinion would quite rightly slaughter us if we let this incident go by default and received General de Gaulle in Ottawa as though nothing had happened. We did not tell the General that in view of what had happened in Montreal it would be preferable if he went home. But I had no illusions in my own mind that de Gaulle would come to Ottawa after he had read my statement. That evening I went on the air to deliver it. I first made it clear that de Gaulle's words were "unacceptable" to the Canadian people and government. The statement went on:

The people of Canada are free. Every province of Canada is free. Canadians do not need to be liberated. Indeed, many thousands of Canadians gave their lives in two world wars in the liberation of France and other European countries.

Canada will remain united and will reject any effort to destroy her unity.

We also sent a copy to the French Embassy. I understand that when General de Gaulle received a copy (after he had retired for the night), he immediately said: "Get the plane ready: we're going home."

Mike: Memoirs of Lester B. Pearson,
Volume 3, John A. Munro and Alex. I. Inglis, eds., 1975

Giving it All Up

The change-over took place Saturday, 20 April, when I went to Rideau Hall to resign, as I had done once before after St Laurent's government was defeated. I went by myself for the last time as Prime Minister to greet my friend, Governor General Michener, and have a drink with him. The press gave me a great deal of attention going in; I got none at all going out. I offered my resignation, then Mr. Trudeau arrived, and the three of us went through the necessary and time-honoured formalities. Mr. Trudeau and the new Cabinet were sworn in, and very suddenly I was in the corner. I slipped home. There was not very far to go as I was still the occupant of 24 Sussex Drive, and did not have to stop by the grocery store as I had in 1957, when my wife told me to pick up some hamburger on my way home. My departure had been arranged so as to give me a few days in the House as a private member. I did not want to take any active political part, but I wanted to see what it would be like and wondered where they would seat me.

The new Prime Minister appeared before the Liberal caucus on Tuesday morning, 23 April, before the House reassembled in the afternoon. There they were, the new Cabinet behind the table, while I was down with the back-benchers and having a great time. The Prime Minister asked if there was any business we wished to take up. I, for the first and last time, got the floor and demanded in no uncertain terms that this new government do something about the importing of American turkeys into Canada which was destroying the turkey trade on Manitoulin Island; if something was not done, there would be a question in the House. Such a speech on my part caused great merriment.

Then Trudeau spoke. He told the caucus that he would dissolve the House that afternoon and announce an election for 25 June. Gasps.

Then he very forcefully made his case for this action, and won over the doubters. It was a great performance.

That afternoon at 2:30 I took my seat in the House on the front-bench toward the end, the same place where I had sat when I first entered Parliament. The most junior Cabinet Minister was on my left and I remember very vividly that I was looking at George Hees right opposite me. Everyone was jovial and I was wondering what I should say when, as I expected he would, the Prime Minister declared this was the time to recognize the incomparable services to Canada, to the world, to the interplanetary system, of his predecessor. But I was relieved of that oratorical problem. The Prime Minister quietly announced dissolution and the Opposition were shocked into complete silence. Of course no one could speak, since there was no Parliament to speak to. The Governor General had ended it a few hours before. Stanley Knowles later complained that Trudeau had not allowed the House to pay me a deserved tribute! I noted in my last prime ministerial diary, "Tough."

Mike: Memoirs of Lester B. Pearson,
Volume 3, John A. Munro and Alex. I. Inglis, eds., 1975

Lost Soul

I must say that my main impression after I was out of office was a sense of great relief at being able to wake up in the morning in our own house and without things pressing in on me from all directions, knowing it was going to be like that until at least eleven o'clock that night. I missed the excitement, of course, but not nearly as much as some people assured me I would. I was very happy—happy for my family and especially my wife. I knew that she had been looking forward to the day when her husband would no longer be Prime Minister and I was gratified to see her relieved and happy. I think she was amused at my wandering around the house those first few days like a lost soul with nothing to do. In fact, I had lots to do but gone was the urgency that had surrounded everything I had been doing for years. Of course, staying home for lunch required a little readjustment! I had no trouble, however, moving from the private car to the upper berth and I enjoyed it exceedingly.

Mike: Memoirs of Lester B. Pearson,
Volume 3, John A. Munro and Alex. I. Inglis, eds., 1975

Walter Gordon

Walter Lockhart Gordon (1906–1987)was Pearson's Minister of Finance from 1963 to 1965. Throughout his life he was a leading Canadian nationalist.

My relationships with Mr. St. Laurent had always been warm and friendly. One day in the late spring of 1954, he asked me to come and see him. I guessed what he might have in mind and decided to have a talk with Mike Pearson beforehand. He agreed that Mr. St. Laurent might be about to ask me to join the government.

After a long discussion with Pearson, we agreed I should very seriously consider an offer to accept one of the senior portfolios, specifically finance or trade and commerce, but that I should decline anything else. Mike did not seem to think this would be in any way presumptuous on my part, only realistic. After all, he would not have joined the government himself more than five years before this except as foreign minister.

I went to see Mr. St. Laurent and, as expected, he invited me to join his government. He said they badly needed a minister from Toronto and that he personally would be very pleased if I would fill this vacancy. It was clear, and quite understandable, of course, that he did not have me in mind for one of the senior portfolios. I felt rather relieved about this, as it permitted me to decline his invitation without any doubts or reservations. Before doing so, I explained the kind of work I had been doing in the firm, my great interest in it, and my disinclination to give it up for an uncertain and possibly less interesting life in politics.

Mr. St. Laurent asked me to have a talk with Mr. Howe before finally making up my mind. I found Mr. Howe ready to receive me, and after a few preliminaries asked him what he liked about his experience in politics. He replied: "Where else could I get as big a job?" It was as simple as that. He could not seem to understanding why I was hesitating. I tried to explain that I had a rather independent turn of mind, that I was my own boss more or less, and that I was uncertain what my position would be if I joined the government. I said, "If, for example, Mr. Howe, you were to bring a proposal to cabinet and as a new member I questioned it, what would your reaction be?" His reply was one of astonishment: "You'd do what, young man?" I had all the answer I required. Mr. Howe was not going to change, and neither was the government.

Walter Gordon, *A Political Memoir*, 1977

Walter Gordon and Ross Thatcher

Wilbert Ross Thatcher (1917-1971) was Liberal Premier of Saskatchewan from 1964 to 1971. He had previously been a CCF Member of Parliament.

I was on good terms with Ross Thatcher in those days, mainly because I had agreed we would send him a little more election money from the central funds than he had expected. He had made me promise to speak at three nomination meetings in Saskatchewan, which I did, including Hazen Argue's in Assiniboia. It was quite an experience for someone who was completely new to politics. On March 20, I drove down to Assiniboia, which is about one hundred miles south of Regina, with Davy Steuart, one of the funniest men in active politics. We arrived about 11.30 a.m. to find the meeting in full swing. Steuart explained that the farmers had little to do in winter and would expect the meeting to continue until midnight, with time out for refueling at noon and again about 6.00 p.m. When I came on to speak at about 9.30 p.m. I confessed to Steuart that I would only be good for about half an hour. He looked horrified, as in Saskatchewan that is considered as being just a warm-up, but volunteered to make a second speech himself if necessary.

After the meeting, two elderly ladies came up and complimented me upon my speech, which they said reminded them of Social Credit! They said they were members of the Social Credit Party and apparently had time on their hands that evening. After some suitable acknowledgement, I asked them if they understood what Social Credit stood for, and if so, would they explain it to me. But they were not be trapped so easily. They replied, "We don't really understand what Social Credit is all about, but that is what makes it so intriguing."

Walter Gordon, *A Political Memoir*, 1977

Living in Public

The colourful Julia Verlyn LaMarsh (1924-1980) was Minister of National Health from 1963 to 1965 and Secretary of State from 1965 to 1968.

I grew tired of being the woman's watchdog. I was always expected to be present when we had women's delegations attending upon the Cabinet. I was, further, expected to be particularly diligent in attending conventions of the party's women, and to make regular rounds in speaking to any and every women's organization which proffered me an invitation. I was the usual invitee whenever any organization, anywhere in Canada, held its annual "ladies night." I was asked to fashion shows, award dinners, and meetings of the professions in which women were a dominant group. My clothes, my stockings, my wigs were a matter of public discussion. (Until Pierre Elliott Trudeau, I do not remember any other member's style of dressing ever discussed in the public print). My weight, my age, my home, my cooking, my hobbies, my friends, my tastes, my likes and dislikes, all became public property to a degree suffered by none of my colleagues, including the Prime Minister. I was two or three times named "Woman of the Year" (not because of anything I did which was important, but because more lines of type appeared about me than about any other woman). Reporters followed me into the hairdressers, photographers tagging along. Executive women followed me into washrooms, wives clustered about me in airports to receive me as I stumbled, bedraggled and exhausted, from an aircraft for yet another meeting. Children and teachers wrote me for recipes and for tips on how to get along as a woman. Columnists asked me about anything and everything—except about my job. Women's magazines and women's pages featured articles about me—sometimes without bothering to interview me.

Cartoonists delighted in sketching me and my clothes and swelling girth. And always the whispers and speculation about my sex life—how much, and with whom? Every member with a pack of eager schoolchildren visiting sought out the lady minister to talk; every member with a group of women politicians in tow asked me to meet with them; every woman politician from another country who visited Ottawa was at once shown in to me. I could not stop without being recognized and spoken to, my purchases eyed, the prices I was paying assessed. I could not walk down the street in Ottawa, or elsewhere, without being constantly on parade. Although most of these encounters were pleasant, the curiosity of the public took the greatest toll on me of anything in politics. For a while I talked freely on television and to the press, hoping that once my views were thoroughly known, I would be an object of curiosity no longer, but the publicity seemed to increase it. When I was first elected to Parliament, I was approached by Gerald Waring, a columnist and reporter to my hometown newspaper. One of the first things he asked me, as we sat in the noisy madhouse of the parliamentary cafeteria, was "Are you a politician, or a woman?" Just as though the two were mutually exclusive! And that inquisitiveness only reflected what others thought.

Judy LaMarsh, Bird in a Gilded Cage, 1968

Outrageous

I sometimes delighted in wearing what others might consider rather outrageous stockings and sometimes coloured wigs into the House. Once I was whistled at in my dark-blonde wig (I think it was the only time in my life I earned such approval), so it was well worth whatever complaints people had. Paul Martin couldn't stand the stockings or the wig, and complained frequently about them, even though Maryon Pearson finally came to wear some discreetly patterned stockings in public.

Judy LaMarsh, Bird in a Gilded Cage, 1968

The Truth Squad

Few campaign gimmicks ever failed as miserably as the Liberal Party's truth squad, briefly in operation during the 1963 general election.

It was clear in the 1963 campaign that we had the best of the main issue. But no one discounted Diefenbaker's ability to skirt the limit and distort the truth as often as he could get away with it. Diefenbaker spoke mainly without notes, and memory being as uncertain as it is, even if he meant to deal only in the truth he might be expected to stray. He wasn't above embroidery. It is hard to pin down just what he is saying, since his sentences rarely end. To read a transcript of one of his speeches is to find that he has left you with hard impressions, but really hasn't said much that you can pin him down with.

In the 1963 election, we wanted him to stick to defence policy and to the truth. He was able to see he couldn't wage much of a campaign if he did. It is my understanding that it was decided that someone would have to pin him down. The idea of the Truth Squad was gleaned by my old political friend, Keith Davey, from *The Making of the President*, where it was obscurely mentioned as a technique adopted during Kennedy's election run in 1960 to keep "Tricky Dick" Nixon on the path of honesty. I suppose the idea appealed to Keith, and ultimately was sold to Pearson, because of our shared recollection of the motto of our mutual alma mater, Victoria College of the University of Toronto: "The Truth Shall Make You Free."

The Truth Squad was to attract publicity and keep Diefenbaker on the defensive. An M.P. would be best who could be spared from his riding. Who would do it? Me, that's who.

One afternoon, about mid-campaign, I checked into my legal office (probably to have a talk to my banker who was long-suffering, but getting anxious) when I received a telephone call from Keith Davey. He explained the problem and the proposal that I head up the Truth Squad. I didn't like the sound of it, and I had already been out of the riding too much, making speeches. I still had a two-or three-day speaking trip to the Maritimes, and my campaign committee would understandably balk at the idea of any more absences from my own riding. But Keith was insistent. Here was another dirty job and there was no one else to do it. I weakened enough to ask him to call back later that day and, in the meantime, I called in Jack Burnett, my campaign Manager, and Del Taylor, my riding president, and had them present for the long-distance call when it came in. We were all opposed to it, but by the time Keith had wrung our hearts, despite our arguments, they had agreed to cover my absence while I was away.

Our first assignment was in Moncton, at a Diefenbaker rally. Early in the evening, we three assembled our papers and notebooks, Jack's (MacBeth) typewriter, and Fred's (Belair) suitcase of reference material, old speeches, up-to-date D.B.S. reports. (The Dominion Bureau of Statistics publishes dry-as-dust reports, but they tell the factual story to those who take time to read them.) The men went down to the meeting hall to reconnoitre it, and returned for dinner to tell me that a special table had been set up for us in the front of the hall, beside the stage, and that a big and derisive welcoming banner had been draped over it. We had to decide whether to try and slip in quietly and take our seats with the rest of the audience or to brazen it out by taking the seats "reserved" for us. Our releases would have to generate publicity and this was one way to assure it. I would have preferred to sit at the back of the hall, but we didn't want to risk being accused of skulking into the meeting. We entered the hall well before the platform party. The news-papermen wouldn't meet our eyes as they filed past us to take their seats, and some pretty ribald comment was made by members of the audience as they squeezed by. The were mostly in good temper, and some of those who spoke to us even indicated they were Liberals who had come for a good show.

Diefenbaker, as might have been anticipated, had a field day. I had never before attended a Conservative rally, nor had I even been in the audience to hear the P.M. make a partisan address. I knew then what I had missed, even if I was the butt of much of the joking. He was in rare form. The Truth Squad was a bonanza for him—a red-herring he could use against the Opposition. It certainly gave him the second wind he needed in his campaign. From that night on, his constantly reworked refrain was the Truth Squad. In Moncton, he was merciless. I never made any record of his witticisms at my expense (I hope no one ever did) but I still bear their scars. For a politician to be laughed at is the most hurtful thing; to be laughed with, the most intoxicating. I was soon numb.

Judy LaMarsh, *Bird in a Gilded Cage*, 1968

Oath of Office

One by one, we were invited into the next room. It was the Governor General's bedroom! My impression was of a bright cheerful yellow room, dominated by a low bed in which lay Canada's most distinguished citizen, his beard and hair combed carefully, his eyes twinkling with amusement as I curtseyed to him. I wonder if anyone else, at any time, in Canada, has had occasion to publicly curtsey to a man while he lies propped in his bed?

This was later often a cause of joking between Madame Vanier and myself. She told me that she had only permitted me into his bedroom for that limited purpose. Shades of the days when a Court waited upon its Queen to announce to the world the birth of a prince of the true blood! I was amused, but felt a little silly. The room was large, but crowded around the Governor General's bed was a semi-circle of Esmond Butler and perhaps an equerry, Gordon Robertson, with his stock of Bibles, and the twenty-six of us, twenty-five men, and one woman. And, of course, I was the only one of whom a curtsey was required. The Bibles were shared around (later the Governor General sent each of us one with an inscription as a memento) and we took our oaths and signed the book again for our respective departments. Then we trooped downstairs for a glass of sherry with Madame Vanier, and gathered for a group portrait: the first Pearson Administration.

Judy LaMarsh, *Bird in a Gilded Cage*, 1968

The Pearson Cabinet

We returned to the Cabinet right after lunch, and for the first time took our places around that historic table: a massive oaken table, covered with dark red felt, surrounded by heavy leather-upholstered chairs jammed close together all around, presided over by one at the head of the table with a higher back, obviously reserved for the Queen's First Canadian Minister. There was a placecard before each chair, so that we were quickly settled into the Cabinet pecking order.

The placecards never again appeared, through the five years I was a member of the Cabinet, and with the frequent resignation of ministers and their replacement, very quickly the original pecking order was lost. It was not unusual to see the most junior ministers, all unknowing, pick seats as high up toward the salt as they dared. But no one took the chairs of the most senior ministers, who were jealous of their positions. On the Prime Minister's right were Paul Martin and Paul Hellyer; on his left, Jack Pickersgill, Walter Gordon, George McIlraith. Later Mitchell Sharp moved from the other side of Paul Hellyer to take Gordon's place. All of us were ranged lower—I was lucky enough to draw a seat beside Guy Favreau, and for most of the Cabinet meetings thereafter we sat together. There wasn't enough room for all the chairs in that small room, designed for much smaller cabinets, and so the most junior of the ministers would perch on one window sill, or sometimes a chair crammed into a corner. The Secretary of the Cabinet, first Robert

Bryce, a carry-over from Diefenbaker's administration (now Deputy Minister of Finance), then Gordon Robertson, and, in his subsequent year-long absence in Quebec City to crash learn French, Gerry Stoner was permanently perched on a chair near a wide window, his papers spread on the window ledge beside him, symbolically near the Prime Minister's right hand. Each minister had in front of him a couple of water glasses and a pitcher of ice water, and sharpened pencils. At first, there were no ashtrays (Diefenbaker did not permit smoking), but from the beginning our people smoked without asking permission. The Prime Minister made one or two peevish references to it, but gave it up and ashtrays appeared. The Cabinet room was often blue with smoke. The chairs were old and almost indestructible, but hard on tender backs. Before long, Walter Gordon, Maurice Sauvé, and I (and later others) had straight chairs brought to replace them for the long hours of Cabinet. Over the years, it became more and more common to order coffee in paper cups brought into the meetings, and often the messenger who answered the bell had no more secure work to do than run in and out repeatedly for coffee. No one ever bought a round for everyone at the table—though little cliques of three or four developed and they would buy for one another. Benson, Drury, and Connolly were the "big spenders" in this department. The Prime Minister acquiesced in this by having his own china cup of coffee brought in frequently, and during a later period this was replaced by an ugly gold plastic thermal cup. Coffee was never arranged on a sensible basis, although from time to time when Cabinets had to meet over the lunch or dinner hour, sandwiches, fruit, cheese, and coffee would be brought in and eaten at the table. We, however, were billed for our share.

Once someone brought in a bottle for a drink before a Cabinet meeting, and once, although on a much later occasion, when George McIlraith was celebrating something, I did arrange to bring in several bottles of chilled champagne, and the proper glasses, which were passed around at the end of the meeting.

Judy LaMarsh, *Bird in a Gilded Cage*, 1968

Mrs. Michener's Flowers

By custom, the wife of the Prime Minister greets the Governor General-designate and his wife with a bouquet of flowers, welcoming her to the Hill. For some reason Mrs. Pearson refused to do that, and the officials of my Department thought they could easily resolve this obstinacy by having me present Mrs. Michener's flowers. I resented this because I am sure that no one would expect a male Secretary of State to perform this pretty function. I suggested they get a woman who was not a member of the Cabinet to do so. They could not think of an appropriate one. Since no one knew what to do with the flowers, they were sent to 7 Rideau Gate to Mrs. Michener herself. Unfortunately, Esmond Butler, who had been Secretary to the late General Vanier, had briefed Mrs. Michener that she would be presented with flowers at Parliament. When they arrived at 7 Rideau Gate, they were rearranged into a bouquet which satisfied her, but there they lay forlornly in a box when I called that morning. I asked her what she intended to do with them, and she told me pathetically that she would just carry them, as apparently no one wanted to make her a presentation of them. I was mad clear through that a morning which should have been so special in the life of this woman was to be spoiled by Mrs. Pearson's pettiness. I seized them from her and said, "Don't worry, they will be presented to you at Parliament Hill, even if I have to do it myself," and sped off. While many of the Governor General-designate's staff ran around trying to find his grey topper (they didn't find it and he wore a black one), I dashed out of the House and sped off to the Parliament Hill. As my car pulled up above the steps to the Senate door, the Micheners arrived below the steps. The Prime Minister and his wife and Senator John Connolly and his wife passed immediately in front of our car down the steps to greet the Micheners. I had from 7 Rideau Gate telephoned a message to Senator Connolly to ask him to have Mrs. Connolly present the flowers, as the wife of the Leader of the Senate. He had received this message but they did not see me in the car, nor the flowers. I scooped up the bouquet, jumped out of the car, ran around it and down the steps to present them. The Connollys and the Prime Minister and his wife had already greeted the Micheners, and they had all started back up the steps when I arrived and thrust the bouquet into the startled Mrs. Michener's hands, saying "Welcome back to Parliament!" and pelted back up the steps ahead of them, racing to the anteroom where other members of the Cabinet had gathered to enter the Senate for the ceremony. To my chagrin, one of my colleagues acidly remarked to another, "Trust a woman to be late."

Judy LaMarsh, *Bird in a Gilded Cage*, 1968

Curtsy, Curtsy, Curtsy

It was decided that the time had come to dispense with the curtsy in Canada for the Queen's representative. The Prime Minister so advised the Governor General-designate. This appeared to be the Prime Minister's own idea. I had complained on more than one occasion about the curtsy. Even though I held an office usually held by a man, I must, as a woman, conform to the archaic custom of bending the knee. I think it was probably Maryon Pearson who complained most often and who did not wish to curtsy to her contemporary. She, no doubt, persuaded her husband to give this advice. In any event, that was the advice Pearson tendered. It could have been a very interesting constitutional point had the Governor-General-designate decided not to adopt the first piece of official advice tendered to him by his Prime Minister. There were two private rehearsals of the ceremony in the Senate chamber to familiarize the Vice-Regal party with their positions and their roles. The first woman to cross in front of the Governor General after he was to be sworn in was his own wife. On both rehearsal occasions Mrs. Michener curtsied and on both occasions my staff gently reminded her not to do so. She argued with them that she wished to curtsy, that this was her husband and she wanted to pay him homage no less than had been paid to his predecessors. Despite the fact the order of dress was to be gentlemen in lounge suits or director's suits, and women in short afternoon dresses, Mrs. Michener chose to wear a long formal dress. It was neither the first nor the last time she didn't stick to the order or dress indicated, causing some embarrassment to others, but she did feel more comfortable, and I suppose it added more formality to the occasion.

Judy LaMarsh, *Bird in a Gilded Cage*, 1968

Shuttle Diplomacy

LaMarsh's centennial year duties included greeting innumerable dignitaries.

It was only just as the first visitors arrived that I learned that I was expected as Secretary of State of Canada to appear to greet each state visitor—and this to be added to my already heavy Centennial schedule! If the visitor was a Head of Government, those receiving would be the Prime Minister, the Secretary of State for External Affairs, and the Secretary of State, and wives as appropriate. What was involved was meeting either outside, on the lawn at the pretty little pagoda set up for the welcoming speeches and the review of the guards of honour, or, as seemed to happen more frequently in inclement weather, within the confines of the Great Hall of Parliament, where the guard's review was curtailed by space, but the speeches of welcome unhappily were not.

By the arrival of the first visitors, the curtsy had been dropped for Canadians to their Excellencies the Governor General and his wife, but the rule adopted for state visits was that we would curtsy if the Head of State appeared to expect it. For each visit we were given a little booklet which listed those who would be in the visitor's entourage, and advice as to whether or not we should curtsy. No one else in the official parties was more cursed by this curtsying than I, for I had to execute more of them during the year than any other woman. Perhaps it was symbolic that I could rarely, in performing a curtsy, manage to land on the right foot.

Although I did not have far to go from my office, in the south-west corner of the Parliament Buildings, to the pagoda drawn up beside the Centennial flame, after once or twice trying to break through the crowd on the way to my prescribed position I always went by car. Very often this was by military vehicle, with a uniformed driver, but from time to time it was in my own car, driven by my messenger. One day I noticed a newspaper report describing the ceremony of greeting in which it was mentioned that a "dirty white Thunderbird" arrived to take away the Secretary of State.

Judy LaMarsh, Bird in a Gilded Cage, 1968

Trudeau and LaMarsh

There was flare-up between Trudeau and me, which stemmed from a judicial appointment of a man I had known years earlier, and to whom I objected on the basis of that knowledge. Our exchange got pretty heated, and he lost his temper when he saw me doodling on my note pad. I was, and am, an inveterate doodler. I let words falling on my ears flow through my mind to my pencil and onto paper. Usually the doodles are pretty harmless, often sketches. This time I wrote: "Arrogant bastard." He inquired to whom the words referred, and I suggested he was bright enough to deduce the answer to that. He went ahead and made the appointment anyway.

That matter might soon have been forgotten, but he made an equally insulting reference to my integrity that I will not soon forget. The ministers present were embarrassed, and some thought he had gone too far—perhaps both of us had. However, Trudeau makes a virtue of never acknowledging a past mistake nor of "looking back". He never apologized, and I didn't expect him to.

Judy LaMarsh, *Bird in a Gilded Cage*, 1968

Cabinet Leaks

John James Greene (1920-1978) was Minister of Agriculture from 1965 to 1968.

When the Prime Minister was complaining about the leaks from cabinet, Joe [Greene] interrupted to say it would be a very simple matter to stop them. Looking directly at a certain minister, he said, "We all know where the leaks come from. If one of our colleagues were to receive a sentence of five years in the penitentiary, I expect the whole problem would be resolved." After a rather pregnant silence, we proceeded to discuss another subject.

On another occasion, I raised the question of cabinet leaks but in a lighter vein. One morning before cabinet began, several ministers commented on an article by Peter Newman which had appeared in the Toronto Star and other newspapers the previous day. Newman, an extremely talented writer as well as an able and industrious reporter, had quoted with remarkable accuracy what was said by a number of ministers at a recent cabinet meeting. This was still the topic of conversation when the Prime Minister arrived. I asked him if it would not be a kindness to give Newman a chair on the grounds that it was most uncomfortable for him to have to crouch for several hours under the table while cabinet meetings were in session. I was delighted to notice two ministers looking surreptitiously under the table to see if Peter was really there.

Walter Gordon, *A Political Memoir*, 1977

Robert Thompson

Robert Norman Thompson (1914-   ) was Leader of the Social Credit party from 1961 to 1967.

A sad-eyed introvert, Thompson presented a sharp contrast to the not-too-distant past, when his party used to rave against the international conspiracy of bankers and Zionists. But if he wasn't anti-Semitic Thompson often gave the impression of being anti-semantic, especially when trying to explain the theories of Social Credit. With a dogged but curiously impersonal fluency, phrases spilled out of him in an unanswerable gush that left his listeners either totally convinced or totally baffled.("For every dollar in circulation, we will create a matching dollar of consumer goods, so that production to satisfy the wants of the people will control the money system, instead of money controlling production.")

He advocated many things that few responsible Canadian politicians would oppose, but most of his declarations somehow came out as convoluted cliches, flavoured by a wistful candour that made it impossible to dislike the man. Certainly his most memorable contribution to Canadian politics was the statement that "the Americans are our best friends, whether we like it or not." Another Thompsonism was his comment that "Parliament is being turned into a political arena," and he once attempted to silence an interjecting MP by telling him: "You've buttered your bread, now you have to lie in it." During a debate on February 1, 1965, while trying to explain why Social Credit could not take the same position as it had with the Diefenbaker minority administration in 1963, he declared: "We've had not one but two elections since then, and two rights do not make a wrong."

Peter C. Newman, *Home Country*, 1973

Bob's Bright Boys

Everything went wrong in that last campaign. Thompson was fogbound over Toronto airport during the press conference called to announce his party platform, and later, on a flight to Calgary, his baggage wound up in Chicago. At a small rally in Regina on October 3, he begged for votes with the appeal: "You can't be any worse off than you are now."

His party printed a million comic books glorifying his career, distributed recordings of his voice and handed out pills labelled "Social Credit—your prescription for curing Canada's ills."

He even had his own brain trust of fifty bow-tied BBBs (Bob's Bright Boys) helping him, but nothing really helped, and at the end of his campaign, there was only the sense of an exhausted man with blood running through his shoes. "People haven't quite accepted the notion of giving us power," he confessed, then added wistfully: "But they're toying with the idea."

Peter C. Newman, *Home Country*, 1973

Guy Favreau

Guy Favreau (1917-1967) occupied various Cabinet posts in Pearson administrations before succumbing to a sudden illness.

My first impression of Favreau was of his unabashed friendliness, and that never failed. He had a most active intelligence and the greatest capacity for work, although his big frame was deceptive in that it hid a delicate health. He was a spendthrift, especially of his own energies. He loved good food, good wine, good company. He loved ideas and things. He was well tailored, yet even when he appeared in a freshly pressed suit and gleaming shoes and linen, he still looked as rumpled as a big bear. He had tremendous loyalty to his Leader, his country, his people. He was a Canadian of French ancestry, born into a big family, who had, by dint of his own extraordinary ability, passed through college to law school and quickly made his mark as an outstanding counsel. He loved the law, and it showed. Lawyers had the utmost respect and regard for him and he for them. His agile mind was always working until his illness, when his agonized friends could hardly bear to watch its brilliance fade.

Judy LaMarsh, Bird in a Gilded Cage, 1968

Three Men and a Leg

Major C.R. Lamoureux was Gentleman Usher of the Black Rod from 1947 to 1970.

Gentleman Usher from the Senate, Major Lamoureux, a double amputee, had a tough problem. He had to walk the length of the Commons Chamber, make his announcement, bow, turn and retire to the door, stopping twice to turn and bow. For a man with two wooden legs, this was no mean feat. When he finally reached the door, he was given loud applause by the Members. Officially, it's a mark of respect for the Senate messenger. For him, it was acclaim for successfully manoeuvering the obstacle course. On one memorable occasion, a couple of years later, we had another brilliant display of parliamentary leg work. Col. Pierre Sevigny, Associate Minister of Defence, and a war amputee, accompanied the Prime Minister to greet new Governor General Vanier. From the main door, General Vanier led off the procession with a regal limp, followed heavily by Col. Sevigny, with Major Lamoureux bringing up the rear.

Gordon Aiken, Backbencher, 1974

Gilles Grégoire

Gilles Grégoire (1926-   ) was the Member for Lapointe, Quebec from 1962 to 1968.

As the end of the session approached, the annual spending spree began. Every year it was the same. With time running out, great gobs of departmental spending were unexamined and unvoted. As Saturday, December 21st began, there was half a billion dollars of spending to approve in three major departments, Health and Welfare, Public Works and Finance. But it had been a long hard year for everyone. The session which began in September 1962 had ended suddenly in an election early in 1963. Pearson's "60 days of decision" had resulted in the immediate recall of parliament after the election, and it was still going. All Members were under strain, and a break was necessary. The mood was to vote the money and prorogue that day.

Gilles Grégoire, however, proclaimed that he would not be rushed. He had quite a lot to say on the Finance estimates, which the government was holding until last. It was necessary, he assured everyone gravely, to explain once again how Social Credit policies could save the nation. And with the House in Committee, there was no limit on the number of times he could speak. He could hold things up until Sunday; and he would if he felt like it.

A feeling of desperation hit the other Members. Train and plane reservations would have to be cancelled, and it was doubtful they could be replaced. Members from far East and far West might not even make it home for Christmas.

The presence of hockey great "Red" Kelly on the government back benches gave someone a bright idea. About 3:00 p.m. at great expense, two rare front row tickets to the hockey match in Montreal that night appeared on Grégoire's desk. He had until 4:30 to catch the train. Word spread around. Members sat at their desks, stood behind the curtains, paced the lobby, watching nervously for some reaction from Grégoire. But he said nothing; and did nothing.

At 4:00 p.m. he got up and went out. Someone followed to make sure he was gone. But he only went to the washroom. On his way back, he talked to some Members standing around about the long speeches he intended to make. Was he serious or playing everyone along?

At 4:15 p.m. he got up again, causing sidelong glances in his direction. But he just went to get a book from the Table, and sat down again.

At 4:25 he left his seat and went over to speak to Minister of Finance Walter Gordon. Then he wished some colleagues a Merry Christmas and was gone. This time he left the building and took the train. The Finance estimates came up at 5:00 and were completed by 6:09. After dinner, and the closing formalities, the session ended at 11:00 p.m. Everyone got home for Christmas.

Gordon Aiken, *Backbencher*, 1974

302

Learning English

Joseph Jacques Jean Chrétien (1934-   ) was first elected a Member in 1963 for the riding of St. Maurice, Quebec. He was a Cabinet Minister under Pearson, Trudeau, and Turner.

When I arrived I hardly spoke any English. I could read it a bit but communicating and understanding were very difficult. I was determined to learn, however. Since there were no language teachers on Parliament Hill, I had to develop by myself. One way was to read *Time* and *Newsweek* thoroughly every week, which also helped me learn about American issues. I kept a dictionary at hand and I got assistance on pronunciation from my wife, who was bilingual.

The more practical and enjoyable way was to become friends with many of the anglophone parliamentarians, guys such as Rick Cashin from Newfoundland, Ron Basford from British Columbia, and Donald Macdonald and "Mo" Moreau from Toronto. We were part of a group of ambitious young mavericks who used to meet regularly, usually in Rick Cashin's office. Cashin was a lively Newfoundlander whom we called "Prime Minister" because he supplied the booze. I didn't drink—that was one of the promises I had made to my wife when I went into politics—but I spent hours listening to the talk in order to improve my English. For a long while I never knew whether they were laughing at me when they were making jokes, but I picked up new words and I was never shy about trying out my English. That led to many funny incidents.

Once there was a big argument between Cashin and Gerry Regan, a Liberal MP from Halifax who became Premier of Nova Scotia and later a Trudeau cabinet minister, about whether Newfoundland or Nova Scotia produced the best lobsters. So I was called upon to be a judge at a party at the Cashins'. There was a lot of white wine that night so nobody cared about who won. The talk was all about politics, and since most of the guests were from the Maritimes, the talk was in English. Someone asked me how I had won my riding in spite of the huge Créditiste majority of the previous election. I answered falteringly.

"Work hard, vary hard," I said. "I went to all the fact-or-ies and I shake hands with every-body. Sometimes when the work was finish at five o'clock, the man and the woman were passing by so fast that I did not have the time to shake their hand, so I just touched them on the bras." Of course I meant "arms." Everyone roared with laughter. "So that's how you won your election, you damn Frenchman!" they said.

Another time I was asked about Claude Ryan, then the editor of *Le Devoir.* "Vary important," I said. "Every politician read him. He love to be consulted and he give good advice. But he can be a little bit pompous. When you are in the presence of Mr. Ryan, you feel you are in front of a bishop. You almost have to put your knee on the floor and kiss his bague." The word "bague" had come into my head instead of "ring." People were laughing so hard that I couldn't continue speaking, but I didn't know what I had said that was so funny.

Jean Chrétien, *Straight from the Heart*, 1985

Chrétien and Finance

Chrétien was named parliamentary secretary to Minister of Finance Mitchell Sharp in 1966.

The first day after my appointment Mitchell invited me into a meeting where there were nothing but big shots: the Governor of the Bank of Canada, the Deputy Governor, the Deputy Minister of Finance, and so on. For an hour and a half they discussed bond issues and tariff rates and balance of payments, and I listened with wonder and awe. Finance was still a very mysterious thing for me. After the meeting Mitchell came up to me and said, "Jean, what you have heard today is very secret. You must not say a word to anybody about it."

"Don't be worried, Mitchell," I said. "I didn't understand a bloody thing."

Jean Chrétien, *Straight from the Heart*, 1985

Robert Stanfield

Robert Lorne Stanfield (1914–   ) was Leader of the Opposition from 1967 to 1976.

The Conservatives did not know what to make of their new leader. He was friendly, but he discouraged intimacy. They did not know what to call him. They could not very well call him the "Chief" as long as Diefenbaker was still around. Heath Macquarrie tried to persuade his colleagues to address Stanfield as "Skipper"—in honour of his Maritime connection—but Stanfield firmly discouraged that. Some of the other Easterners liked "Old Hickory," for no apparent reason. In the press gallery, they called him "Big Thunder" presumably because the reporters could come up with no nickname that was less appropriate to the Stanfield style. None of the nicknames stuck. Those in the caucus who felt they knew him called him Bob; to others, he remained "Mr. Stanfield." He seemed like a decent enough fellow, but many Tory M.P.s concluded that he lacked political acumen. He was unclear in his view, ineffectual in Parliament, and innocent of any sense of political time or tactics. Tories who had been raised to despise Grits could not fathom a leader who prefaced his attacks on the Government with an apology: "I don't want to be offensive, but...."

Geoffrey Stevens, Stanfield, 1973

Robert Stanfield

It was mid-1971 and the Leader of Her Majesty's Loyal Opposition was making another of his incessant political pilgrimages to British Columbia, flying this time in a small single-engined plane. Suddenly, the motor stalled and, as the plane fell earthward, the Leader's senior assistant, Tom Sloan, screwed his eyes tightly closed and entertained a fleeting wish that he had a God with whom he could make his peace. The Leader was vexed—though for quite a different reason. Glancing out the window at the ground rushing up to meet him, he commented in a stern and disapproving voice: "This is going to play hell with my schedule." An instant later, the confused pilot located the reserve-fuel switch and the motor coughed back to life, thereby saving the Leader's schedule, among other things.

Geoffrey Stevens, Stanfield, 1973

Sorry, I'm Paired

Bob Stanfield was elected to Parliament on November 6, 1967; nine days later he arrived on Parliament Hill to take over officially.

The following week Stanfield make his maiden speech and in it he moved his first non-confidence motion, in the form of an amendment to a government supply resolution. The amendment stated: "This House regrets that the mismanagement of this government has endangered the rate of economic growth, the prospects of satisfactory levels of employment, and the ability of individual Canadians to meet their own commitments." That was pretty standard rhetoric for an opposition motion, but it was Stanfield's first big moment in Parliament.

The next day, however, Lester Pearson told Stanfield he had to be away on government business and inquired whether Stanfield would "pair" with him when the amendment was put to a vote that night. "Pairing" is an informal convention of Parliament. A government or opposition member who finds he has to be absent for a vote, arranges with a member of the other side to abstain from voting. In this way an absent M.P. does not affect the voting balance in the House. Of course, a member never "pairs" if his own motion is being voted on. But, still ignorant of the ways of Parliament, Stanfield readily agreed to Pearson's request.

Lowell Murray was horrified when he heard what Stanfield had done. "You're crazy," he told the person who brought him the news. "Stanfield wouldn't do that. He's got more sense than that." A little later, Murray went up to Stanfield in the Opposition lobby: "By the way, somebody says that you've paired." "I did," said Stanfield sheepishly. That night he had to sit in his seat in doleful embarrassment as his first non-confidence motion went down to defeat on a vote of 119 to 105. The Liberals were delighted. They had, they congratulated themselves, found an easy mark.

Geoffrey Stevens, *Stanfield*, 1973

Soft Stanfield

Delegations of old Diefenbaker M.P.s waited on Stanfield to insist that he retain the men who had worked for the Chief. Exasperated, Murray told Stanfield: "Look, we've only got so many positions and it's easier to let people out now when you're coming in, rather than a month or two from now when it appears to be a reflection on their ability." Stanfield agreed to have a heart-to-heart talk with one of Diefenbaker's aides, Thomas Van Dusen. When he came back from talking to Van Dusen, Murray asked him; "Did you see Tommy?" "Yeah," replied Stanfield slowly. "Shall I go ahead and fill that position?" Murray asked. "Well," said Stanfield, "I don't think he got what I was driving at." "What do you mean?" demanded Murray. "Didn't you tell him?" "Well," Stanfield confessed, "I asked him what his plans were and I guess he indicated he'd like to stay on." Van Dusen stayed on for more than a year.

Geoffrey Stevens, *Stanfield*, 1973

Stanfield's French

Arriving at Montreal International Airport late one night at the end of 1972, he hopped into the mini-bus carrying passengers to the Airport Hilton, and decided to show off his French to the girl driving the bus. "Est-ce que vous conduisez toute la nuit?" inquired the Leader of Her Majesty's Loyal Opposition. Mistaking a pleasantry for a proposition, the girl turned with a willing smile. "Non, M'sieu," she replied. "Je finis à minuit."

Geoffrey Stevens, *Stanfield*, 1973

Plain Bob

For most of the years of his leadership of the Conservative party, Stanfield carried his own baggage at airports, railway stations, and bus depots. Often he travelled unaccompanied and was unmet upon arrival, even when he was guest of honour at some function. Once he flew from Ottawa to Vancouver for a luncheon in his honour, only to find that none of the other guests had shown up. Another time he went on a hotline show in Ontario, and in the space of two hours on the air, not a single person called in. He always drove his own car, and he liked to mow his own lawn and tend his own garden, resenting the intrusion when public works crews took over the maintenance of the grounds at Stornoway, the official residence of opposition leaders.

Charles Lynch, *You Can't Print That*, 1983

Pierre Elliott Trudeau

Pierre Elliott Trudeau (1919-   ) became Prime Minister in 1968 after a stint as Minister of Justice. He retired in 1984 after serving some 16 years as Prime Minister.

When he comes into a room, the room is somehow different. He has that incandescent glow that thousands of photographers' flash bulbs impart to the flesh. He looks remote and austere, his very presence generates an undercurrent of the unexpected. In one of the workshops he was addressing, the solid cadre of photographers and television men who follow his every move was blocking the view of the delegates. Finally, an exasperated member of the audience stoop up and yelled: "Down in front." Trudeau instantaneously barked back: "How far in front?"—quizzically implying that they wanted him to sit down. It was a small joke, but it relaxed the audience, persuaded the photographers to move back, and won him a round of applause.

Peter C. Newman, *Home Country*, 1973

First Impressions

The Prime Minister had arrived for lunch at one-thirty, half an hour behind schedule, bounding into the room with a broad smile of welcome, looking extremely natty in a well-tailored conservative brown suit, a striped tie, and a blue shirt that exactly matched his eyes. He is a slim, athletic man of medium height. His receding brown hair is just beginning to gray, and there is a small bald patch at the back. His features are pleasantly irregular—high cheekbones, which give his face a faintly Oriental cast; a slightly aquiline nose; and a large mouth with very white, even teeth. His eyes are luminous, and of a blue so brilliant that the effect of his gaze is startling to some people, even a bit frightening. He looks at one with such intensity, seeming to listen with his eyes, that the object of his attention is apt to feel that every word spoken must be significant.

The Prime Minister apologized for his tardiness, and offered his visitor a cocktail. He was delighted when it was refused. "Good!" he said, "Then we can go right in and eat." He sat down at the lunch table and poured chilled dry white wine into small cut-crystal glasses, remarking that he drank very little and didn't smoke at all. "I'm not willing to sacrifice the control of physical and mental ability that drinking and smoking take away for what they give in return." He said, "I used to tell myself that smoking impaired the memory, and in time I believed that it did. I have always thought, Why should I lose even a little bit of my memory, since it is not all that good? Also, in my early boyhood I was frailer than most boys and I thought I had to be more careful. I still have to average eight hours' sleep. I think I just have to have that. I can go for weeks or months on five hours or so of sleep, as I did during the election campaign, but afterward I have to make up for it by sleeping twelve or thirteen hours."

Edith Iglauer, New Yorker, 1969

The Very Model of a Modern Minister of Justice

Once, leaving the Chateau Laurier through service stairs and finally a rear entrance, he leaped up onto a metal bannister and, legs straight out, arms raised high, went swooping down it and flying off the end.

There were gasps of fright from a group of women standing at the top. And as they recovered, one said, "Imagine having a Prime Minister who'd do a thing like that!" It was said with adoring admiration.

And there are two other women in Ottawa who must have similar feelings about a little incident one night in the street to the side of the Skyline Hotel.

It was dark. They were driving slowly. Across from the hotel a car was parked, and a group came out of a side door to go across to it. One of the men, all at once, just as their car was approaching, went down onto his knees in a sort of Al Jolson type of pose, his arms raised with clasped hands in a plea for them to stop the car so he could cross the street.

They stopped, he leaped up, bowed gallantly, and as he crossed in their headlights their hands went up to their mouths in astonishment. It was the Justice Minister.

Douglas Stuebing, Trudeau: A Man For Tomorrow, 1968

Brother Can You Spare a Tie?

John Diefenbaker derided the Justice Minister in the House early in July, 1967, when Trudeau appeared in a sport jacket with an open-necked yellow shirt, and yellow ascot with red polka dots. The Opposition Leader suggested that Mr. Trudeau was not showing proper respect for the dignity of the Commons. Although External Affairs Minister Paul Martin cut off any reply by Trudeau, the Justice Minister was questioned outside by even more casually-dressed newsmen about what he was going to do. Trudeau replied: "Get another tailor I guess, but it won't be yours."

Robert Stanbury, the Member for York Scarboro, remembers the day very well. There had been a long caucus which ended just before the Commons was called to order. The two men came out of the caucus together. Trudeau was wearing the open-necked shirt. "He said to me: 'God, I've got to get a tie.' His office was quite close to the caucus room and he dashed in to get something. When he came out he was wearing the polka-dot thing, I don't think it was even an ascot. It was a scarf or something."

Douglas Stuebing, *Trudeau: A Man For Tomorrow*, 1968

Eccentric Trudeau

Rideau Club denizens were fond of telling each other the story about the time he turned up on a Saturday morning at the Privy Council office dressed in desert boots and a boiler suit and the commissionaire on duty, convinced he was a plumber who had his worksheets jumbled, turned him away at the door. When his name was mentioned casually in the early speculative talk about candidates, it was dismissed as a joke. ("How could anybody who combs his hair like that be a Canadian prime minister?")

Peter C. Newman, *Distemper of Our Times*, 1968

Trudeau's Parsimony

His parsimony, except to those to whom he is emotionally attached, is legendary. In Montreal, in mid-winter, he would run coatless to restaurants, to save the checkroom tip. He seldom pays for someone's meal, nor carries enough money to cover the bill. At the state funeral for Pierre Laporte, an aide had to slip him a $10 bill when the collection plate was passed: Trudeau looked at the amount, and frowned. In 1975, as Prime Minister, he disputed in public an $8 tax increase on his Laurentian estate imposed by the municipality of St. Adolphe D'Howard. Yet when his close friend Jacques Hébert faced a jail term for his book, *J'Accuse les Assasins de Coffin*, Trudeau took on the full legal burden of defending Hébert, for free; he funded the literary projects of friends, and once sent $3,000 to a penniless friend in Paris.

Richard Gwyn, *Northern Magus*, 1980

Trudeau's Discipline

Even more than his body, Trudeau disciplined his mind. Blessed with an exceptional memory, he read omnivorously and with a ferocious, head-down tenacity. "I was never satisfied with reading eight chapters of a book, I had to read twelve." Even when teachers recommended it, he never skipped. He has never altered this linear approach. Early in 1979, when members of the Task Force on National Unity gave Trudeau an advance copy of their report and met with him privately to discuss it, he asked them questions only about the first three chapters—all he'd had time to read. By contrast, Marc Lalonde at the same meeting hopped all over the map because, as most of us would when pushed for time he had read only the summary of recommendations.

Richard Gwyn, *Northern Magus*, 1980

Trudeau's Concentration

At times, his concentration comes close to being obsessive. He will allow no one, nor anything, to interrupt him. When he became Prime Minister, dinner guests, once even his close friend Jean Marchand, were informed they must leave by 9.45 p.m. so that he could spend an hour alone with his documents boning up for the next day's round of committee meetings. Passengers in his official car were instructed to stay silent while he worked on his papers in the back; once, near the end of a two-hour drive to Montreal, his press secretary, Pat Gossage, exclaimed in delight at the autumn colours. "Pat, you promised," came the reprimand from the bowed head in the back. Trudeau's chauffeur, forbidden also from turning on the radio, at last secured permission to install a tape deck with an ear plug.

Richard Gwyn, Northern Magus, 1980

Trudeau and Chrétien

Chrétien encounters Trudeau for the first time.

The artificial division of the Quebec Liberal MPs into the "old" and "new" guard—essentially pre-1963 and post-1963—was unfair and arbitrary; but the press had established the distinction and everyone was aware of it. So when there was an election for the chairman of the Quebec caucus, the two groups tended to line up behind their own candidates. A friend of mine, Gérald Laniel, ran for the "new guard" and I supported him; indeed I proposed him. As it happened, he lost by one vote. Trudeau hadn't voted. Had it been a tie, the chairman had been expected to vote for our guy. In other words, Trudeau lost us the election. I went over and gave him hell.

"But Jean," he said, "I don't know these guys. They didn't make any speeches, so how could I have decided to vote for one or the other?"

"But you should have had some indication when you saw me propose Laniel," I said. "That was a sign that he's the 'new guard' guy."

"Pardon me," Trudeau replied. "There is no 'new guard' or 'old guard' for me. I didn't know those guys, so I didn't vote for either of them."

"But weren't you impressed by the fact that I proposed Laniel?"

"I wasn't impressed at all," he said.

"Gee, Pierre," I said, "you'd better learn something about politics or you won't go very far." I was disappointed, and all the "new guard" guys were angry at this beatnik. The worst part was that, in his logic and his objectivity, he was right.

Jean Chrétien, Straight from the Heart, 1985

Everybody's Idea of a Cabinet Minister

Prime Minister Pearson had been persuaded by Lalonde and Gibson that Trudeau should pave the way—for the constitutional reforms and for his candidacy—by taking a cross-country trip and meeting with the premiers. Pearson had also suggested that Carl Goldenberg, a leading constitutional lawyer, accompany him. Trudeau made an excellent impression on most of the provincial politicians, once they had figured out which of the two men who debarked from the plane at each stop was the Minister of Justice. Goldenberg, a youthful sixty-one, is small, gray-haired, and dignified, and wore a black hat and blue topcoat, so that he looked like everyone's idea of a Cabinet minister, while Trudeau had on a short leather coat and a fur cap. Goldenberg has said, "Trudeau always insisted I walk out of the plane first, and then he'd follow, carrying the bags. So naturally I would be greeted as the Minister of Justice. When we got back to Ottawa, he was still carrying my bags, right into the hotel where we were staying, and the clerk gave him a very simple room. When Pierre saw mine, he was astonished. 'I didn't know they had rooms like this!' he said".

Edith Iglauer, New Yorker, 1969

Trudeau and Smallwood

As Minister of Justice, Trudeau visited Premier Joey Smallwood of Newfoundland.

I had hardly heard of the man but I invited him to lunch and asked him what he wanted. He said he wanted my views on the constitution. So I told him, for Quebec—nothing. Nothing. I don't mean almost nothing. I mean nothing whatsoever, Quebec should have nothing that Prince Edward Island doesn't have—that Newfoundland doesn't have. But I said, for the French people in Canada, anywhere in Canada—everything. Everything. Everything that the English Canadians have, rights, education, everything. Trudeau listened and then remarked that he might as well go home because I had expressed his views so clearly and so forcefully. And he told me he only wished he could have made his views so clear, that as a French Canadian he wished he could use the English language like that. And I didn't know that I was talking to a man with such facility, such powers of exposition in the English language. Why there aren't four or five men in the country who can express themselves in English like this man and here I was, using my meat

axe like a clumsy elephant with arthritis and he tells me he wished he
could express himself so clearly!

Joey Smallwood,
quoted in Peter C. Newman, *Distemper of Our Times*, 1968

Three Wise Men

We three were opposed to having American nuclear weapons established in Canada. A few weeks before the election, Pearson changed
his mind and announced he would accept such weapons on Canadian
soil, so we refused to run. The Liberals were elected as a minority
Government, and everything seemed to be disintegrating. In November, 1965, there was another general election. Again Pearson insisted
that I run.

The nuclear warheads were no longer a public issue, so I made the
same condition. I said, "I'll run if you accept Trudeau and Pelletier."
Pearson's people were again reluctant, but finally succeeded in getting
them ridings—constituencies in which to run. For Pierre, they chose
Mount Royal, a suburb of Montreal. We were all elected. Right away
I became Minister of Manpower and Immigration. I started working at
once to get ministerial offices for the others. So in January, 1966, Pierre
was appointed Parliamentary Secretary to the Prime Minister. This was
a very difficulty step for Pearson to take, because Pierre had been so
critical of him a couple of years earlier, and the reaction in the caucus
of the Liberal Members of Parliament was violent. Some of them said
that Pierre was not a Liberal and the Party shouldn't have accepted him.
Well, in the spring of 1967, the Minister of Justice retired, and I thought
that afforded a good opportunity to put Pierre in the Cabinet. After a
few weeks, Mr. Pearson agreed, and there was a second violent reaction
in the Liberal caucus. In December, the Prime Minister told his Cabinet that he intended to resign as soon as a qualified successor could be
chosen. A few friends in the Cabinet had been meeting together, including Trudeau and me. We were looking for a prospective leader.
They were unanimous that I should run. No one mentioned Pierre
Trudeau's name. That December, Pierre introduced his bill on divorce
in the House of Commons, and made such a big case for it that almost
overnight he became a public figure. I had always been the prospective
candidate, but I had always refused. I am deeply rooted in Quebec, and

I see that fact as deeply dangerous, because as Prime Minister I would have to represent the whole of Canada. So I had a conversation with Pierre. I said, "The situation is changing, and you have become a potential candidate." Pierre refused. He said, "It's not the reason we came— to take over the Party and the government," and he said we had plenty of time. I said to him, "In politics, there is the opportunity, and if we miss it it may not recur." Pierre left for Tahiti over the Christmas holidays for some scuba diving with Tim Porteous, and I left for a vacation in Florida. I came back before I had intended, to gather support for Pierre. Then Pierre had a second chance to reach the Canadian public—as Minister of Justice at the first of the federal-provincial conferences on constitutional reform. He performed there particularly well. There was no doubt in my mind then that he was a serious candidate. What he had been lacking six months before he now had. Besides, he was intelligent, a good lawyer, a good economist, perfectly bilingual, healthy, rich, young, and a bachelor. The Liberal Party in Montreal was still hesitant, but the "Draft Trudeau" movement increased in strength. Pierre formally became a candidate on a Thursday night in February when a group of us met in his office in the Parliament Buildings. Pierre took out a large trick coin and flipped it, and then, without looking at how it had come up, said, "O.K.!" And we started the show.

Jean Marchand, quoted in Edith Iglauer, *New Yorker*, 1969

The Coin

The coin I tossed was a great big green-and-red one given me by Pearson's Secretary of State, Judy LaMarsh, in a Cabinet meeting. It said 'Yes' on the green side and 'No' on the red one. She was telling me to make up my mind to run or not to run. But at the meeting where I tossed the coin I had already made up my mind. I had done that a day or so before, while walking around the Parliament Buildings until two o'clock in the morning. How did I make up my mind? I was pushed.

Pierre Elliott Trudeau, quoted in Edith Iglauer, *New Yorker*, 1969

Trudeaumania

Trudeau led a triumphal procession from shopping centre to shopping centre, where he was gaped at, flower-bedecked, sung to, applauded, heckled, admired, all the time being magnified in the public eye by the crowd's intense awareness of his style. The Trudeau crowds are sprinkled with teeny-boppers, running with long manes blowing like banners in the wind, full of vitality, excitement, laughter, shrieking in a kind of ecstasy that rises to a squawk when one of their number is kissed. What is probably more significant is the presence of scores of toddlers, held on the shoulders of their parents being admonished to "remember him" the way in other years the very young were brought out to behold royalty. Trudeau seems to enjoy each of these occasions, accepting the flowers thrust at him with a shrug, bounding up on the backs of trucks to give voice to his cause. But he is at his best away from the howling mobs, at press conferences, where he is transformed into a first-rate teacher who can turn tentative, vaguely articulated questions into something intelligent, reworking them so that each answer becomes a lucid lecture, a precis of the problem at hand, its ramifications, other possible solutions and the difficulties involved.

Peter C. Newman, *Home Country*, 1973

Dissolution, Trudeau Style

Near noon on Tuesday, April 23, Trudeau, for the first time as Prime Minister, met with the Liberal caucus. They cheered him, sang "Happy Birthday" to Lester Pearson and then got down to debating whether or not there should be a June election. The Commons was due to sit at 2:30 p.m.

At 1:05 p.m., Trudeau walked out of the West Block caucus room and down the hall to his third-floor Justice Minister's office. He was accompanied by several party leaders: Transport Minister Paul Hellyer, House Leader and Health Minister Allan MacEachen, national Liberal President Senator John Nichol and constitutional advisor Marc Lalonde, among others.

Would he see the Governor-General today? "I have nothing to say," the Prime Minister replied as he entered his office.

If he was going to have Parliament dissolved this afternoon he had fewer than 85 minutes left in which to do it.

Inside, Trudeau conferred briefly with his colleagues and at 1:15 p.m. the Prime Minister, accompanied by his aide, Gibson, slipped down the office's secret staircase which had been built by Prime Minister Alexander Mackenzie in the 19th Century as a means of avoiding favour-seekers. According to legend it was used also by Sir John A. Macdonald for the same reason.

Trudeau found it a useful device for giving the Press the slip.

While Trudeau was inside, Senator Paul Martin was walking down the regular stairs of the West Block, apparently on his way to lunch, when he met a reporter he knew well. "Better get back to Trudeau's office," the Senator counselled. "That's where the action is going to be." A gaggle of reporters and cameramen camped outside the door.

Meanwhile, Martin climbed into his chauffeured limousine which moved just a few yards ahead to the secret staircase entrance. Trudeau and Gibson jumped in and the car sped off to Rideau Hall.

Upstairs, ministers and aides, in clusters or individually, came out of the office every few minutes. "You'll have to ask the Prime Minister," they all said in response to any question. "I have nothing to say."

As Martin's car arrived at the rear of Government House property at 1:30 p.m., reporters staked out in front of the building (Mounties would not permit them to wander) were kept busy by the sudden arrival at the front door of the Governor-General's limousine.

Trudeau walked across the grounds in back, through the greenhouse and into the main building. He was met by Mr. Michener's secretary Esmond Bulter and immediately escorted into His Excellency's study.

Fifteen minutes later he left by the same route and attention was again diverted when Mrs. Michener got into the official car, ostensibly for a shopping trip. At the same time outside the Justice Minister's office, a few reporters remembered the secret staircase and ran downstairs to keep an eye on that entrance.

At 2 p.m. an aide came out of the office and asked innocently: "Are you looking for the Prime Minister? Well, he's probably back in his Centre Block office by now."

Sure enough, his car had just driven up to the front entrance of the Centre Block. "Where have you been, sir?" a reporter inquired. "Out to lunch," Trudeau grinned and walked into his office.

Moments after 2:30 p.m. Mr. Speaker called the Commons to order.

Then the new Prime Minister rose on a question of privilege. For almost two minutes the Green Chamber echoed with thunderous applause from the Liberal benches and occasionally from the Opposition.

Trudeau did not acknowledge the welcome. Unsmiling he leaned against a desk with his arms crossed and waited for silence. When it came he said he wanted to give thanks "for the messages of congratulations and encouragement from all parts of the House."

There was a brief pause before the pronouncement came: "In view of the announcement I am about to make, Mr. Speaker, I feel any further comment by me on any other subject would be improper."

Members leaped to their feet and cheered and pounded their desks as Trudeau continued: "This afternoon I called on the Governor-General to request him to dissolve Parliament and to have writs issued for a General Election on June 25. By proclamation under the Great Seal of Canada dated April 23, 1968, the present Parliament is dissolved and members and senators are discharged from attendance. I thank you, Mr. Speaker."

Douglas Stuebing, *Trudeau: A Man For Tomorrow*, 1968

Trudeau in Cabinet, I

When his ideas were challenged or when he wanted to get to the heart of a matter in cabinet, Trudeau could be ruthless in debate, asking probing questions that demolished the logic underlying the counter-arguments, and applying the full force of his intellect and knowledge. Occasionally I saw him get his way simply by interjecting a phrase that indicated his position. Since most ministers assumed that Trudeau had thought through everything, and since even more ministers wanted to please the boss, he was able to rally a majority to his side without much difficulty. That was human nature, of course, but it could be annoying when ministers constantly played to Trudeau, sensed his direction, and automatically followed. At times Trudeau tested for sycophancy by suddenly supporting the opposite argument and seeing who really believed what they had held.

Jean Chrétien, *Straight from the Heart*, 1985

Trudeau in Cabinet, II

Debate in full cabinet centres on four of five items each session. The sessions are intended to last from ten a.m. to one p.m., but often the ministers lunch on sandwiches and work through until the House of

Commons convenes at two p.m. Trudeau is addressed as "Prime Minister", other colleagues by their first names. The debate is not formal, but is normally polite. Trudeau notes the names of ministers who want to speak—they signal by raising their hands—and calls them in order of the hand-raising. Kierans said, "there is not much interruption, the way there is in the cabinet committees. Once in a while you say 'Wait a minute, John, that's not right and you know it's not right,' but mostly you hold your peace and wait your turn."

Walter Stewart, *Shrug: Trudeau in Power*, 1971

Trudeau Eclectic

"A lot of guys thought that Lord Acton was the great forming influence on me," he said. "The truth is that I liked Acton's approach and several of his essays but probably read less of him than several newspaper people studying his influence on me have read since—and less of de Tocqueville, too. Quite frankly, I didn't read de Tocqueville's entire works, and I was well into my thirties by the time I found confirmation in him of my theories of checks and balances. I am very eclectic. I can quote from Plato and from the theories of de Tocqueville and from Montesquieu's 'Laws' but it would be a mistake to single any one of them out. I bet many people in my position have read more than I have in the field of history and economics. I have probably read more of Dostoyevski, Stendhal, and Tolstoy than the average statesman, and less of Keynes, Mill, and Marx. The point I am making is that I am not a scholar of any of these disciplines. I haven't read as much as a good economist, and, being eclectic, I have done a lot of other reading and travelling."

Edith Iglauer, *New Yorker*, 1969

Trudeau's Intellect

By his mind alone, Trudeau dominates almost everyone who meets him. "Pearson was merely one of us," Mitchell Sharp has said, "whereas Trudeau was not—he was someone extraordinary." A former aide, himself uncommonly intelligent says, "I loved him for that marvellous, marvellous mind."

Memory is the single most impressive component. Almost everyone likens Trudeau's mind to a computer: capacious, inexhaustible, and precise. He could (and frequently did) quote back passages of a memorandum six months after receiving it. An aide remembers him giving a political speech that reproduced, word for word, a text he'd read only twice before (once in the car en route to the rally). In argument, he can use his memory to devastating effect, recalling statements an opponent made months before which contradict whatever he happens now to be saying.

Trudeau devotes the same total attention to analyzing each successive problem as he does to any task, whether this is polishing up his scuba diving technique, or boning up on Tibetan culture in advance of his trip there. At cabinet meetings, Trudeau invariably knew as much or more about the issue at hand as the minister responsible—although as the years passed, this phenomenon became less marked. To prepare himself, Trudeau performed like a workaholic mandarin. Night after night, at home, he ploughed his way through the "damned brown boxes" as Margaret called them. Predictably, the real mandarins took advantage of Trudeau's single-mindedness and piled more and more briefing notes and memoranda into the boxes; to their delight all this paper burden would come back to their desks, underlinings and annotations in Trudeau's bold, declarative handwriting on every page.

Trudeau's mind is ordered, sequential, linear. When he's reading, he never skips. When he's analyzing a problem, he never slides past a part of the problem that seems unresolvable, nor fails to pursue to the uttermost limit all the consequences, political and intellectual, of any solution that comes to his own or to anyone else's mind. The observation he makes most frequently in cabinet discussions is, "But if we do X, surely Y will happen." An aide recalls, "Those pitiless, pitiless questions. He was not interested in showing you to be wrong, but in making certain that you were right." One of Trudeau's ministers, Francis Fox, says: "His ability to think things right through, to foresee the implications of proposals, was uncanny and unnerving."

Richard Gwyn, *Northern Magus*, 1980

Trudeau Nonchalant

In his first four years as Prime Minister, Trudeau seemed quite unconcerned about the moods he created. The opposition, he felt, was angry most of the time anyway. One day he came in for question period reading a book. It was insulting to everyone there. When he was asked questions, he half stood to answer, still reading. He seemed to be saying: "I can answer your stupid questions without disturbing my train of thought."

Finally, tired of being hassled by midgets, he picked up his book and left before the question period ended. There were no great accomplishments by the government that day.

Yet, he was often quick to respond to challenges. In April 1972, Opposition House Leader Ged Baldwin, Member for Peace River, was twitting him for not calling an election.

"When will the Prime Minister take the one major initiative to restore public confidence?" he asked.

"I would be prepared to call a by-election in Peace River," replied the Prime Minister.

And he was direct.

"What are you babbling about?" he asked one Member, who interrupted a statement he was making.

"I'm not babbling," replied the Member, "you are waffling." The fast response brought a brief smile.

Sometimes he was too smart with his answers. "Bud" Simpson, Member for Churchill, Manitoba, was pressing him one day about improvements to the port of Churchill. He made no response.

"He doesn't know where Churchill is," called out heckler Don MacInnis.

"He is dead, Mr. Speaker," responded the Prime Minister.

Gordon Aiken, Backbencher, 1974

Trudeau and the House

Whenever Robert Stanfield got up to ask a question, they would sit there, row upon row of Liberal ministers, hooting with derisive laugher, looking not like sober men conducting the nation's business but like a clutch of obnoxious prefects from the upper forms of some expensive private school, sneering at a drudge. And in their midst sat their leader, the existential hero, clad in a dark suit from London, a yellow rose from the Governor-General's greenhouse and an air of elegant boredom, turning his attackers off with quips, non sequiturs, and historical allusions. He complained about "the whiny demands of the Opposition" and put everybody down, making fun of their pretension in questioning his wisdom. He acted as if he really believed that Opposition MPs were "nobodies," a fairly risky assumption since even after the 1968 election the opposition side of the House represented 54 per cent of Canadian voters. Trudeau was just as rude to MPs outside the House. After his son was born on Christmas Day, 1971 one of the most popular MPs in the House, a Conservative from the Maritimes, decided to send Trudeau a congratulatory wire. He went down to his local telegraph office only to find that the operator, a staunch Tory, was prepared to give him a hot fight about transmitting the message. The MP finally persuaded her to send it anyway and filed the episode away in his mind as a wryly amusing, if apt, reflection of his riding's political style. A few weeks later, back in Ottawa, he saw Trudeau at a cocktail party, and thinking the PM might be amused as well he went over to tell him what happened. Trudeau stared back at him, bored beyond endurance, and said offhandedly, "Oh, I never saw any of the wires. There were so many hundreds, we decided not to be bothered."

Peter C. Newman, *Home Country*, 1973

Trudeau Under Stress

Trudeau, during, after, and through all the months leading up to that cataclysm, gave the nation and indeed the world, a demonstration of superhuman grace under inhuman pressure of a kind almost no one else could have brought off. He never once complained. He never once explained. He defended Margaret on every occasion. "I do not indulge in guilt by association," he said in reply to a question about Margaret's relationship to the Stones. When a reporter pushed too hard, he batted him down. "A gentleman would not ask such questions" and then took away the sting by quipping that Margaret in fact preferred the Beatles as musicians, "though I hope she doesn't start seeing the Beatles."

In hindsight, cabinet ministers and aides, looking back over the two years of unceasing tension that led up to the break, cannot recall his ever showing any sign of it at work, except for occasionally looking tired because Margaret had insisted he stay up with her to watch late movies on television. It was only right at the end, after Margaret had made him look like a cuckold in public, that the nerve ends began to show. "You could see it in his eyes," says a former aide, "a look of bewilderment.

For the first time in his life something was happening that was affecting him directly and personally, and there was absolutely nothing he could do about it." Yet before 1977 was out, the aide continues, Trudeau was back in control. He'd found, somehow, an emotional compartment in which to stuff the pain. "Suddenly something must have gone click in his mind, and he bounced back." Alone, he poured out his love to his sons, and found solace in them.

Richard Gwyn, *Northern Magus*, 1980

Trudeau Challenged

I particularly remember one occasion during the Commonwealth Conference in 1973 at Mont Tremblant, when all the leaders had gone back to Ottawa on the special airplanes we had for them, and the PM had asked me to stay behind and come back with him in the helicopter. And in that interval between the airplanes' leaving and the helicopter's departure, he said: "Let's go water-skiing." Neither of us had water-skied all that summer, but each of us—it was unstated—was determined he was going to outdo the other guy. We went at it until we almost sank into the lake. For example, he was determined that he could do a deep-water single-ski start. Now that's a tough thing to do until you've got the knack of it, and if you haven't practiced it for a while....But he stayed at that, I don't know whether it was six, seven, or eight times, until his arms must have been just about pulled out of their sockets. And the next day, he must have felt like I did—that his legs were just about falling off him, that his arms were terrible, the worst neck-ache that you've ever had—and he was in an intolerable mood and so was I. But he just had to do it.

The bobsled run in St. Moritz was the same kind of thing. He didn't know how dangerous it was, but insisted on doing it because he was challenged. And when he did it, I was crazy enough that I wasn't going to permit a guy ten years older than me to do it, I had to do it better than him. As soon as he saw that my time was better than his, he insisted on doing it again, and this is the kind of person he is.

Ivan Head, quoted in George Radwanski, *Trudeau*, 1978

Trudeau at the Ballet

It was intermission during a performance of Les Grands Ballets Canadiens that I had come to review for the *Globe and Mail*. In the VIP foyer at Salle des Arts, where the critics and special guests of the company had gathered, I saw him away in the corner talking animatedly to a bunch of ballet groupies. I sauntered over towards them to eavesdrop, when I heard him give an analysis of the first ballet that was as good as anything I was going to be able to come up with. He has a seemingly instinctive skill to get to the heart of a problem with an adroit question for which he clearly knows the answers, but with which he solicits genuine debate. It is, I know, part of the formal process of Logic, but he always seems to do it with grace and style, even when he has no intention of changing his mind.

When we finally talked, he learned for the first time that I was the dance critic for Canada's national newspaper.

Mr. Trudeau, as is known to some, is a dance fan. A former dancer with the National Ballet had told me of classes he and Pierre had taken together in Montreal during the Forties. Right there and then I decided this would be a great occasion to make a pitch for an interview based on his balletic past.

"C'mon, c'mon," he said. "We can't do that. I've got enough problems with the West as it is. But you, tell me about you. Is this your job, travelling around the country and taking in all the dance?"

I could tell from the tone of mock admiration that this was what he wanted my job to be, so I didn't bother him with the details of late-night editing and fighting the mournful feature ideas of the assistant editor. "Sure," I said, "that's it. That's all I do."

The bell went to summon us back to our seats.

"I want your job," he said, "Right now."

I trust all this now puts into a far happier perspective his later and allegedly disrespectful pirouette behind the Queen's back. When the band plays, a guy's gotta dance.

John Fraser, Telling Tales, 1986

Eric Kierans

Eric William Kierans (1914-) was Minister of Communications and Postmaster General during most of the first Trudeau administration.

Kierans had a disconcerting habit of butting into other departments, particularly those concerned with economics. (There are eight economic portfolios, none held by anyone with Kierans' qualifications—former head of the Montreal and Canadian stock Exchanges, former Revenue Minister for the Province of Quebec, and a self-made millionaire.) Worse, he did his homework, and often knew more than the minister involved. In one case, a colleague proposed offering a huge government contract to an American-owned company operating in Quebec. Without such a contract, company officials had argued, the firm would go bankrupt, throwing hundreds of Quebeckers out of work. Kierans investigated—nothing fancy, he simply looked up the company involved on data cards supplied by the Financial Post—and discovered that the U.S. firm owned stocks worth $46 million in another, and profitable, Canadian company. "That money came out of the Canadian economy," he said, "let them use that to keep the thing afloat." His colleague was not pleased to receive the information. His officials would check the details, he informed the cabinet stiffly, but for his own part he resented the fact that Kierans had raised such a matter in full cabinet, rather than coming to him privately. "There wasn't time," Kierans responded blandly, "I was in the Parliamentary Library at nine o'clock, where the information is readily available, and left to come straight to this meeting."

Walter Stewart, *Shrug: Trudeau in Power*, 1971

James Jerome

James Jerome (1931-) was Speaker of the House of Commons from 1974 until 1979. Léo Robitaille was his steward throughout that period.

Each day, the Sergeant-at-Arms, the Clerk, Table Officers, and the Speaker form a procession through the Hall and down the south corridor into the main entrance of the Chamber to signal the start of the sitting. Léo immediately noticed that I had reading glasses in my jacket pocket which I couldn't carry dressed in the Speaker's regalia, and he offered to polish them and to place them on the arm of the Speaker's Chair while we were in the procession.

On my second day, when I got into the Chair and looked to my right, I cannot remember looking at a more forlorn human being than Léo, cradling my broken glasses in his hands. I couldn't read my list, the floor plan, or anything else without them, so the only answer was to borrow a pair from the nearest Member—who unfortunately had a head the size of a football. I couldn't help but laugh to myself all during Question Period at what must have looked like something out of Vaudeville, as I tried to get accustomed to the strange surroundings, gathering my funny looking garb around me, and trying to hold on the over-sized pair of pince-nez reading glasses.

James Jerome, *Mr. Speaker*, 1985

Honourable Jack

John Henry Horner (1927-   ) was first elected to the Commons in 1957 as a Progressive Conservative. In 1977 he crossed the floor of the House and entered the Trudeau Cabinet as Minister of Industry Trade and Commerce.

After my swearing in, we went out to meet the press. I guess Trudeau was watching me very closely to see how I would handle the questions. He commented later, "The press don't bother you at all. You like to play with them." At cabinet later that morning, Trudeau introduced me as the cabinet minister from Alberta. He was absolutely fair and straight with me; he told cabinet that any appointments in or from Alberta were to be cleared through me. As Alberta's representative in cabinet, I could veto any appointment related to my province. This statement did much to reassure me that I would have a full part to play in cabinet and would not be merely a pawn to be used by Trudeau and the Liberal party. I greatly appreciated his introduction; it kind of set my mind and heart at ease that this whole thing was going to work, that Trudeau and I, maybe to a lot of people's surprise, were going to get along. And that's about the way it turned out.

Jack Horner, *My Own Brand*, 1980

Miami

*Thomas Charles Cossitt (1923-1982) represented Leeds, Ontario, for the
Conservatives from 1972 until his death.*

Tom Cossitt, the Tory member from Leeds, used to make a specialty of
questioning all of the ministers about their travels. He loved to get indignant about the expense and so on; he knew it was good publicity.
Most of the time he left me alone, but there was one occasion back in
1974 when Tom really thought he had me. It was the time I flew to
Miami.

After I got back from the trip Cossitt sent me a written question
which I'd replied to in writing, as is customary. In my reply I told him,
"Yes, I did fly to Miami." Period. So the next day Tom got up in the
House and made a statement. He said something like "It's disgraceful
that this minister flew to Miami at the taxpayers' expense." I didn't respond; I just sat there with a big grin on my face and didn't say a thing—
just like the time our new elementary school teacher Miss Donnelly told
us how she was going to whip all us bushwacker kids into shape. Cossitt
should have known by the way I was acting that he was getting himself
into trouble.

The next day the story hit the headlines—"Whelan Flies Free to
Miami"—but I still didn't do anything to defend myself. Afterwards
when the reporters asked me about the trip, I simply confirmed that I
had indeed flown to Miami and they rushed off to meet their deadlines.
Tom must have thought I was just hoping the whole thing would blow
over. But a couple of days later a reporter finally thought to come and
check out the story with me. He asked me what I had to say about flying to Miami on a government plane and I said, "Well, the only thing
I've got to say is that it was cold as hell in Miami the day I was there and
when I left the next morning it was forty below zero." The reporter
looked baffled, then said, "It was never that cold in Florida." "Whoever
said anything about Florida?" I said. "I'm talking about Miami, Manitoba. I was there to give a speech at the annual Manitoba Corn Awards
Banquet. Over four hundred people were there." In all the fuss no one

had ever checked to see where Miami was and I chided the reporter for not reading a copy of my speech beforehand. To give Tom Cossitt credit, he laughed about the whole thing afterwards.

Eugene Whelan, *Whelan*, 1986

Prime Ministers

All the prime ministers under whom I served developed an individual style of chairing the cabinet. My earliest impression was that Mackenzie King had not read the cabinet documents — at least not with sufficient care to discuss them comprehensively. He would go around the table asking his ministers' views on any particular matter. When his time came to speak, he had absorbed enough to be able to pronounce with some conviction.

Louis St. Laurent, on the other hand, knew more about what was in a cabinet document than the minister who presented it. His technique at the cabinet table reflected his professional skill as a great lawyer. From the document, he gleaned an appreciation of what was involved and frequently would outline the proposal before the minister had spoken. Stealing the show in this way irritated me. I greatly admired St. Laurent's capacity, but I wanted to state my own case. Often, in his recital of "the facts," St. Laurent revealed his own reaction to the proposals and this had the effect of encouraging many ministers to agree with him.

Pearson's modus operandi was much more informal. I am certain that he always did his homework and he encouraged the fullest discussion — sometimes unnecessarily so. The pace with Mike was always easy, if, on occasion, less orderly.

No one liked discussion more than Pierre Trudeau. He is a born seminar leader. Sometimes I felt that, as in Pearson's time, there was too much discussion in Trudeau's cabinet. A lot of time was spent on cabinet committee work that often duplicated the work of the full cabinet or vice versa. No one was more tolerant of the right of discussion than Trudeau, but nobody was less sympathetic to ideas that he thought irrelevant, unsound or unintelligible. When I compare the different styles of each prime minister, the most satisfactory results were those that issued from the skilful management of Louis St. Laurent.

Paul Martin, *A Very Public Life*, I, 1983

Sources

Aberdeen, Lord and Lady. *"We Two": Reminiscences of Lord and Lady Aberdeen, Volume II.* London: W. Collins Sons & Co. Ltd., 1925

Aiken, Gordon. *The Backbencher: Trails and tribulations of a Member of Parliament.* Toronto: McClelland and Stewart Limited, 1974. Repinted by permission of McClelland and Stewart.

Beal, John Robinson. *The Pearson Phenomena.* Toronto: Longmans Canada Limited, 1964.

Beaverbrooke, Lord. *Friends: Sixty Years of Intimate Personal Relations with Richard Bedford Bennett, PC, KC, LLB, Hon LLD, FRSC, Viscount Bennett of Mickleham, Surrey, and of Calgary and Hopewell, Canada - - A personal memoir with an appendix of letters.* London: William Heineman Ltd., 1959.

Biggar, E.B. *Anecdotal Life of Sir John Macdonald.* Montreal: John Lovell & Son, 1891.

Bilkey, Paul. *Persons, Papers and Things: Being the Casual Recollections of a Journalist with Some Flounderings in Philosophy.* Toronto: The Ryerson Press, 1940.

Bishop, Charles. "Years Around Parliament: Thoughts, Men, Memories." *Ottawa Evening Citizen*, 1945.

Borden, Henry, ed. *Robert Laird Borden: His Memoirs.* Toronto: The MacMillan Company of Canada Ltd., 1938. Reprinted by permission of the editor.

Borden, Sir Robert L. *Letters to Limbo.* Edited by Henry Borden. Toronto: University of Toronto Press, 1971. Reproduced by permission of University of Toronto Press.

Bosc, Marc. Canada. House of Commons. *Debates.*

Bothwell, Robert, and Kilbourn, William. *C.D. Howe: A Biography.* Toronto: McClelland and Stewart, 1979. Repinted by permission of McClelland and Stewart.

Bowman, Charles A. *Ottawa Editor: The Memoirs of Charles A. Bowman.* Sidney: Gray's Publishing Ltd., 1966.

Bown, John. Canada. House of Commons. *Debates.*

Boyd, John. *Sir George Etienne Cartier, Bart.: His Life and Times.* Toronto: The Macmillan Company of Canada ltd., 1914.

Bridle, Augustus [Domino, pseud.] *The Masques of Ottawa.* Toronto: The Macmillan Company of Canada Ltd., 1921.

_____, *Sons of Canada: Short Stories of Characteristic Canadians.* Toronto: J.M. Dent & Sons Ltd., 1916.

Brown, Robert Craig. *Robert Laird Borden: A Biography. Volume II: 1914-1937.* Toronto: Macmillan of Canada, 1980.

Camp, Dalton. *Gentlemen, players and politicians.* Toronto: McClelland and Stewart, 1970. Reprinted by permission of the author.

Careless, J.M.S. *Brown of the Globe. Volume Two: Statesman of Confederation 1860-1880.* Toronto: The Macmillan Company of Canada Ltd., 1963. Reprinted by permission of the author.

Cartwright, Sir Richard. *Reminiscences.* Toronto: William Briggs, 1912.

Casgrain, Therese F. *A Woman in a Man's World.* Translated by Joyce Marshall. Toronto: McClelland and Stewart, 1972. Repinted by permission of McClelland and Stewart.

Charlesworth, Hector. *Candid Chronicles: Leaves from the Note Book of a Canadian Journalist.* Toronto: The Macmillan Company of Canada Ltd., 1925.

Chaudiere [pseud.] "From the Capital." *Canadian Illustrated News,* 1874.

_____, *More Candid Chronicles: Further leaves from the Note Book of a Canadian Journalist.* Toronto: The Macmillan Company of Canada Ltd., 1928.

_____, *I'm Telling You: Being the Further Candid Chronicles.* Toronto: The Macmillan Company of Canada Ltd., 1937.

Chrétien, Jean. *Straight from the Heart.* Toronto: Key Porter Books, 1985. Reprinted by permission of Key Porter Books.

Cook, Fred. *Fifty Years Ago and Since.* Ottawa: Library of Parliament Collection, n.d.

_____, *Giants and Jesters in Public Life.* Ottawa: Library of Parliament Collection, n.d.

Cross, Austin. *The People's Mouths.* Toronto: The Macmillan Company of Canada Ltd., 1943.

Dafoe, John W. *Laurier, A Study in Canadian Politics.* Toronto: Thomas Allen, 1922. Reprinted by permission of Thomas Allen & Son Ltd. Publishers.

_____, *Clifford Sifton in Relation to his Times.* Toronto: The Macmillan Company of Canada Ltd., 1931.

Dawson, R. MacGregor. *William Lyon Mackenzie King: A Political Biography.* Toronto: University of Toronto Press, 1958. Reproduced by permission of University of Toronto Press.

Debates

Diefenbaker, John G. *One Canada: Memoirs of the Right Honourable John G. Diefenbaker. The Crusading Years 1895-1956.* Toronto: Macmillan of Canada, 1975. With the permission of the Rt. Hon. John G. Diefenbaker Centre.

_____, *One Canada: Memoirs of the Right Honourable John G. Diefenbaker. The Years of Achievement 1957-1962.* Toronto: Macmillan of Canada, 1976. With the permission of the Rt. Hon. John G. Diefenbaker Centre.

One Canada: Memoirs of the Right Honourable John G. Diefenbaker. The Tumultuous Years 1962-1967. Toronto: Macmillan of Canada, 1977. With the permission of the Rt. Hon. John G. Diefenbaker Centre.

Douglas, Thomas C. "Recollections of a Parliamentarian." *Canadian Parliamentary Review,* Volume 4, Number 2 (Summer 1981). Reprinted by permission of Canadian Parliamentary Review.

Figler, Bernard. *Sam Jacobs, Member of Parliament.* Ottawa: Bernard Figler, 1959. Reprinted by permission of the author's estate.

Ford, Arthur R. *As The World Wages On.* Toronto: The Ryerson Press, 1950.

Fraser, John. *Telling Tales.* Toronto: Collins Publishers, 1986. Reprinted by permission of McClelland and Stewart Ltd.

Graham, Roger. *Arthur Meighen. Volume I: The Door of Oppourtunity.* Toronto: Clarke, Irwin & Company Ltd., 1960. Reprinted by permission of the author.

_____, *Arthur Meighen. Volume II: And Fortune Fled.* Toronto: Clarke, Irwin & Company Ltd., 1963. Reprinted by permission of the author.

_____, *Arthur Meighen. Volume III: No Surrender.* Toronto: Clarke, Irwin & Company Ltd., 1965. Reprinted by permission of the author.

Gwyn, Richard. *The Northern Magus. Pierre Trudeau and Canadians.* Gwyn. Toronto: McClelland and Stewart Ltd., 1980. Reprinted by permission of McClelland and Stewart Ltd.

Hall, D.J. *Clifford Sifton. Volume Two: A Lonely Eminence.* Vancouver: University of British Columbia Press, 1985. Reprinted by permission of University of British Columbia Press.

Ham, George H. *Reminiscences of A Raconteur Between the '40's and the '20's.* Toronto: The Musson Book Company Ltd., 1920.

Hamilton, Lord Frederic. *The Days Before Yesterday.* New York: George H. Doran Company, 1920.

Hammond, M.O. *Confederation and its Leaders.* Toronto: McClelland, Goodchild & Stewart, 1917.

Hardy, H. Reginald. *Mackenzie King of Canada.* Toronto: Oxford University Press, 1949.

Heaps, Leo. *The Rebel in the House. The Life and Times of A.A. Heaps, M.P.* Markham: Fitzhenry and Whiteside Ltd., 1984 (revised and enlarged edition). Reprinted by permission of Fitzhenry and Whiteside Ltd.

Heeney, Arnold. *The Things That Are Caesar's: Memoirs of a Canadian Public Servant.* Edited by Brian D. Heeney. Toronto: University of Toronto Press, 1972. Reproduced by permission of University of Toronto Press.

Horner, Jack. *My Own Brand.* Edmonton: Hurtig Publishers Ltd., 1980. Reprinted by permission of the author.

Hutchison, Bruce. *The Incredible Canadians. A Candid Portrait of Mackenzie King: His Works, His Times, and His Nation.* Toronto: Longmans, Green and Company, 1952.

_____, *Mr. Prime Minister.* Toronto: Longmans Canada Ltd., 1964.

Iglauer, Edith. *"Profiles: Prime Minister/Premier Ministre."* The New Yorker, July 5, 1969.

Jerome, James. *Mr.Speaker.* Toronto: McClelland and Stewart Ltd., 1985. Reprinted by permission of McClelland and Stewart Ltd.

Kendle, John. *John Bracken: A Political Biography.* Toronto: University of Toronto Press, 1979. Reproduced by permission of University of Toronto Press.

LaMarsh, Judy. *Memoirs of a Bird in a Gilded Cage.* Toronto: McClelland and Stewart Ltd., 1968. Reprinted by permission of McClelland and Stewart Ltd.

Lewis, David. *The Good Fight: Political Memoirs 1909-1958.* Toronto: Macmillan of Canada, 1981. Reprinted by permission of Macmillan of Canada.

Lounger [pseud.] "The Lounger at Ottawa." *Canadian Illustrated News,* 1873.

Lynch, Charles. *You Can't Print That! Memoirs of a Political Voyeur.* Edmonton: Hurtig Publishers Ltd., 1983. Reprinted by permission of the author.

Manior, Robert J. *Life is an Adventure.* Toronto: The Ryerson Press, 1936.

Martin, Paul. *A Very Public Life. Volume I: Far From Home.* Ottawa: Deneau Publishers, 1983. Reprinted by permission of Deneau Publishers.

_____, *A Very Public Life. Volume I: So Many Worlds.* Ottawa: Deneau Publishers, 1985. Reprinted by permission of Deneau Publishers.

Massey, Vincent. *What's Past is Prologue. The Memoirs of the Right Honourable Vincent Massey, C.H.* Toronto: The Macmillan Company of Canada Ltd., 1963.

Munro, John A. and Inglis, Alex I., eds. *Mike: The Memoirs of the Right Honourable Lester B. Pearson. Volume 2: 1948-1957.* Toronto: University of Toronto Press, 1973. Reproduced by permission of University of Toronto Press.

Munro, John A. and Inglis, Alex I., eds. *Mike: The Memoirs of the Right Honourable Lester B. Pearson. Volume 3: 1948-1957.* Toronto: University of Toronto Press, 1975. Reproduced by permission of University of Toronto Press.

Macdonald, E.M. *Recollections, Political and Personal.* Toronto: The Ryerson Press, 1938.

Macdonald, Sir John A. Canada. Parliament. *Scrapbook Debates.*

McIlraith, George. "Looking Back at Parliament: Interview with George McIlraith." *Canadian Parliamentary Review,* Volume 7, Number 4 (Winter 1984-85). Reprinted by permission of Canadian Parliamentary Review.

MacInnis, Grace. *J.S. Woodsworth: a Man to Remember.* Toronto: The Macmillan Company of Canada Ltd., 1953.

MacLean, Andrew D. *R.B. Bennett: Prime Minister of Canada.* Toronto: Excelsior Publishing Company Ltd., 1934.

McNaught, Kenneth. *A Prophet in Politics: A Biography of J.S. Woodsworth.* Toronto: University of Toronto Press, 1959. Reprinted by permission of the author.

Neatby, H. Blair. *William Lyon Mackenzie King: 1924-1939, The Prism of Unity.* Toronto: University of Toronto Press, 1976. Reproduced by permission of University of Toronto Press.

Newman, Peter C. *Renegade in Power: The Diefenbaker Years.* Toronto: McClelland and Stewart Ltd., 1963. Reprinted by permission of McClelland and Stewart Ltd.

Newman, Peter C. *The Distemper of Our Times. Canadian Politics in Transition: 1963-1968.* Toronto: McClelland and Stewart Ltd., 1968. reprinted by permission of McClelland and Stewart Ltd.

Newman, Peter C. *Home Country: People, Places, and Power Politics.* Toronto: McClelland and Stewart Ltd., 1973. reprinted by permission of McClelland and Stewart Ltd.

O'Leary, Grattan. *Recollections of People, Press and Politics.* Toronto: Macmillan of Canada, 1977.

O'Sullivan, Sean (with Rod McQueen). *Both My Houses: From Politics to Priesthood.* Toronto: Key Porter Books, 1986. Reprinted by permission of Key Porter Books.

Pargue, J. Sambert (contributor). *Giants and Jesters in Public Life.* Ottawa: Library of Parliament Collection, n.d.

Pearson, Lester B. *Mike: The Memoirs of the Right Honourable Lester B. Pearson. Volume 1, 1897-1948.* Toronto: University of Toronto Press, 1972. Reproduced by permission of University of Toronto Press.

Pickersgill, John W. *My Years with Louis St.Laurent: A Political Memoir.* Toronto: University of Toronto Press, 1975. Reprinted by permission of the author.

Pope, Sir Joseph. *Memoirs of the Right Honourable Sir John Alexander Macdonald, G.C.B., First Prime Minister of the Dominion of Canada.* Volume II. London: Edward Arnold, Publisher to the India Office, 1894.

_____, *The Day of Sir John Macdonald. A Chronicle of the First Prime Minister of the Dominion.* Toronto: Glasgow, Brook & Company, 1915.

Preston, W.T.R. *My Generation of Politics and Politicians.* Toronto: D.A. Rose Publishing Company, 1927.

Radwanski, George. *Trudeau.* Toronto: Macmillan of Canada, 1978.

Roberts, Leslie. *C.D.: The Life and Times of Clarence Decatur Howe.* Toronto: Clarke, Irwin & Company Ltd., 1957.

Ross, Sir George W. *Geting Into Parliament and After.* Toronto: William Briggs, 1913.

Saywell, John T., ed. *The Canadian Journal of Lady Aberdeen, 1893-1898.* Toronto: The Champlain Society, 1960.

Sevigny, Pierre. *This Game of Politics.* Toronto: McClelland and Stewart Ltd., 1965.

Shackleton, Doris F. *Tommy Douglas.* Toronto: McClelland and Stewart Ltd., 1975. Reprinted by permission of McClelland and Stewart Ltd.

Skelton, Isabel. *The Life of Thomas D'Arcy McGee.* Gardenvale: Garden City Press, 1925.

Skelton, Oscar D. *Life and Letters of Sir Wilfrid Laurier. Volume I.* Toronto: Oxford University Press, 1921.

Slattery, T.P. *The Assassination of D'Arcy McGee.* Toronto: Doubleday Canada Ltd., 1968. Reprinted by permission of Doubleday Canada Ltd.

Stanley, Geroge F.G. *Louis Riel.* Toronto: The Ryerson Press, 1963. Reprinted by permission of McGraw-Hill Ryerson Ltd.

Stevens, Geoffrey. *Stanfield.* Toronto: McClelland and Stewart Ltd., 1973. Reprinted by permission of McClelland and Stewart Ltd.

Stewart, Walter. *Shrug: Trudeau in Power.* Toronto: New Press, 1971.

Stubbs, Roy St.George. *Prairie Portraits.* Toronto: McClelland and Stewart Ltd., 1954.

Stuebing, Douglas (with John Marshall and Gary Oakes). *Trudeau: A Man for Tomorrow.* Toronto: Clarke, Irwin & Company Ltd., 1968.

Stursberg, Peter. *Diefenbaker: Leadershop Gained, 1952-62.* Toronto: University of Toronto Press, 1975. Reproduced by permission of University of Toronto Press.

Stursberg, Peter. *Diefenbaker: Leadershop Lost, 1962-67.* Toronto: University of Toronto Press, 1976. Reproduced by permission of University of Toronto Press.

Thomas, Lewis H. ed. *The Making of a Socialist: The Recollections of T.C. Douglas.* Edmonton: The University of Alberta Press, 1982. Reprinted by permission of the University of Alberta Press.

Thomson, Dale C. *Louis St.Laurent: Canadian.* Toronto: Macmillan of Canada, 1967. Reprinted by permission of the author.

Trofimenkoff, Susan Mann. *Stanley Knowles: The Man from Winnipeg North Centre.* Saskatoon: Western Producer Prairie Books, 1982. Reprinted by permission of the author.

TWA (Timothy Warren Anglin). *New Brunswick Freeman*, 1868.

Van Dusen, Thomas. *The Chief.* Toronto: McGraw-Hill, 1968. Reprinted by permission of the editor.

Ward, Norman, ed. *A Party Politician: The Memoirs of Chubby Power.* Toronto: Macmillan of Canada, 1966. Reprinted by permission of the editor.

Watkins, Ernest. *R.B. Bennett: A Biography.* London: Secker & Warburg, 1963.

Whelan, Eugene (with Rich Archbold). *Whelan: The Man in the Green Stetson.* Toronto: Irwin Publishing, 1986.

Willison, Sir John. *Reminiscences, Political and Personal.* Toronto: McClelland and Stewart Ltd., 1919.

_____, *Sir Wilfrid Laurier.* Toronto: Oxford University Press, 1926.

Young, James. *Public Men and Public Life in Canada: The Story of the Canadian Confederacy.* Volume II. Toronto: William Briggs, 1912.

Index